SHINOBU OHTAKA

In Magi volume 30, the new world accelerates!

MAGI

Volume 30

Shonen Sunday Edition

Story and Art by

SHINOBU OHTAKA

Original Japanese edition published by SHOGAKUKAN.
English translation rights in the United States of America, Canada, the United Kingdom, Ireland, Australia and New Zealand arranged with SHOGAKUKAN.

ORIGINAL COVER DESIGN / Yasuo SHIMURA+Bay Bridge Studio

Translation & English Adaptation ◆ John Werry
Touch-up Art & Lettering ◆ Stephen Dutro
Editor ◆ Mike Montesa

Printed in Canada

Published by VIZ Media, LLC
P.O. Box 77010
San Francisco, CA 94107

10 9 8 7 6 5 4 3 2 1
First printing, June 2018

WWW.SHONENSUNDAY.COM

ratings.viz.com RATED T TEEN

PARENTAL ADVISORY
MAGI is rated T for Teen. This volume contains suggestive themes.

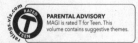

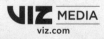

VIZ MEDIA
viz.com

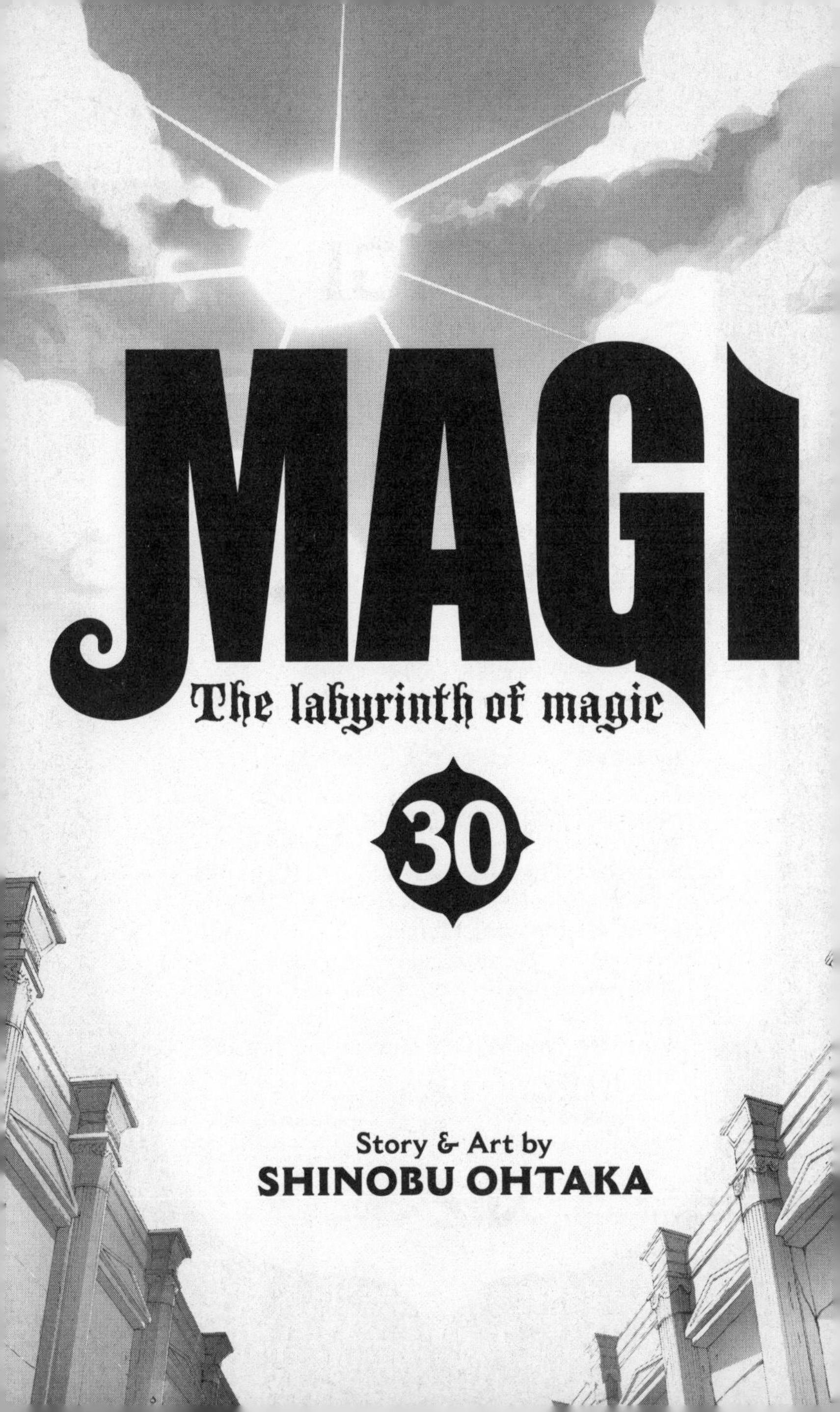

MAGI

The labyrinth of magic

30

Story & Art by

SHINOBU OHTAKA

MAGI
The labyrinth of magic
30

CONTENTS

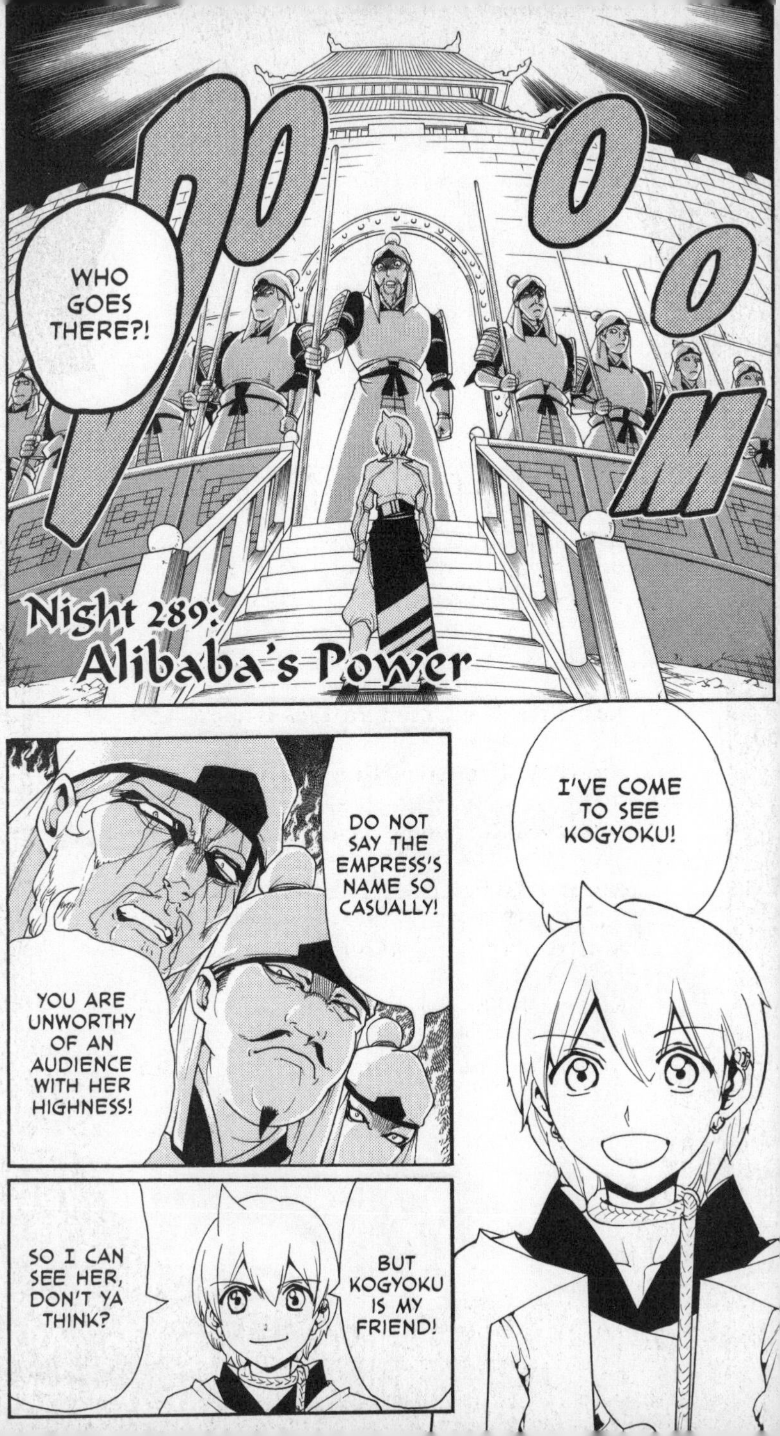
DOOOOM
WHO GOES THERE?!
Night 289: Alibaba's Power
I'VE COME TO SEE KOGYOKU!
DO NOT SAY THE EMPRESS'S NAME SO CASUALLY!
YOU ARE UNWORTHY OF AN AUDIENCE WITH HER HIGHNESS!
BUT KOGYOKU IS MY FRIEND!
SO I CAN SEE HER, DON'T YA THINK?

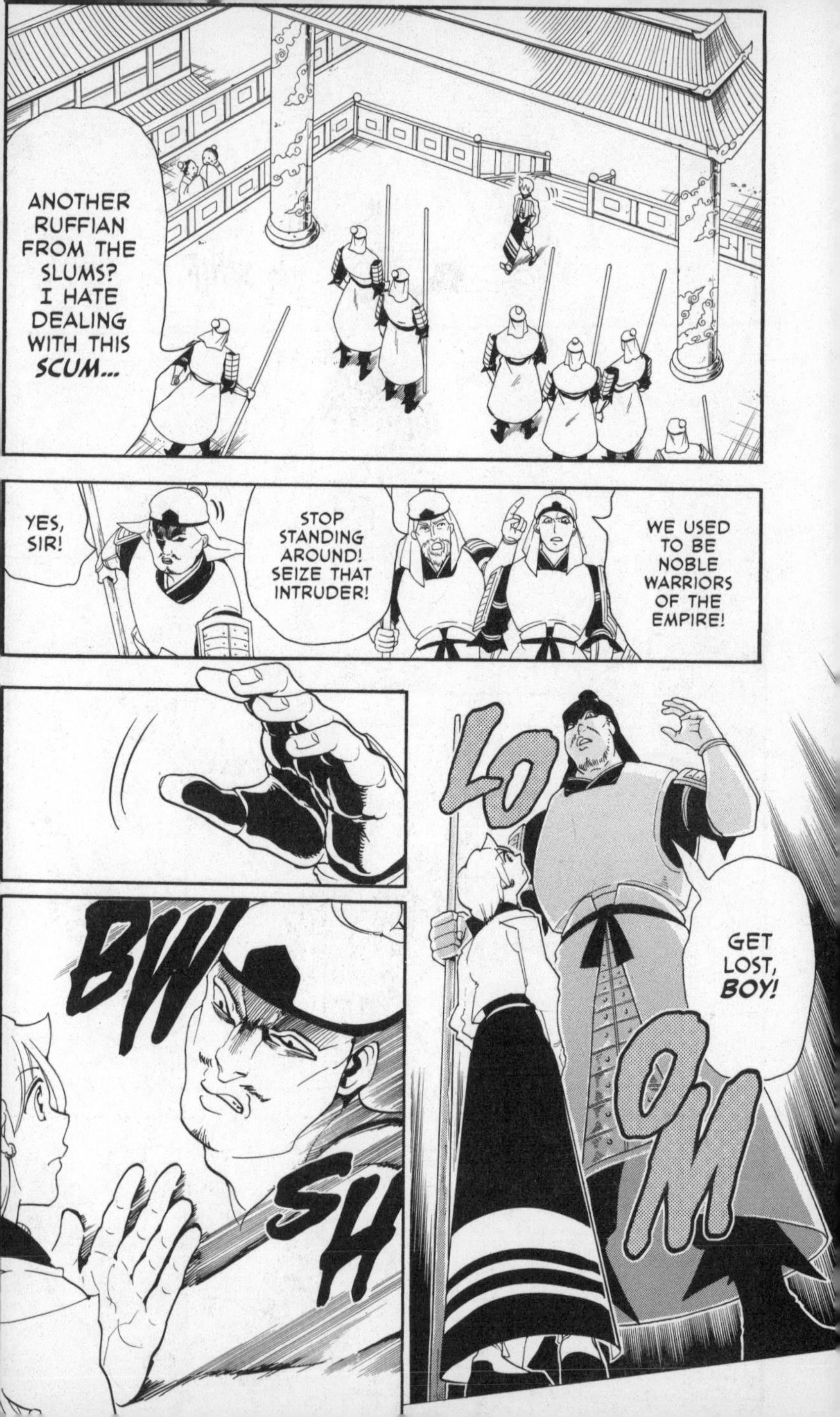
ANOTHER RUFFIAN FROM THE SLUMS? I HATE DEALING WITH THIS *SCUM...*
WE USED TO BE NOBLE WARRIORS OF THE EMPIRE!
STOP STANDING AROUND! SEIZE THAT INTRUDER!
YES, SIR!
LOOM
GET LOST, *BOY!*
BWSH

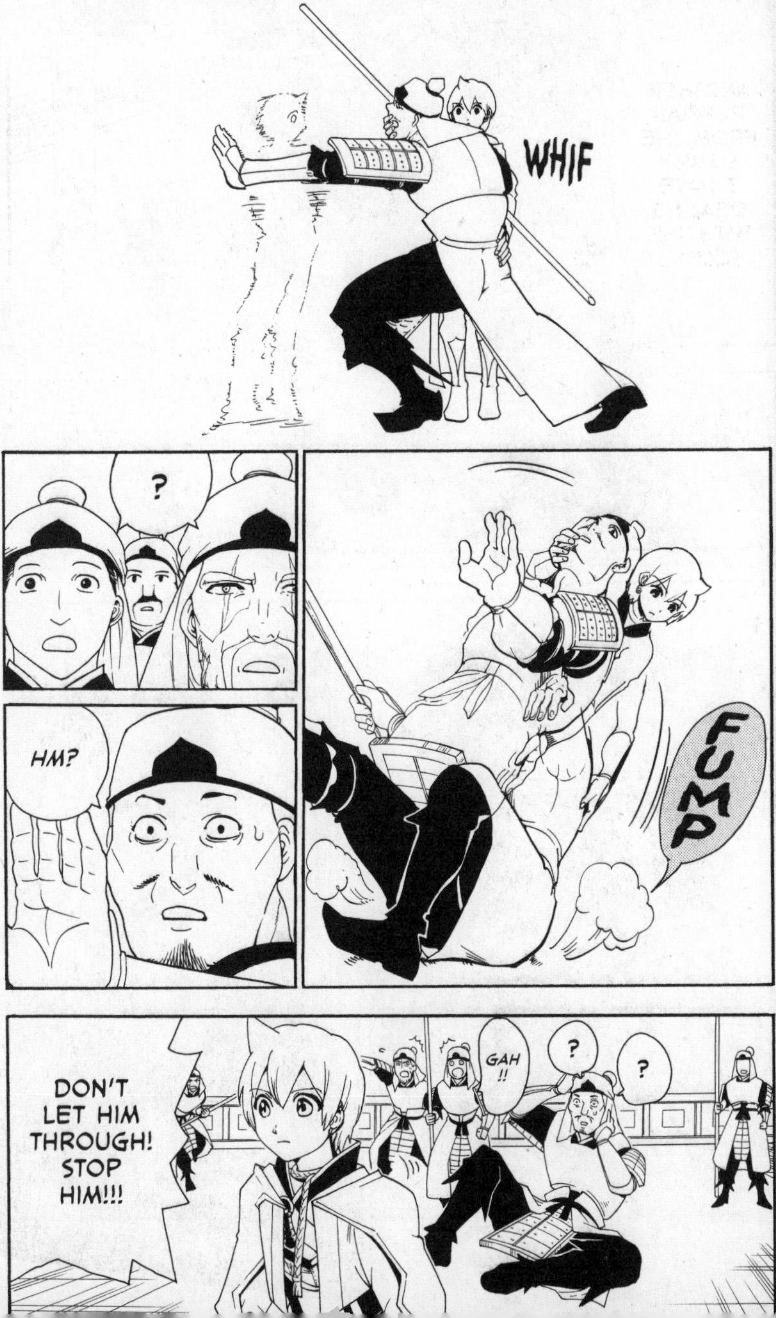
WHIF
FUMP
?
HM?
?
?
GAH !!
DON'T LET HIM THROUGH! STOP HIM!!!

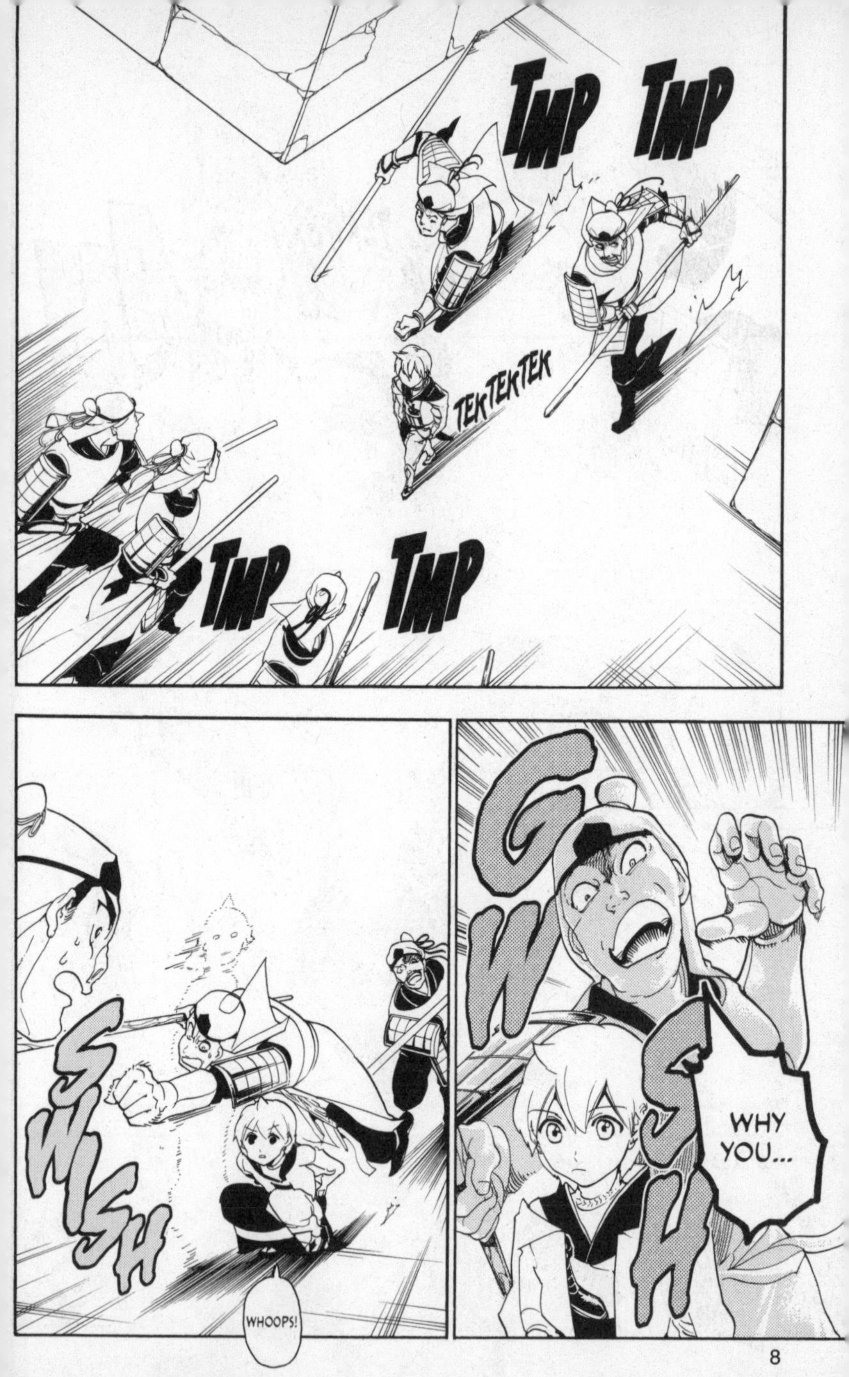

TMP TMP
TEK TEK TEK
TMP TMP
GWSH
WHY YOU...
SWISH
WHOOPS!

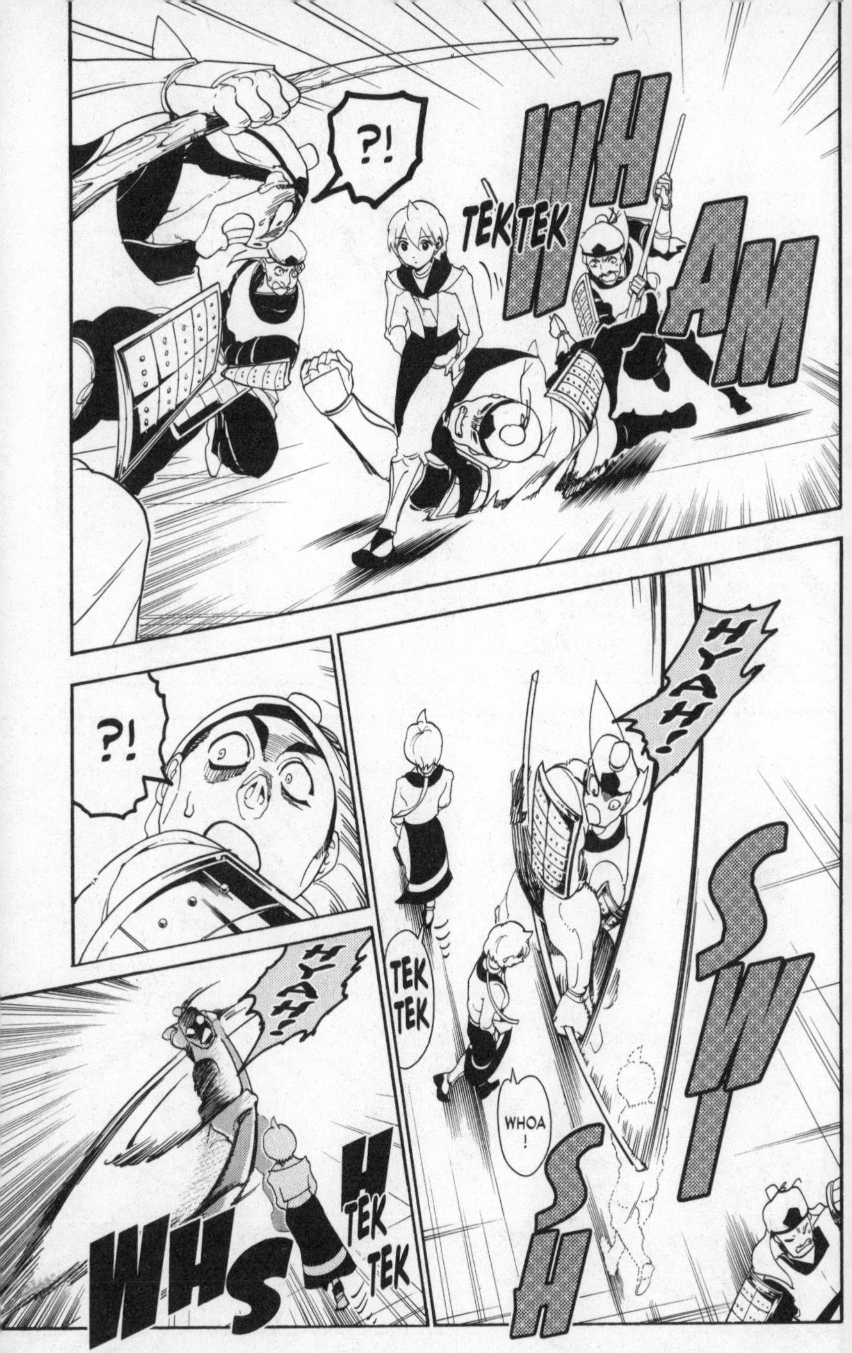
?!
TEK TEK
WHHAM
HYAH!
TEK TEK
WHOA!
SWISH
?!
HYAH!
WHSH
TEK TEK

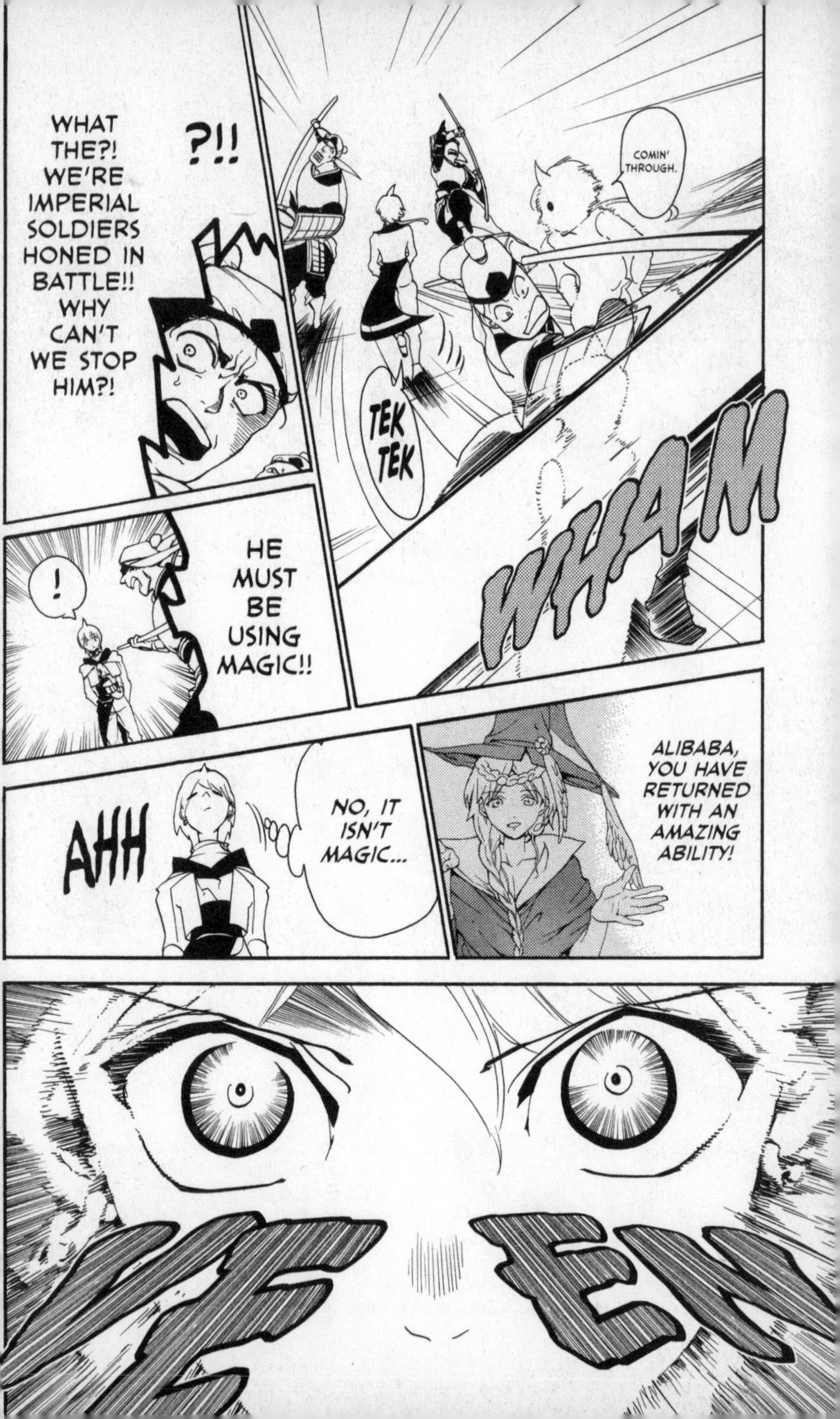
COMIN' THROUGH.
TEK TEK
WHAM
?!!
WHAT THE?! WE'RE IMPERIAL SOLDIERS HONED IN BATTLE!! WHY CAN'T WE STOP HIM?!
HE MUST BE USING MAGIC!!
!
ALIBABA, YOU HAVE RETURNED WITH AN AMAZING ABILITY!
NO, IT ISN'T MAGIC...
AHH

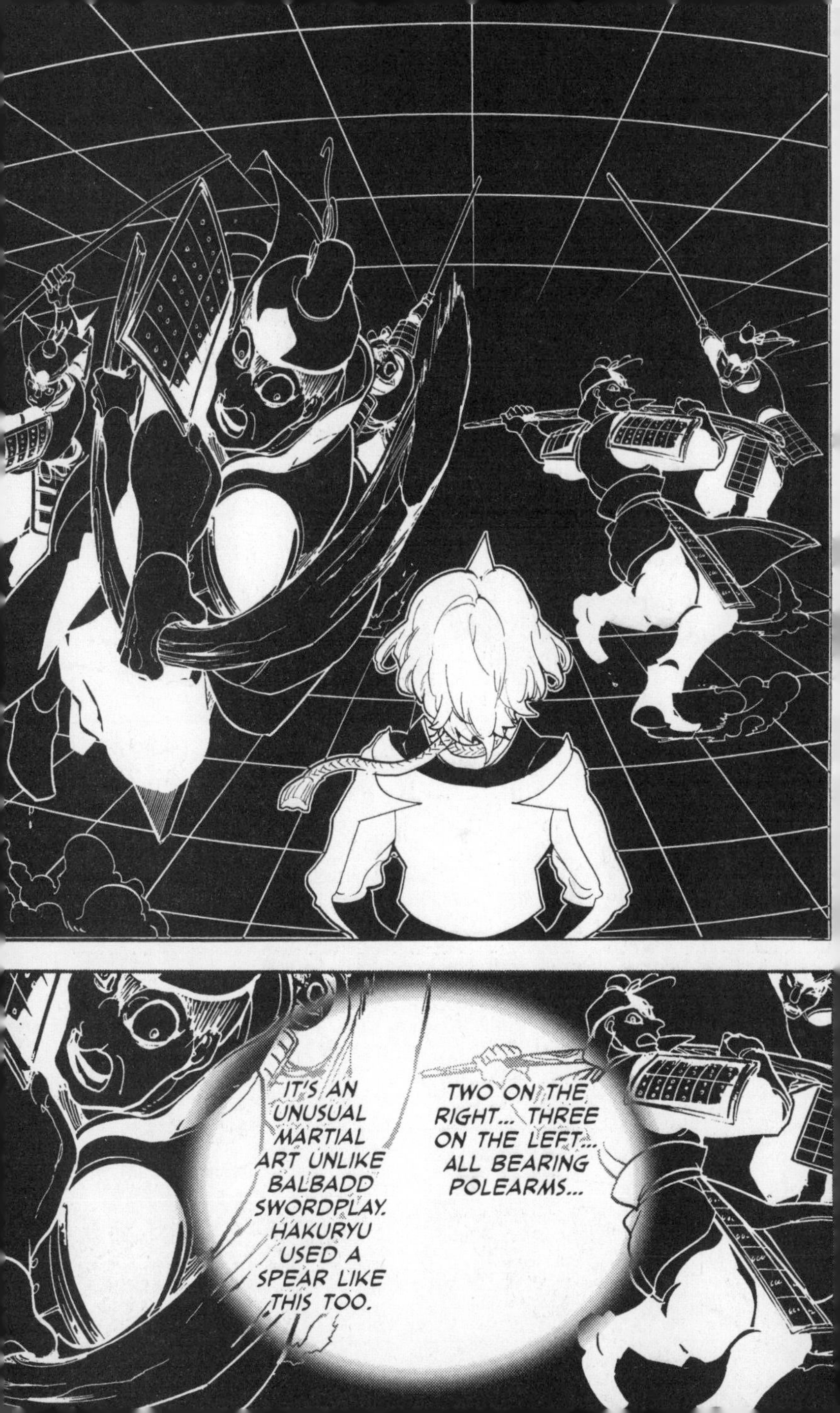
TWO ON THE RIGHT... THREE ON THE LEFT... ALL BEARING POLEARMS...
IT'S AN UNUSUAL MARTIAL ART UNLIKE BALBADD SWORDPLAY. HAKURYU USED A SPEAR LIKE THIS TOO.

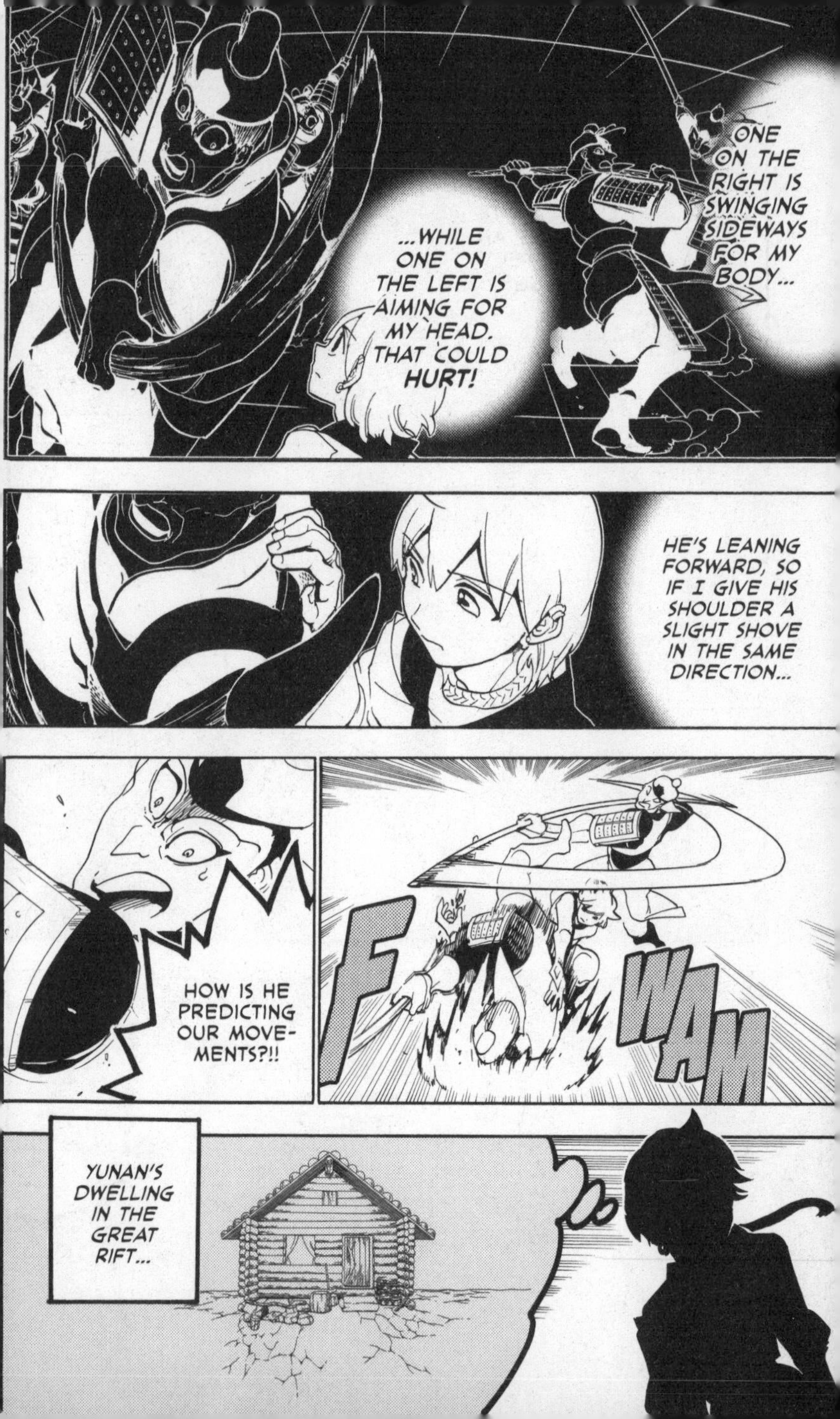
ONE ON THE RIGHT IS SWINGING SIDEWAYS FOR MY BODY...
...WHILE ONE ON THE LEFT IS AIMING FOR MY HEAD. THAT COULD HURT!
HE'S LEANING FORWARD, SO IF I GIVE HIS SHOULDER A SLIGHT SHOVE IN THE SAME DIRECTION...
FWAM
HOW IS HE PREDICTING OUR MOVE-MENTS?!!
YUNAN'S DWELLING IN THE GREAT RIFT...

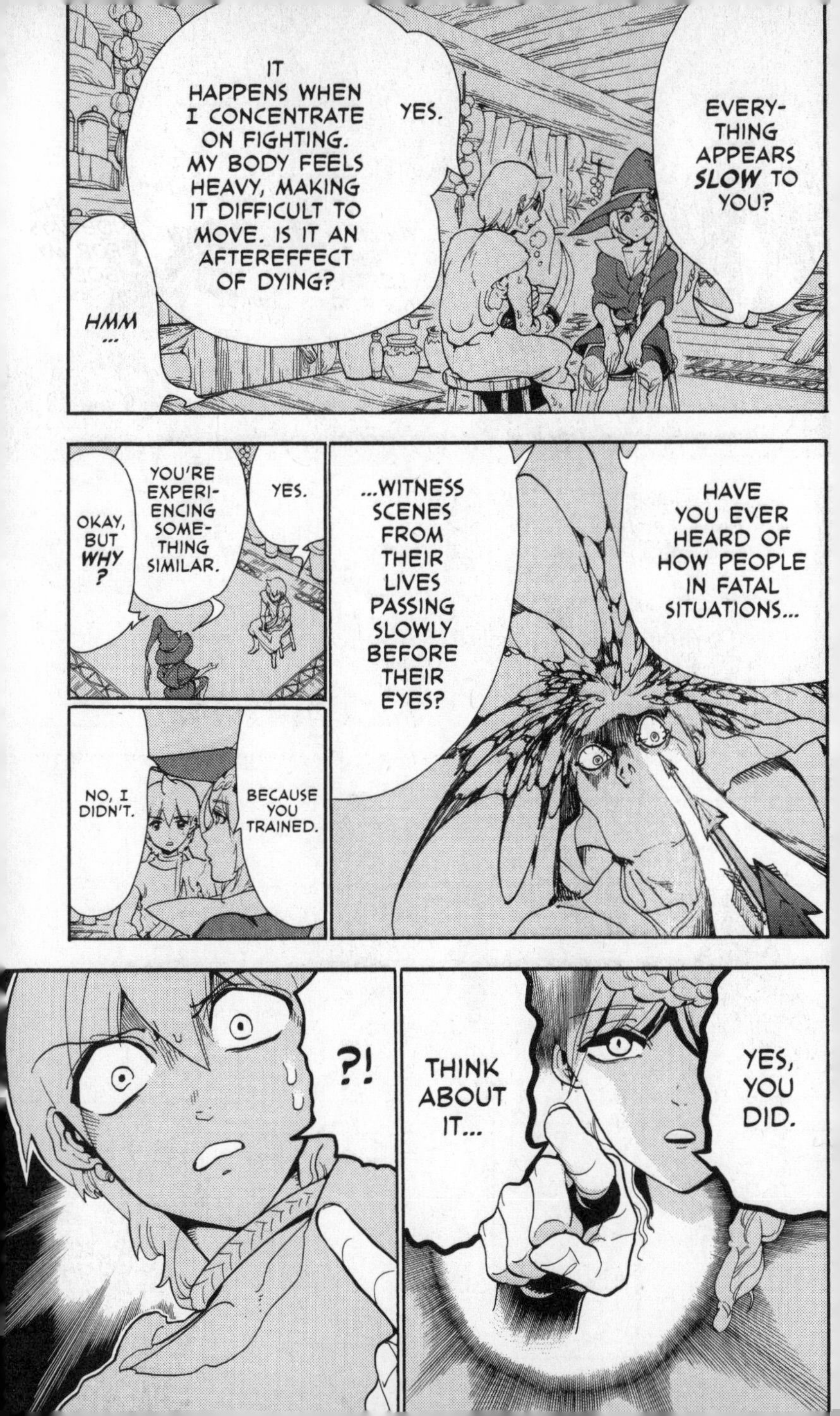
EVERY-THING APPEARS SLOW TO YOU?
YES.
IT HAPPENS WHEN I CONCENTRATE ON FIGHTING. MY BODY FEELS HEAVY, MAKING IT DIFFICULT TO MOVE. IS IT AN AFTEREFFECT OF DYING?
HMM...
HAVE YOU EVER HEARD OF HOW PEOPLE IN FATAL SITUATIONS...
...WITNESS SCENES FROM THEIR LIVES PASSING SLOWLY BEFORE THEIR EYES?
YES.
YOU'RE EXPERI-ENCING SOME-THING SIMILAR.
OKAY, BUT WHY?
BECAUSE YOU TRAINED.
NO, I DIDN'T.
YES, YOU DID.
THINK ABOUT IT...
?!

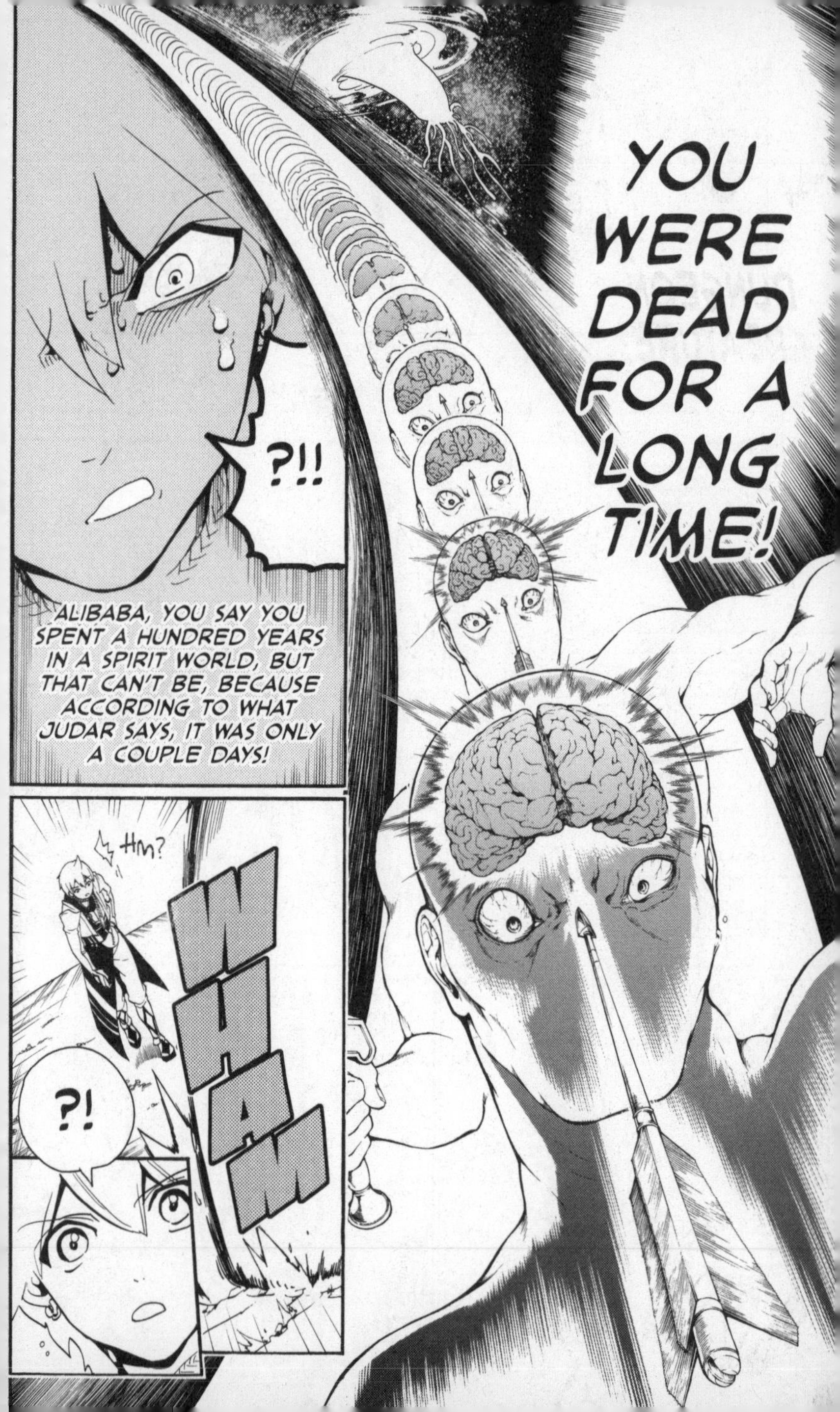
YOU WERE DEAD FOR A LONG TIME!
?!!
ALIBABA, YOU SAY YOU SPENT A HUNDRED YEARS IN A SPIRIT WORLD, BUT THAT CAN'T BE, BECAUSE ACCORDING TO WHAT JUDAR SAYS, IT WAS ONLY A COUPLE DAYS!
Hm?
WHAM
?!

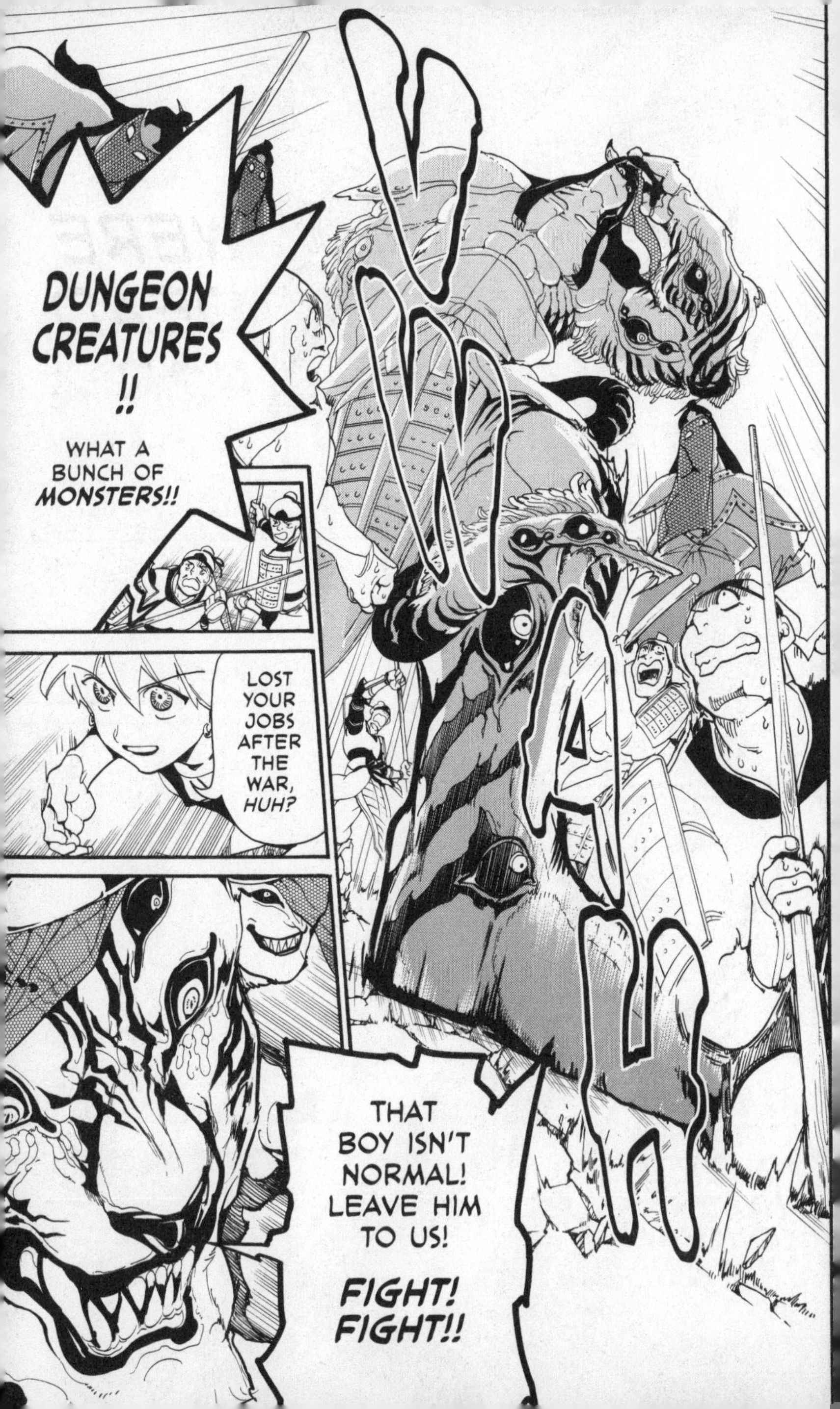

DUNGEON CREATURES!!
WHAT A BUNCH OF MONSTERS!!
LOST YOUR JOBS AFTER THE WAR, HUH?
THAT BOY ISN'T NORMAL! LEAVE HIM TO US!
FIGHT! FIGHT!!

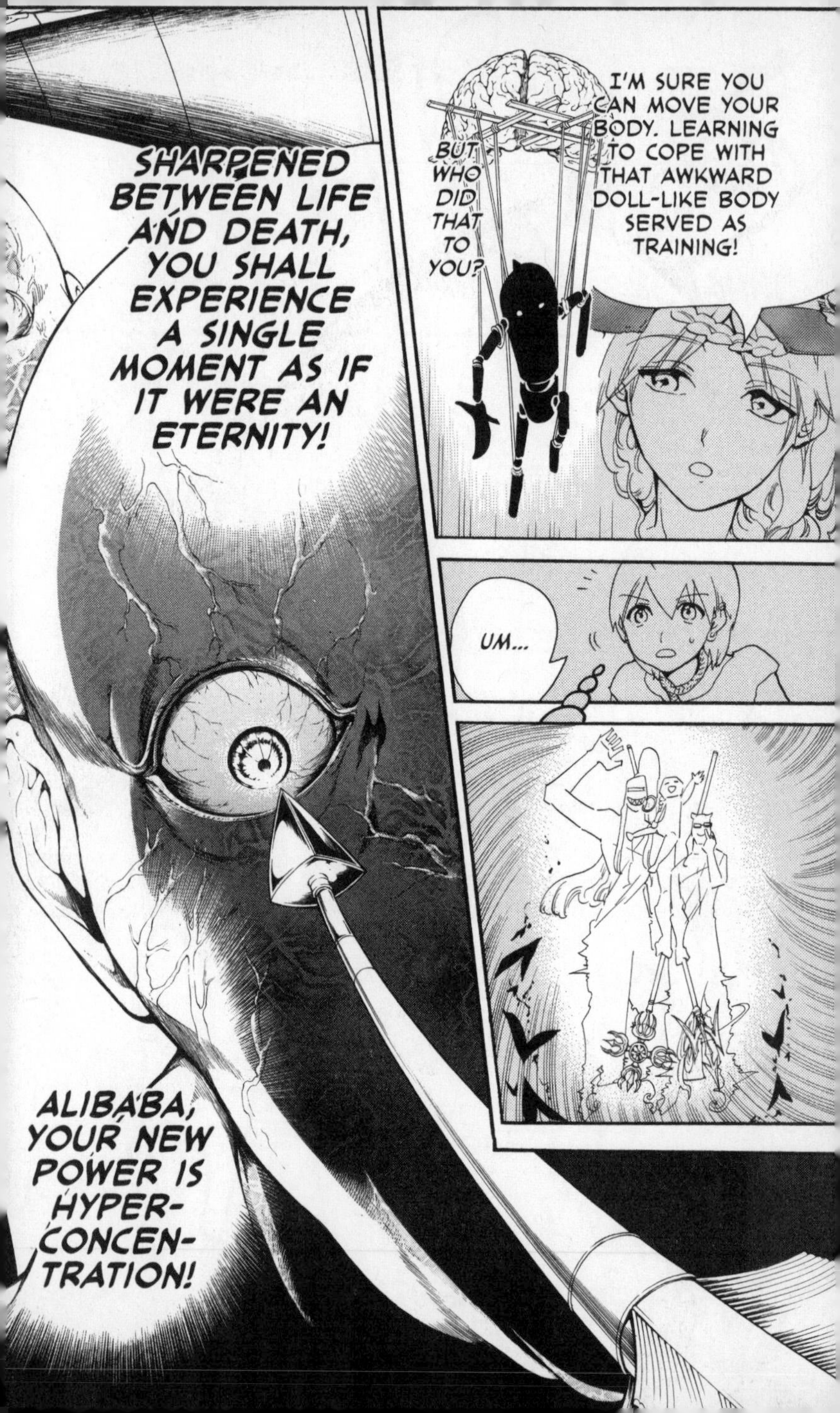
I'M SURE YOU CAN MOVE YOUR BODY. LEARNING TO COPE WITH THAT AWKWARD DOLL-LIKE BODY SERVED AS TRAINING!
BUT WHO DID THAT TO YOU?
UM...
SHARPENED BETWEEN LIFE AND DEATH, YOU SHALL EXPERIENCE A SINGLE MOMENT AS IF IT WERE AN ETERNITY!
ALIBABA, YOUR NEW POWER IS HYPER-CONCENTRATION!

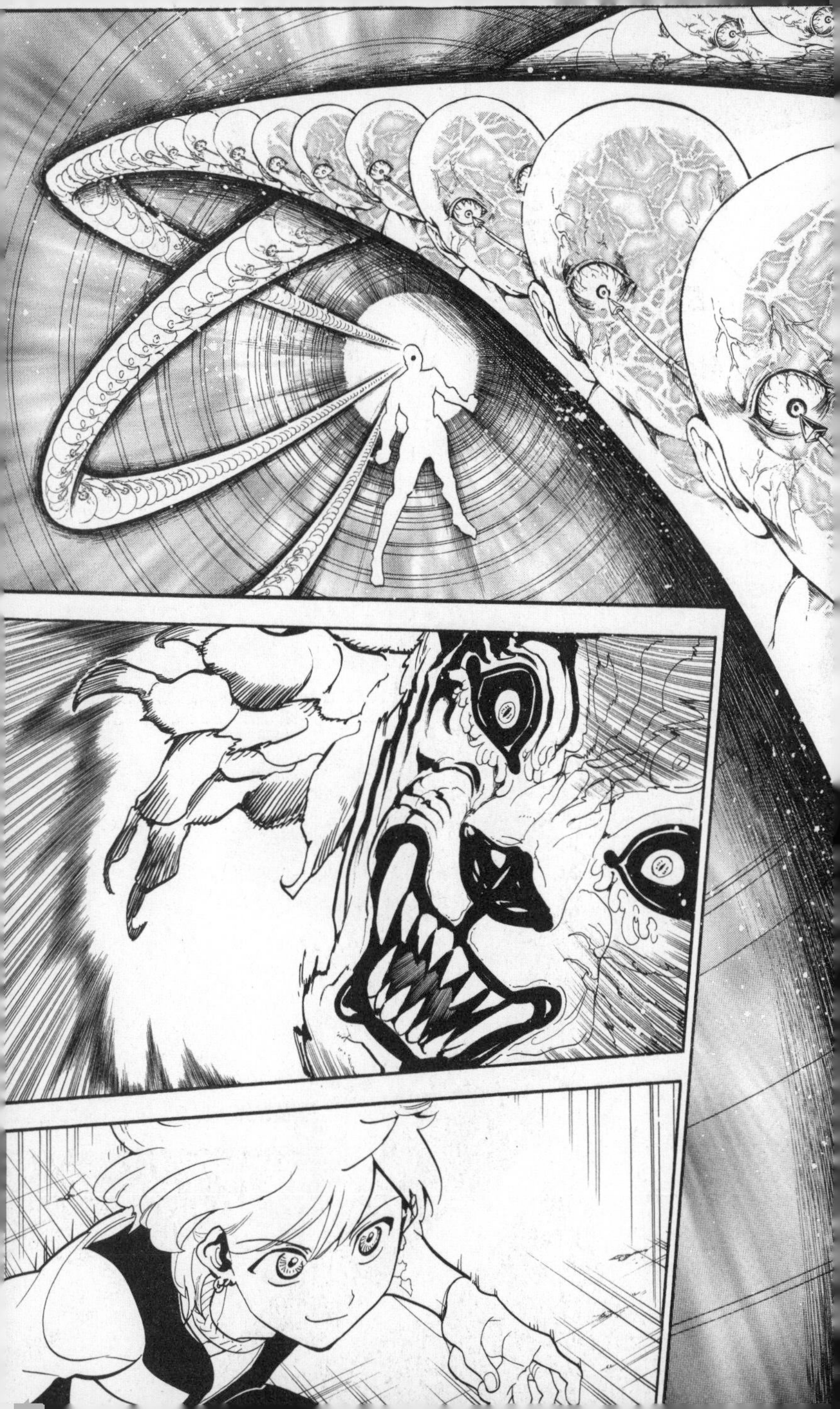

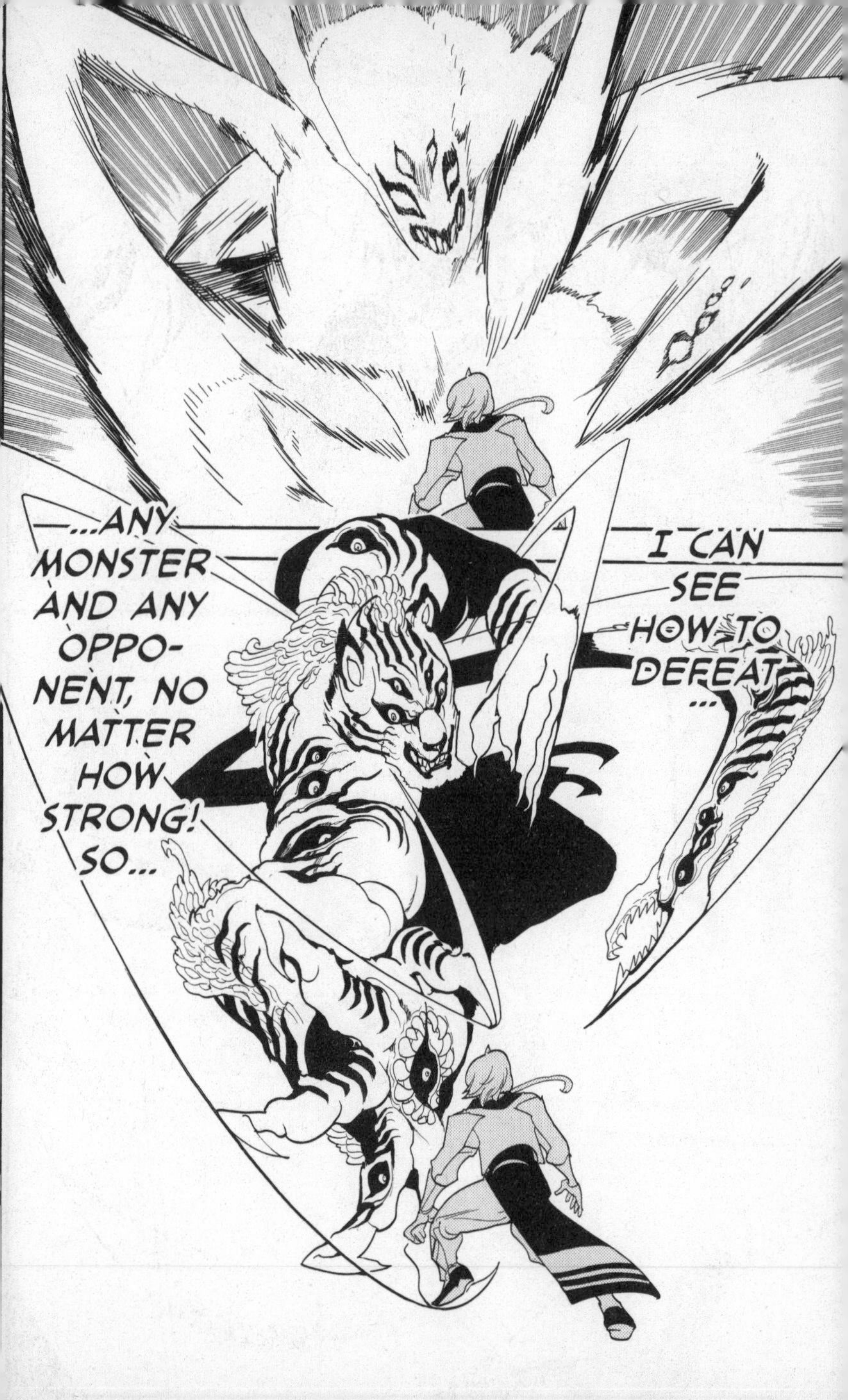
I CAN SEE HOW TO DEFEAT...
...ANY MONSTER AND ANY OPPONENT, NO MATTER HOW STRONG! SO...

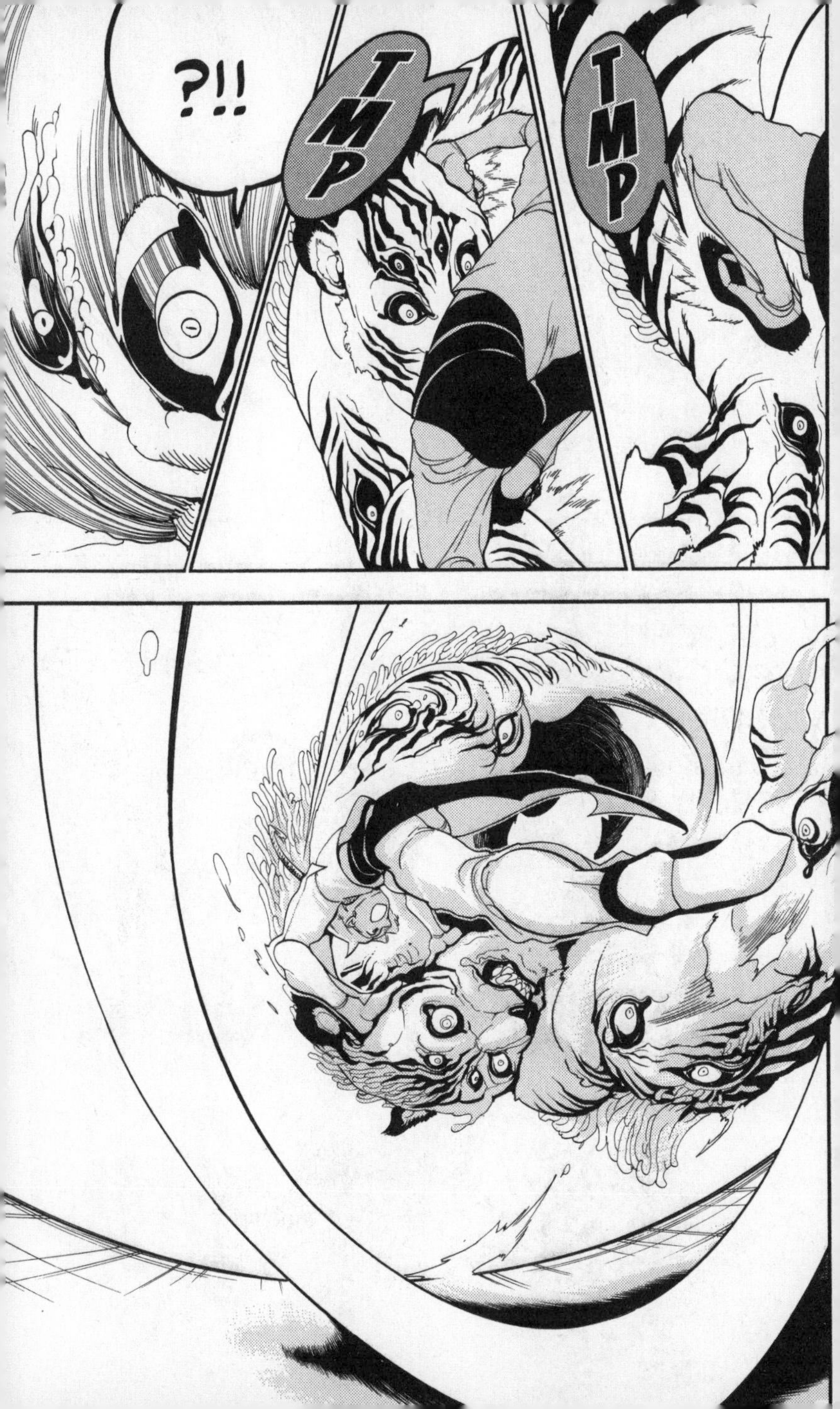
TMP
TMP
?!!

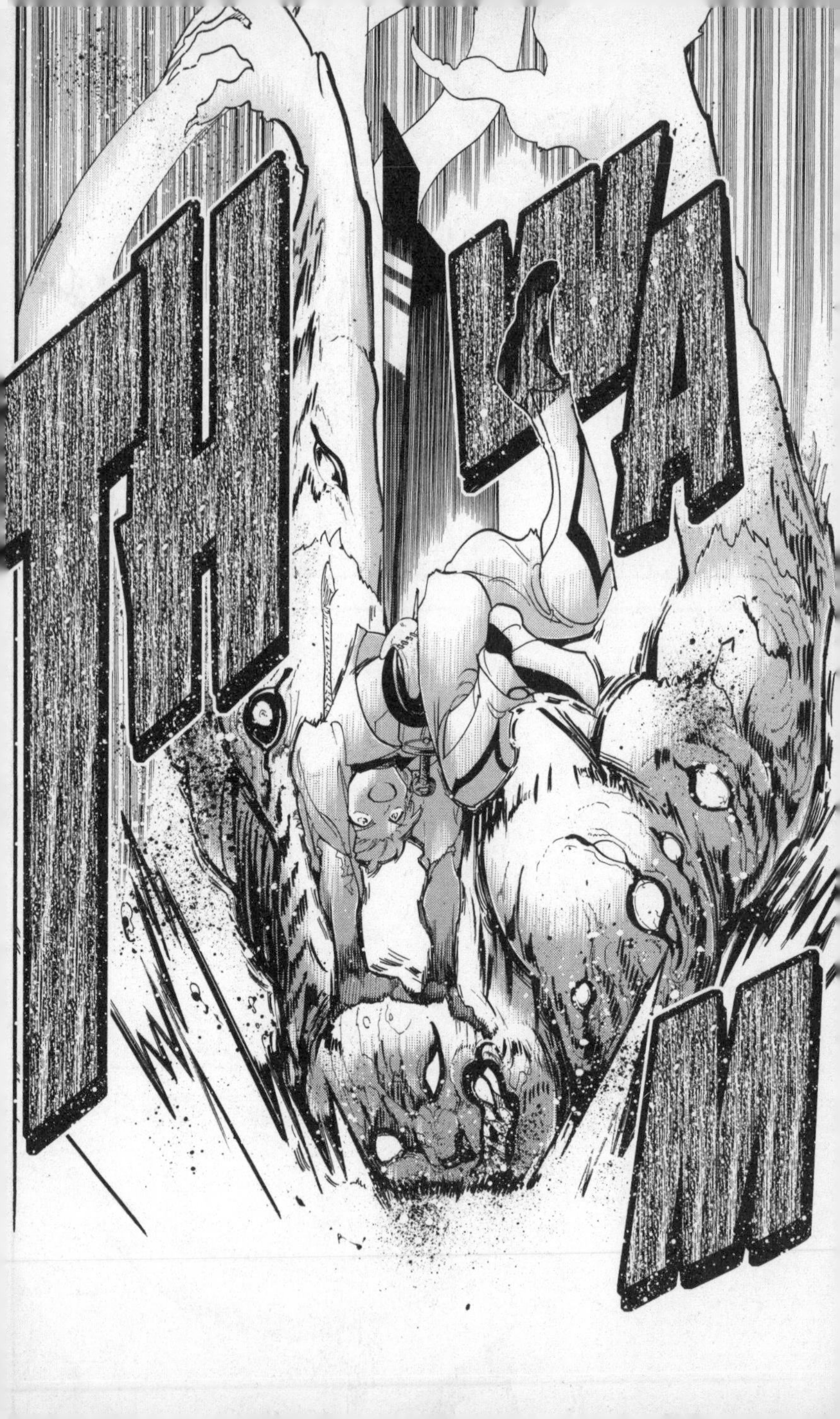
THWAM

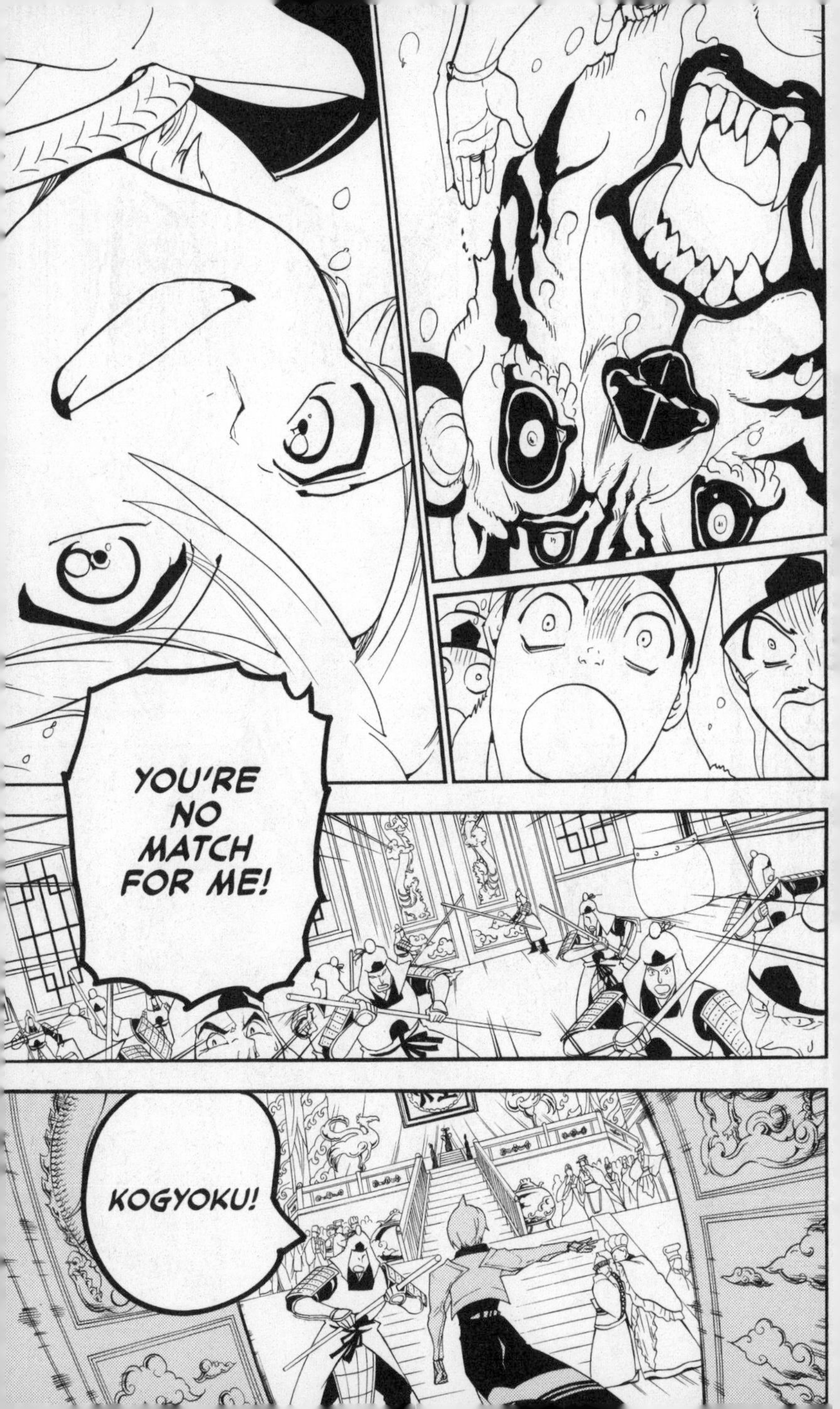
YOU'RE NO MATCH FOR ME!
KOGYOKU!

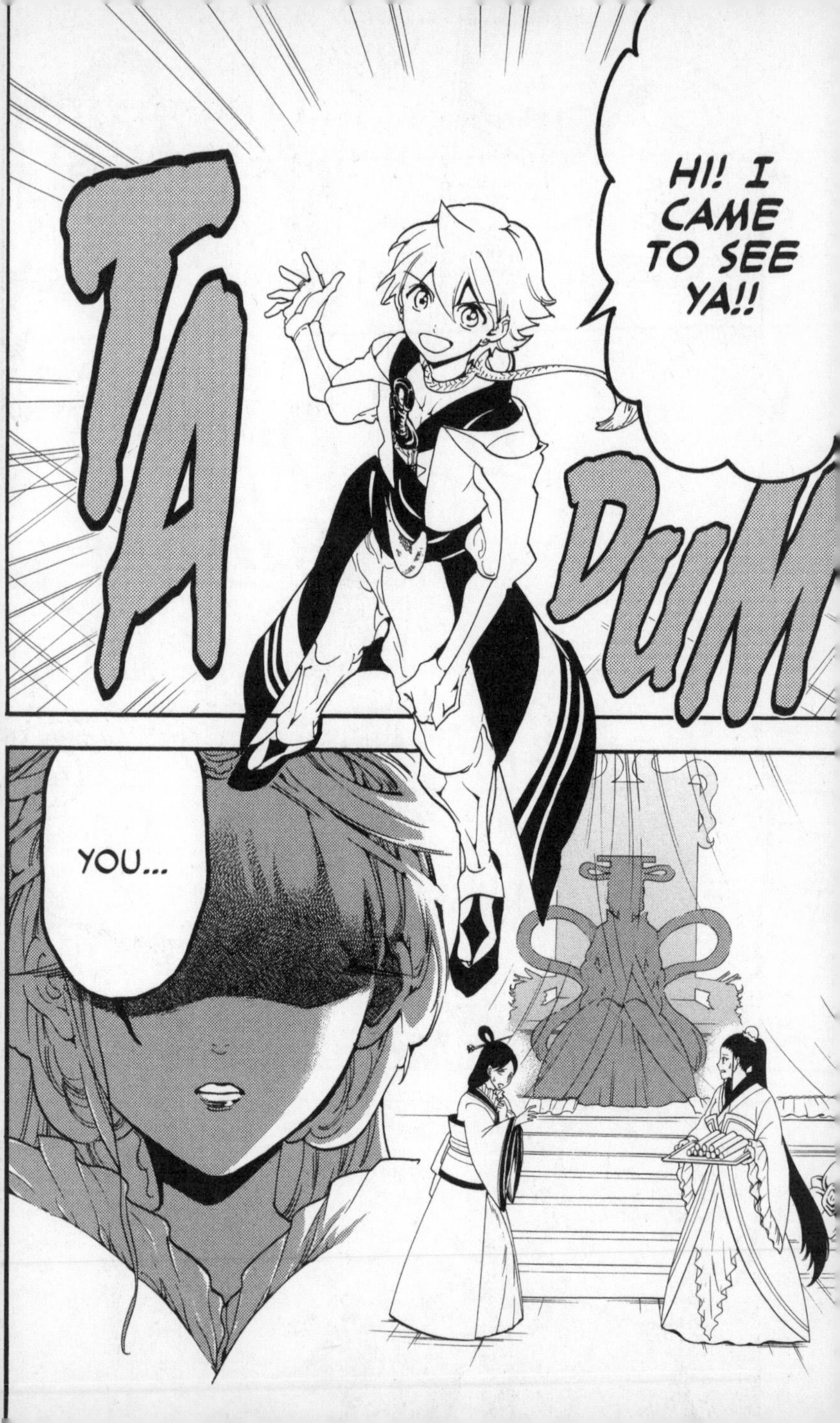
HI! I CAME TO SEE YA!!
TA DUM
YOU...

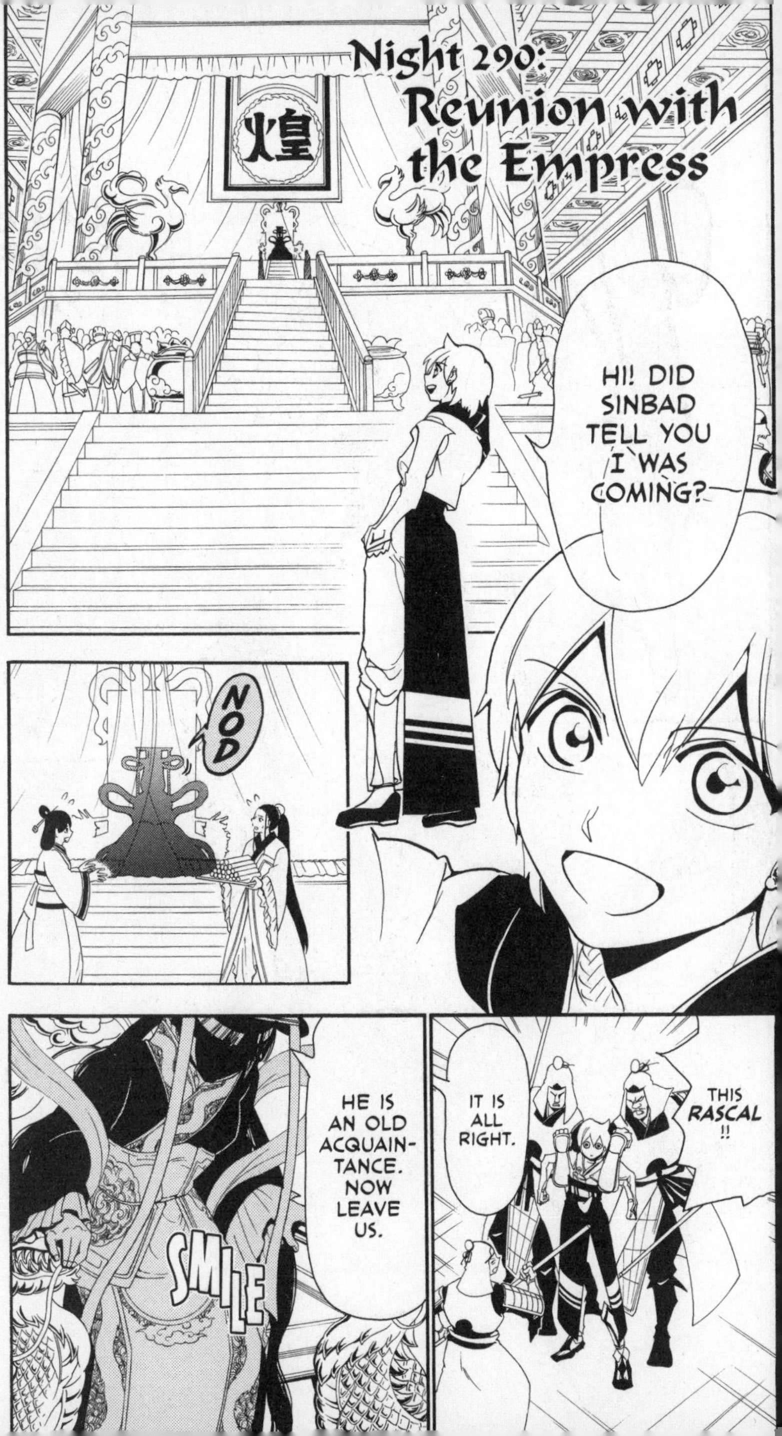
Night 290: Reunion with the Empress
煌
HI! DID SINBAD TELL YOU I WAS COMING?
NOD
THIS RASCAL !!
IT IS ALL RIGHT.
HE IS AN OLD ACQUAIN-TANCE. NOW LEAVE US.
SMILE

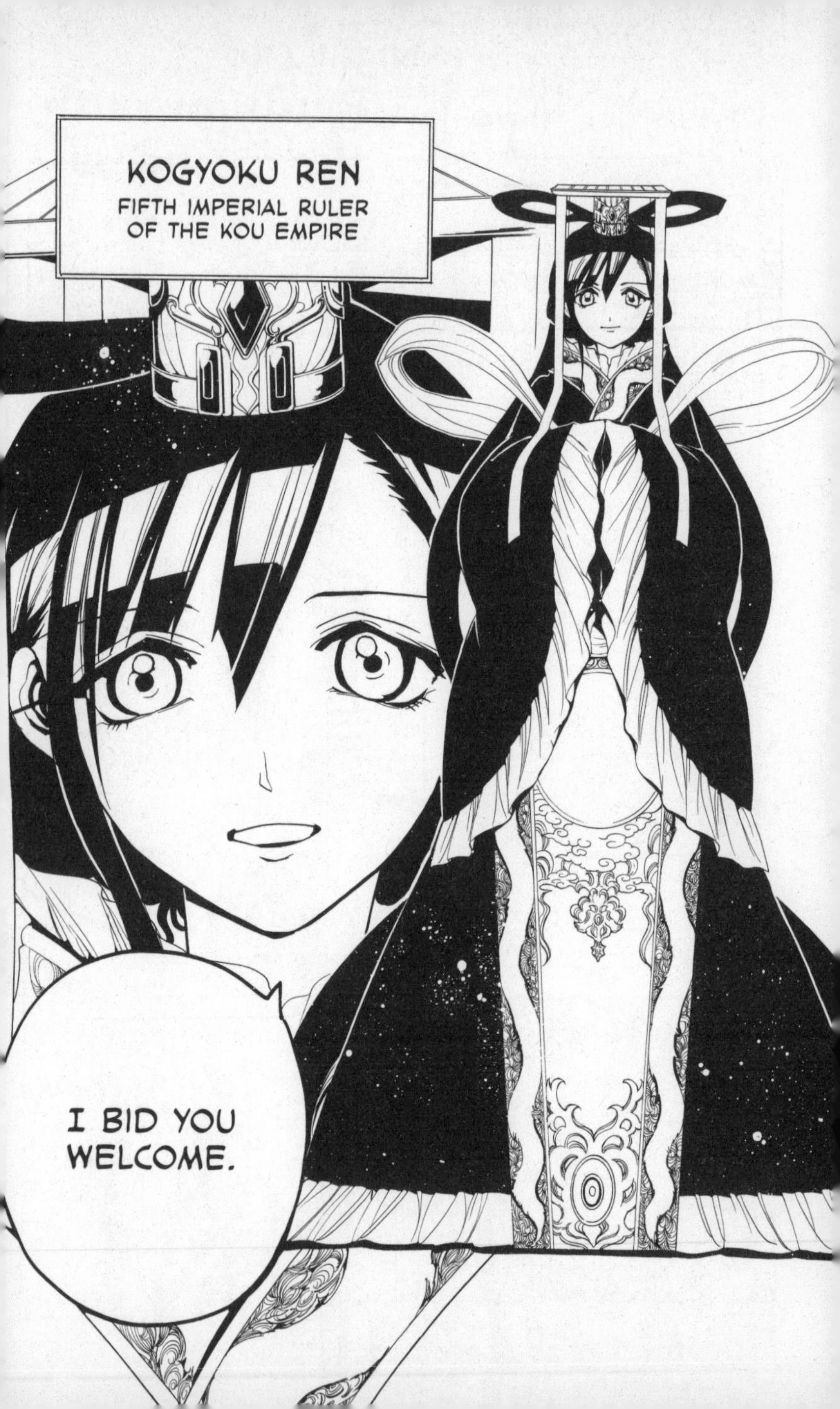
KOGYOKU REN
FIFTH IMPERIAL RULER OF THE KOU EMPIRE
I BID YOU WELCOME.

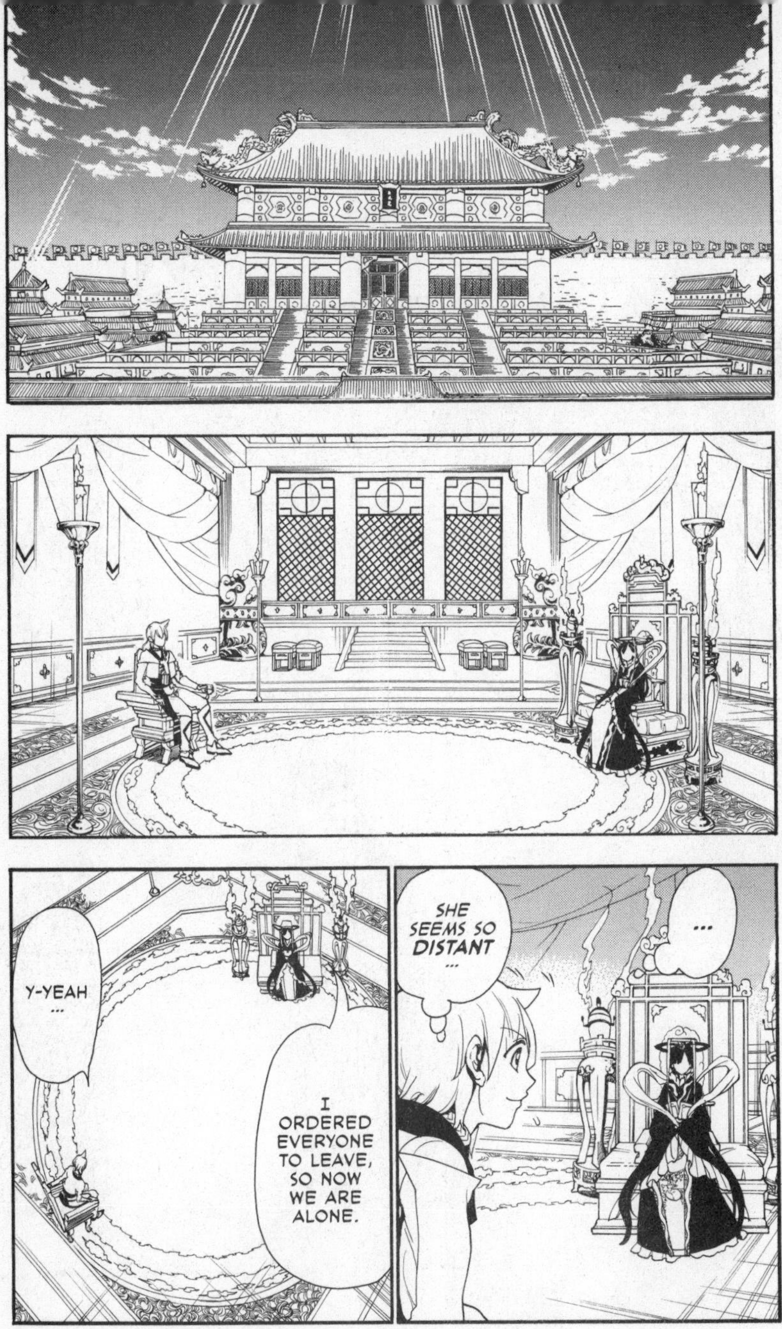
...
SHE SEEMS SO DISTANT ...
I ORDERED EVERYONE TO LEAVE, SO NOW WE ARE ALONE.
Y-YEAH ...

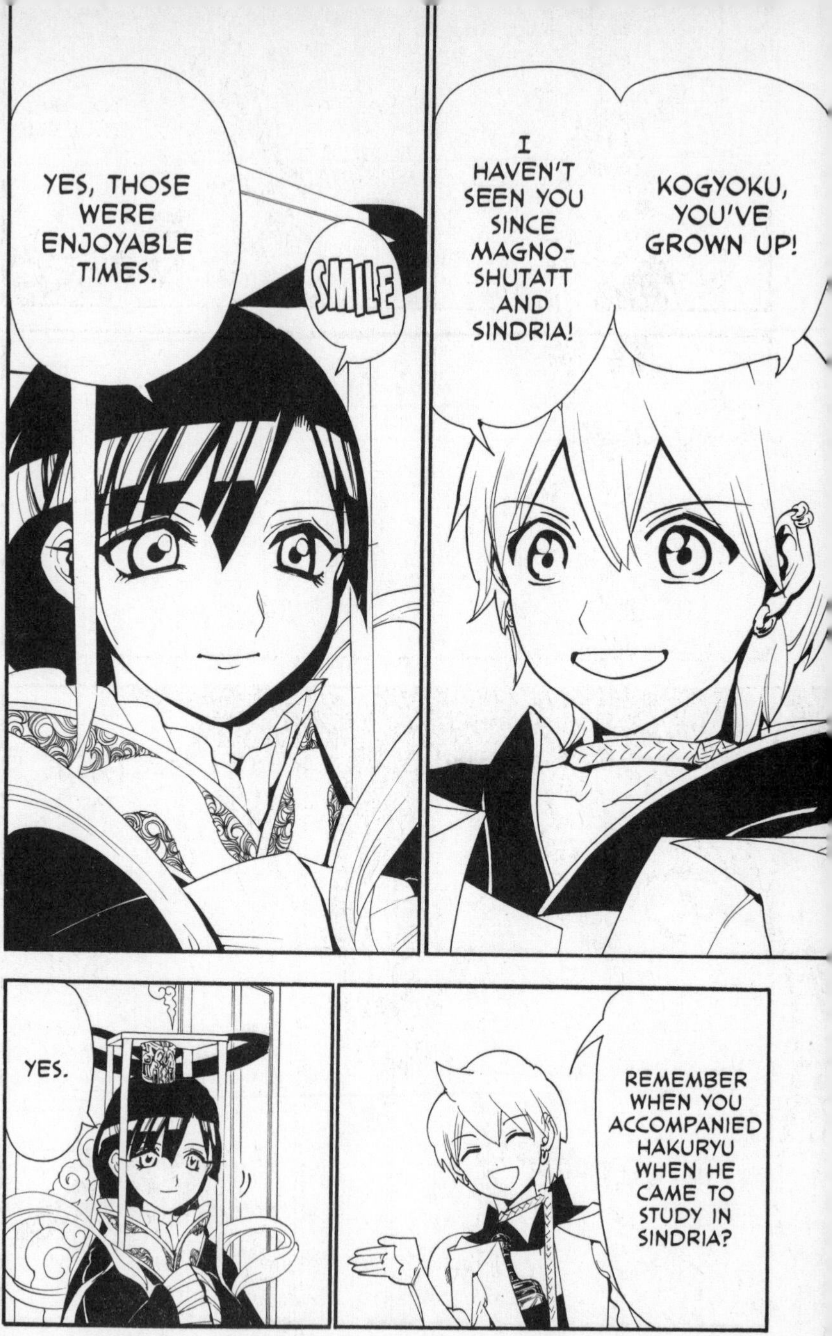
KOGYOKU, YOU'VE GROWN UP!
I HAVEN'T SEEN YOU SINCE MAGNO-SHUTATT AND SINDRIA!
SMILE
YES, THOSE WERE ENJOYABLE TIMES.
REMEMBER WHEN YOU ACCOMPANIED HAKURYU WHEN HE CAME TO STUDY IN SINDRIA?
YES.

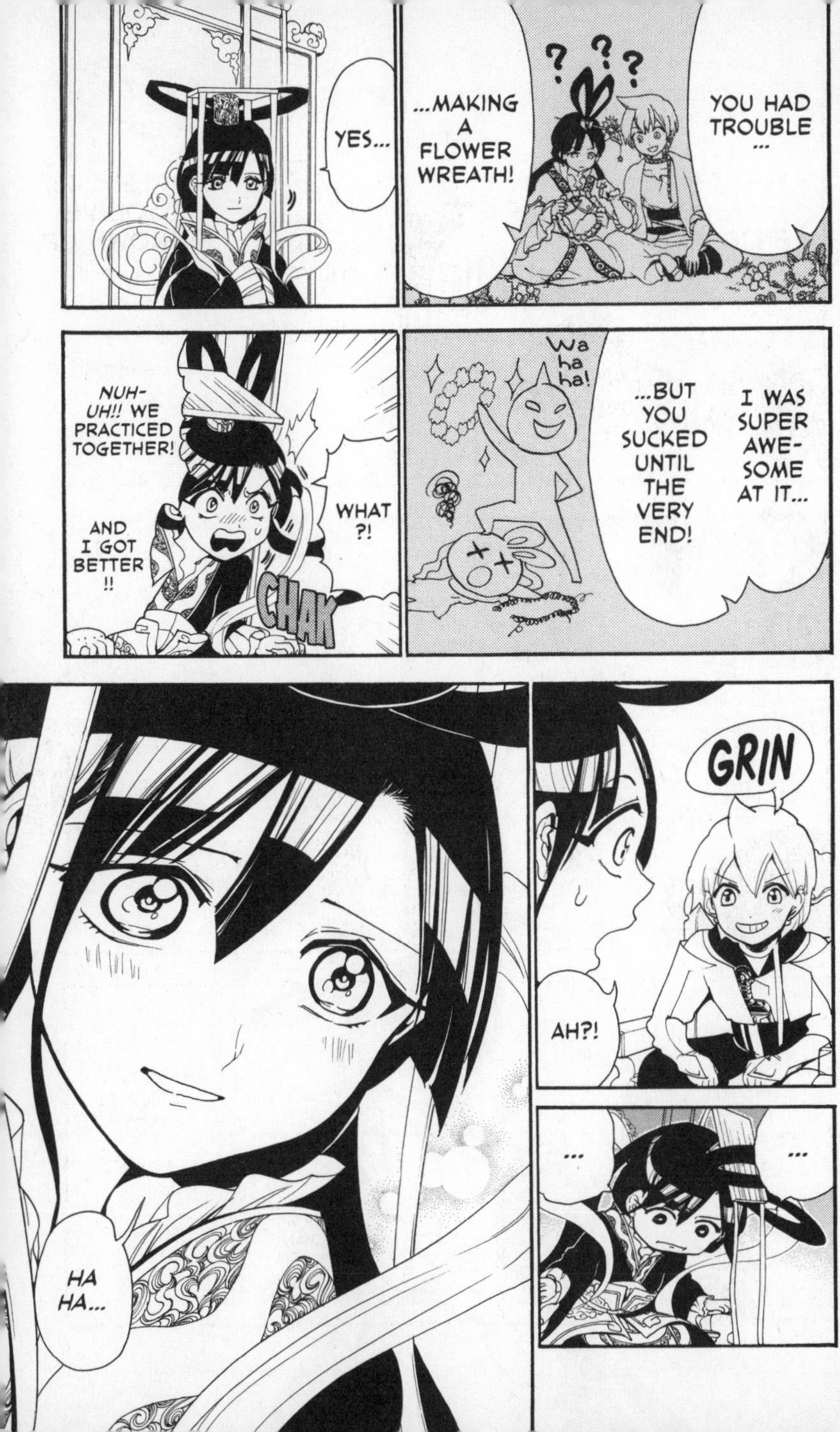
YOU HAD TROUBLE ...
...MAKING A FLOWER WREATH!
YES...
I WAS SUPER AWE-SOME AT IT...
...BUT YOU SUCKED UNTIL THE VERY END!
Wa ha ha!
WHAT?!
NUH-UH!! WE PRACTICED TOGETHER!
AND I GOT BETTER!!
CHAK
GRIN
AH?!
...
...
HA HA...

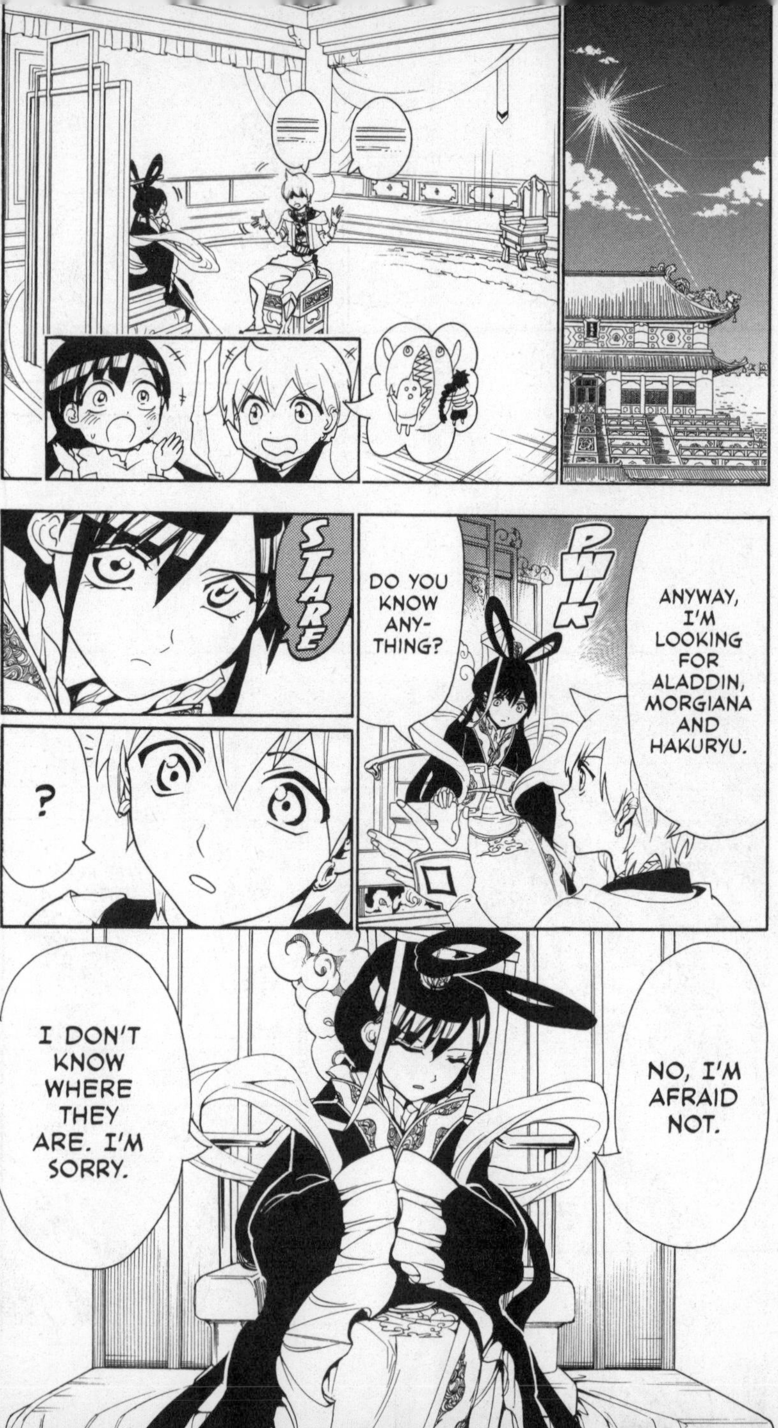
PWIK
ANYWAY, I'M LOOKING FOR ALADDIN, MORGIANA AND HAKURYU.
DO YOU KNOW ANY-THING?
STARE
?
NO, I'M AFRAID NOT.
I DON'T KNOW WHERE THEY ARE. I'M SORRY.

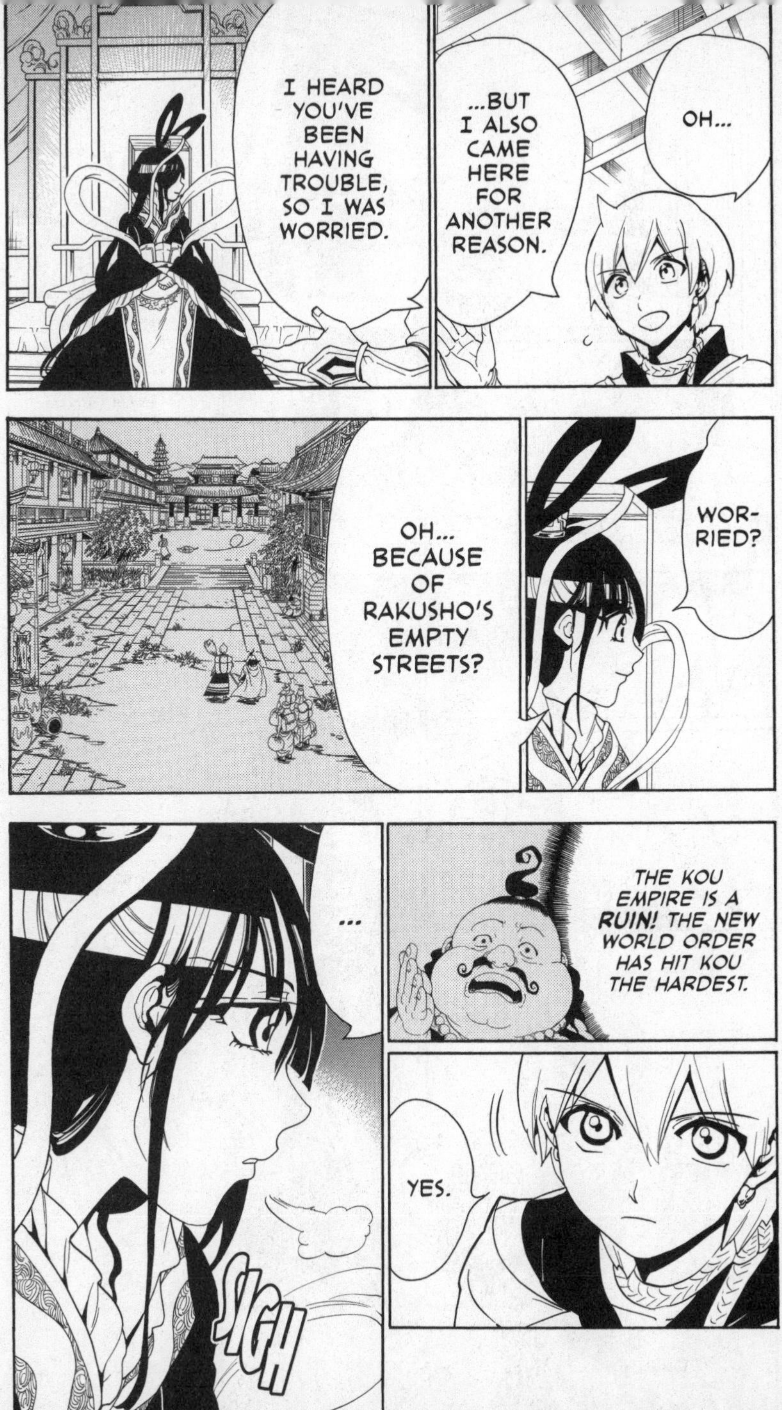
OH...
...BUT I ALSO CAME HERE FOR ANOTHER REASON.
I HEARD YOU'VE BEEN HAVING TROUBLE, SO I WAS WORRIED.
WOR-RIED?
OH... BECAUSE OF RAKUSHO'S EMPTY STREETS?
THE KOU EMPIRE IS A RUIN! THE NEW WORLD ORDER HAS HIT KOU THE HARDEST.
YES.
...
SIGH

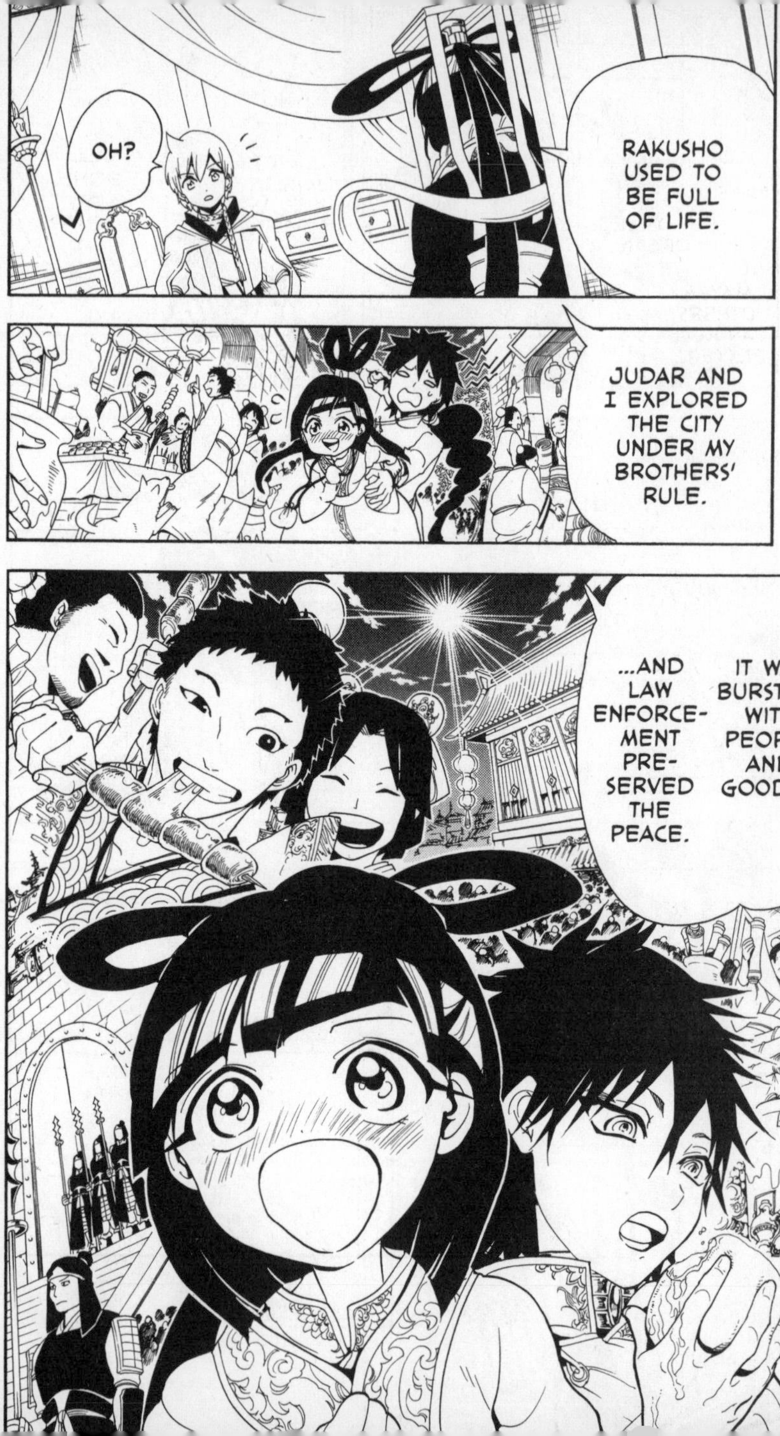
RAKUSHO USED TO BE FULL OF LIFE.
OH?
JUDAR AND I EXPLORED THE CITY UNDER MY BROTHERS' RULE.
IT WAS BURSTING WITH PEOPLE AND GOODS...
...AND LAW ENFORCEMENT PRESERVED THE PEACE.

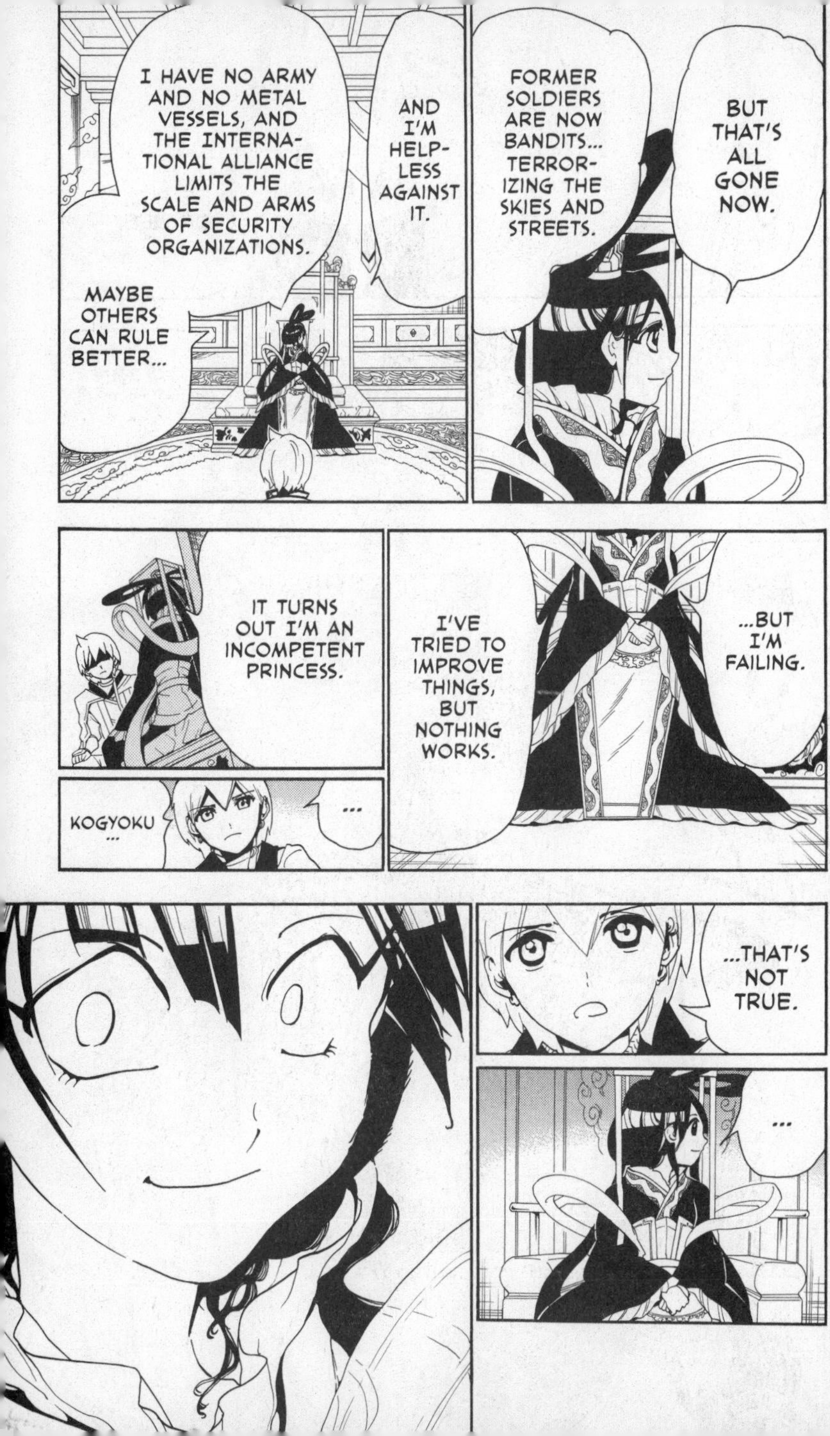
BUT THAT'S ALL GONE NOW.
FORMER SOLDIERS ARE NOW BANDITS... TERRORIZING THE SKIES AND STREETS.
AND I'M HELPLESS AGAINST IT.
I HAVE NO ARMY AND NO METAL VESSELS, AND THE INTERNATIONAL ALLIANCE LIMITS THE SCALE AND ARMS OF SECURITY ORGANIZATIONS.
MAYBE OTHERS CAN RULE BETTER...
...BUT I'M FAILING.
I'VE TRIED TO IMPROVE THINGS, BUT NOTHING WORKS.
IT TURNS OUT I'M AN INCOMPETENT PRINCESS.
...
KOGYOKU ...
...THAT'S NOT TRUE.
...

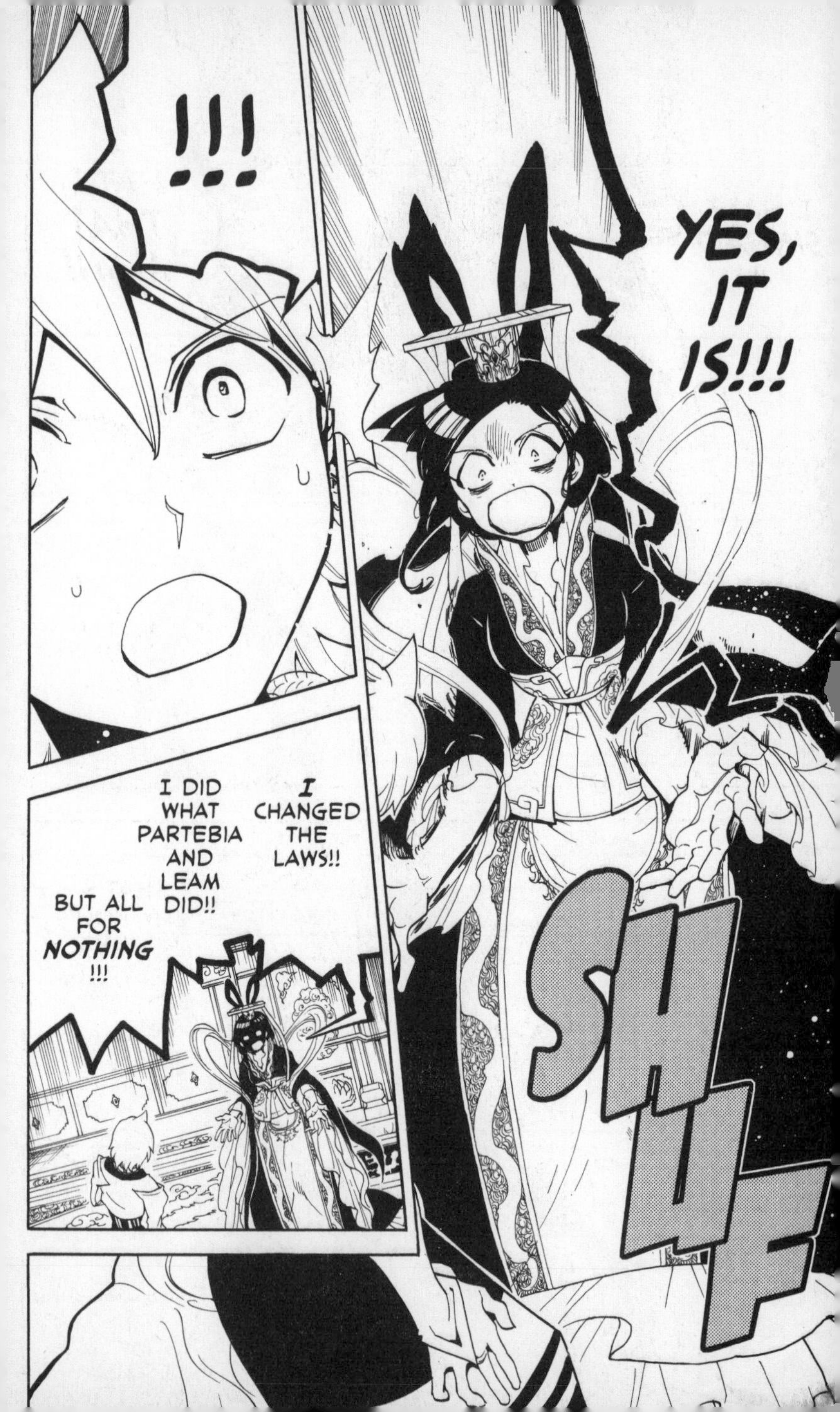
YES, IT IS!!!
!!!
I CHANGED THE LAWS!!
I DID WHAT PARTEBIA AND LEAM DID!!
BUT ALL FOR *NOTHING* !!!
SHUF

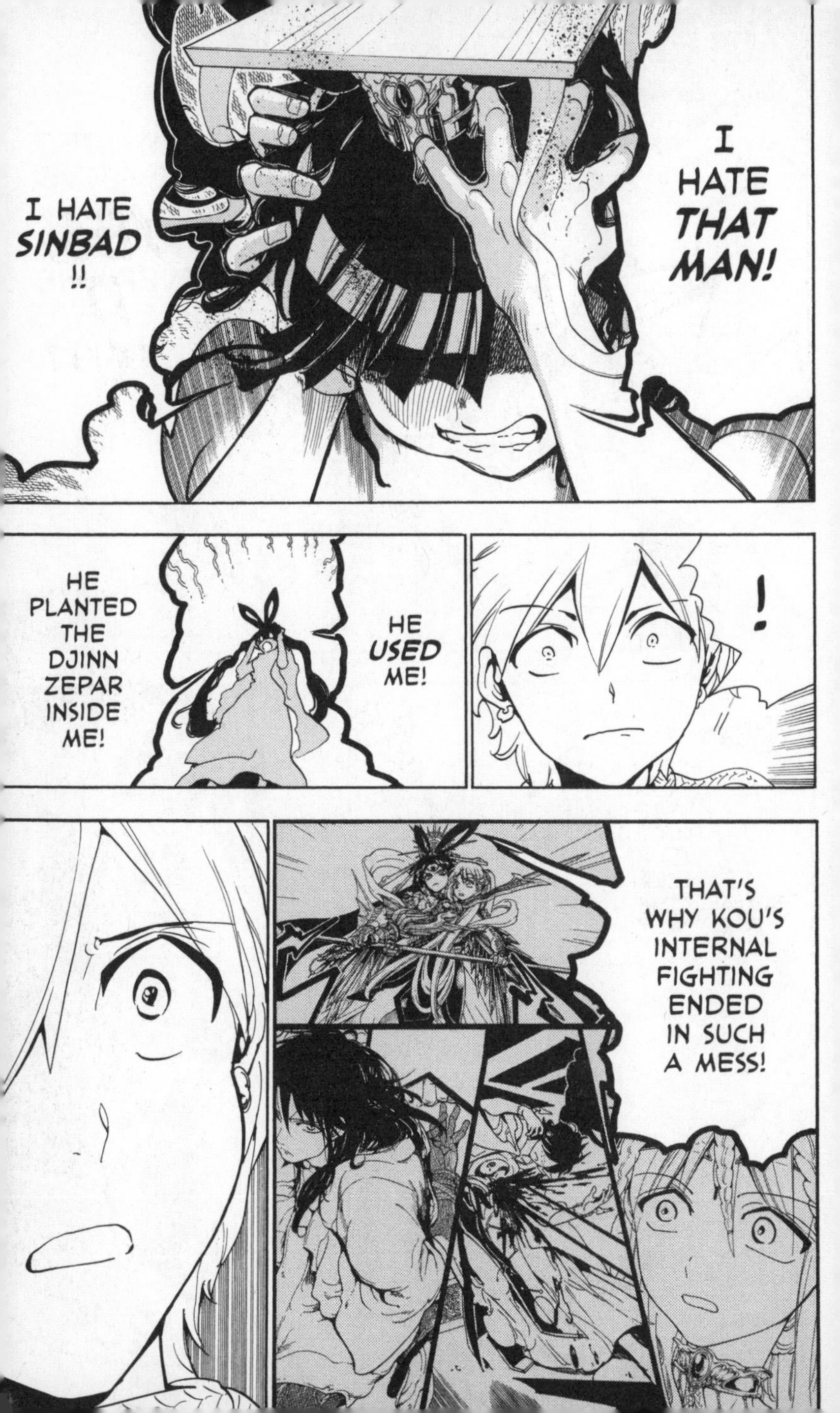
I HATE THAT MAN!
I HATE SINBAD!!
!
HE USED ME!
HE PLANTED THE DJINN ZEPAR INSIDE ME!
THAT'S WHY KOU'S INTERNAL FIGHTING ENDED IN SUCH A MESS!

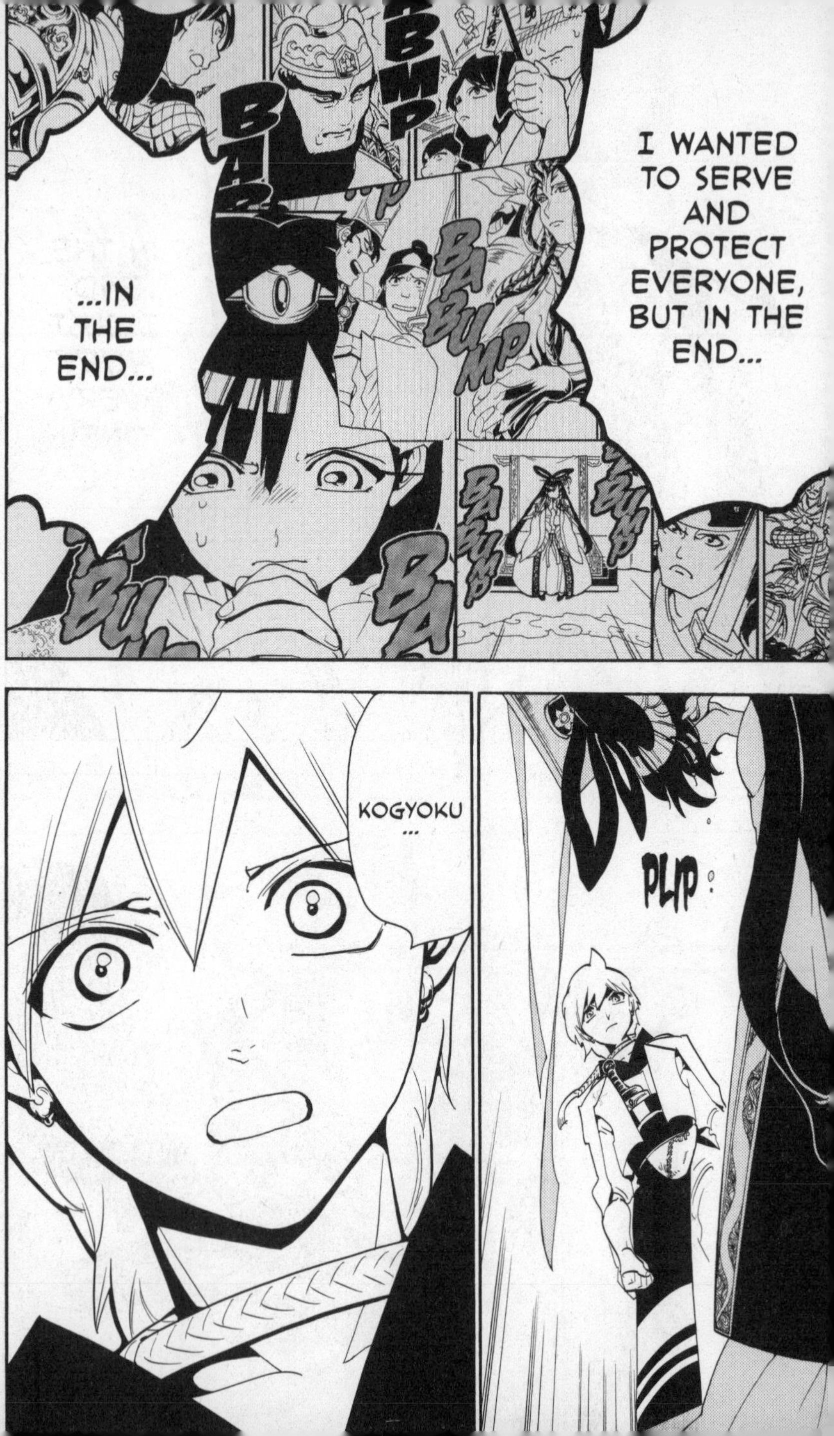

I WANTED TO SERVE AND PROTECT EVERYONE, BUT IN THE END...
BA BUMP
...IN THE END...
BA BUMP
PLIP
KOGYOKU ...

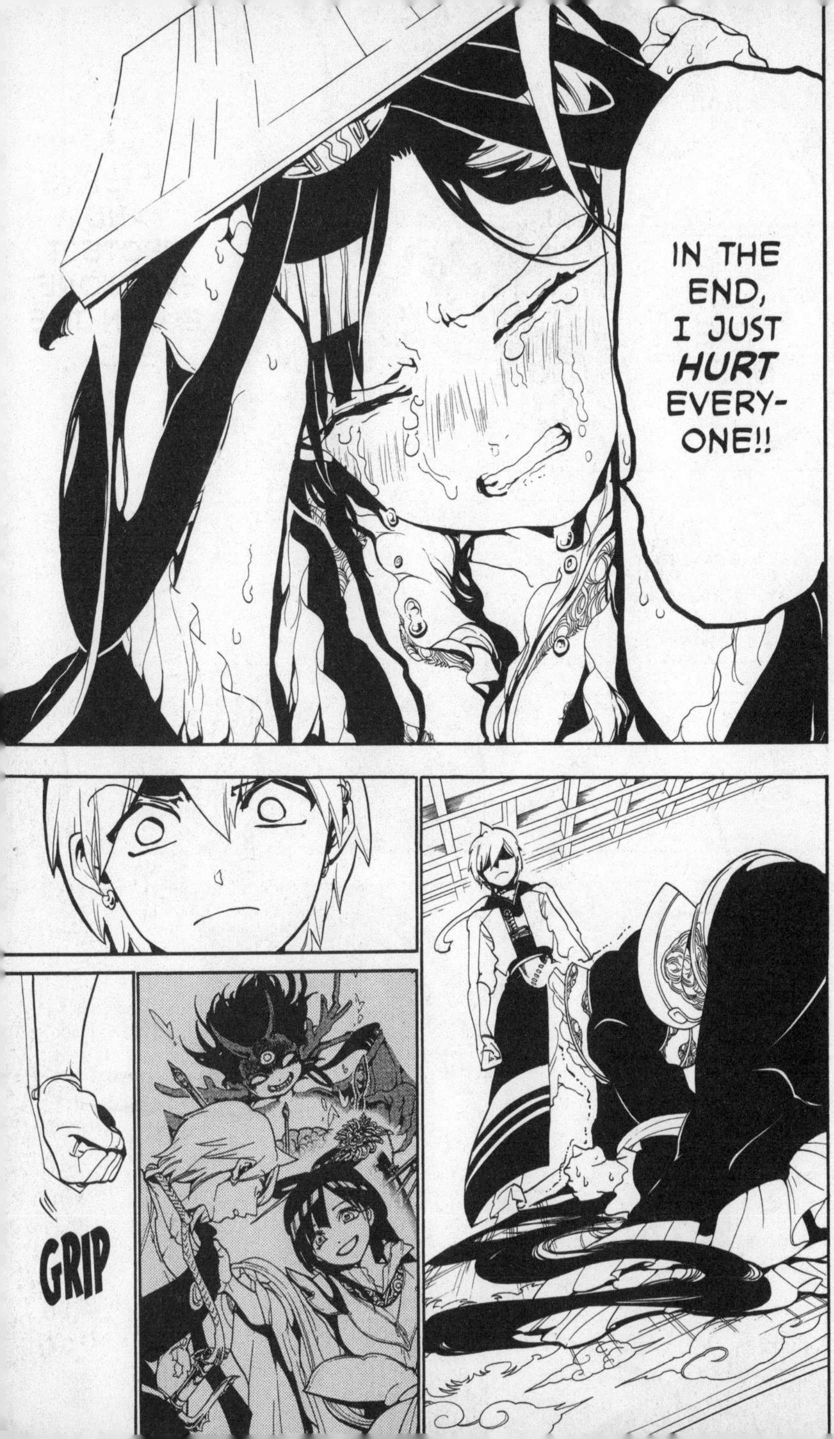
IN THE END, I JUST *HURT* EVERY-ONE!!
GRIP

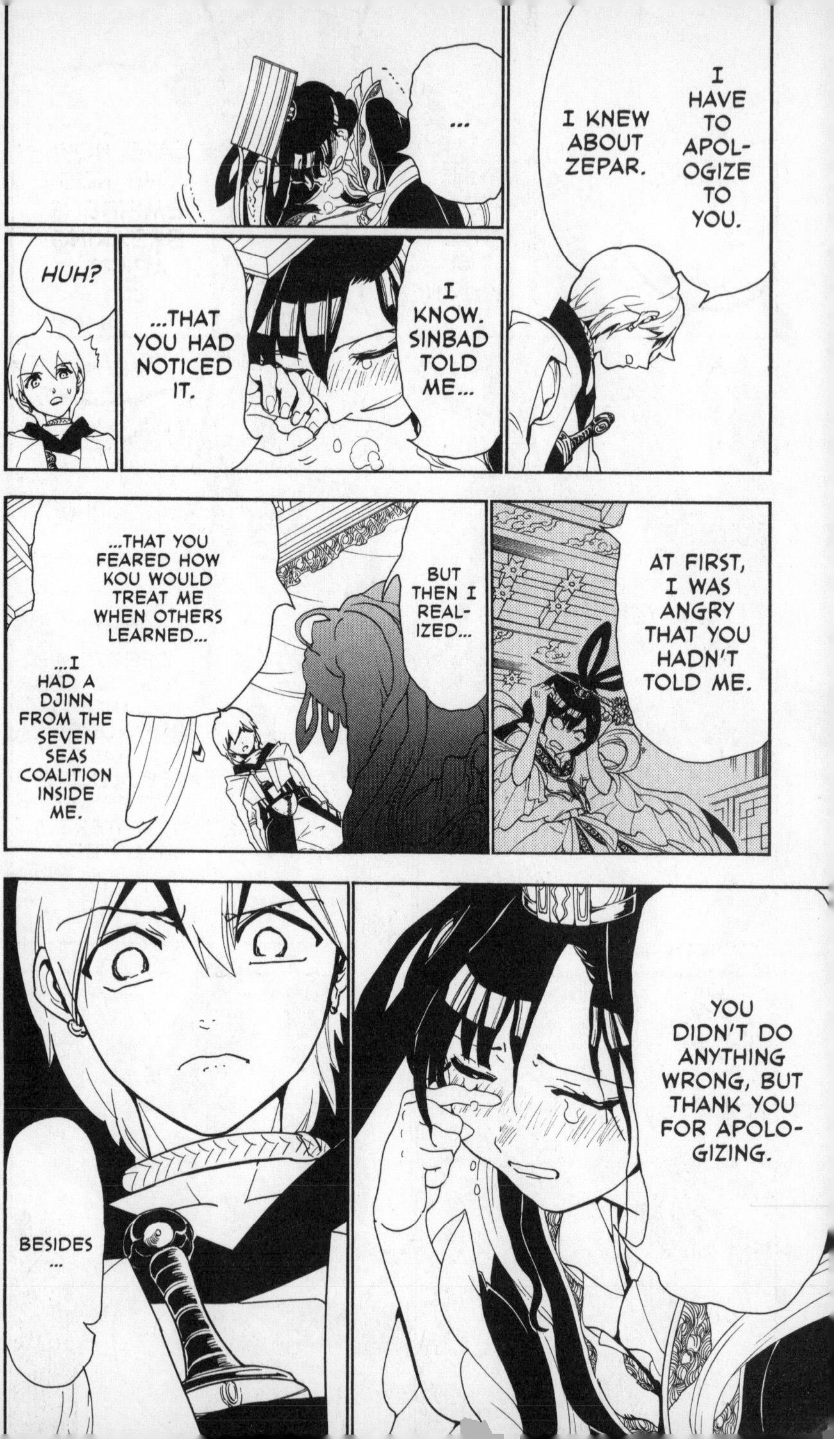
I HAVE TO APOLOGIZE TO YOU.
I KNEW ABOUT ZEPAR.
...
I KNOW. SINBAD TOLD ME...
...THAT YOU HAD NOTICED IT.
HUH?
AT FIRST, I WAS ANGRY THAT YOU HADN'T TOLD ME.
BUT THEN I REALIZED...
...THAT YOU FEARED HOW KOU WOULD TREAT ME WHEN OTHERS LEARNED...
...I HAD A DJINN FROM THE SEVEN SEAS COALITION INSIDE ME.
YOU DIDN'T DO ANYTHING WRONG, BUT THANK YOU FOR APOLOGIZING.
BESIDES...

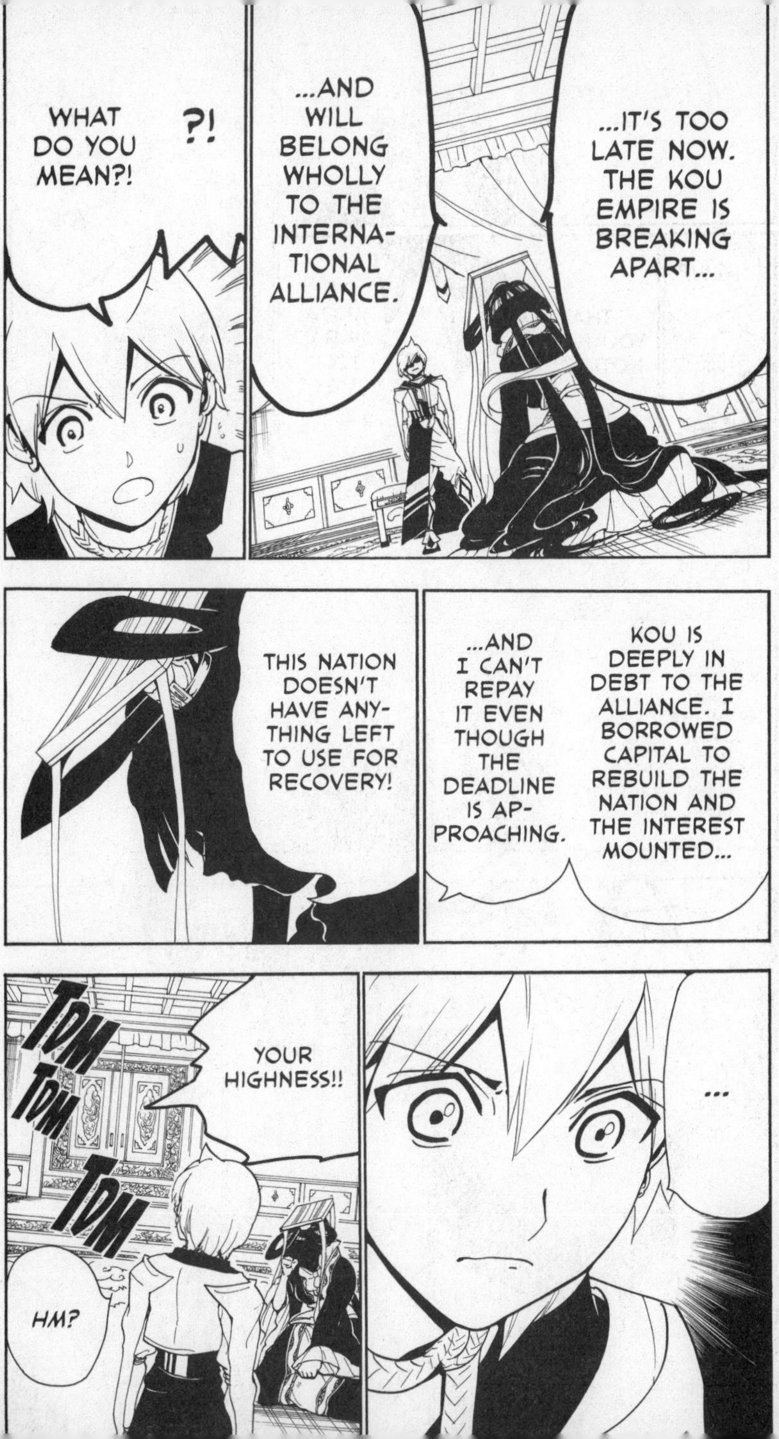

...IT'S TOO LATE NOW. THE KOU EMPIRE IS BREAKING APART...
...AND WILL BELONG WHOLLY TO THE INTERNATIONAL ALLIANCE.
?!
WHAT DO YOU MEAN?!
KOU IS DEEPLY IN DEBT TO THE ALLIANCE. I BORROWED CAPITAL TO REBUILD THE NATION AND THE INTEREST MOUNTED...
...AND I CAN'T REPAY IT EVEN THOUGH THE DEADLINE IS APPROACHING.
THIS NATION DOESN'T HAVE ANYTHING LEFT TO USE FOR RECOVERY!
...
TOM TOM TOM
YOUR HIGHNESS!!
HM?

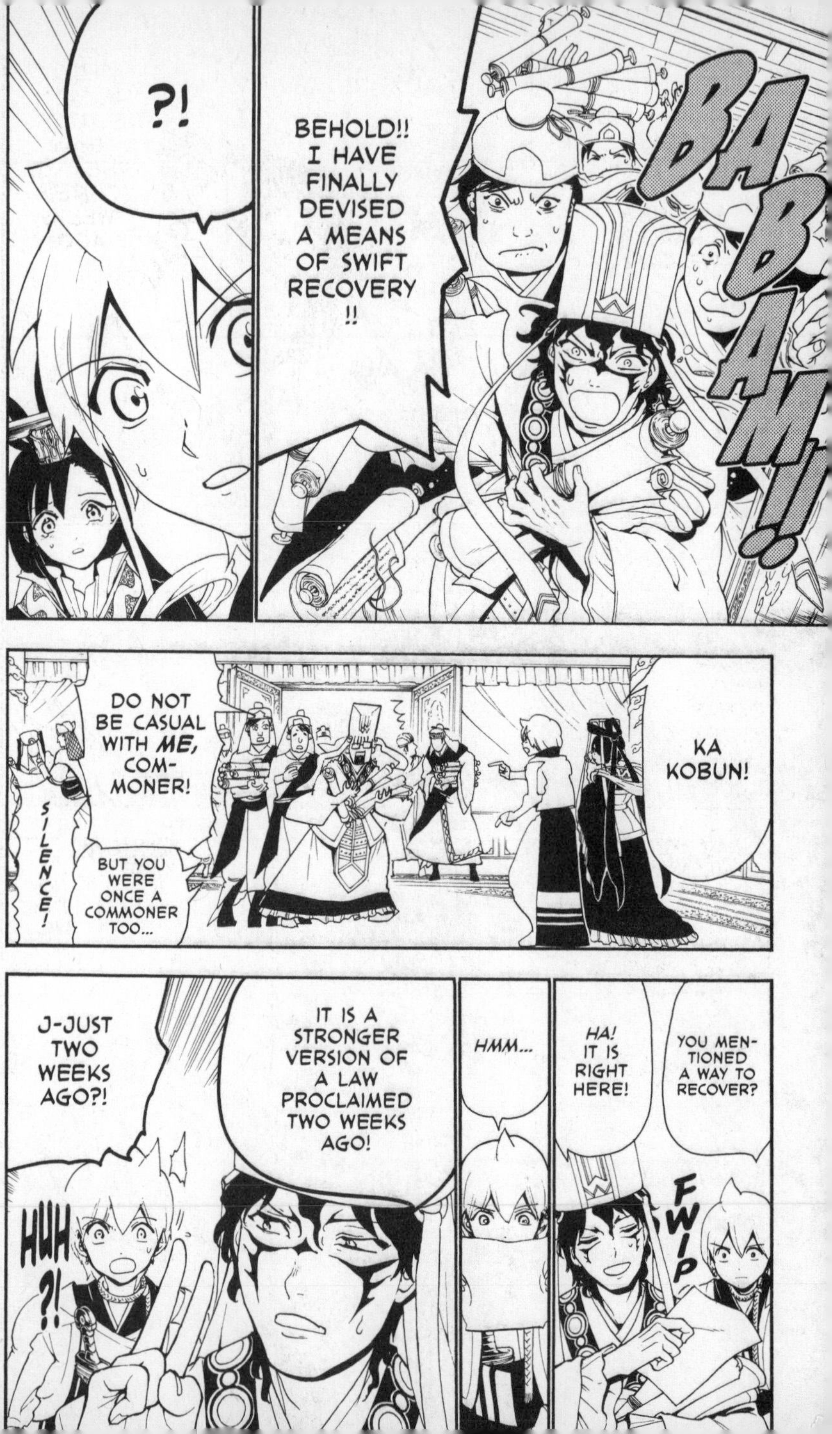
BABAM!!
BEHOLD!! I HAVE FINALLY DEVISED A MEANS OF SWIFT RECOVERY !!
?!
KA KOBUN!
DO NOT BE CASUAL WITH *ME,* COM-MONER!
BUT YOU WERE ONCE A COMMONER TOO...
SILENCE!
YOU MEN-TIONED A WAY TO RECOVER?
HA! IT IS RIGHT HERE!
FWIP
HMM...
IT IS A STRONGER VERSION OF A LAW PROCLAIMED TWO WEEKS AGO!
J-JUST TWO WEEKS AGO?!
HUH ?!

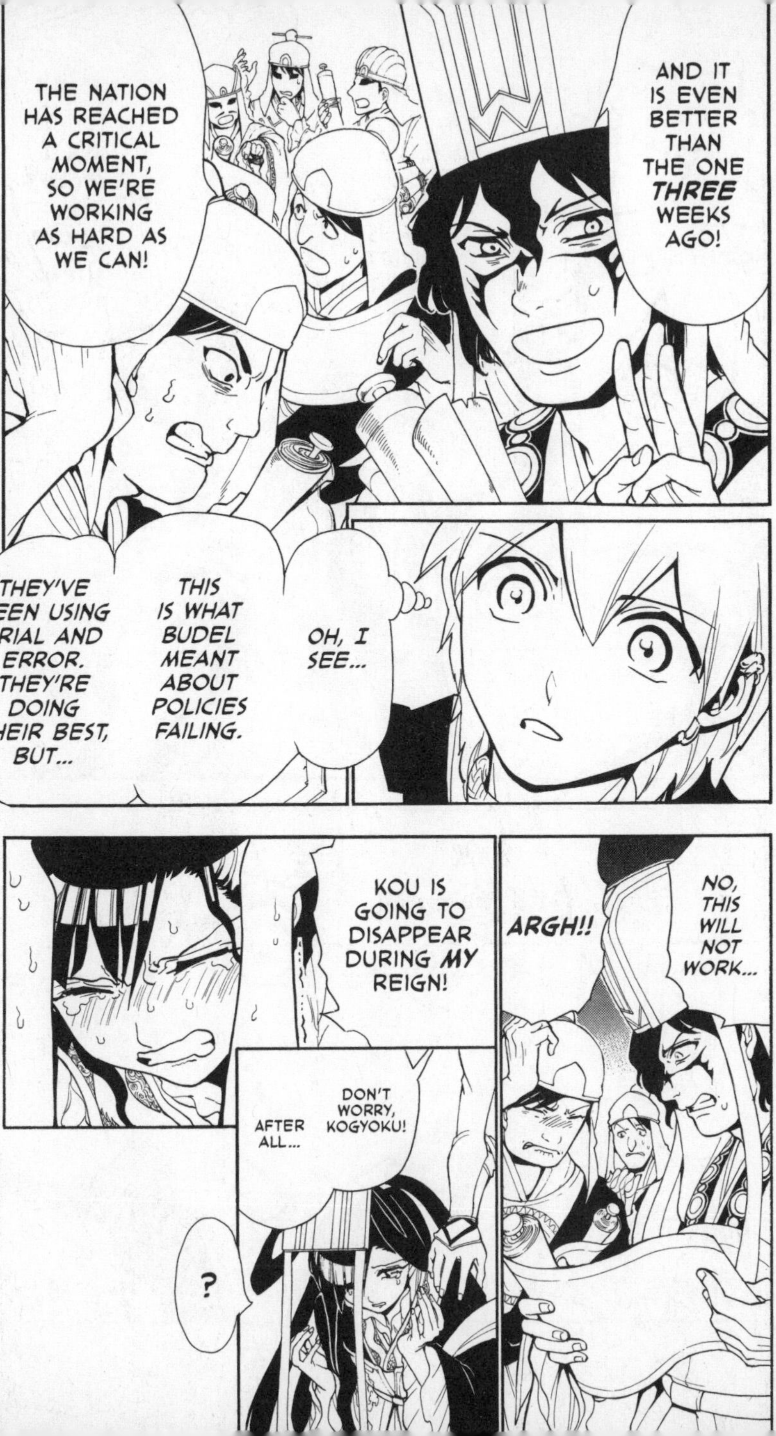
AND IT IS EVEN BETTER THAN THE ONE *THREE* WEEKS AGO!
THE NATION HAS REACHED A CRITICAL MOMENT, SO WE'RE WORKING AS HARD AS WE CAN!
OH, I SEE...
THIS IS WHAT BUDEL MEANT ABOUT POLICIES FAILING.
THEY'VE BEEN USING TRIAL AND ERROR. THEY'RE DOING THEIR BEST, BUT...
NO, THIS WILL NOT WORK...
ARGH!!
KOU IS GOING TO DISAPPEAR DURING *MY* REIGN!
DON'T WORRY, KOGYOKU!
AFTER ALL...
?

...KOU *DOES* HAVE SOME-THING!
?!
W-WHAT ARE YOU TALKING ABOUT?!
GRIN
JUST LEAVE THIS TO ME!

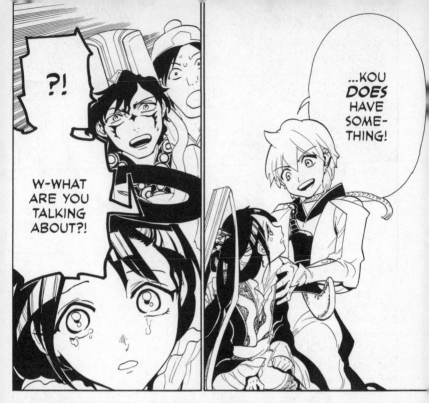

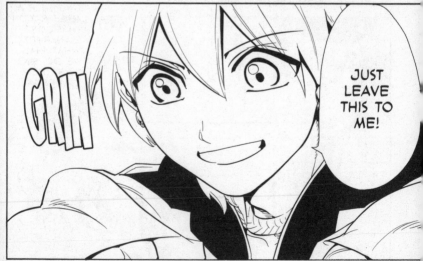

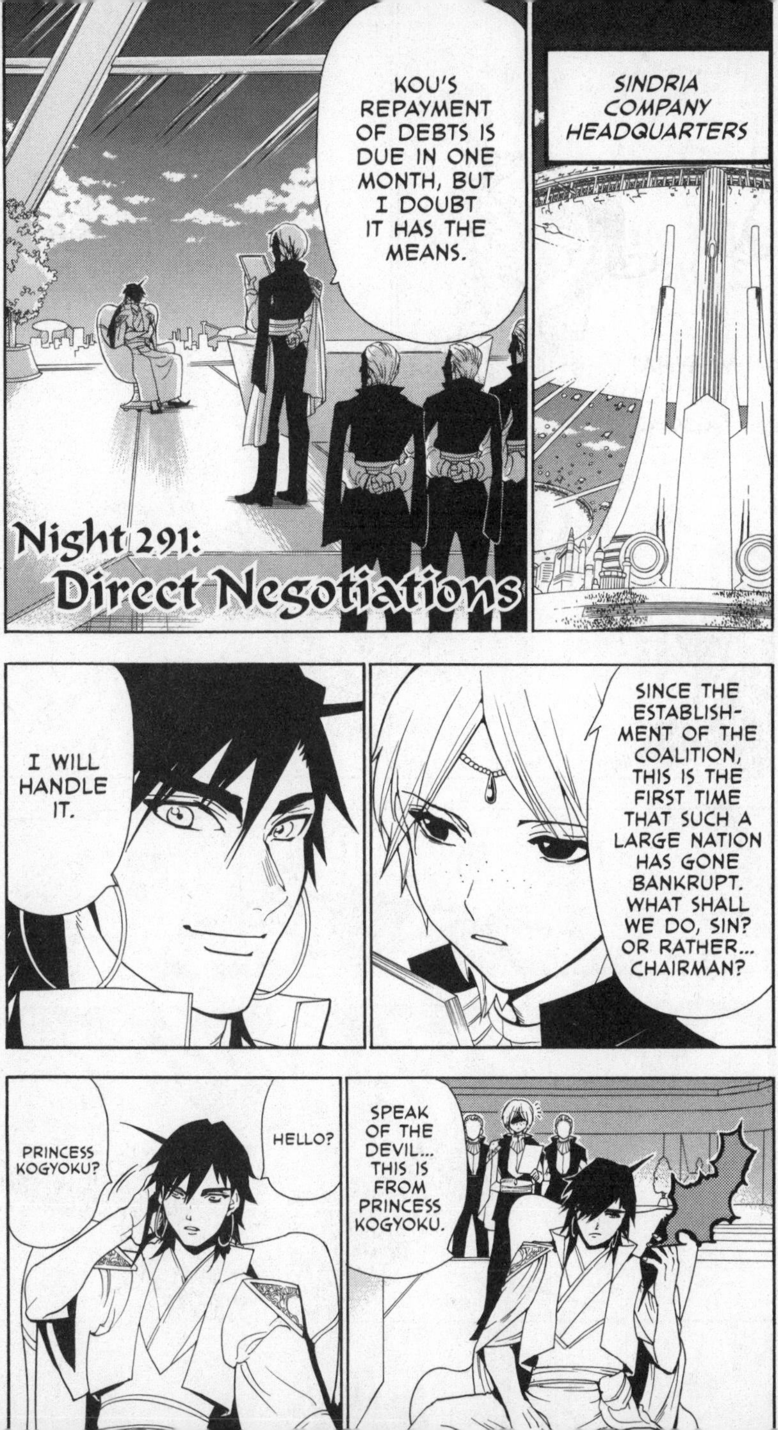
SINDRIA COMPANY HEADQUARTERS
KOU'S REPAYMENT OF DEBTS IS DUE IN ONE MONTH, BUT I DOUBT IT HAS THE MEANS.
Night 291: Direct Negotiations
SINCE THE ESTABLISHMENT OF THE COALITION, THIS IS THE FIRST TIME THAT SUCH A LARGE NATION HAS GONE BANKRUPT. WHAT SHALL WE DO, SIN? OR RATHER... CHAIRMAN?
I WILL HANDLE IT.
SPEAK OF THE DEVIL... THIS IS FROM PRINCESS KOGYOKU.
HELLO?
PRINCESS KOGYOKU?

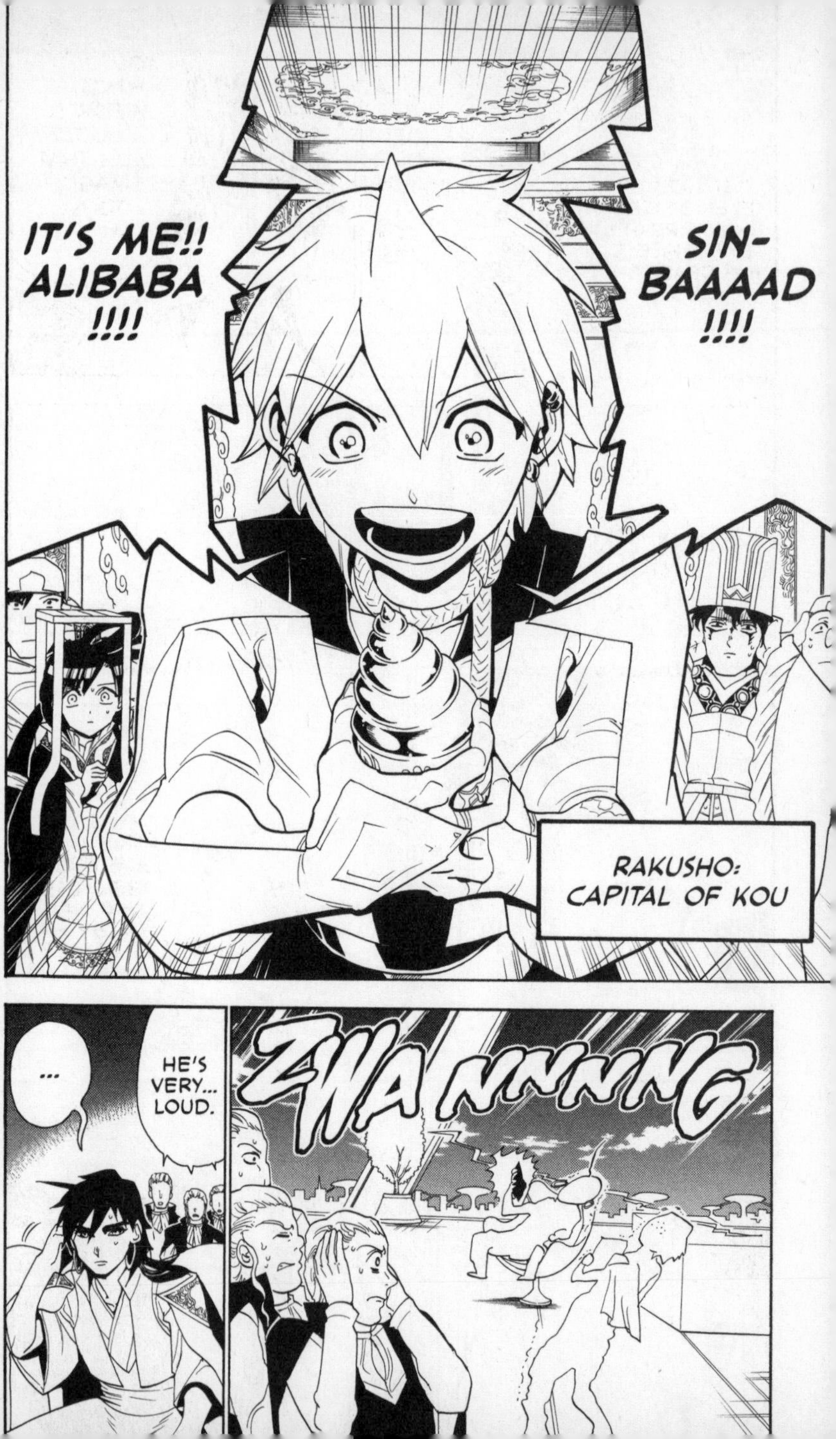
SIN-BAAAAD !!!!
IT'S ME!! ALIBABA !!!!
RAKUSHO: CAPITAL OF KOU
ZWANNNNG
HE'S VERY... LOUD.
...

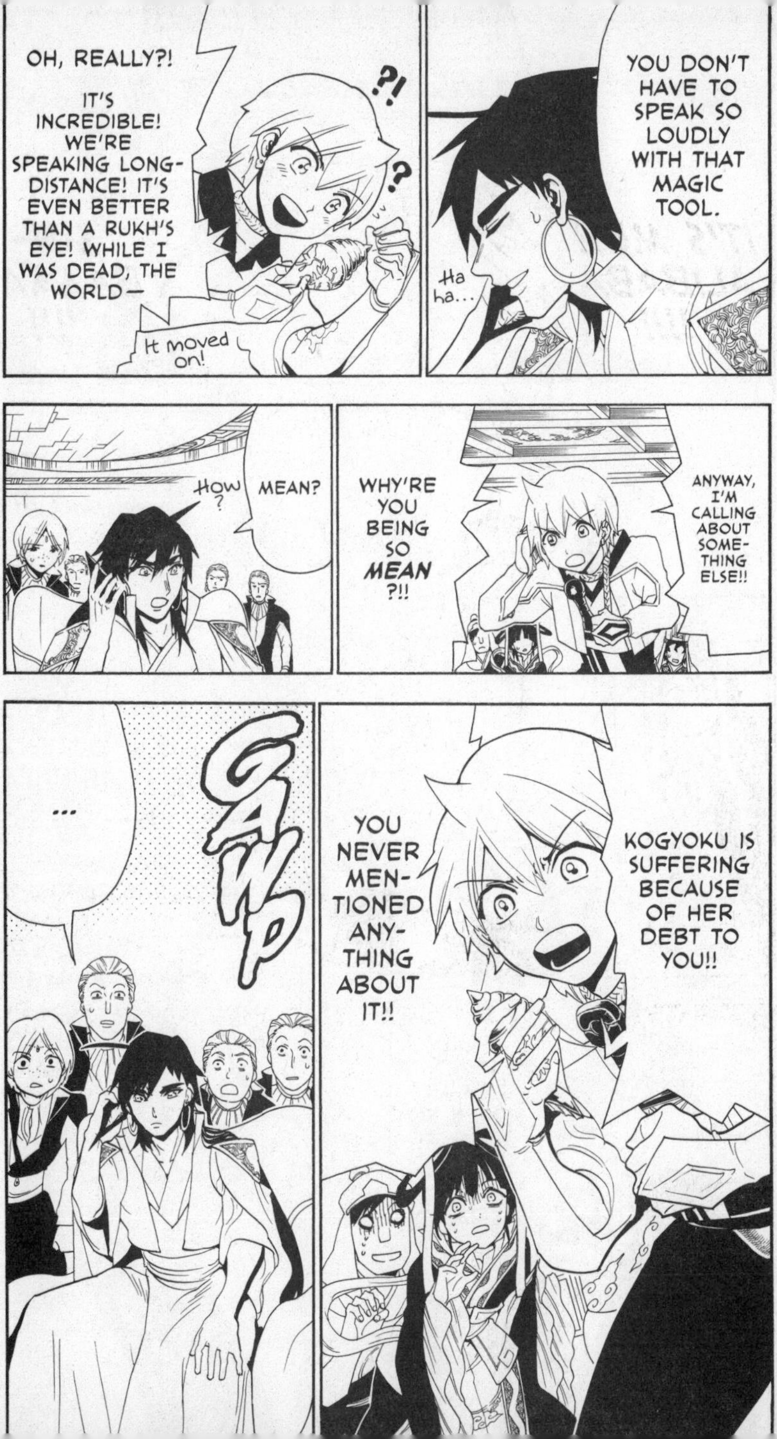
YOU DON'T HAVE TO SPEAK SO LOUDLY WITH THAT MAGIC TOOL.
Ha ha...
?!
?
OH, REALLY?!
IT'S INCREDIBLE! WE'RE SPEAKING LONG-DISTANCE! IT'S EVEN BETTER THAN A RUKH'S EYE! WHILE I WAS DEAD, THE WORLD—
It moved on!
ANYWAY, I'M CALLING ABOUT SOME-THING ELSE!!
WHY'RE YOU BEING SO *MEAN*?!!
MEAN?
How?
KOGYOKU IS SUFFERING BECAUSE OF HER DEBT TO YOU!!
YOU NEVER MEN-TIONED ANY-THING ABOUT IT!!
GAWP
...

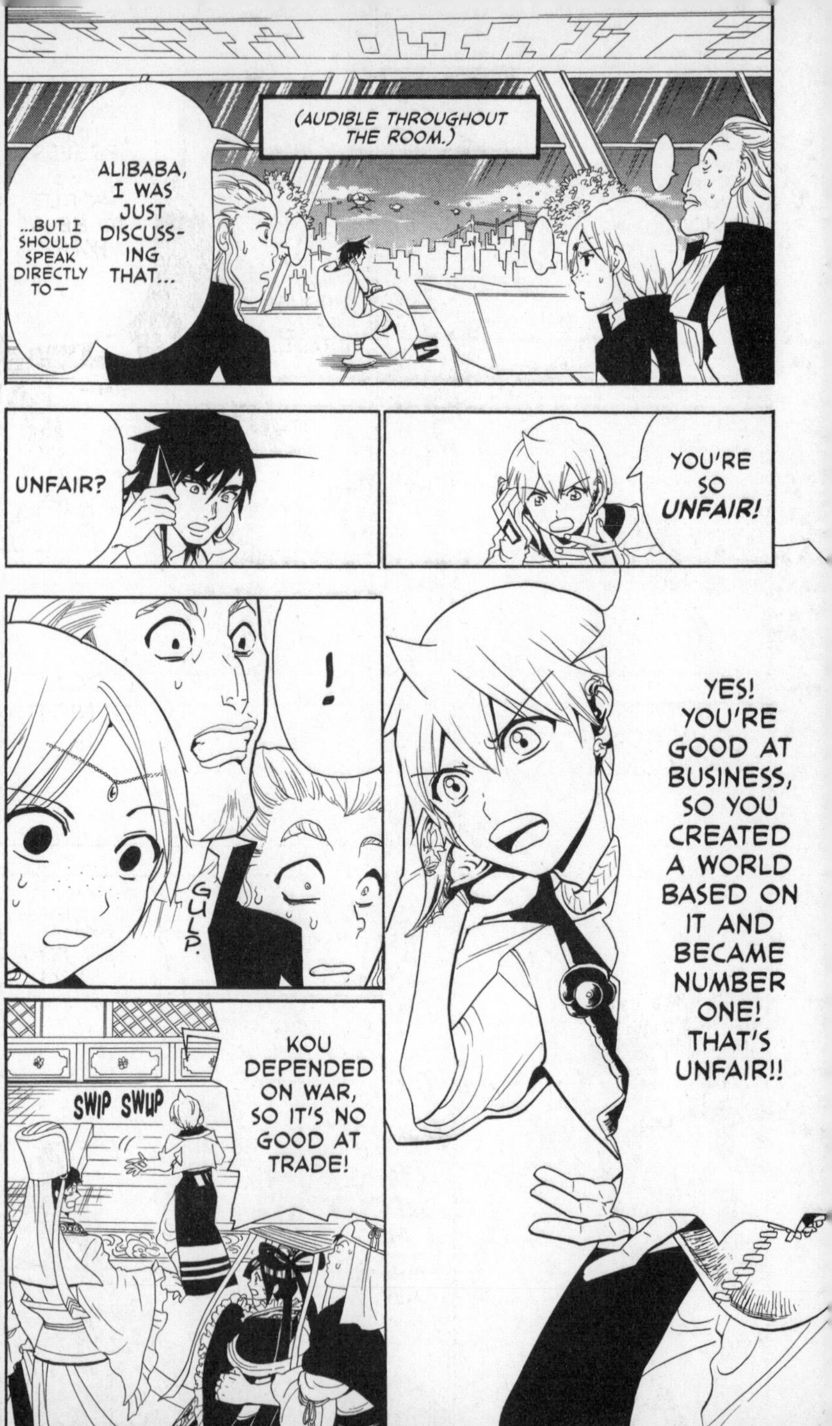
(AUDIBLE THROUGHOUT THE ROOM.)
...
...
...
ALIBABA, I WAS JUST DISCUSSING THAT...
...BUT I SHOULD SPEAK DIRECTLY TO—
YOU'RE SO *UNFAIR!*
UNFAIR?
YES! YOU'RE GOOD AT BUSINESS, SO YOU CREATED A WORLD BASED ON IT AND BECAME NUMBER ONE! THAT'S UNFAIR!!
!
GULP.
KOU DEPENDED ON WAR, SO IT'S NO GOOD AT TRADE!
SWIP SWUP

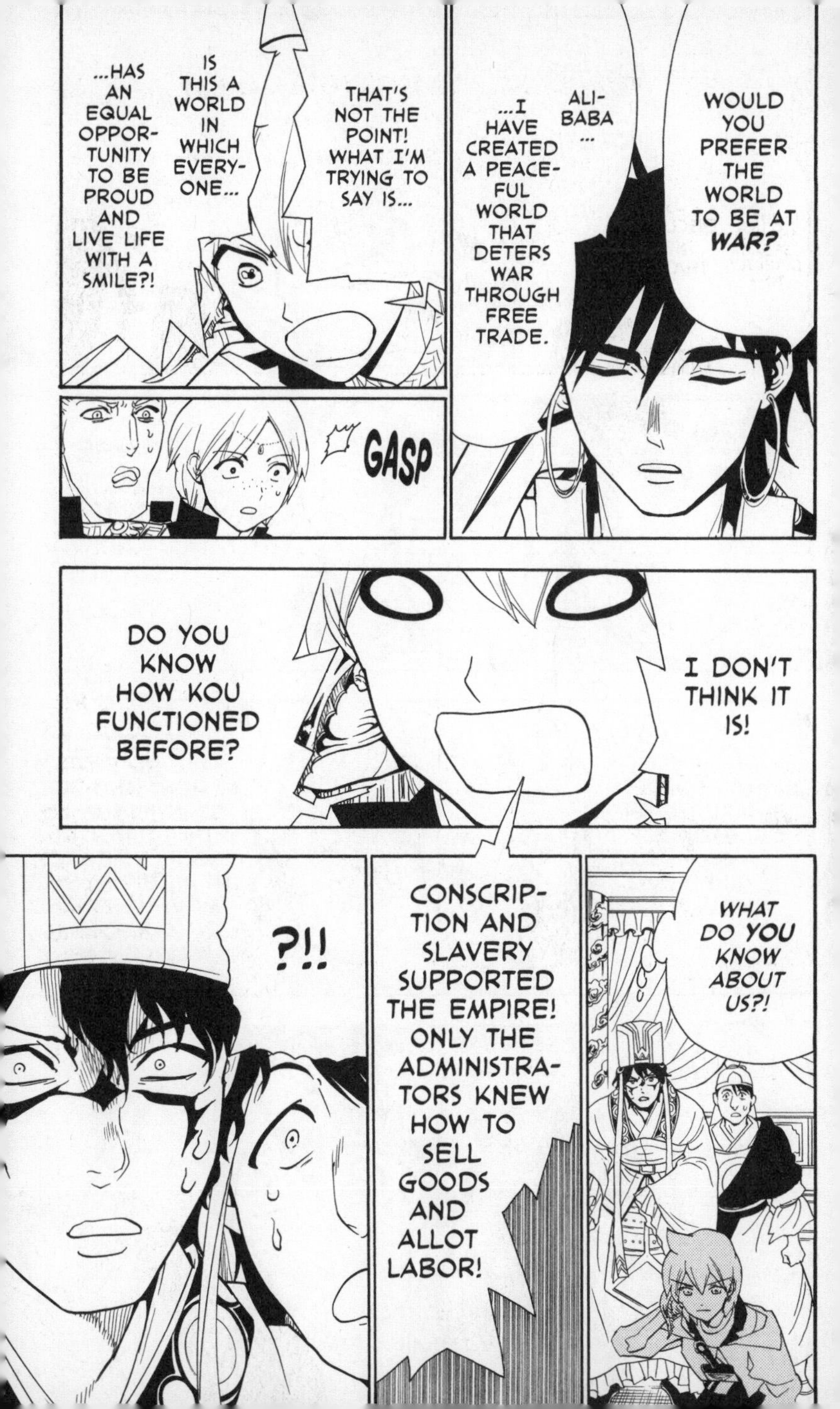
WOULD YOU PREFER THE WORLD TO BE AT WAR?
ALI-BABA...
...I HAVE CREATED A PEACEFUL WORLD THAT DETERS WAR THROUGH FREE TRADE.
THAT'S NOT THE POINT! WHAT I'M TRYING TO SAY IS...
IS THIS A WORLD IN WHICH EVERYONE...
...HAS AN EQUAL OPPORTUNITY TO BE PROUD AND LIVE LIFE WITH A SMILE?!
GASP
I DON'T THINK IT IS!
DO YOU KNOW HOW KOU FUNCTIONED BEFORE?
WHAT DO YOU KNOW ABOUT US?!
CONSCRIPTION AND SLAVERY SUPPORTED THE EMPIRE! ONLY THE ADMINISTRATORS KNEW HOW TO SELL GOODS AND ALLOT LABOR!
?!!

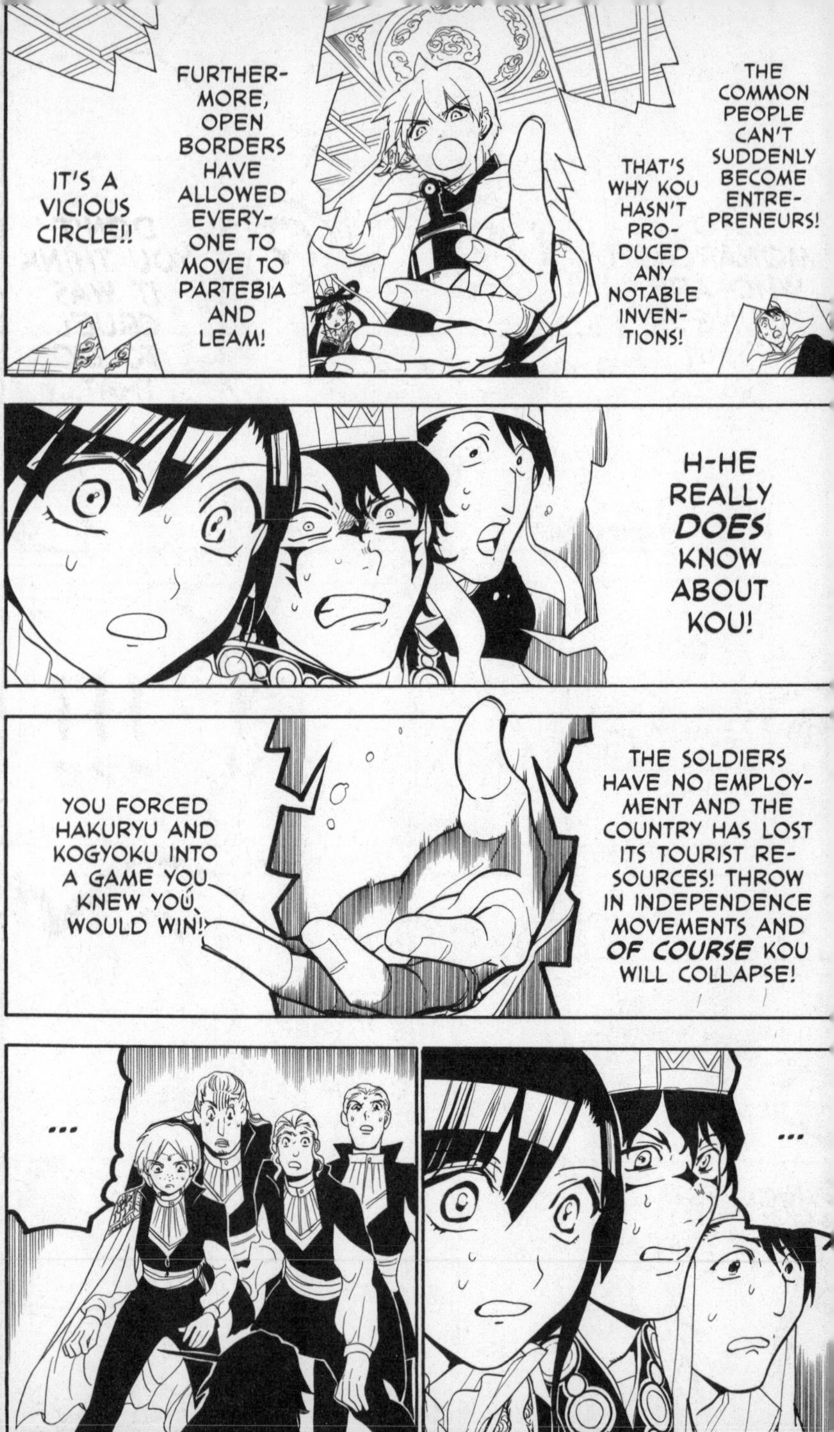
THE COMMON PEOPLE CAN'T SUDDENLY BECOME ENTRE-PRENEURS!
THAT'S WHY KOU HASN'T PRO-DUCED ANY NOTABLE INVEN-TIONS!
FURTHER-MORE, OPEN BORDERS HAVE ALLOWED EVERY-ONE TO MOVE TO PARTEBIA AND LEAM!
IT'S A VICIOUS CIRCLE!!
H-HE REALLY ***DOES*** KNOW ABOUT KOU!
THE SOLDIERS HAVE NO EMPLOY-MENT AND THE COUNTRY HAS LOST ITS TOURIST RE-SOURCES! THROW IN INDEPENDENCE MOVEMENTS AND ***OF COURSE*** KOU WILL COLLAPSE!
YOU FORCED HAKURYU AND KOGYOKU INTO A GAME YOU KNEW YOU WOULD WIN!
...
...

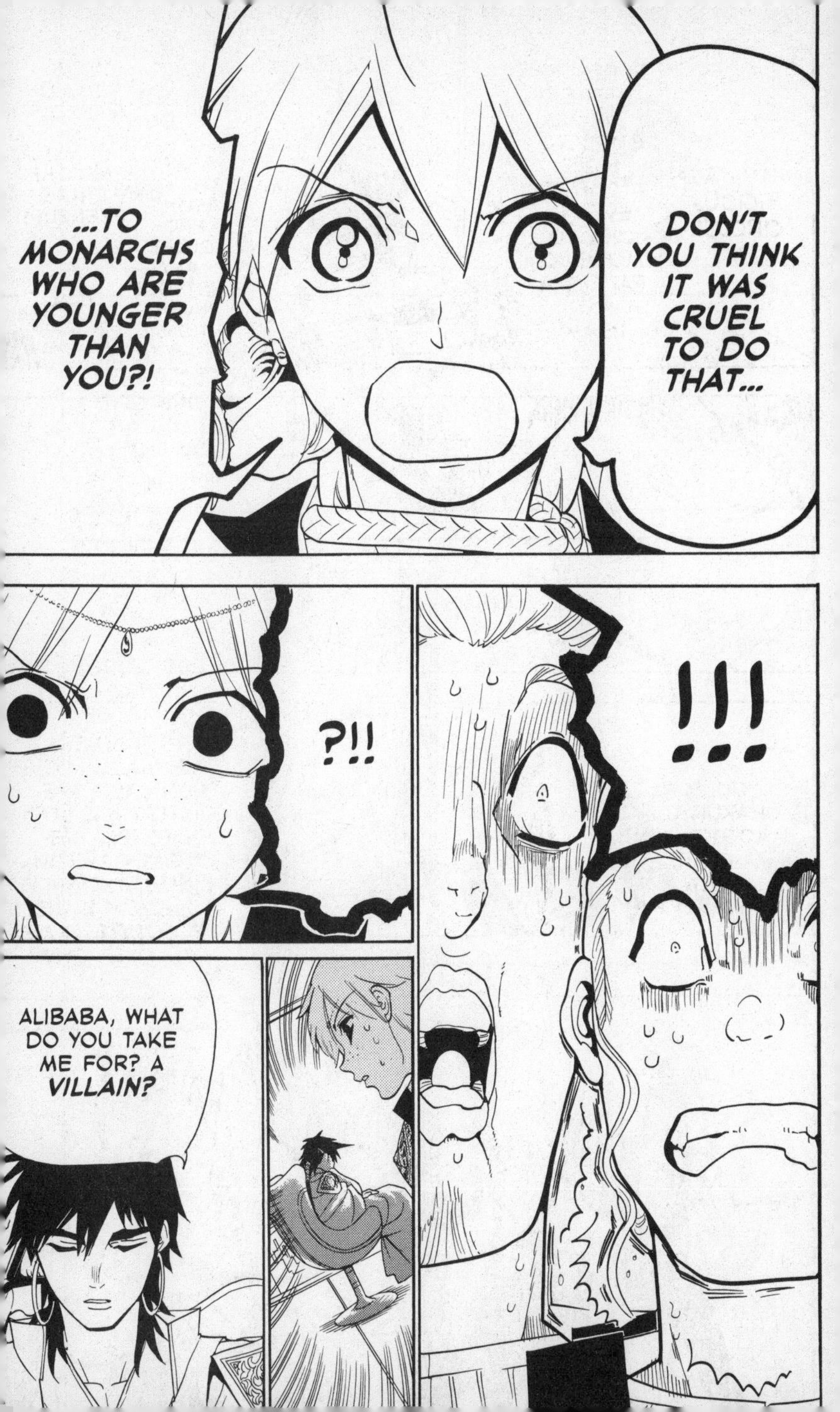
DON'T YOU THINK IT WAS CRUEL TO DO THAT...
...TO MONARCHS WHO ARE YOUNGER THAN YOU?!
!!!
?!!
ALIBABA, WHAT DO YOU TAKE ME FOR? A *VILLAIN?*

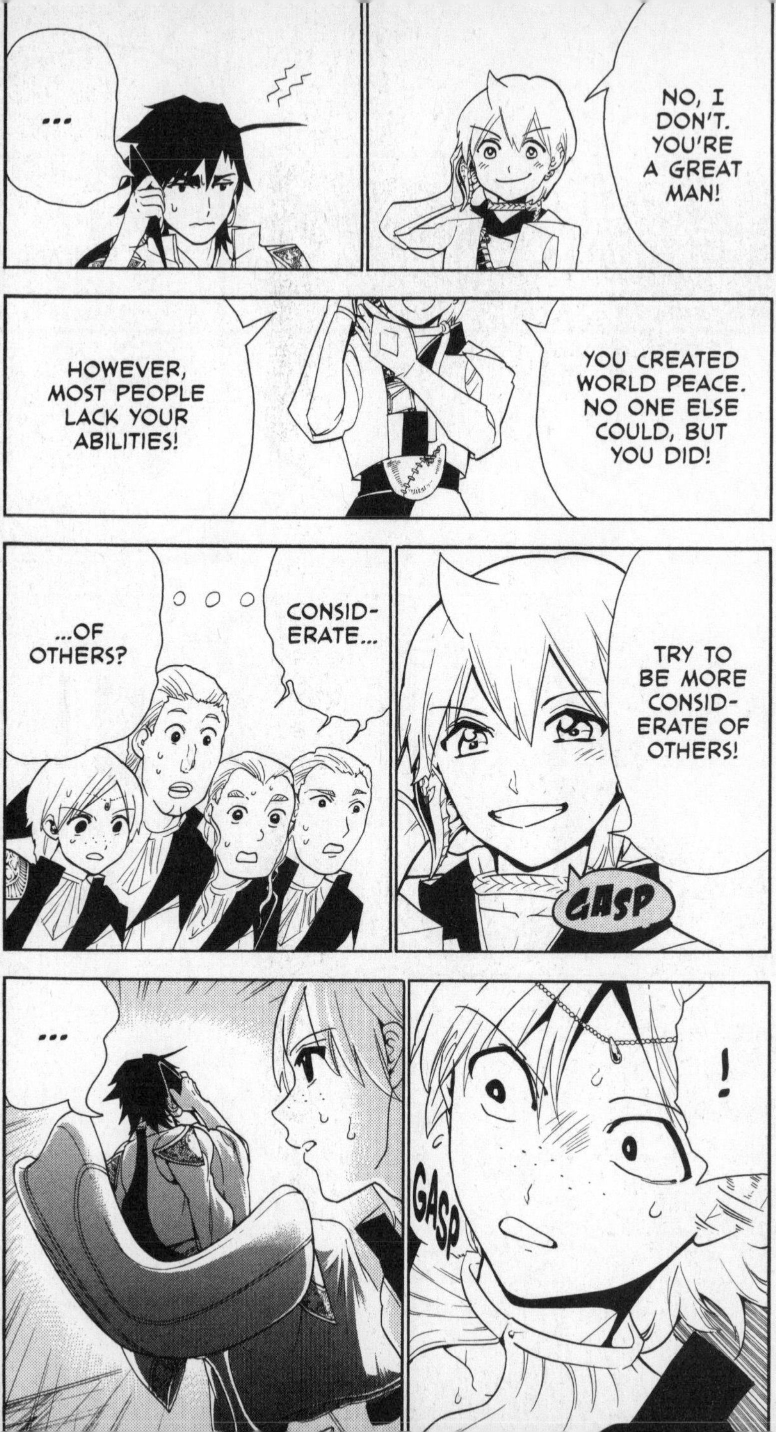
NO, I DON'T. YOU'RE A GREAT MAN!
...
YOU CREATED WORLD PEACE. NO ONE ELSE COULD, BUT YOU DID!
HOWEVER, MOST PEOPLE LACK YOUR ABILITIES!
TRY TO BE MORE CONSID-ERATE OF OTHERS!
GASP
CONSID-ERATE...
...OF OTHERS?
!
GASP
...

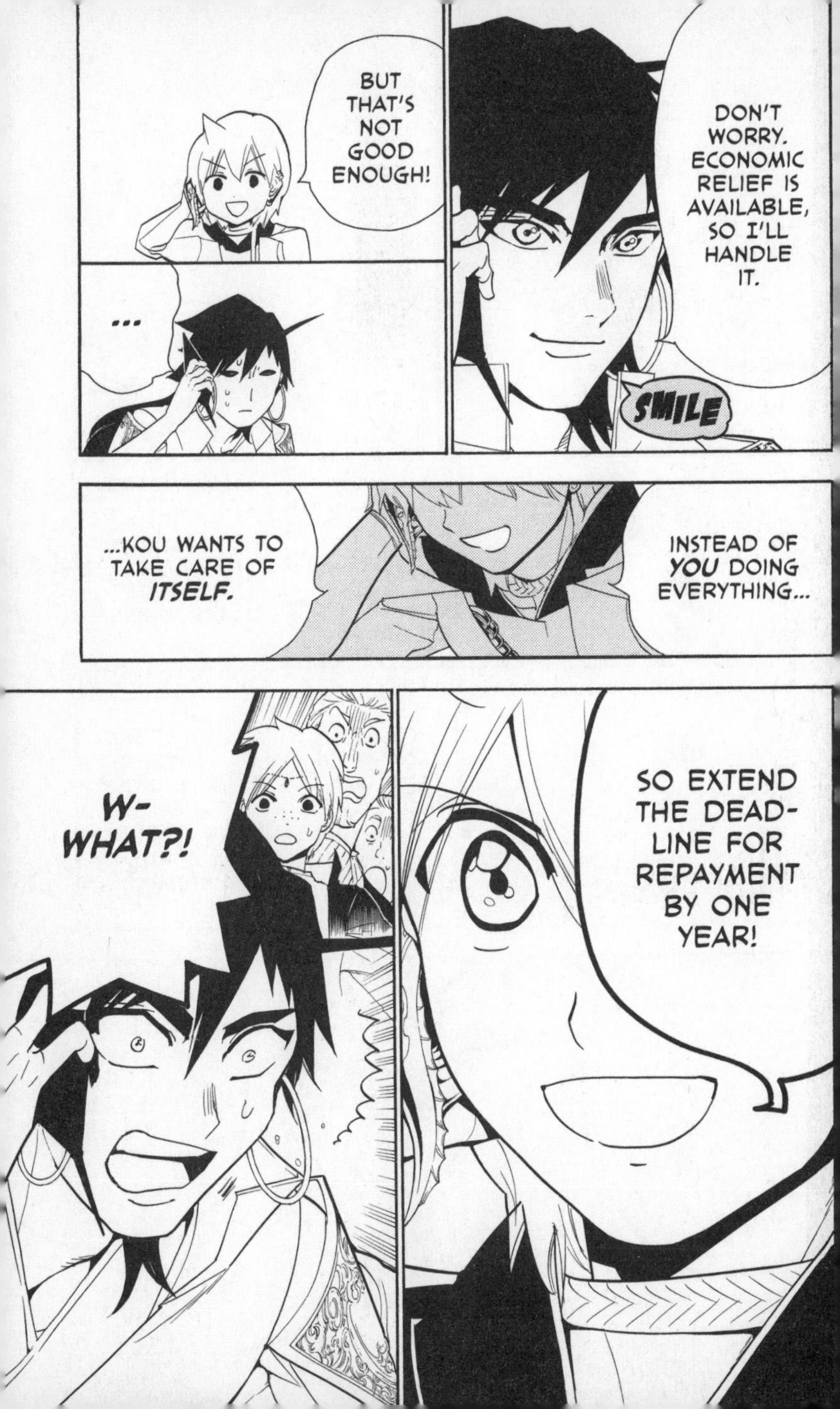
DON'T WORRY. ECONOMIC RELIEF IS AVAILABLE, SO I'LL HANDLE IT.
SMILE
BUT THAT'S NOT GOOD ENOUGH!
...
INSTEAD OF *YOU* DOING EVERYTHING...
...KOU WANTS TO TAKE CARE OF *ITSELF.*
SO EXTEND THE DEAD-LINE FOR REPAYMENT BY ONE YEAR!
W-WHAT?!

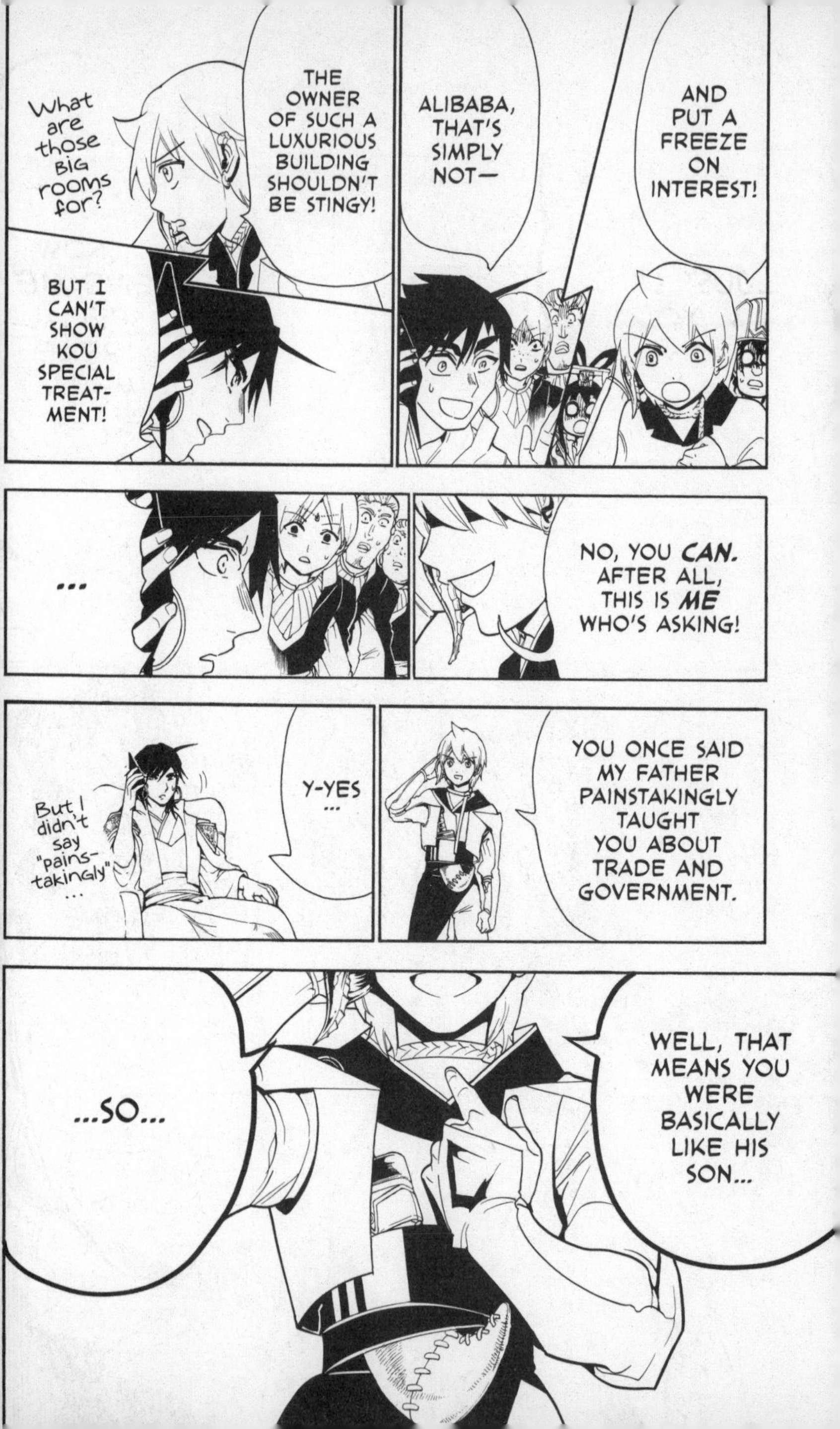
AND PUT A FREEZE ON INTEREST!
ALIBABA, THAT'S SIMPLY NOT—
THE OWNER OF SUCH A LUXURIOUS BUILDING SHOULDN'T BE STINGY!
What are those big rooms for?
BUT I CAN'T SHOW KOU SPECIAL TREATMENT!
NO, YOU *CAN.* AFTER ALL, THIS IS *ME* WHO'S ASKING!
...
YOU ONCE SAID MY FATHER PAINSTAKINGLY TAUGHT YOU ABOUT TRADE AND GOVERNMENT.
Y-YES ...
But I didn't say "painstakingly" ...
WELL, THAT MEANS YOU WERE BASICALLY LIKE HIS SON...
...SO...

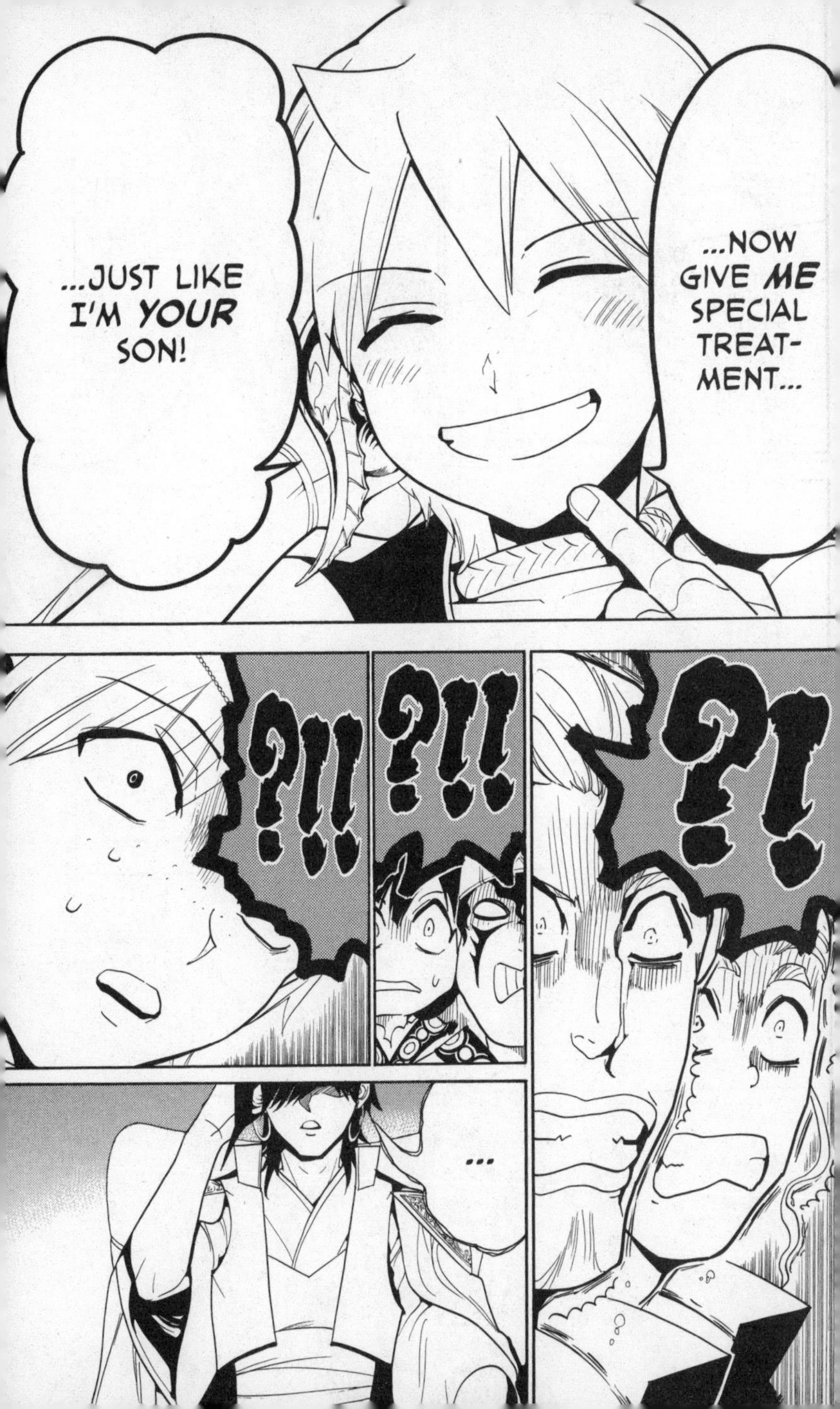
...NOW GIVE ME SPECIAL TREATMENT...
...JUST LIKE I'M YOUR SON!
?!
?!!
?!!!
...

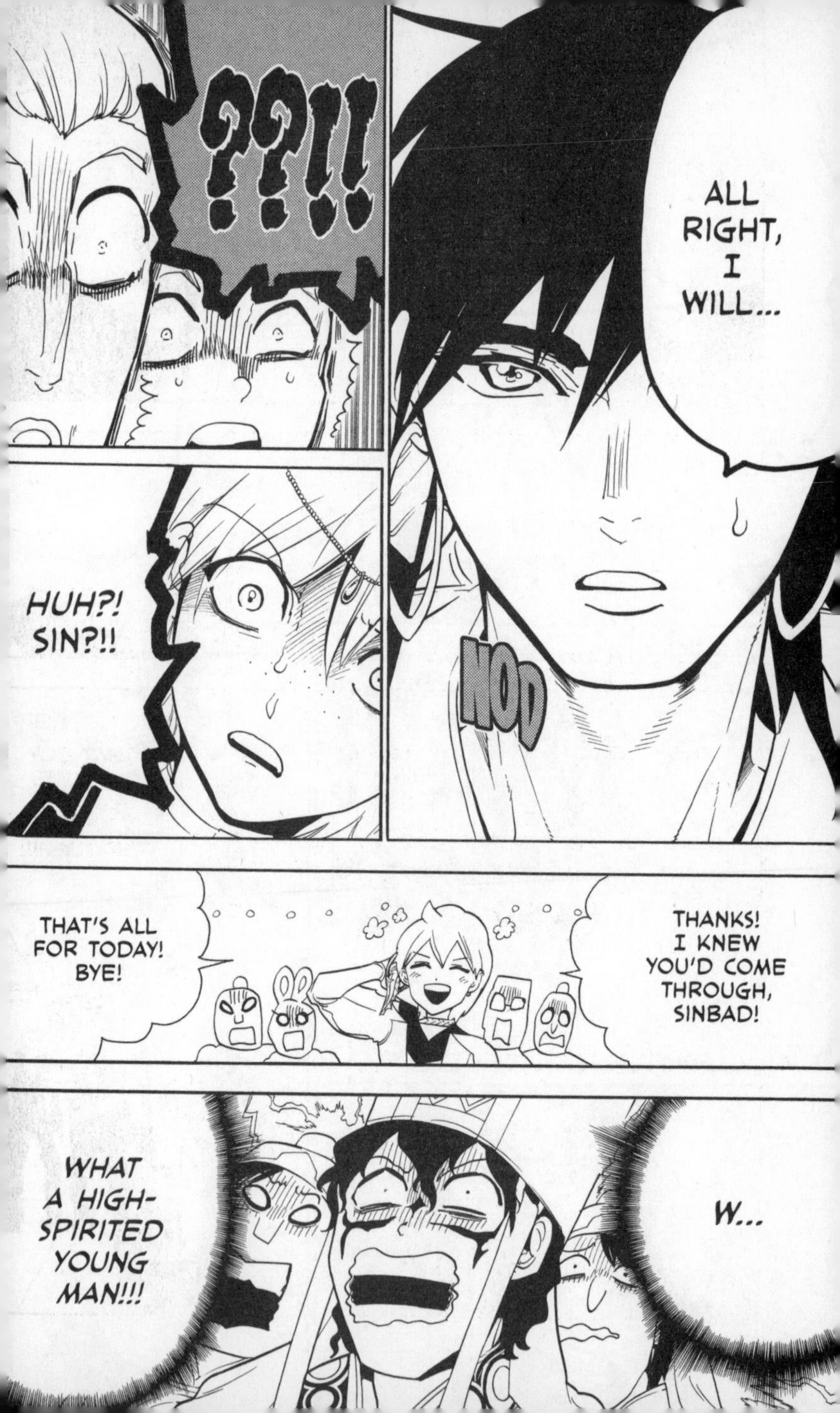
ALL RIGHT, I WILL...
NOD
??!!
HUH?! SIN?!!
THANKS! I KNEW YOU'D COME THROUGH, SINBAD!
THAT'S ALL FOR TODAY! BYE!
W...
WHAT A HIGH-SPIRITED YOUNG MAN!!!

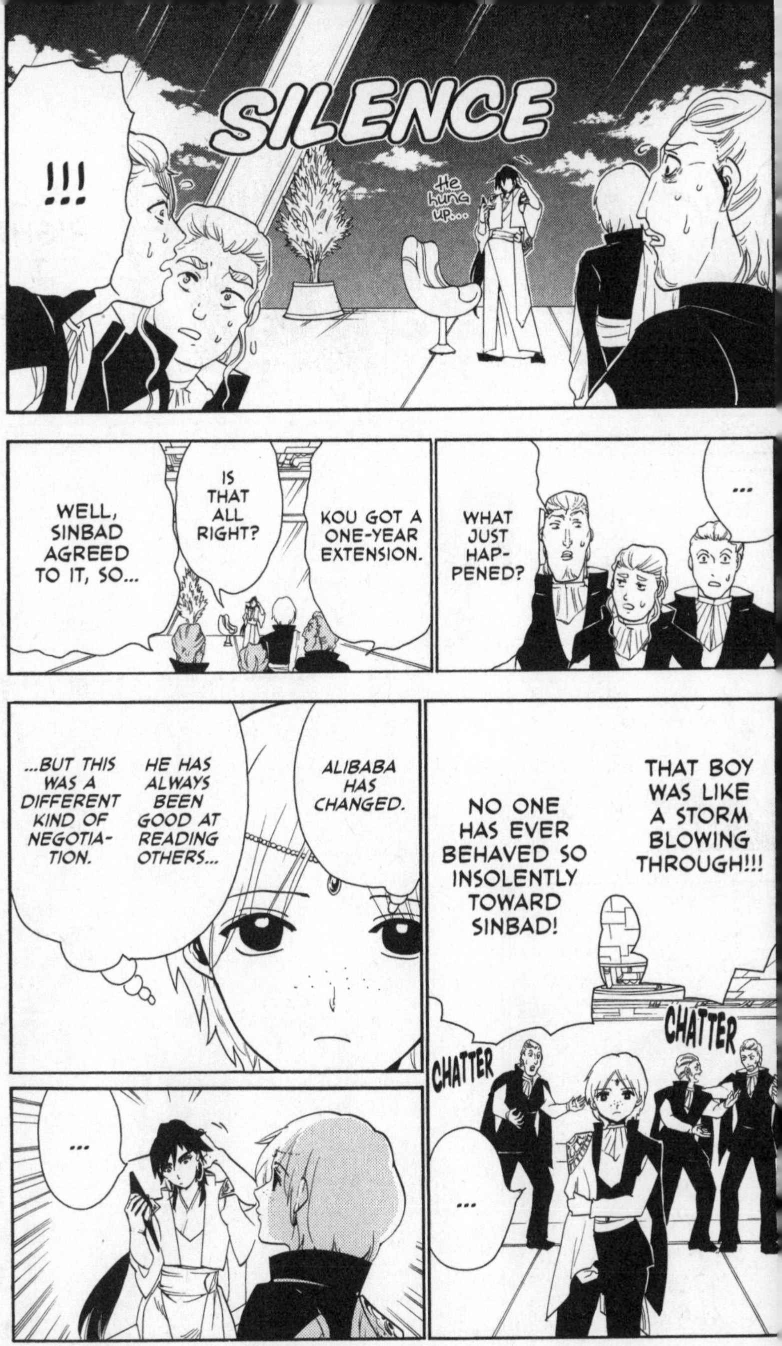
SILENCE
He hung up...
!!!
...
WHAT JUST HAPPENED?
KOU GOT A ONE-YEAR EXTENSION.
IS THAT ALL RIGHT?
WELL, SINBAD AGREED TO IT, SO...
THAT BOY WAS LIKE A STORM BLOWING THROUGH!!!
NO ONE HAS EVER BEHAVED SO INSOLENTLY TOWARD SINBAD!
CHATTER
CHATTER
...
ALIBABA HAS CHANGED.
HE HAS ALWAYS BEEN GOOD AT READING OTHERS...
...BUT THIS WAS A DIFFERENT KIND OF NEGOTIATION.
...

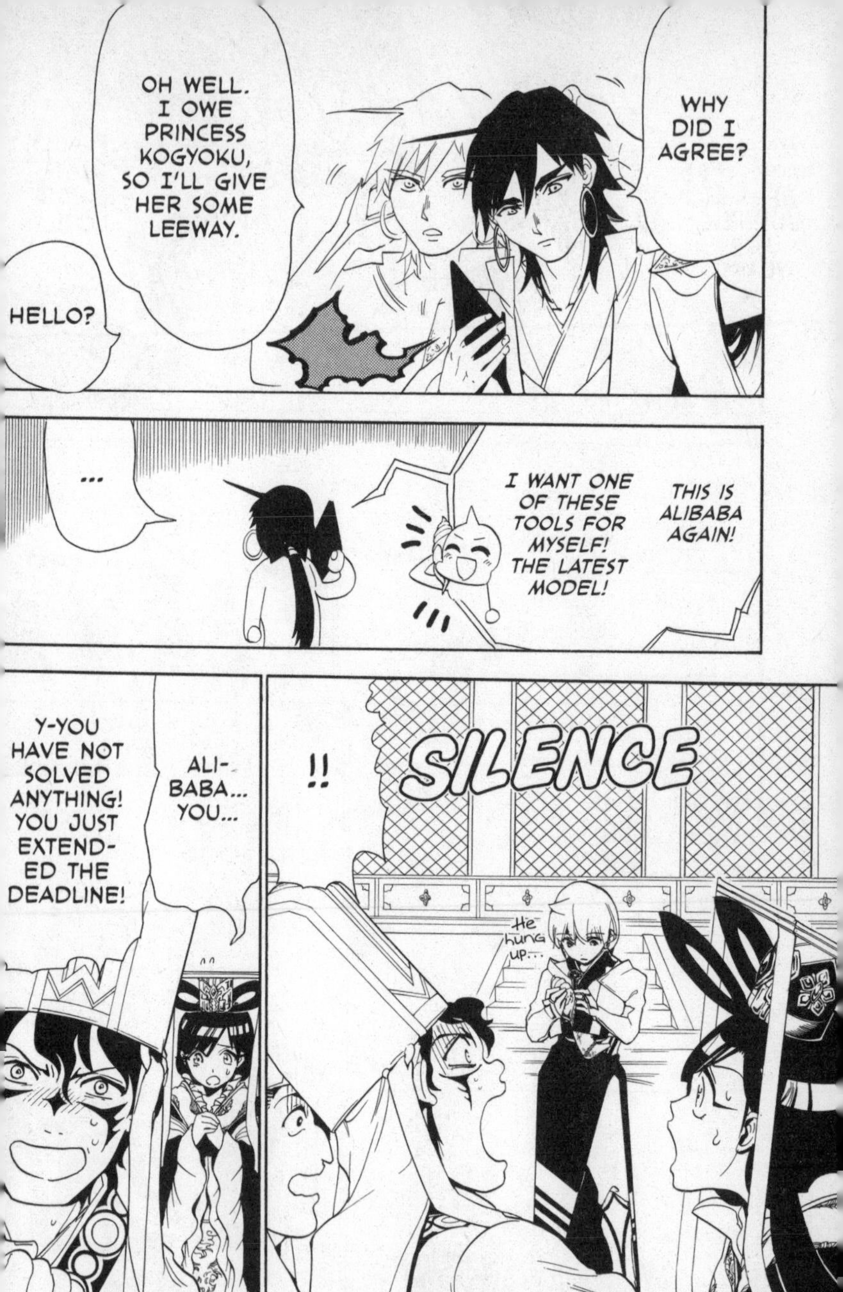
WHY DID I AGREE?
OH WELL. I OWE PRINCESS KOGYOKU, SO I'LL GIVE HER SOME LEEWAY.
HELLO?
THIS IS ALIBABA AGAIN!
I WANT ONE OF THESE TOOLS FOR MYSELF! THE LATEST MODEL!
...
SILENCE
He hung up...
!!
ALI-BABA... YOU...
Y-YOU HAVE NOT SOLVED ANYTHING! YOU JUST EXTEND-ED THE DEADLINE!

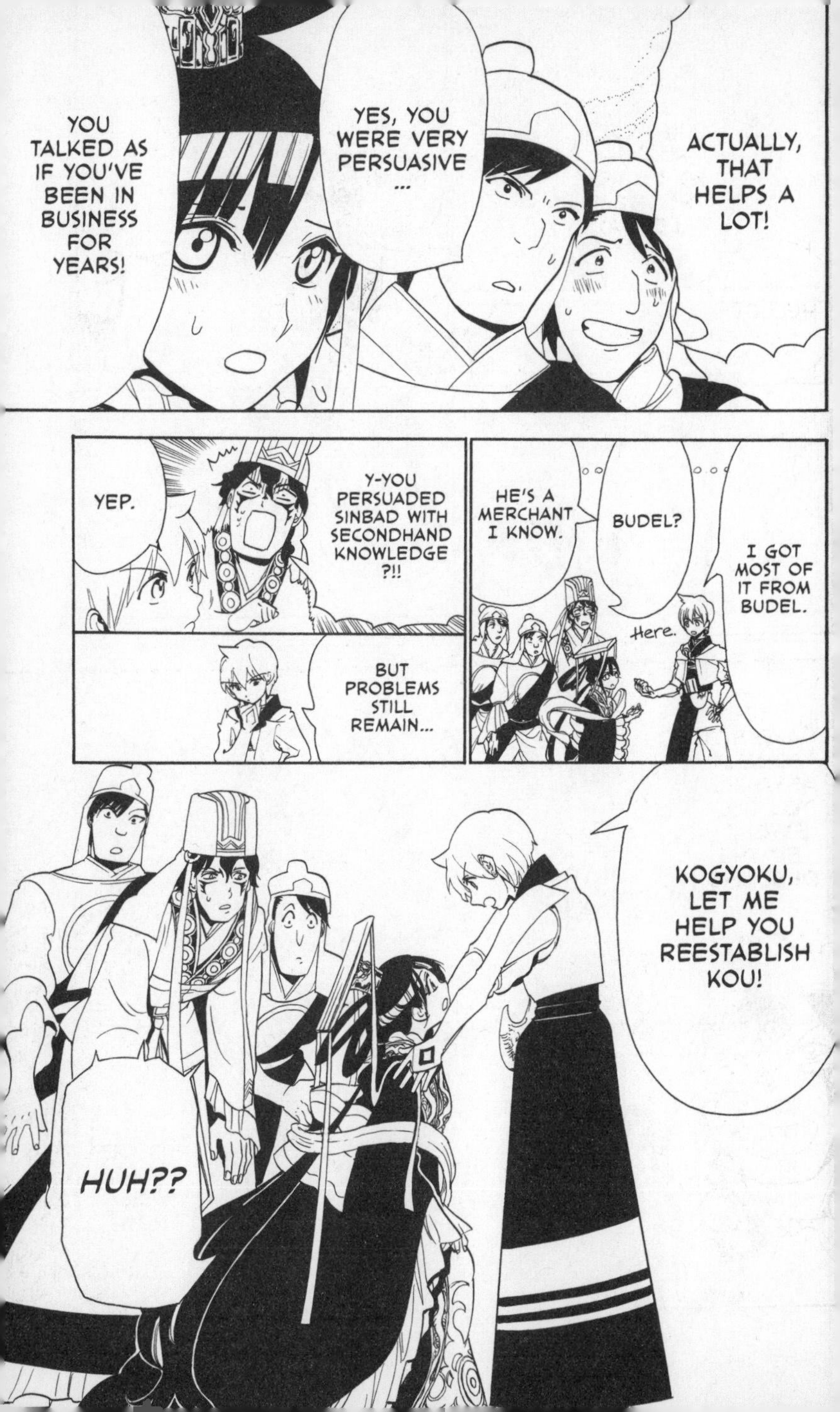
ACTUALLY, THAT HELPS A LOT!
YES, YOU WERE VERY PERSUASIVE ...
YOU TALKED AS IF YOU'VE BEEN IN BUSINESS FOR YEARS!
I GOT MOST OF IT FROM BUDEL.
BUDEL?
HE'S A MERCHANT I KNOW.
Here.
Y-YOU PERSUADED SINBAD WITH SECONDHAND KNOWLEDGE?!!
YEP.
BUT PROBLEMS STILL REMAIN...
KOGYOKU, LET ME HELP YOU REESTABLISH KOU!
HUH??

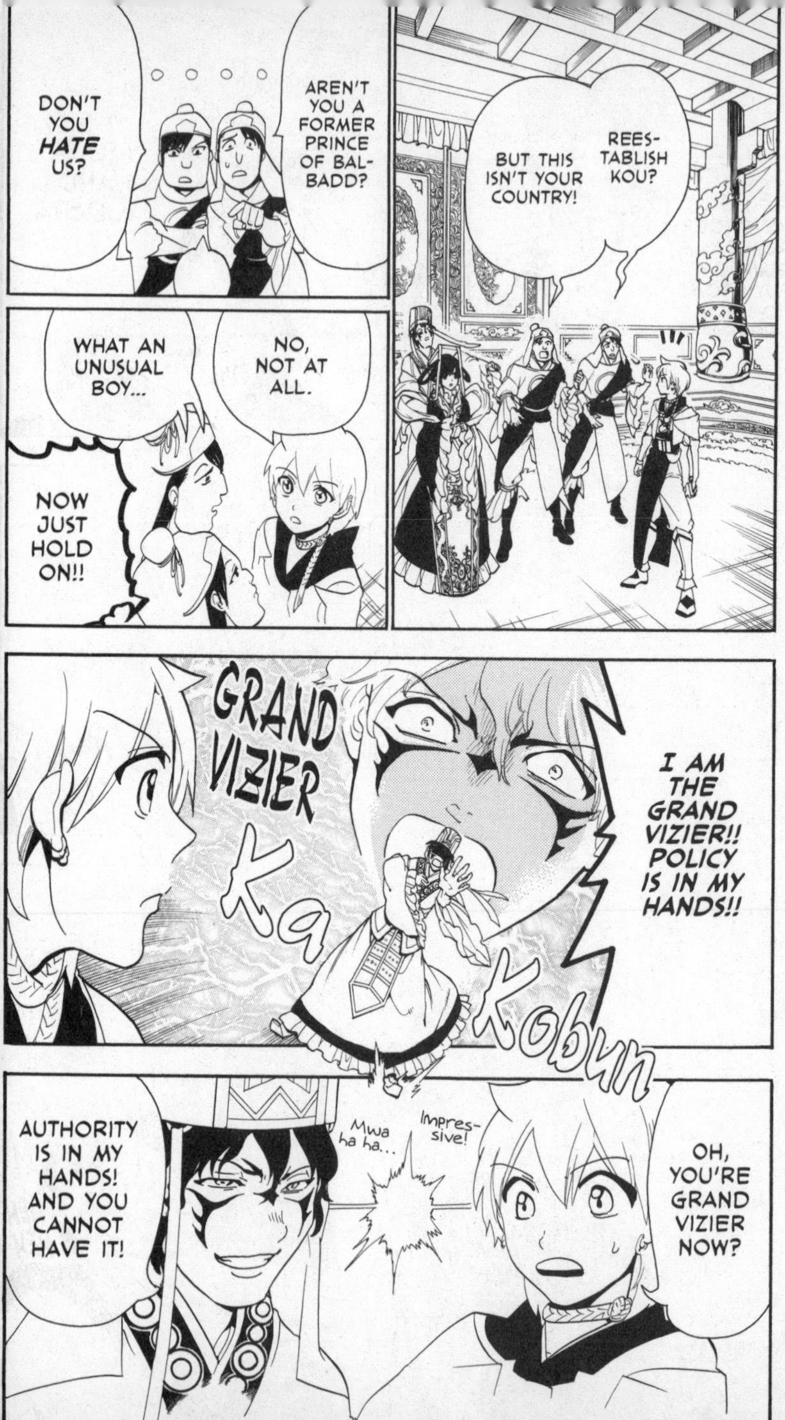
REES-TABLISH KOU?
BUT THIS ISN'T YOUR COUNTRY!
AREN'T YOU A FORMER PRINCE OF BAL-BADD?
DON'T YOU *HATE* US?
NO, NOT AT ALL.
WHAT AN UNUSUAL BOY...
NOW JUST HOLD ON!!
I AM THE GRAND VIZIER!! POLICY IS IN MY HANDS!!
GRAND VIZIER
Ka
Kobun
OH, YOU'RE GRAND VIZIER NOW?
Impres-sive!
Mwa ha ha...
AUTHORITY IS IN MY HANDS! AND YOU CANNOT HAVE IT!

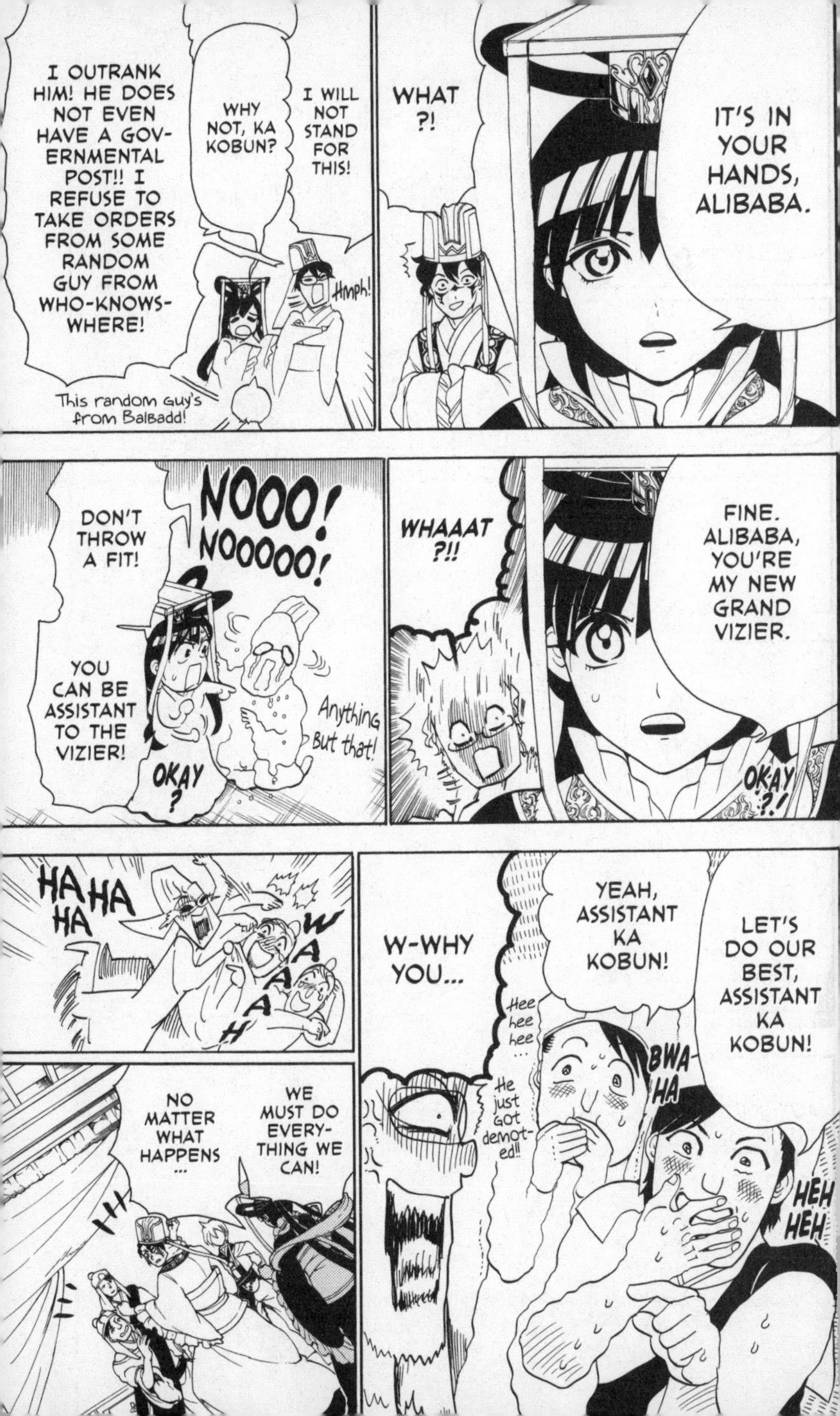
IT'S IN YOUR HANDS, ALIBABA.
WHAT ?!
I WILL NOT STAND FOR THIS!
WHY NOT, KA KOBUN?
I OUTRANK HIM! HE DOES NOT EVEN HAVE A GOVERNMENTAL POST!! I REFUSE TO TAKE ORDERS FROM SOME RANDOM GUY FROM WHO-KNOWS-WHERE!
Hmph!
This random guy's from Balbadd!
FINE. ALIBABA, YOU'RE MY NEW GRAND VIZIER.
WHAAAT ?!!
OKAY ?!
NOOO! NOOOOO!
DON'T THROW A FIT!
YOU CAN BE ASSISTANT TO THE VIZIER!
OKAY ?
Anything but that!
LET'S DO OUR BEST, ASSISTANT KA KOBUN!
YEAH, ASSISTANT KA KOBUN!
W-WHY YOU...
Hee hee hee...
He just got demoted!!
BWAHA
HEH HEH
HAHA HA
WAAAAH
WE MUST DO EVERYTHING WE CAN!
NO MATTER WHAT HAPPENS...

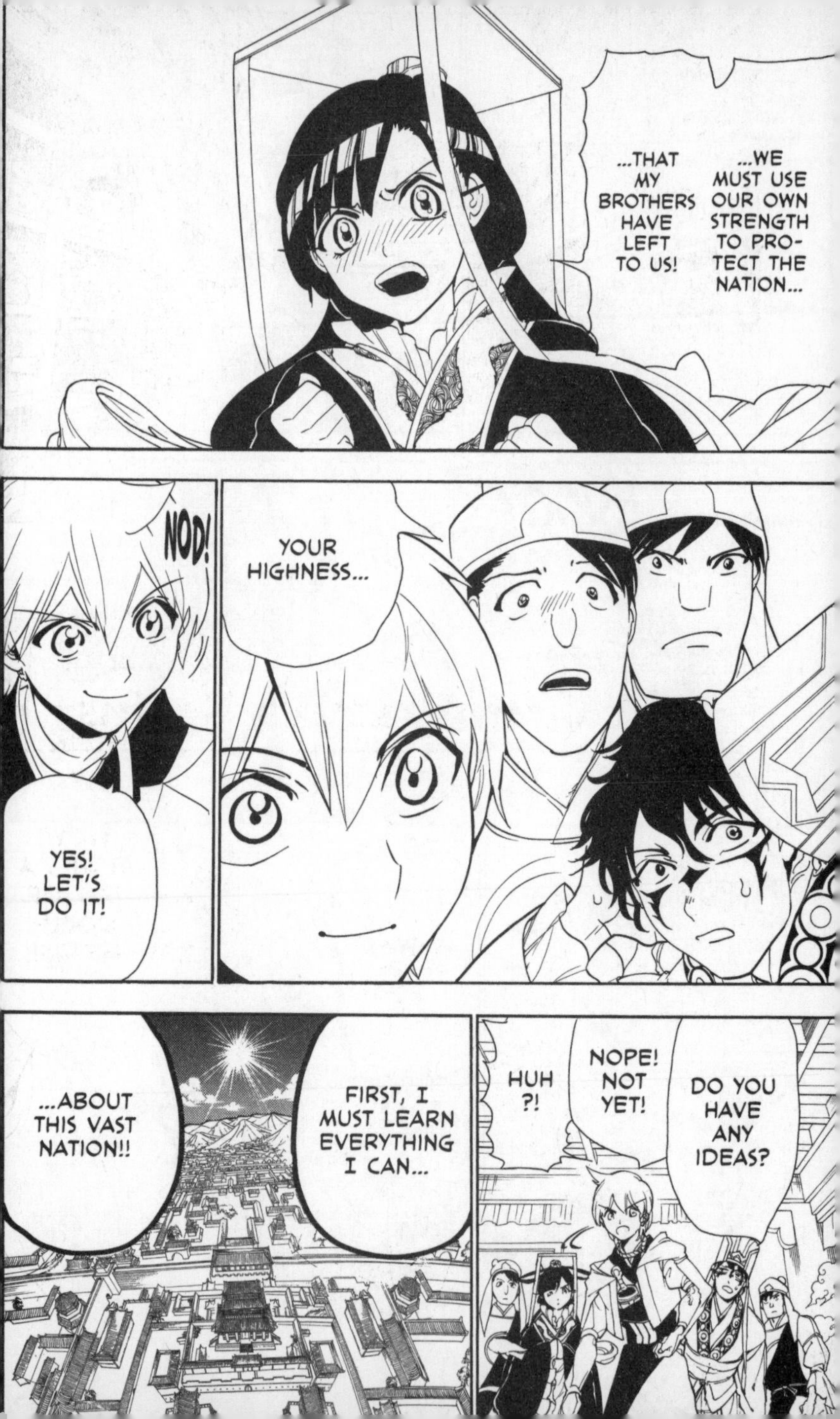
...WE MUST USE OUR OWN STRENGTH TO PROTECT THE NATION...
...THAT MY BROTHERS HAVE LEFT TO US!
YOUR HIGHNESS...
NOD!
YES! LET'S DO IT!
DO YOU HAVE ANY IDEAS?
NOPE! NOT YET!
HUH ?!
FIRST, I MUST LEARN EVERYTHING I CAN...
...ABOUT THIS VAST NATION!!

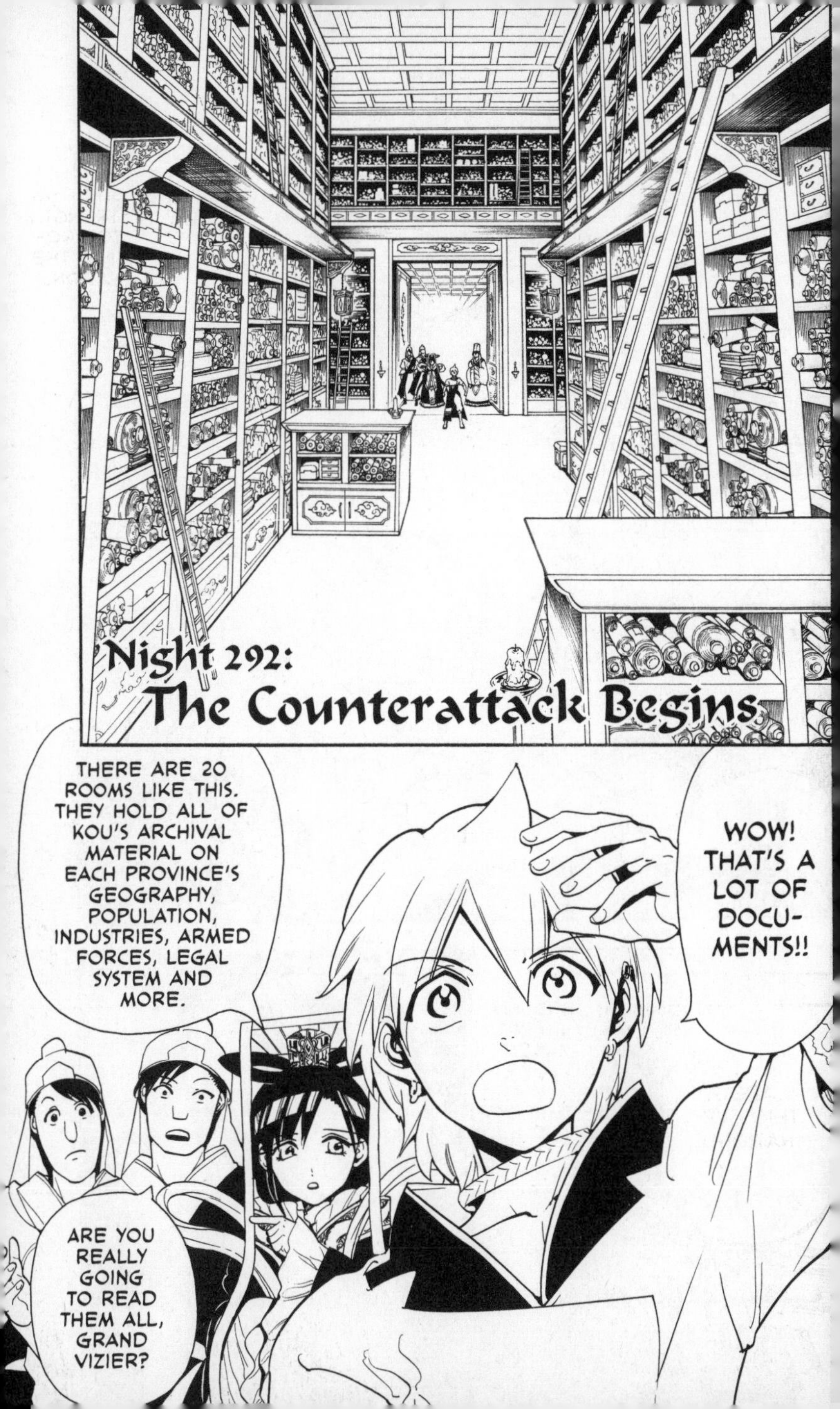
Night 292:
The Counterattack Begins
WOW! THAT'S A LOT OF DOCU- MENTS!!
THERE ARE 20 ROOMS LIKE THIS. THEY HOLD ALL OF KOU'S ARCHIVAL MATERIAL ON EACH PROVINCE'S GEOGRAPHY, POPULATION, INDUSTRIES, ARMED FORCES, LEGAL SYSTEM AND MORE.
ARE YOU REALLY GOING TO READ THEM ALL, GRAND VIZIER?

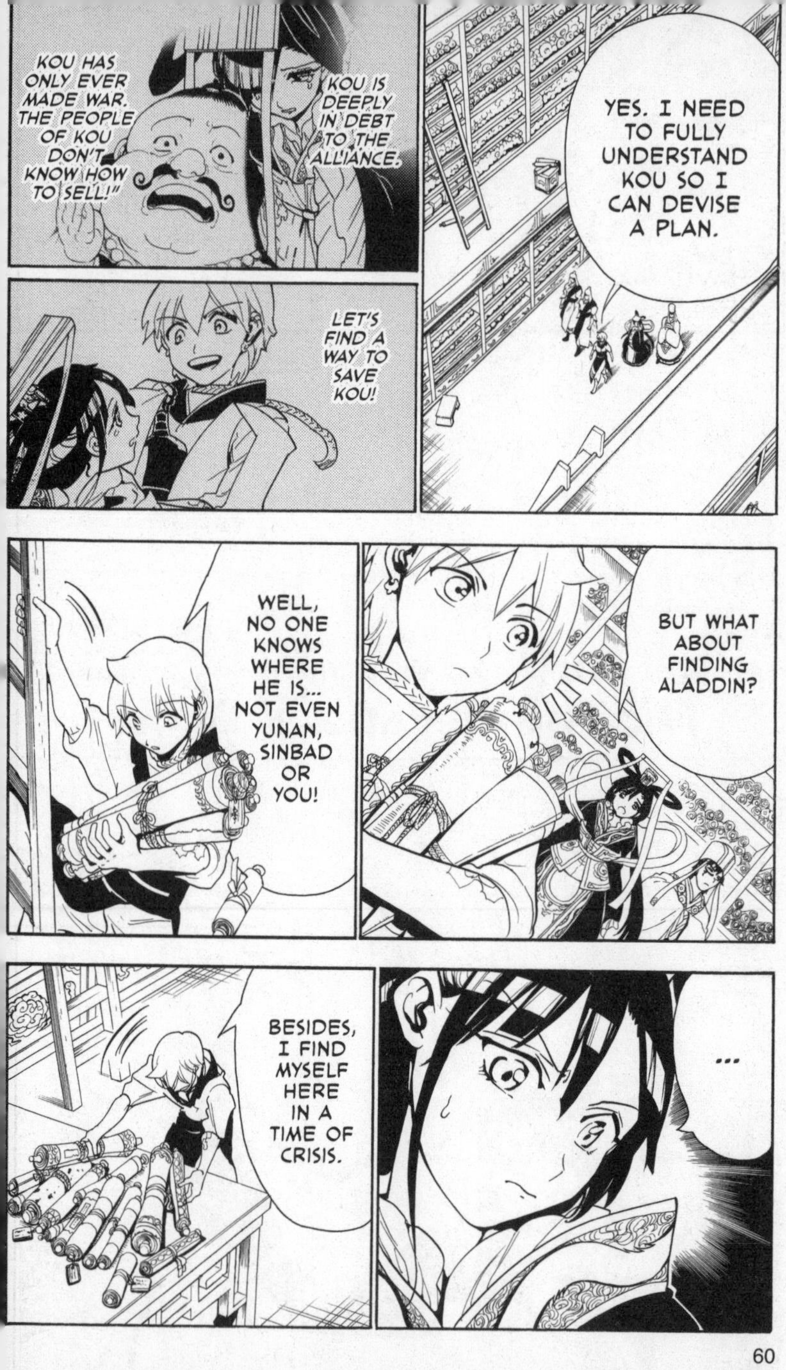
YES. I NEED TO FULLY UNDERSTAND KOU SO I CAN DEVISE A PLAN.
KOU IS DEEPLY IN DEBT TO THE ALLIANCE.
KOU HAS ONLY EVER MADE WAR. THE PEOPLE OF KOU DON'T KNOW HOW TO SELL!"
LET'S FIND A WAY TO SAVE KOU!
BUT WHAT ABOUT FINDING ALADDIN?
WELL, NO ONE KNOWS WHERE HE IS... NOT EVEN YUNAN, SINBAD OR YOU!
...
BESIDES, I FIND MYSELF HERE IN A TIME OF CRISIS.

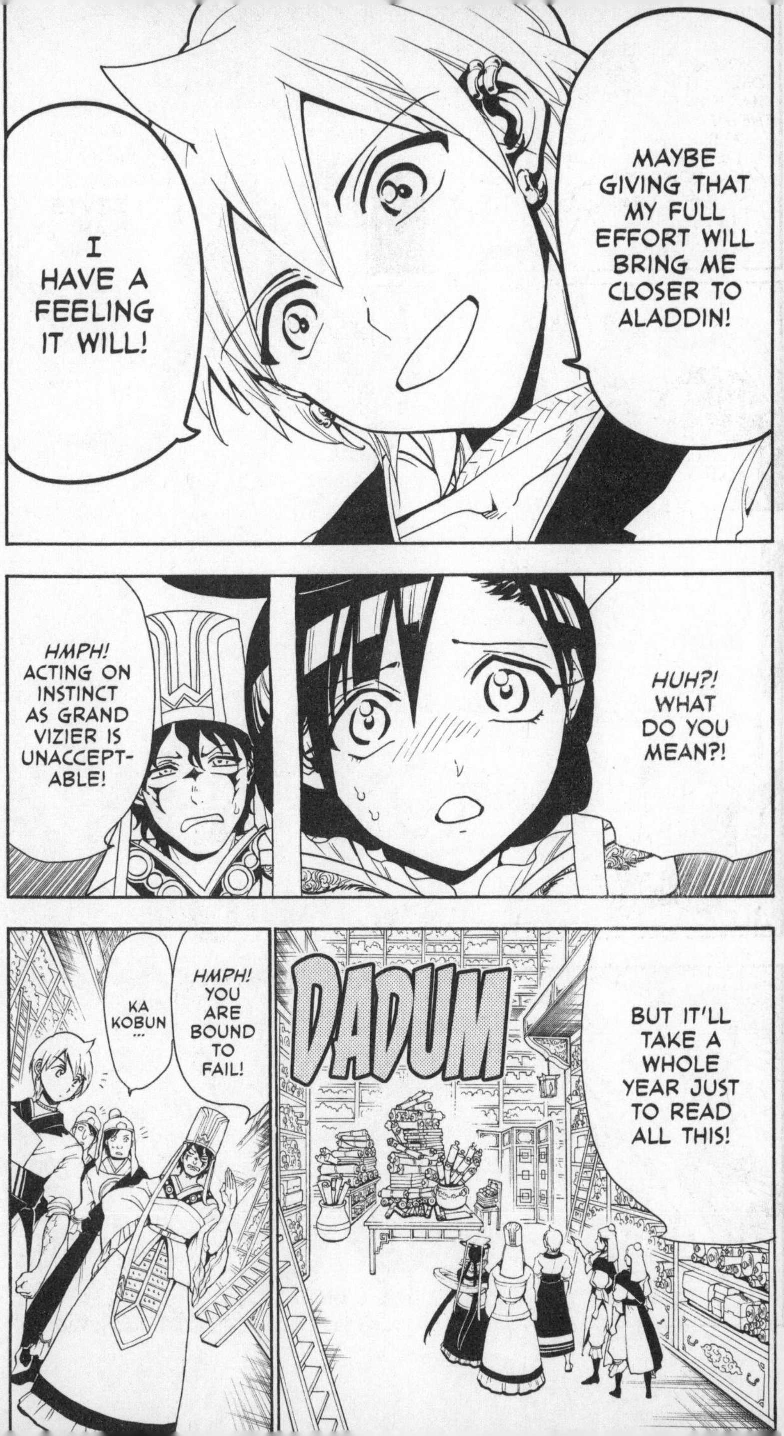
MAYBE GIVING THAT MY FULL EFFORT WILL BRING ME CLOSER TO ALADDIN!
I HAVE A FEELING IT WILL!
HUH?! WHAT DO YOU MEAN?!
HMPH! ACTING ON INSTINCT AS GRAND VIZIER IS UNACCEPT-ABLE!
BUT IT'LL TAKE A WHOLE YEAR JUST TO READ ALL THIS!
DADUM
HMPH! YOU ARE BOUND TO FAIL!
KA KOBUN...

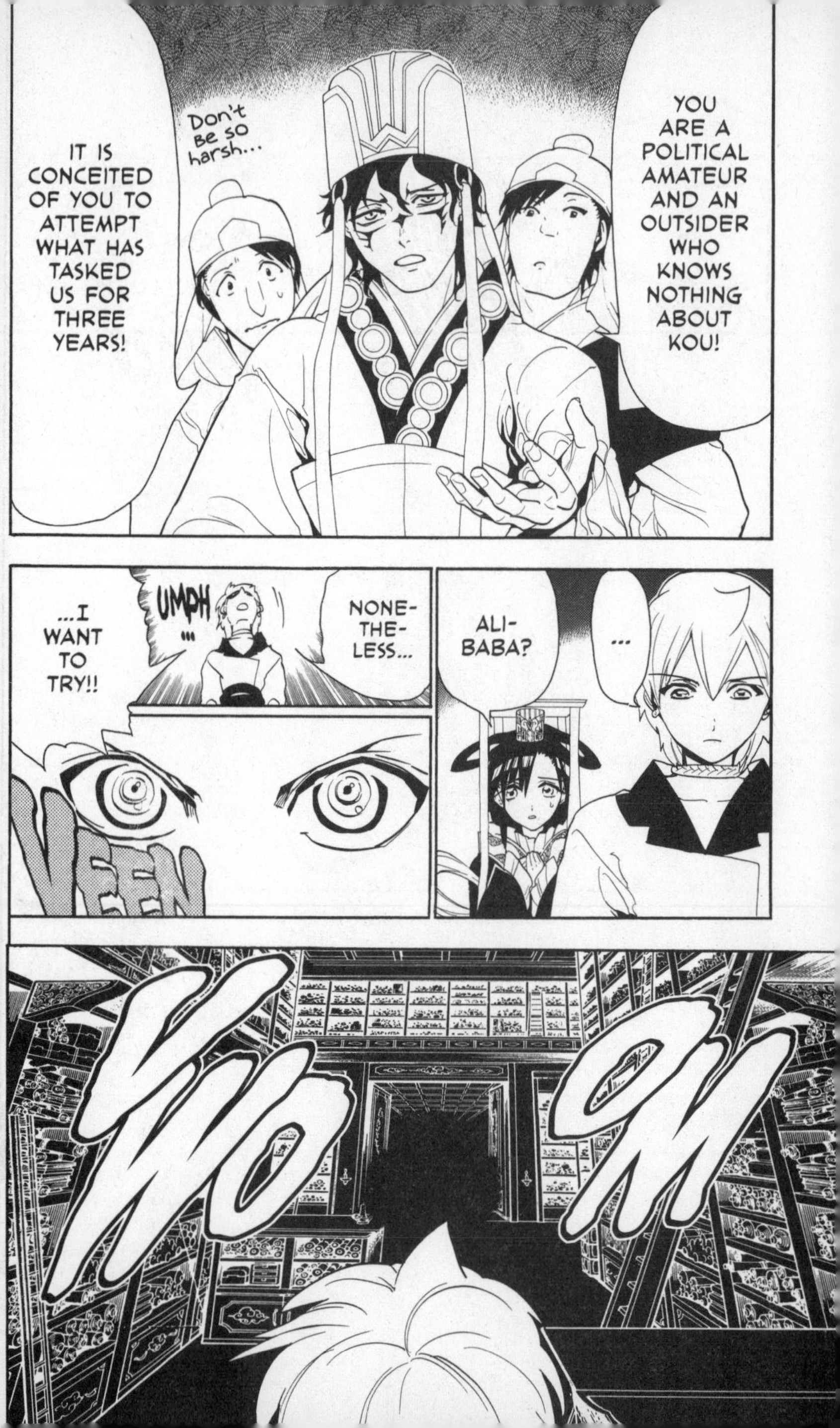

YOU ARE A POLITICAL AMATEUR AND AN OUTSIDER WHO KNOWS NOTHING ABOUT KOU!
Don't be so harsh...
IT IS CONCEITED OF YOU TO ATTEMPT WHAT HAS TASKED US FOR THREE YEARS!
...
ALI-BABA?
NONE-THE-LESS...
UMPH
...I WANT TO TRY!!
VEEN
WOOM

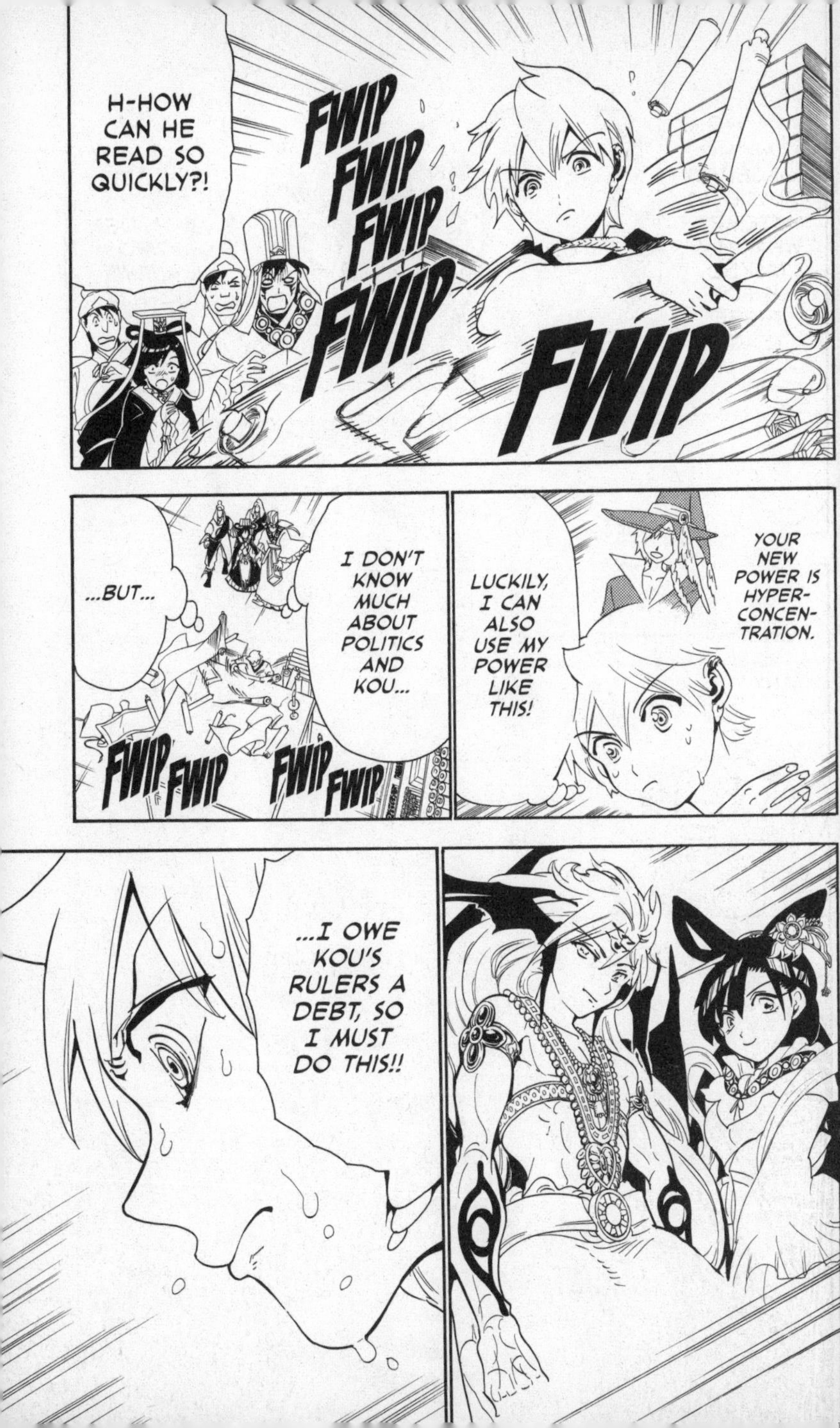
FWIP
FWIP
FWIP
FWIP
FWIP
H-HOW CAN HE READ SO QUICKLY?!
YOUR NEW POWER IS HYPER-CONCENTRATION.
LUCKILY, I CAN ALSO USE MY POWER LIKE THIS!
I DON'T KNOW MUCH ABOUT POLITICS AND KOU...
...BUT...
FWIP FWIP
FWIP FWIP
...I OWE KOU'S RULERS A DEBT, SO I MUST DO THIS!!

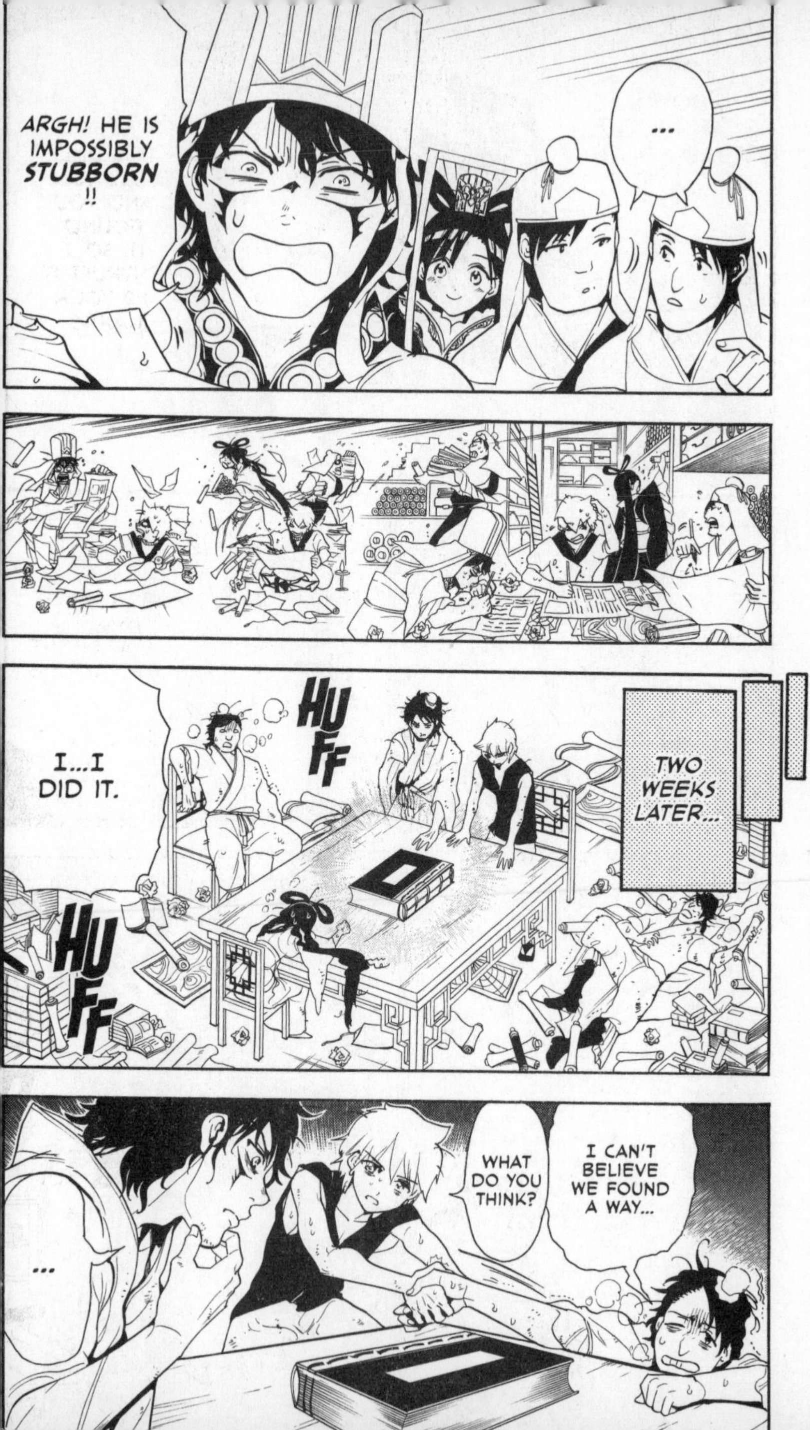
...
ARGH! HE IS IMPOSSIBLY STUBBORN!!
TWO WEEKS LATER...
HUFF
HUFF
I...I DID IT.
I CAN'T BELIEVE WE FOUND A WAY...
WHAT DO YOU THINK?
...

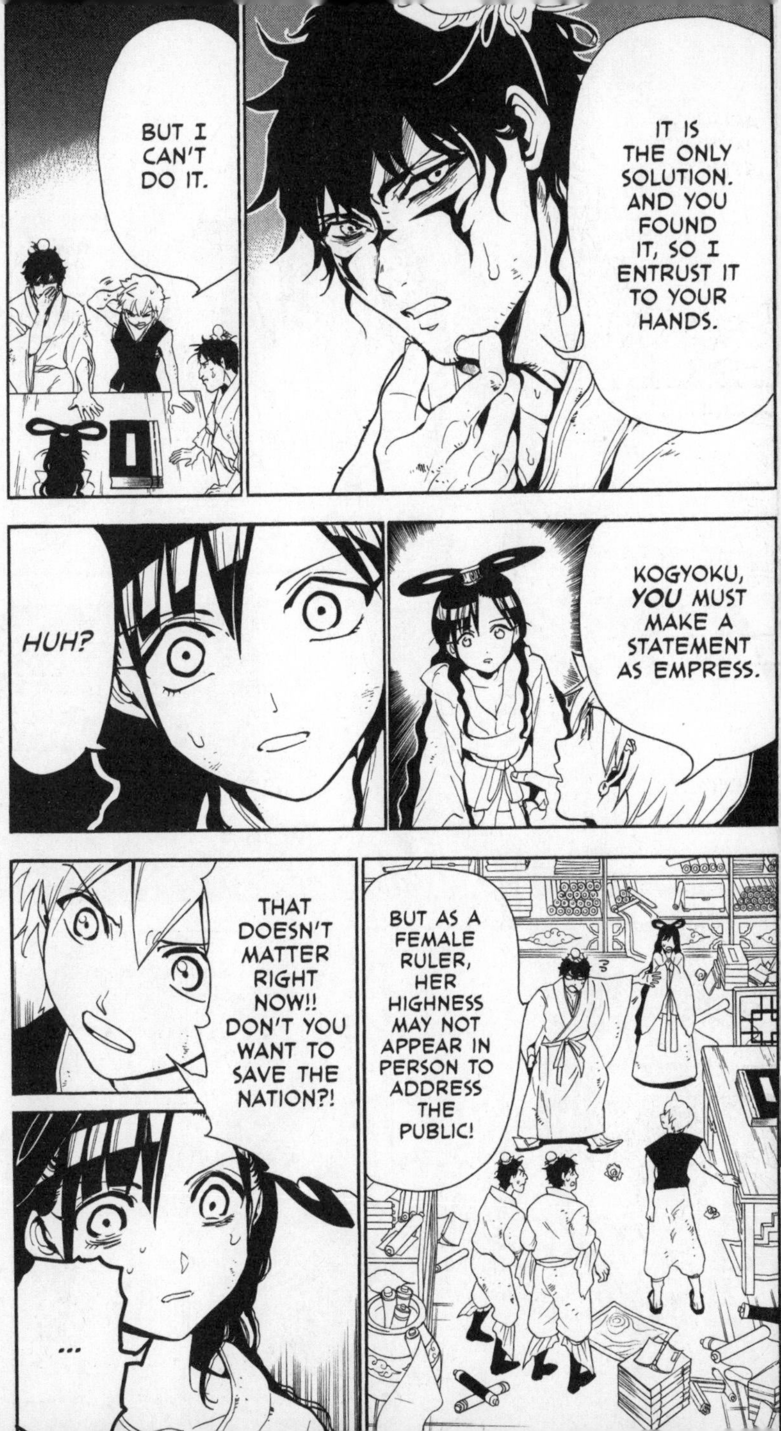
IT IS THE ONLY SOLUTION. AND YOU FOUND IT, SO I ENTRUST IT TO YOUR HANDS.
BUT I CAN'T DO IT.
KOGYOKU, *YOU* MUST MAKE A STATEMENT AS EMPRESS.
HUH?
BUT AS A FEMALE RULER, HER HIGHNESS MAY NOT APPEAR IN PERSON TO ADDRESS THE PUBLIC!
THAT DOESN'T MATTER RIGHT NOW!! DON'T YOU WANT TO SAVE THE NATION?!
...

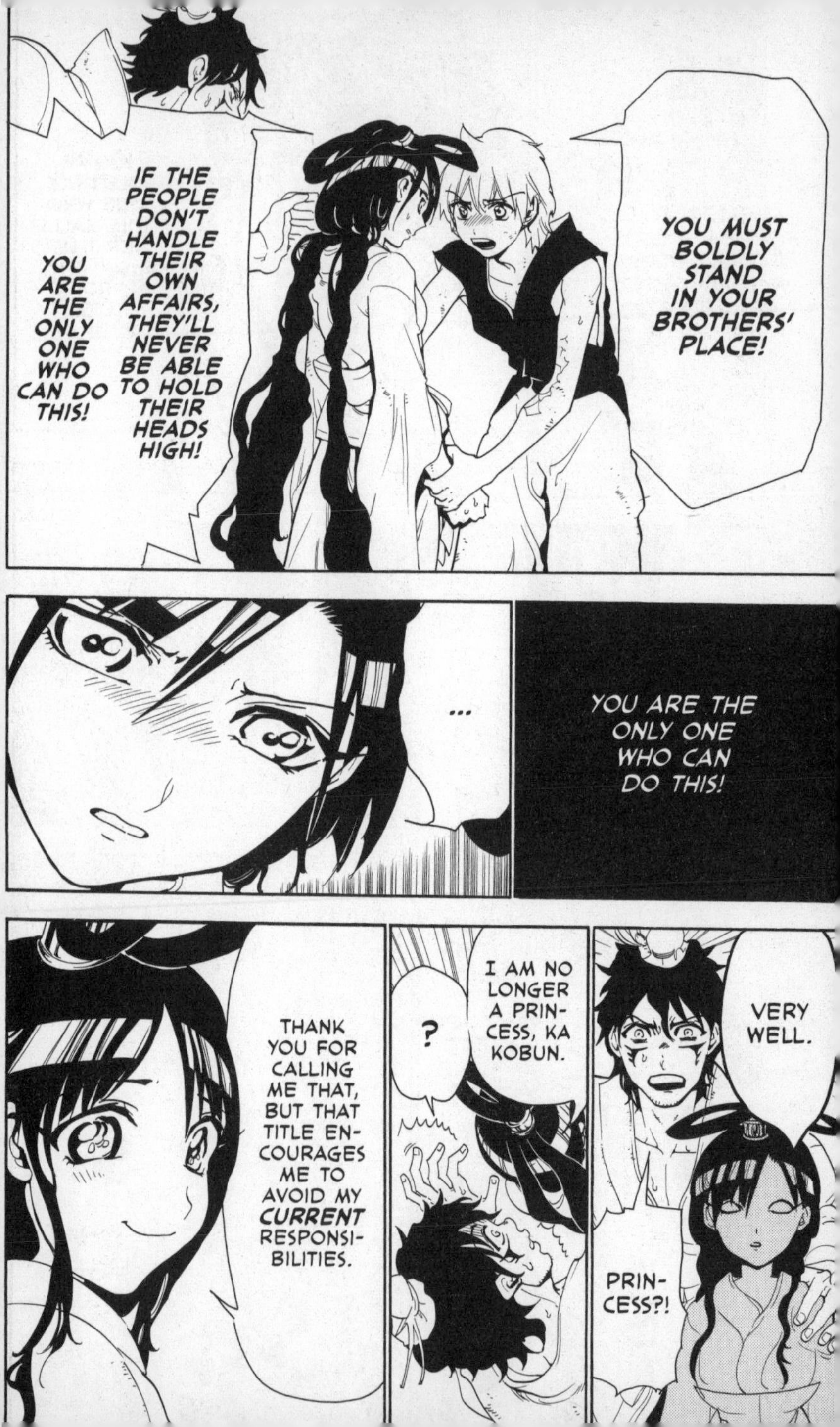
YOU MUST BOLDLY STAND IN YOUR BROTHERS' PLACE!
IF THE PEOPLE DON'T HANDLE THEIR OWN AFFAIRS, THEY'LL NEVER BE ABLE TO HOLD THEIR HEADS HIGH!
YOU ARE THE ONLY ONE WHO CAN DO THIS!
YOU ARE THE ONLY ONE WHO CAN DO THIS!
...
VERY WELL.
PRIN-CESS?!
I AM NO LONGER A PRIN-CESS, KA KOBUN.
?
THANK YOU FOR CALLING ME THAT, BUT THAT TITLE EN-COURAGES ME TO AVOID MY *CURRENT* RESPONSI-BILITIES.

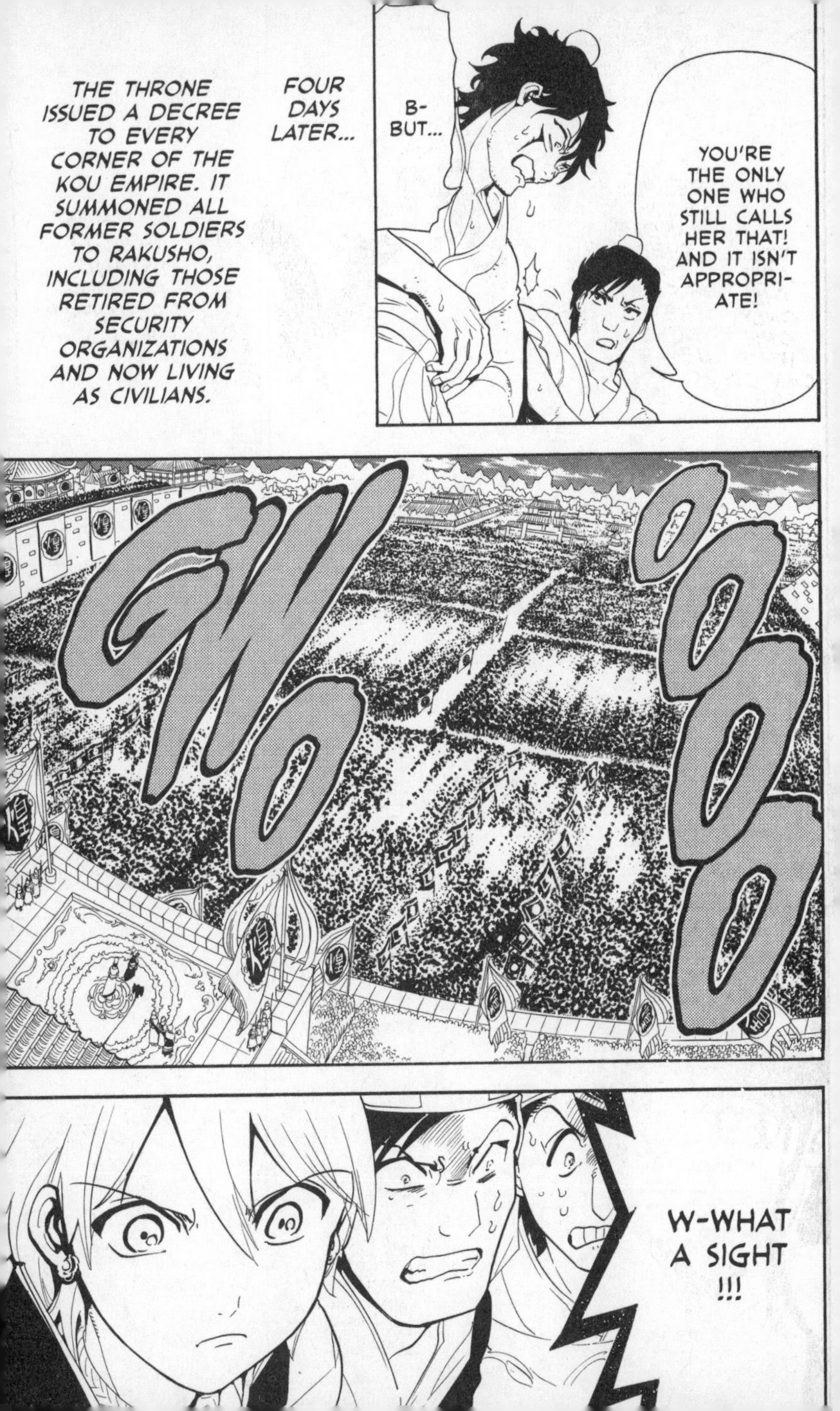

YOU'RE THE ONLY ONE WHO STILL CALLS HER THAT! AND IT ISN'T APPROPRI-ATE!
B-BUT...
FOUR DAYS LATER...
THE THRONE ISSUED A DECREE TO EVERY CORNER OF THE KOU EMPIRE. IT SUMMONED ALL FORMER SOLDIERS TO RAKUSHO, INCLUDING THOSE RETIRED FROM SECURITY ORGANIZATIONS AND NOW LIVING AS CIVILIANS.
GWOOOO
W-WHAT A SIGHT !!!

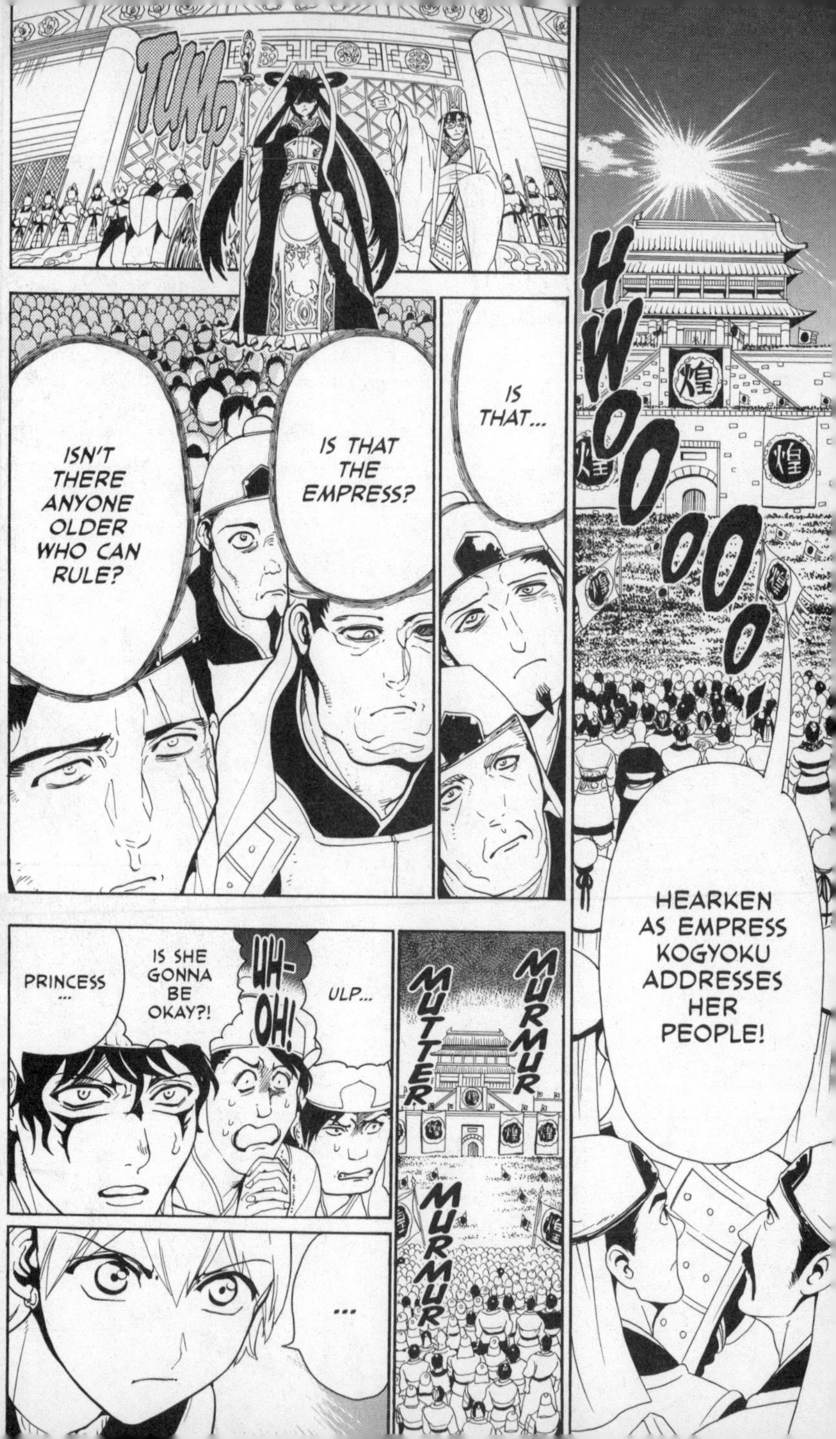
HWOOOOOOO
HEARKEN AS EMPRESS KOGYOKU ADDRESSES HER PEOPLE!
TUMP
IS THAT...
IS THAT THE EMPRESS?
ISN'T THERE ANYONE OLDER WHO CAN RULE?
MURMUR
MUTTER
MURMUR
ULP...
UH-OH!
IS SHE GONNA BE OKAY?!
PRINCESS ...
...

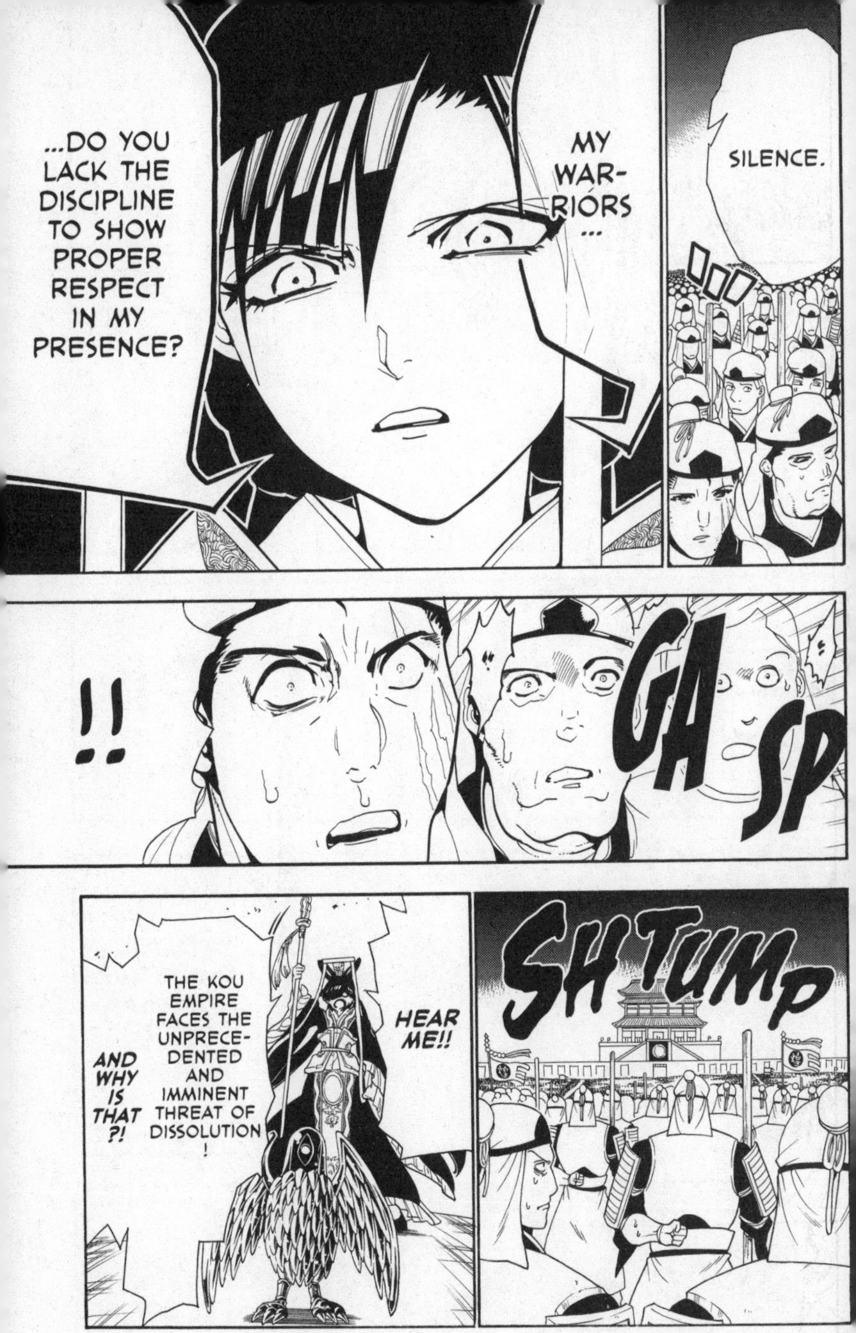
SILENCE.
MY WAR-RIÓRS...
...DO YOU LACK THE DISCIPLINE TO SHOW PROPER RESPECT IN MY PRESENCE?
GASP
!!
SHTUMP
HEAR ME!!
THE KOU EMPIRE FACES THE UNPRECE-DENTED AND IMMINENT THREAT OF DISSOLUTION!
AND WHY IS THAT?!

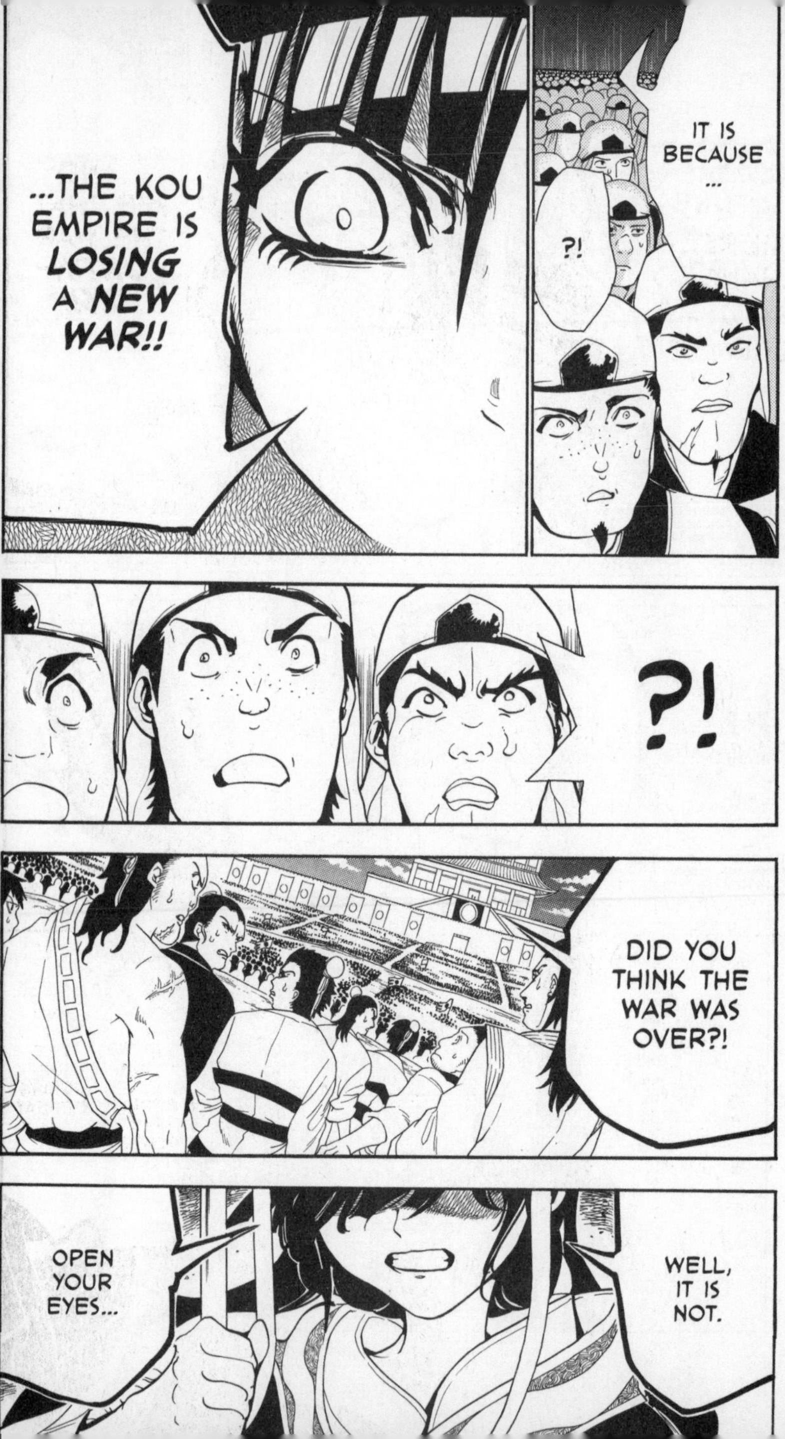
IT IS BECAUSE ...
?!
...THE KOU EMPIRE IS LOSING A NEW WAR!!
?!
DID YOU THINK THE WAR WAS OVER?!
WELL, IT IS NOT.
OPEN YOUR EYES...

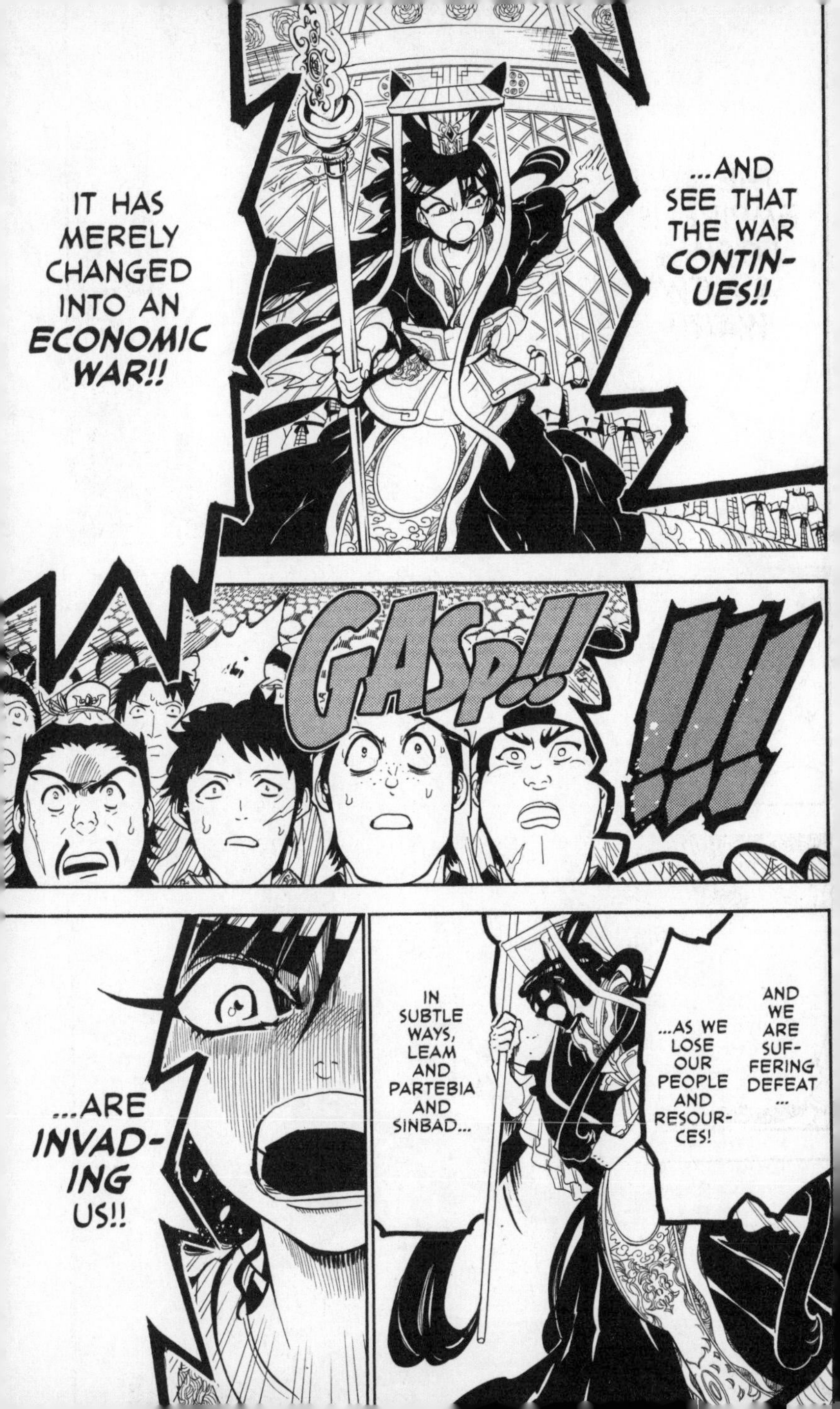
...AND SEE THAT THE WAR CONTINUES!!
IT HAS MERELY CHANGED INTO AN ECONOMIC WAR!!
GASP!!
!!!
AND WE ARE SUFFERING DEFEAT...
...AS WE LOSE OUR PEOPLE AND RESOURCES!
IN SUBTLE WAYS, LEAM AND PARTEBIA AND SINBAD...
...ARE INVADING US!!

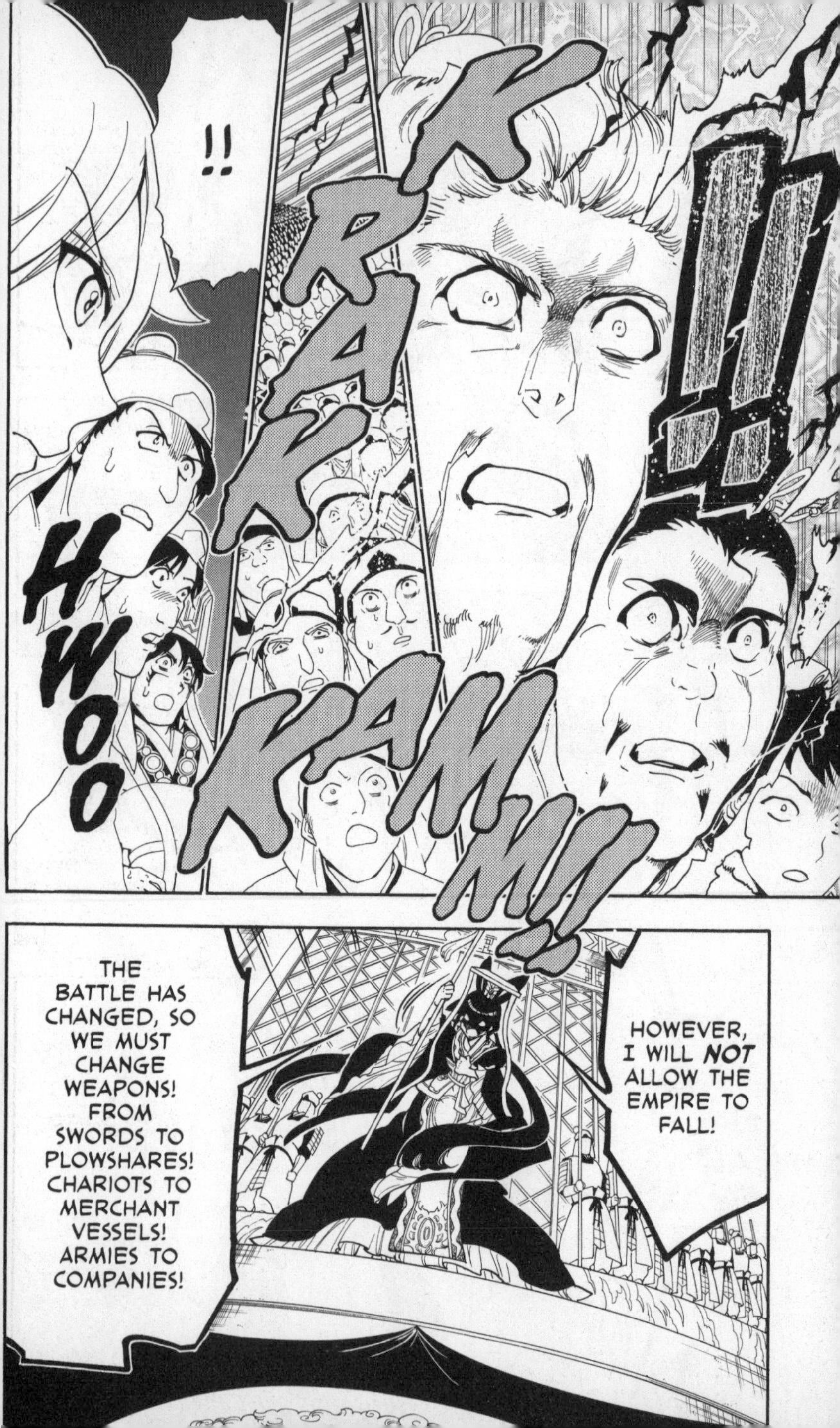
!!
KRAKKAMM!!
!!
HWOOO
THE BATTLE HAS CHANGED, SO WE MUST CHANGE WEAPONS! FROM SWORDS TO PLOWSHARES! CHARIOTS TO MERCHANT VESSELS! ARMIES TO COMPANIES!
HOWEVER, I WILL *NOT* ALLOW THE EMPIRE TO FALL!

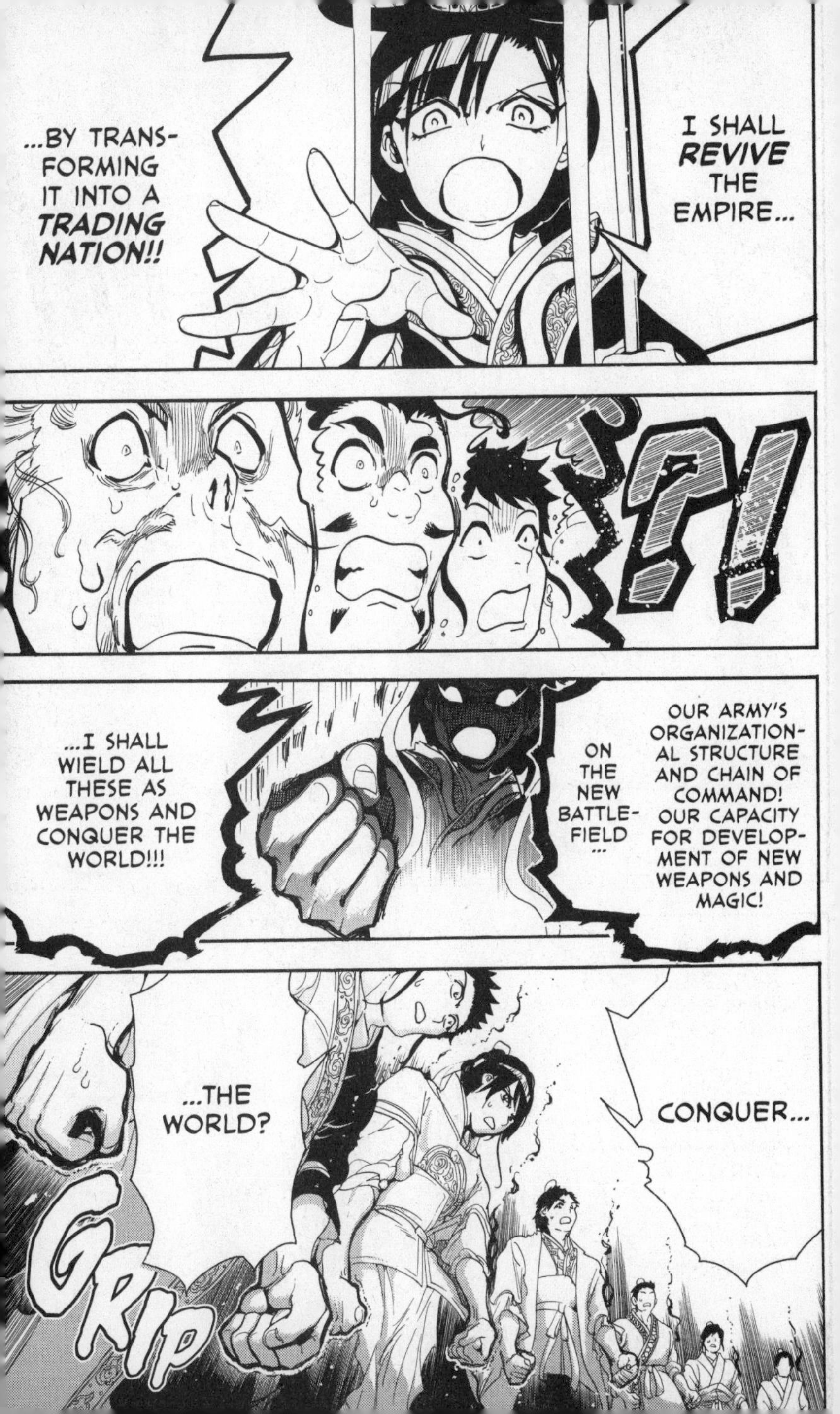
I SHALL REVIVE THE EMPIRE...
...BY TRANS-FORMING IT INTO A TRADING NATION!!
?!
OUR ARMY'S ORGANIZATION-AL STRUCTURE AND CHAIN OF COMMAND! OUR CAPACITY FOR DEVELOP-MENT OF NEW WEAPONS AND MAGIC!
ON THE NEW BATTLE-FIELD...
...I SHALL WIELD ALL THESE AS WEAPONS AND CONQUER THE WORLD!!!
CONQUER...
...THE WORLD?
GRIP

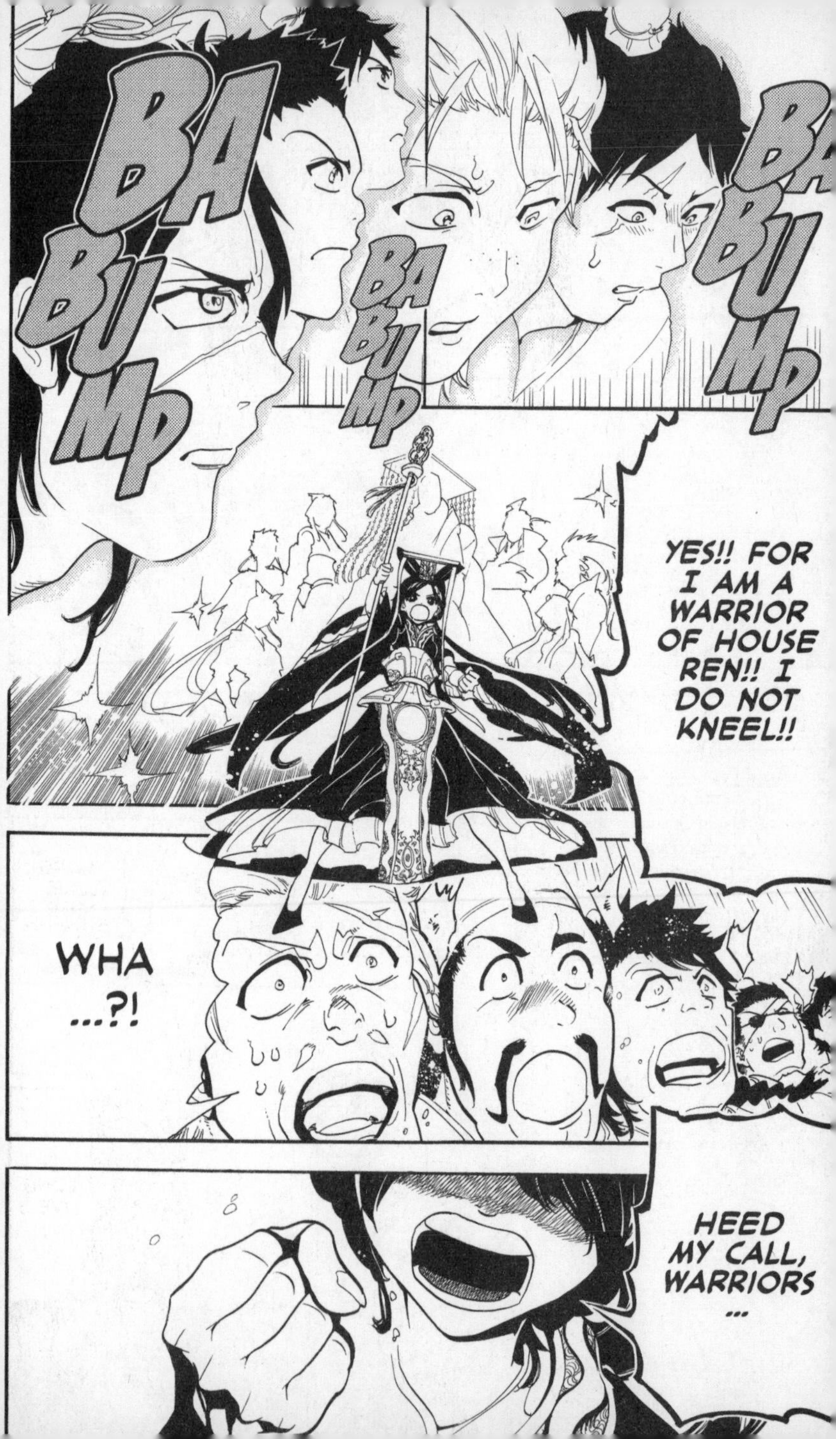
BA BU MP
BA BU MP
BA BU MP
YES!! FOR I AM A WARRIOR OF HOUSE REN!! I DO NOT KNEEL!!
WHA ...?!
HEED MY CALL, WARRIORS ...

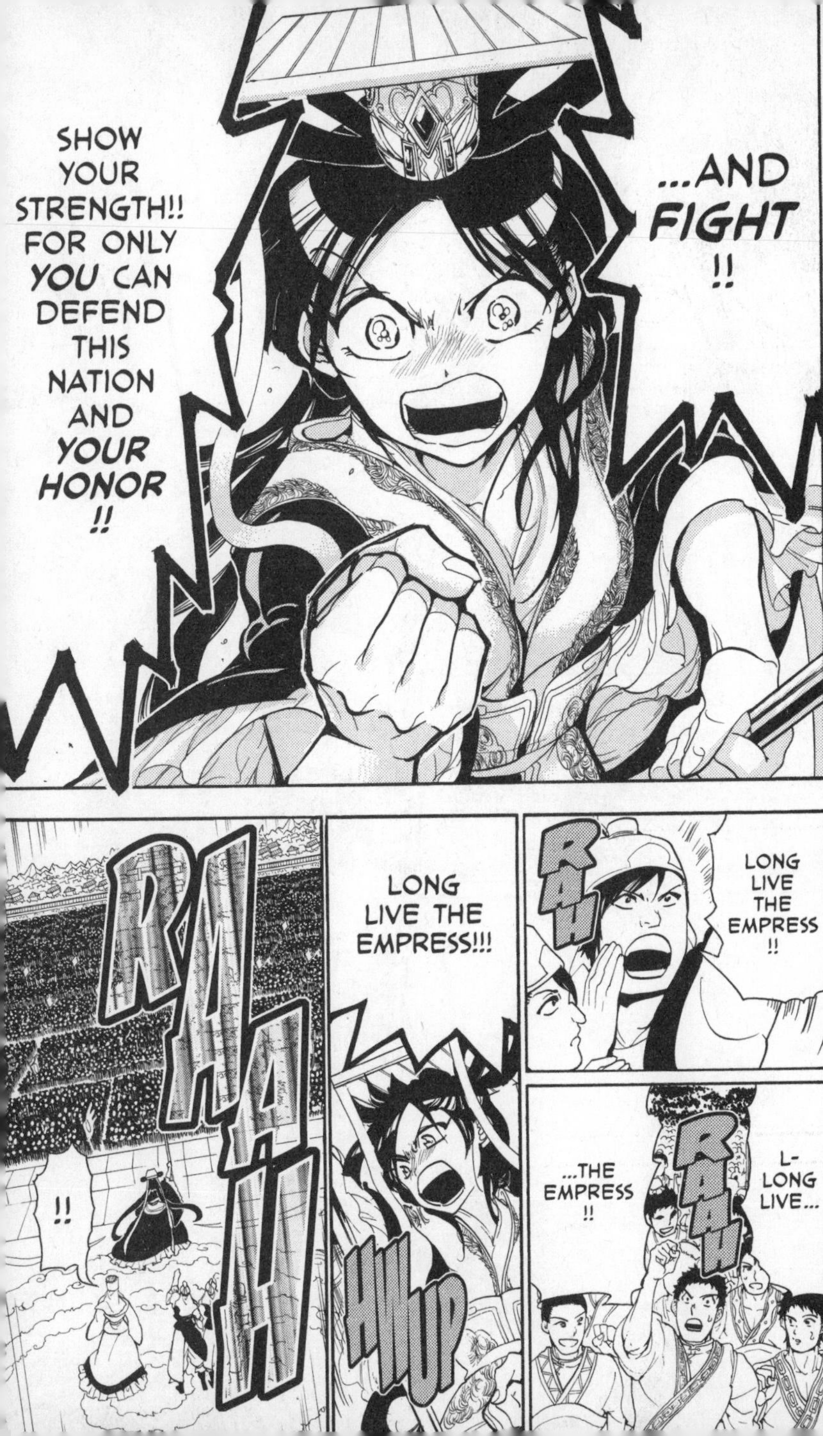
SHOW YOUR STRENGTH!! FOR ONLY YOU CAN DEFEND THIS NATION AND YOUR HONOR !!
...AND FIGHT !!
RAH
LONG LIVE THE EMPRESS !!
L- LONG LIVE...
RAAH
...THE EMPRESS !!
LONG LIVE THE EMPRESS!!!
HWUP
RAAAH
!!

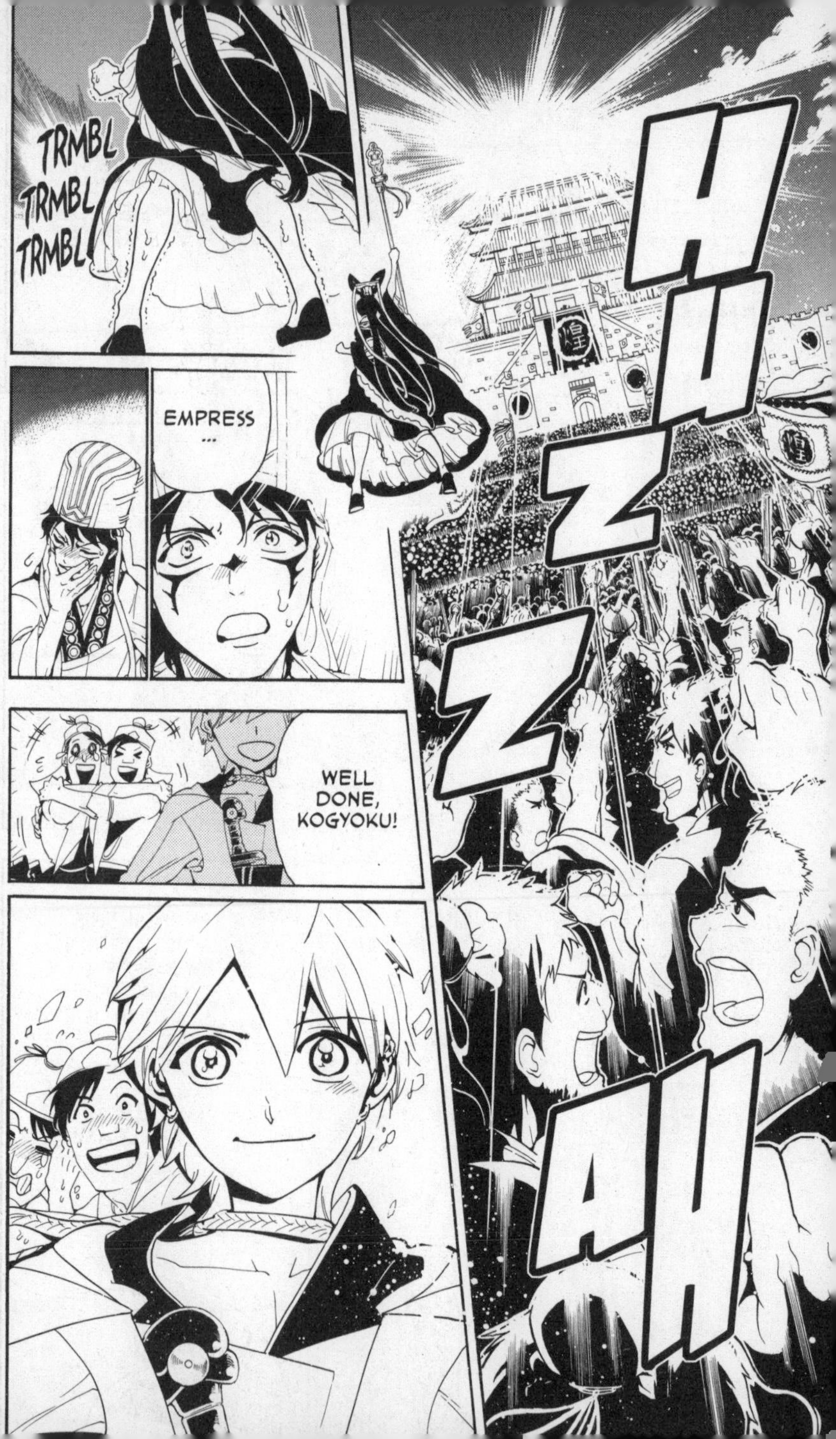
HUZZAH
TRMBL
TRMBL
TRMBL
EMPRESS ...
WELL DONE, KOGYOKU!

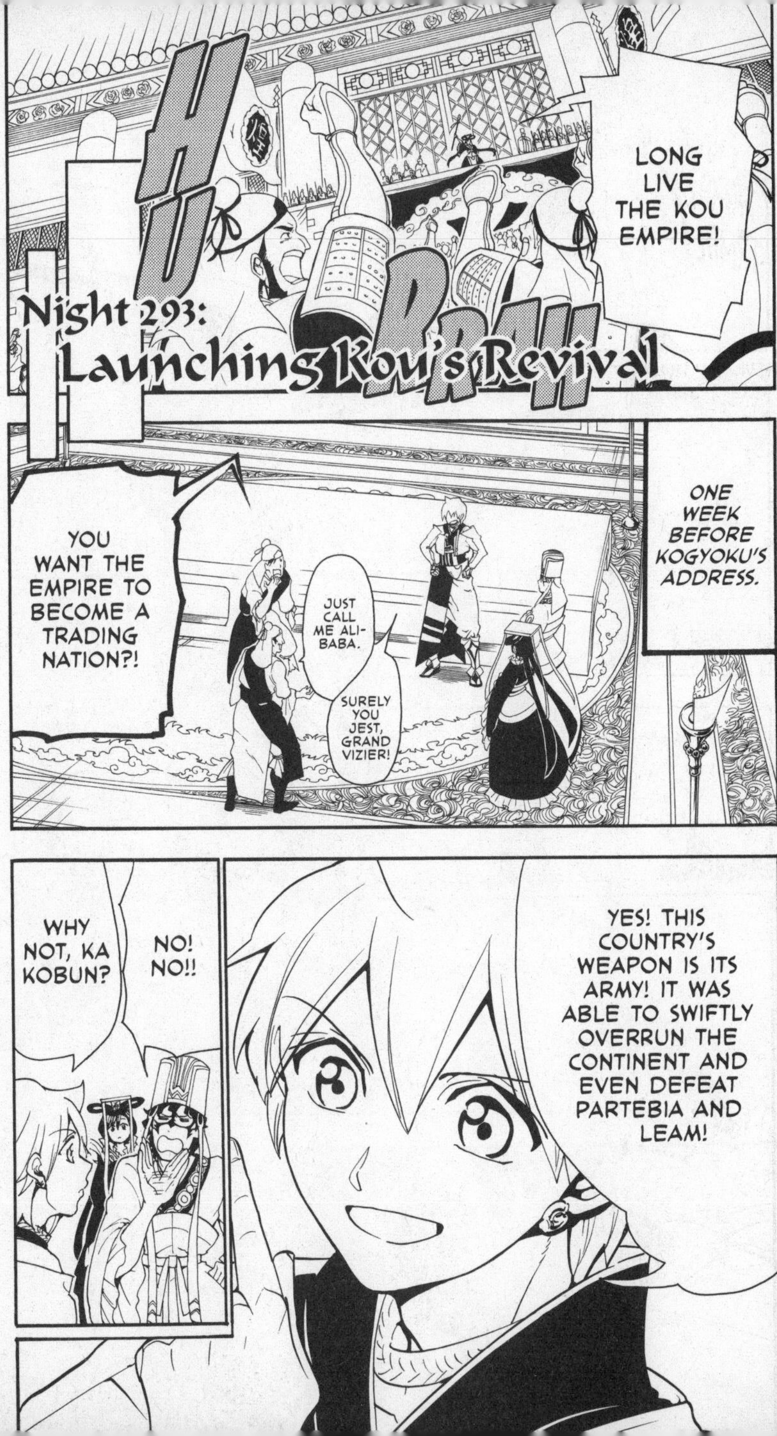
HURRAH
LONG LIVE THE KOU EMPIRE!
Night 293: Launching Kou's Revival
ONE WEEK BEFORE KOGYOKU'S ADDRESS.
JUST CALL ME ALI-BABA.
SURELY YOU JEST, GRAND VIZIER!
YOU WANT THE EMPIRE TO BECOME A TRADING NATION?!
YES! THIS COUNTRY'S WEAPON IS ITS ARMY! IT WAS ABLE TO SWIFTLY OVERRUN THE CONTINENT AND EVEN DEFEAT PARTEBIA AND LEAM!
NO! NO!!
WHY NOT, KA KOBUN?

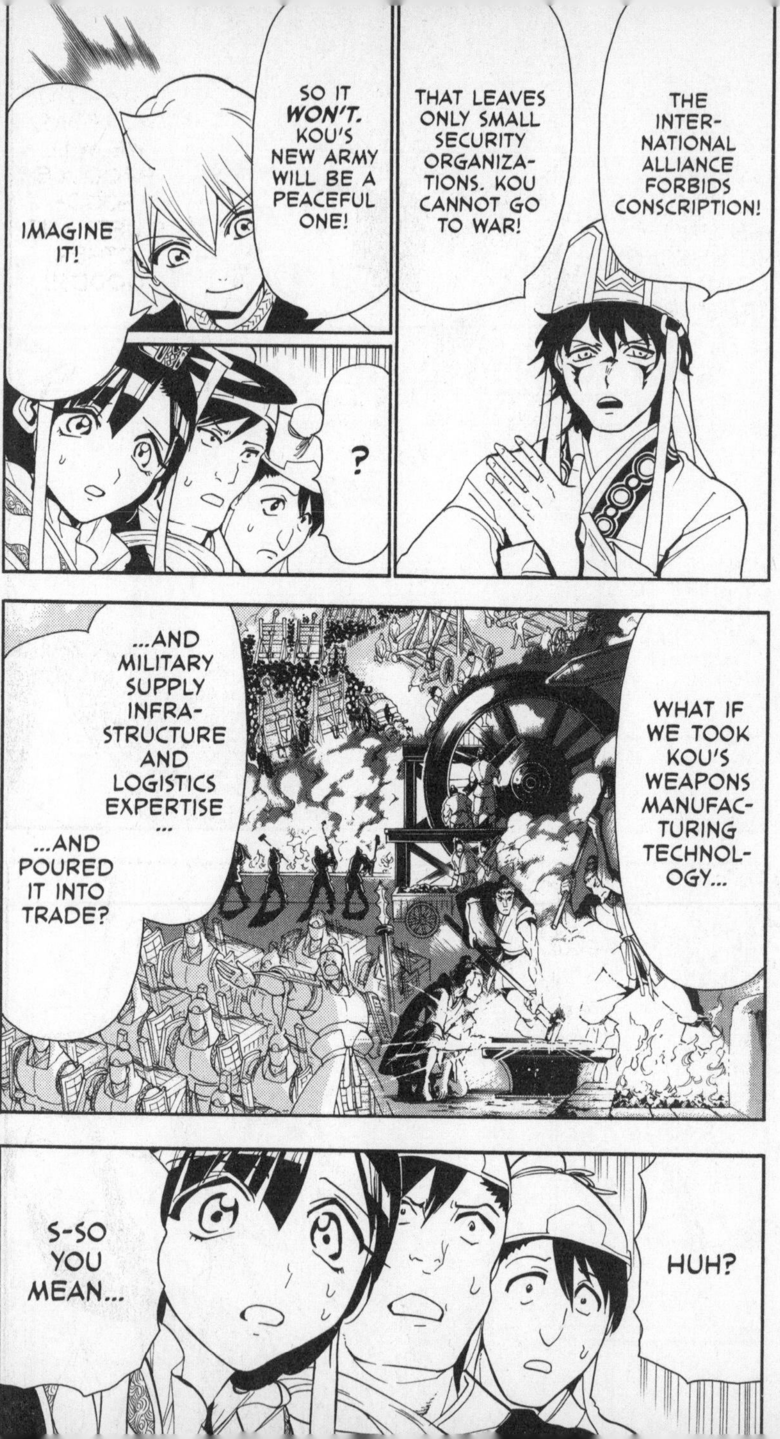
THE INTERNATIONAL ALLIANCE FORBIDS CONSCRIPTION!
THAT LEAVES ONLY SMALL SECURITY ORGANIZATIONS. KOU CANNOT GO TO WAR!
SO IT *WON'T.* KOU'S NEW ARMY WILL BE A PEACEFUL ONE!
IMAGINE IT!
?
WHAT IF WE TOOK KOU'S WEAPONS MANUFACTURING TECHNOLOGY...
...AND MILITARY SUPPLY INFRASTRUCTURE AND LOGISTICS EXPERTISE...
...AND POURED IT INTO TRADE?
HUH?
S-SO YOU MEAN...

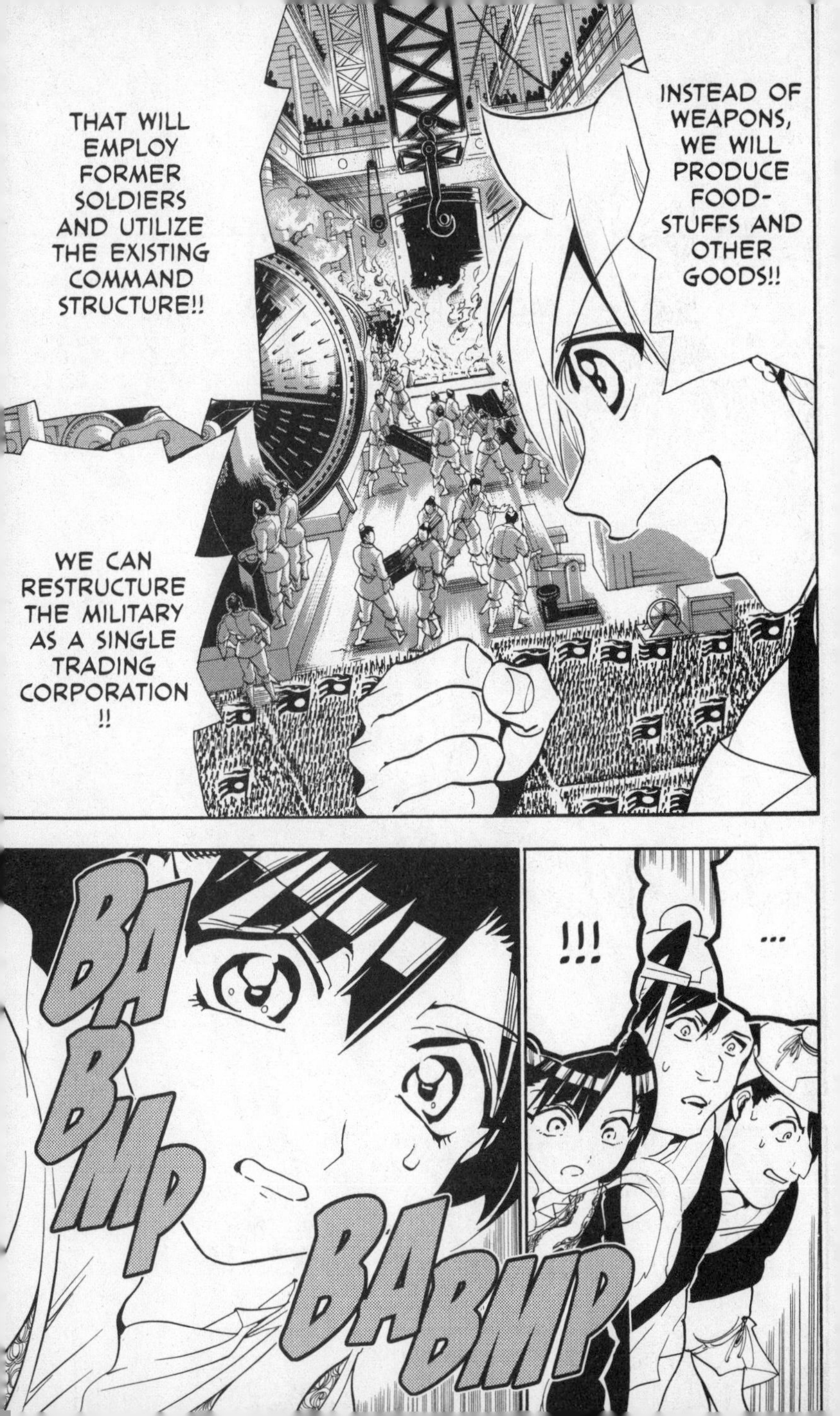
INSTEAD OF WEAPONS, WE WILL PRODUCE FOOD-STUFFS AND OTHER GOODS!!
THAT WILL EMPLOY FORMER SOLDIERS AND UTILIZE THE EXISTING COMMAND STRUCTURE!!
WE CAN RESTRUCTURE THE MILITARY AS A SINGLE TRADING CORPORATION!!
...
!!!
BABMP
BABMP

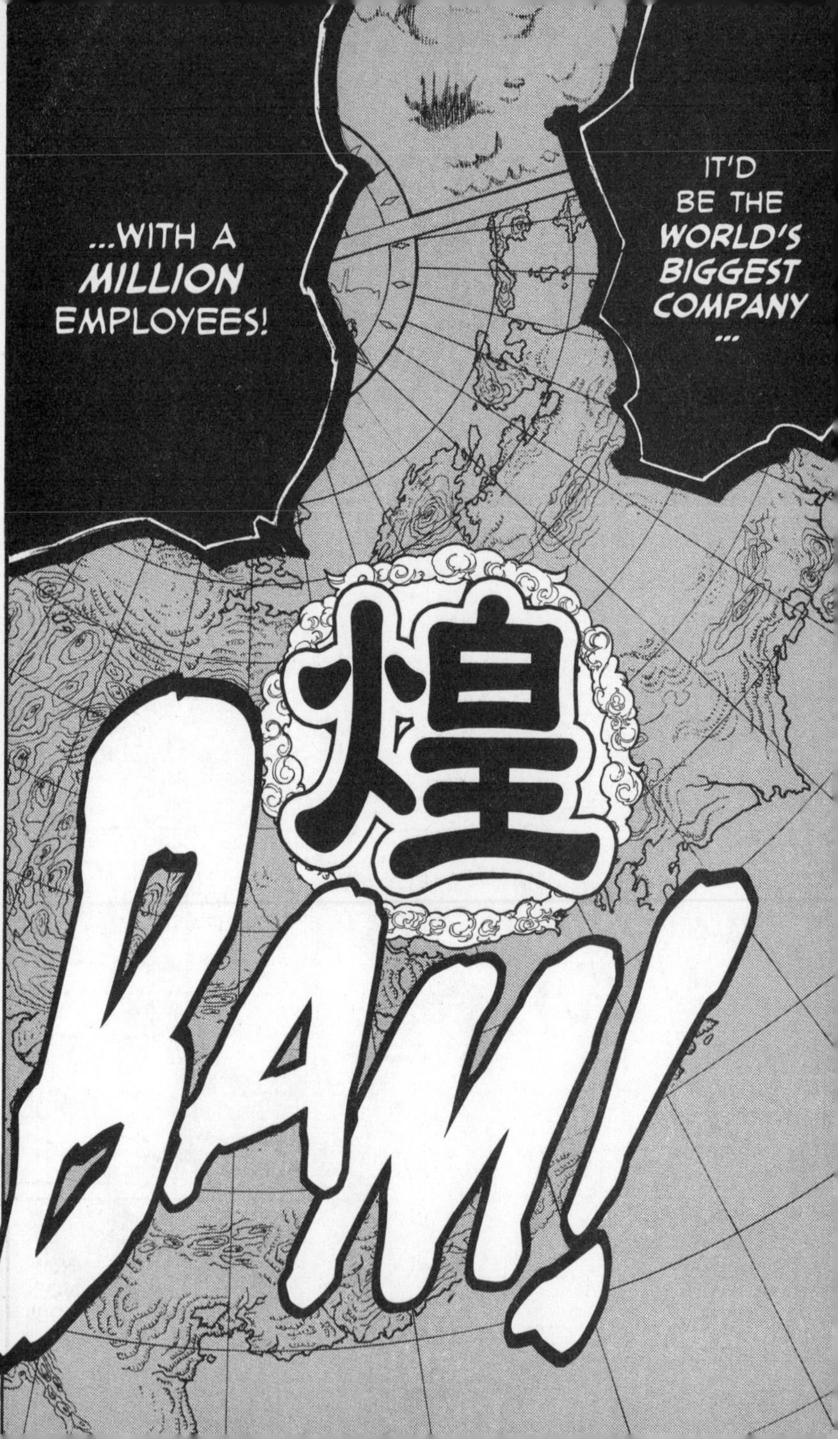
IT'D BE THE WORLD'S BIGGEST COMPANY ...
...WITH A MILLION EMPLOYEES!
煌
BAM!

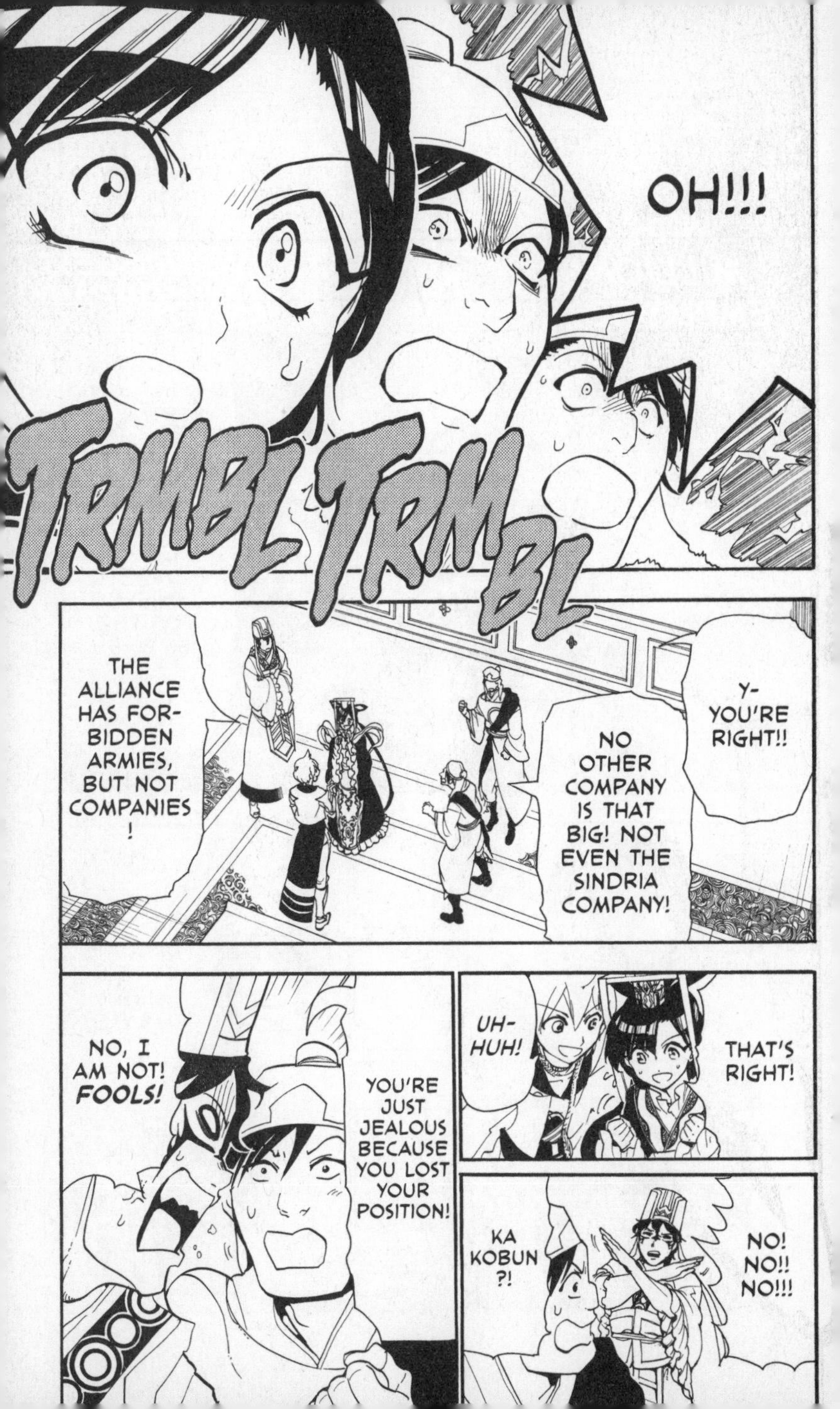
OH!!!
TRMBL TRMBL
Y- YOU'RE RIGHT!!
NO OTHER COMPANY IS THAT BIG! NOT EVEN THE SINDRIA COMPANY!
THE ALLIANCE HAS FORBIDDEN ARMIES, BUT NOT COMPANIES!
THAT'S RIGHT!
UH-HUH!
NO! NO!! NO!!!
KA KOBUN?!
YOU'RE JUST JEALOUS BECAUSE YOU LOST YOUR POSITION!
NO, I AM NOT! FOOLS!

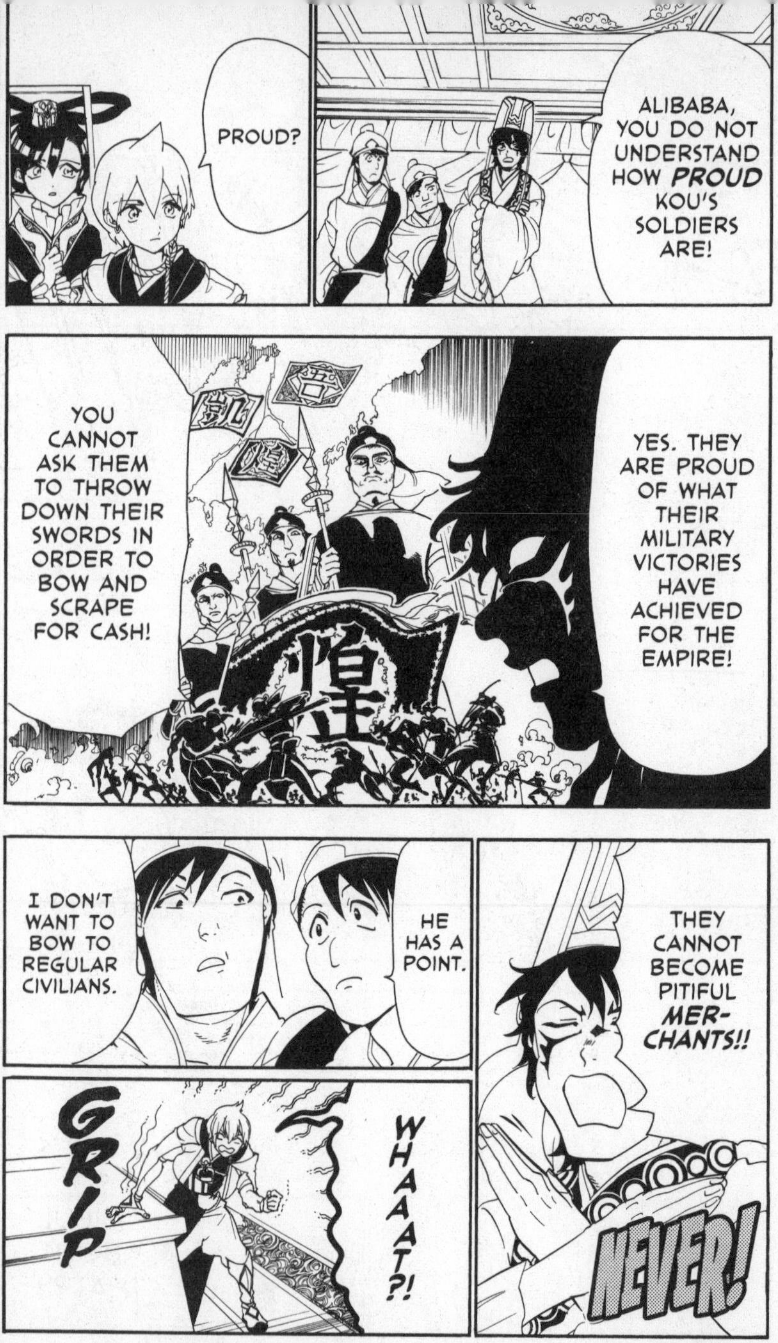
ALIBABA, YOU DO NOT UNDERSTAND HOW PROUD KOU'S SOLDIERS ARE!
PROUD?
YES. THEY ARE PROUD OF WHAT THEIR MILITARY VICTORIES HAVE ACHIEVED FOR THE EMPIRE!
YOU CANNOT ASK THEM TO THROW DOWN THEIR SWORDS IN ORDER TO BOW AND SCRAPE FOR CASH!
THEY CANNOT BECOME PITIFUL MERCHANTS!!
NEVER!
HE HAS A POINT.
I DON'T WANT TO BOW TO REGULAR CIVILIANS.
WHAAAT?!
GRIP

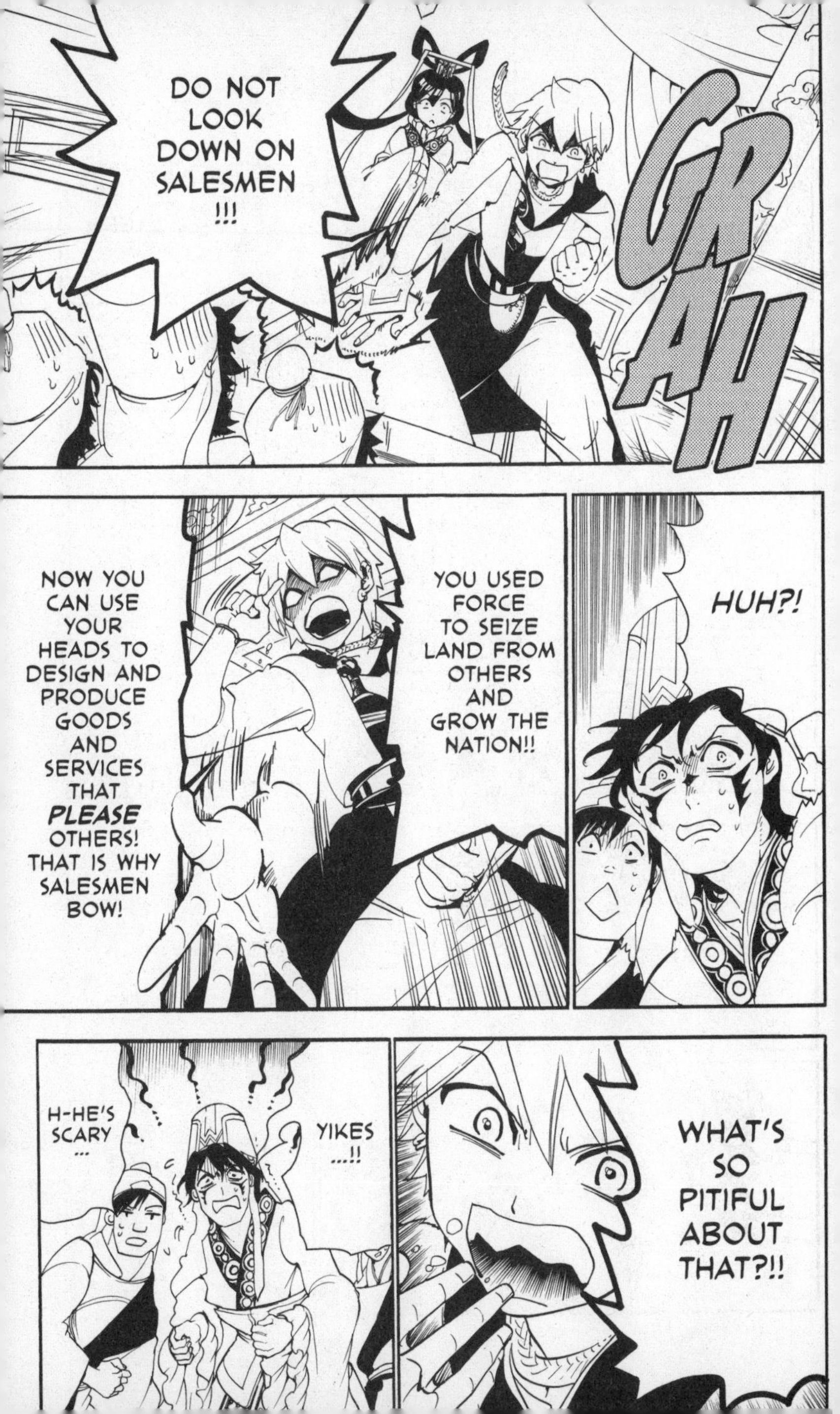
GRAAH
DO NOT LOOK DOWN ON SALESMEN !!!
HUH?!
YOU USED FORCE TO SEIZE LAND FROM OTHERS AND GROW THE NATION!!
NOW YOU CAN USE YOUR HEADS TO DESIGN AND PRODUCE GOODS AND SERVICES THAT *PLEASE* OTHERS! THAT IS WHY SALESMEN BOW!
WHAT'S SO PITIFUL ABOUT THAT?!!
YIKES ...!!
H-HE'S SCARY ...

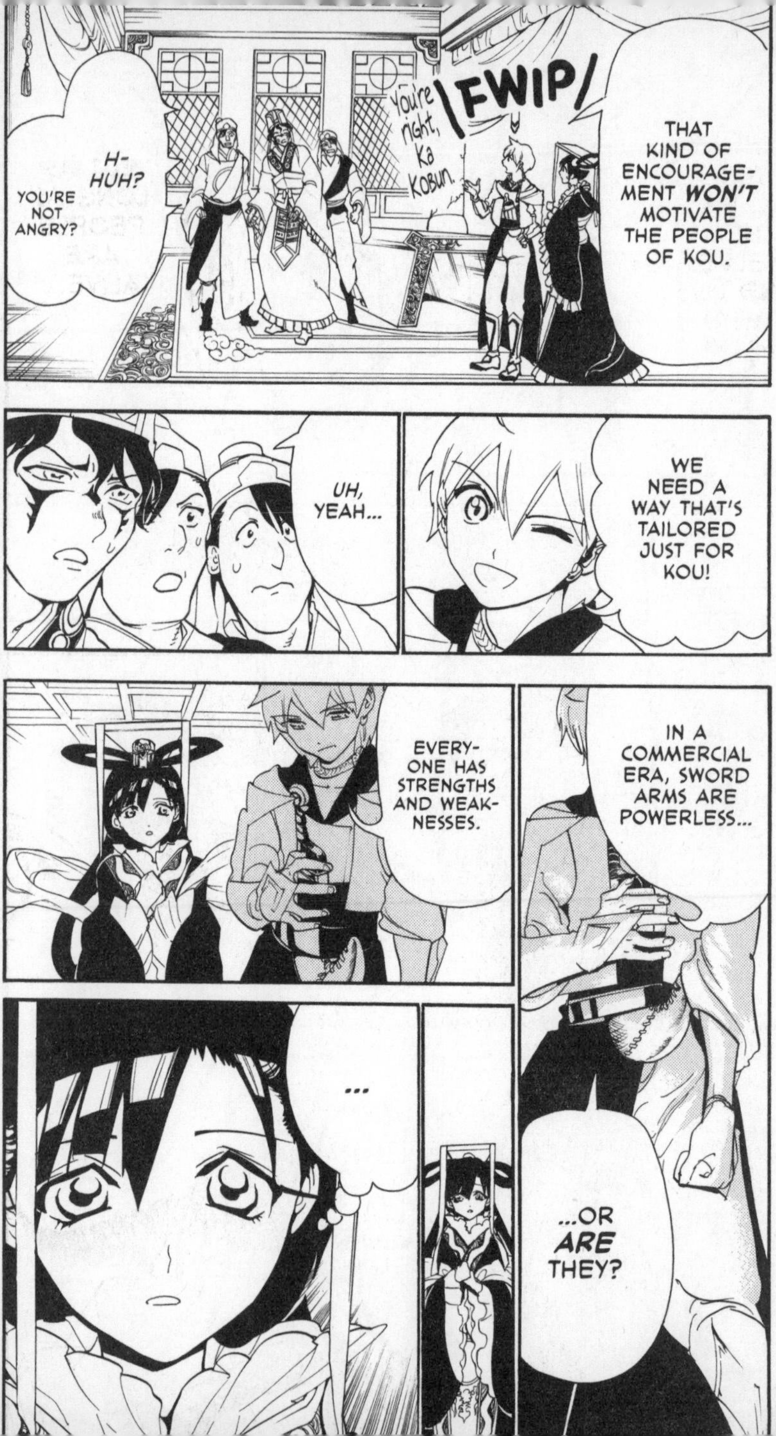
THAT KIND OF ENCOURAGEMENT *WON'T* MOTIVATE THE PEOPLE OF KOU.
FWIP
You're right, Ka Kobun.
H-HUH?
YOU'RE NOT ANGRY?
WE NEED A WAY THAT'S TAILORED JUST FOR KOU!
UH, YEAH...
IN A COMMERCIAL ERA, SWORD ARMS ARE POWERLESS...
...OR *ARE* THEY?
EVERYONE HAS STRENGTHS AND WEAKNESSES.
...

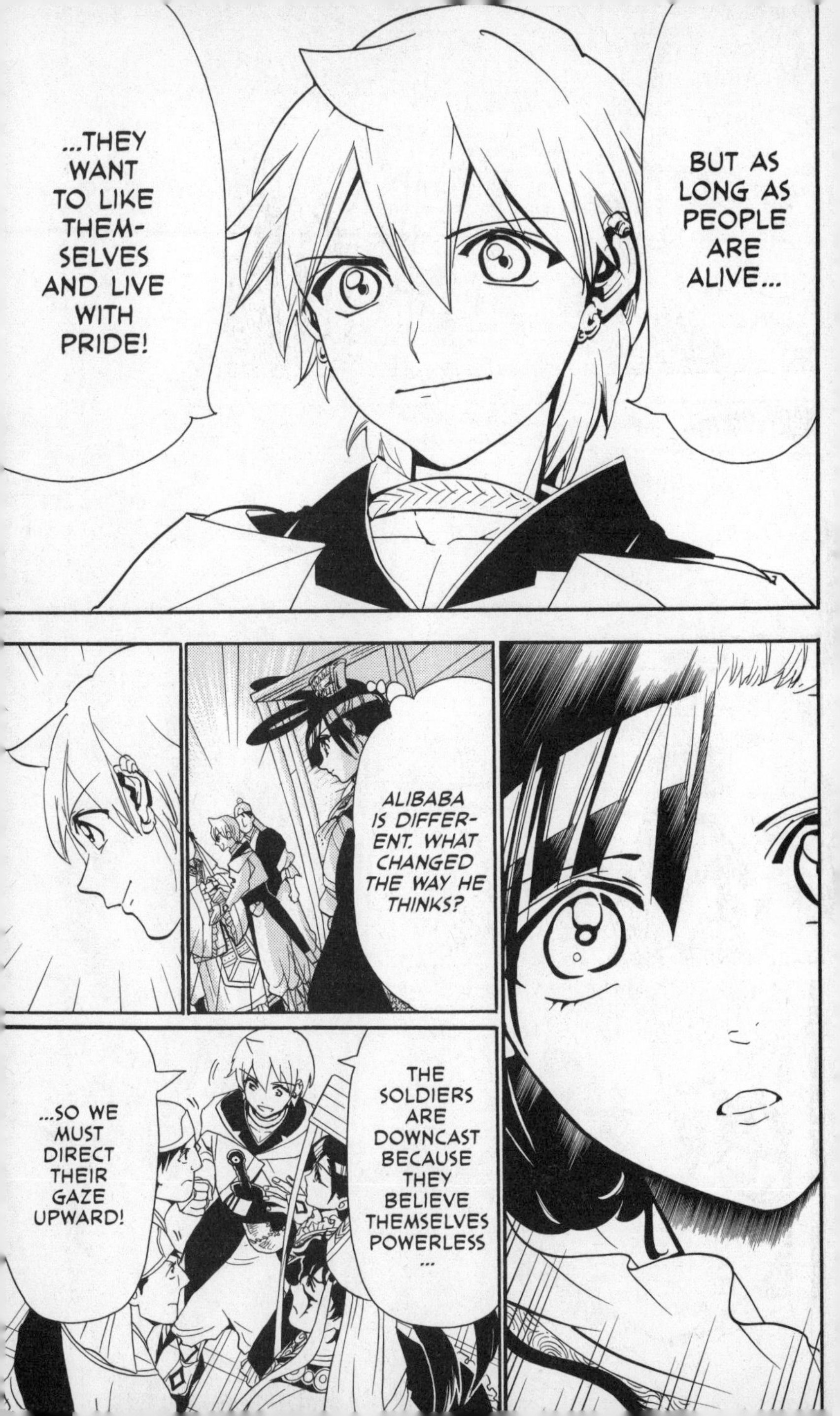
BUT AS LONG AS PEOPLE ARE ALIVE...
...THEY WANT TO LIKE THEMSELVES AND LIVE WITH PRIDE!
ALIBABA IS DIFFERENT. WHAT CHANGED THE WAY HE THINKS?
THE SOLDIERS ARE DOWNCAST BECAUSE THEY BELIEVE THEMSELVES POWERLESS ...
...SO WE MUST DIRECT THEIR GAZE UPWARD!

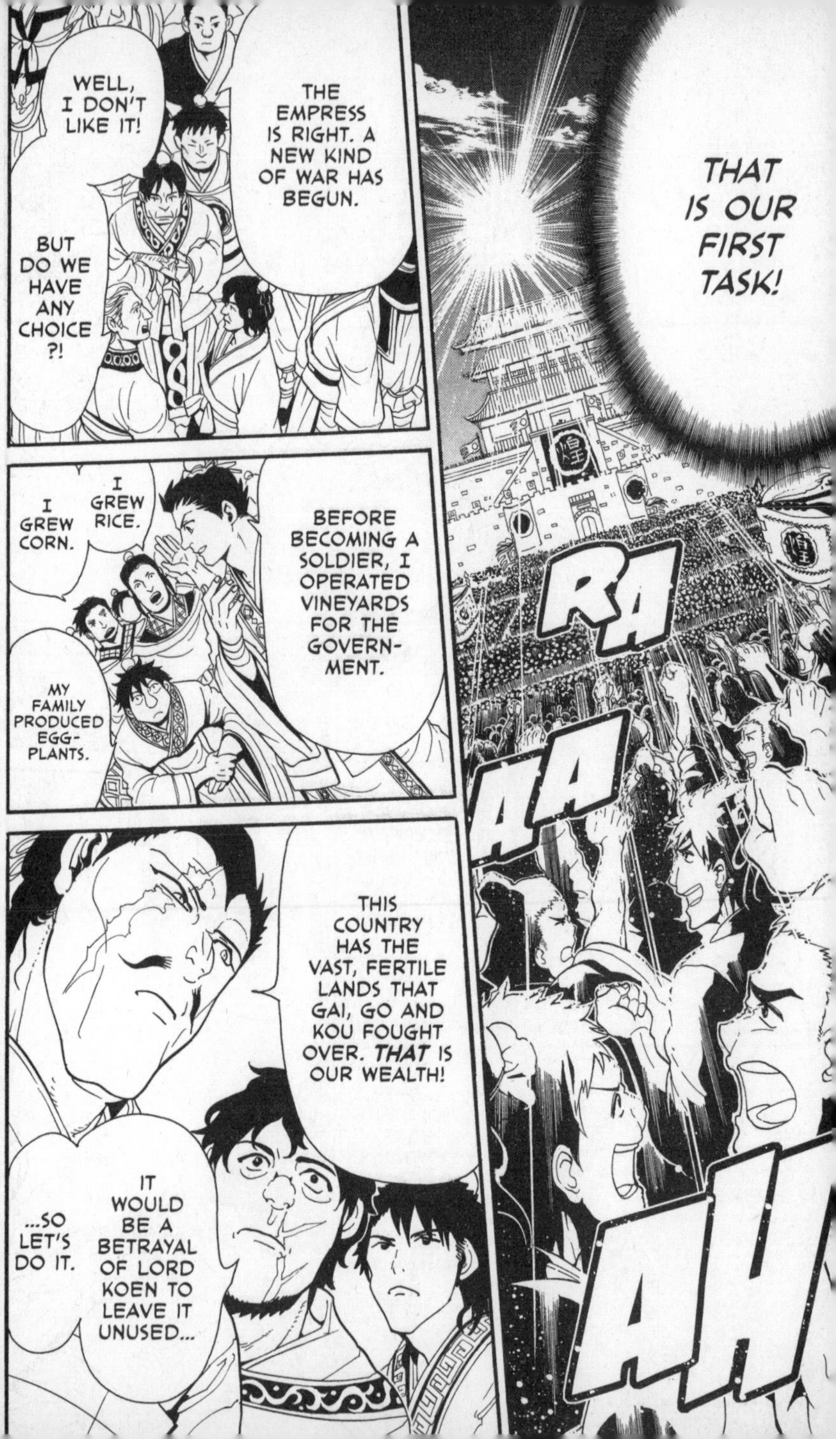
THAT IS OUR FIRST TASK!
RA
AA
AH
THE EMPRESS IS RIGHT. A NEW KIND OF WAR HAS BEGUN.
WELL, I DON'T LIKE IT!
BUT DO WE HAVE ANY CHOICE?!
BEFORE BECOMING A SOLDIER, I OPERATED VINEYARDS FOR THE GOVERNMENT.
I GREW RICE.
I GREW CORN.
MY FAMILY PRODUCED EGG-PLANTS.
THIS COUNTRY HAS THE VAST, FERTILE LANDS THAT GAI, GO AND KOU FOUGHT OVER. *THAT* IS OUR WEALTH!
IT WOULD BE A BETRAYAL OF LORD KOEN TO LEAVE IT UNUSED...
...SO LET'S DO IT.

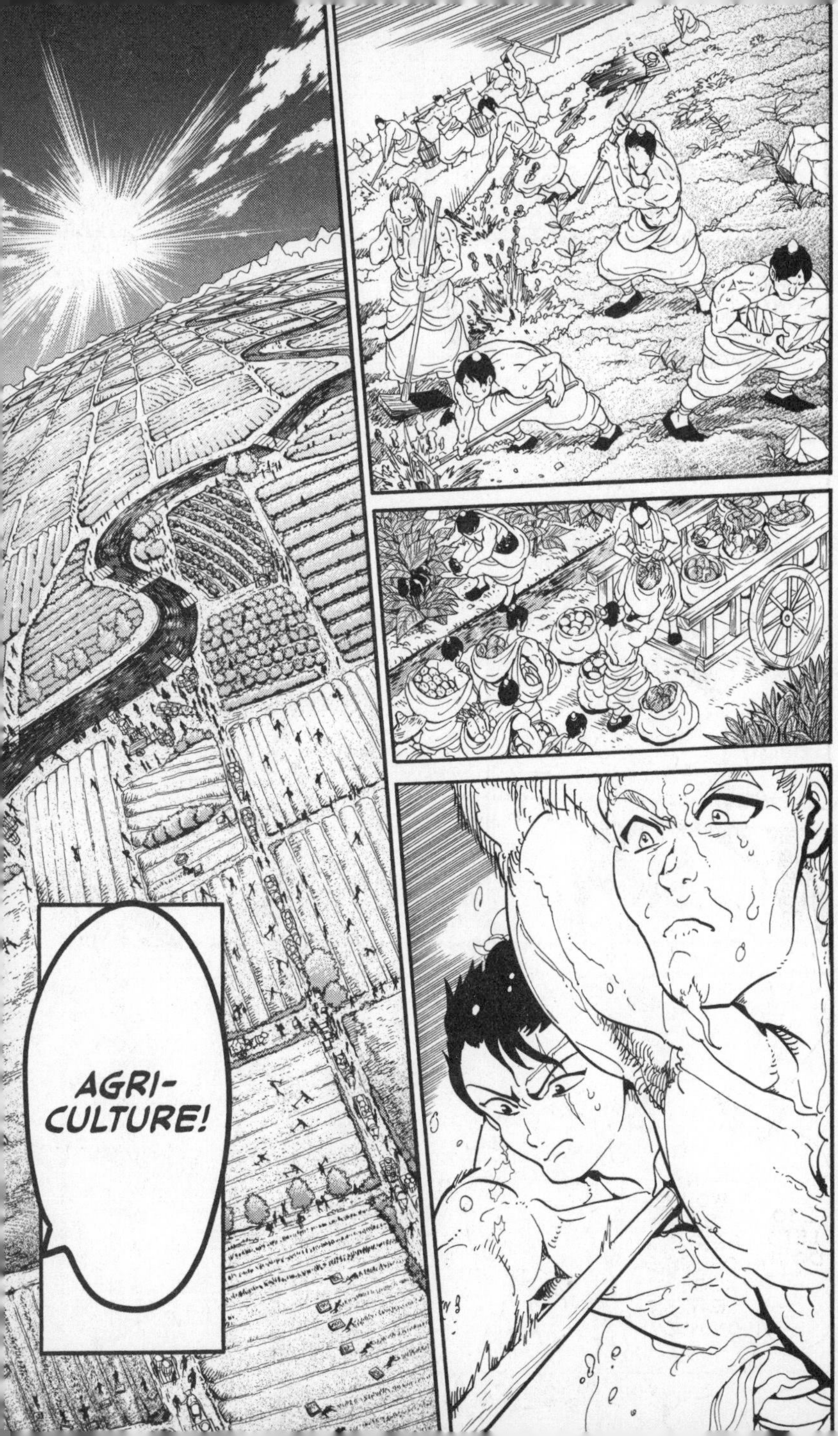
AGRI- CULTURE!

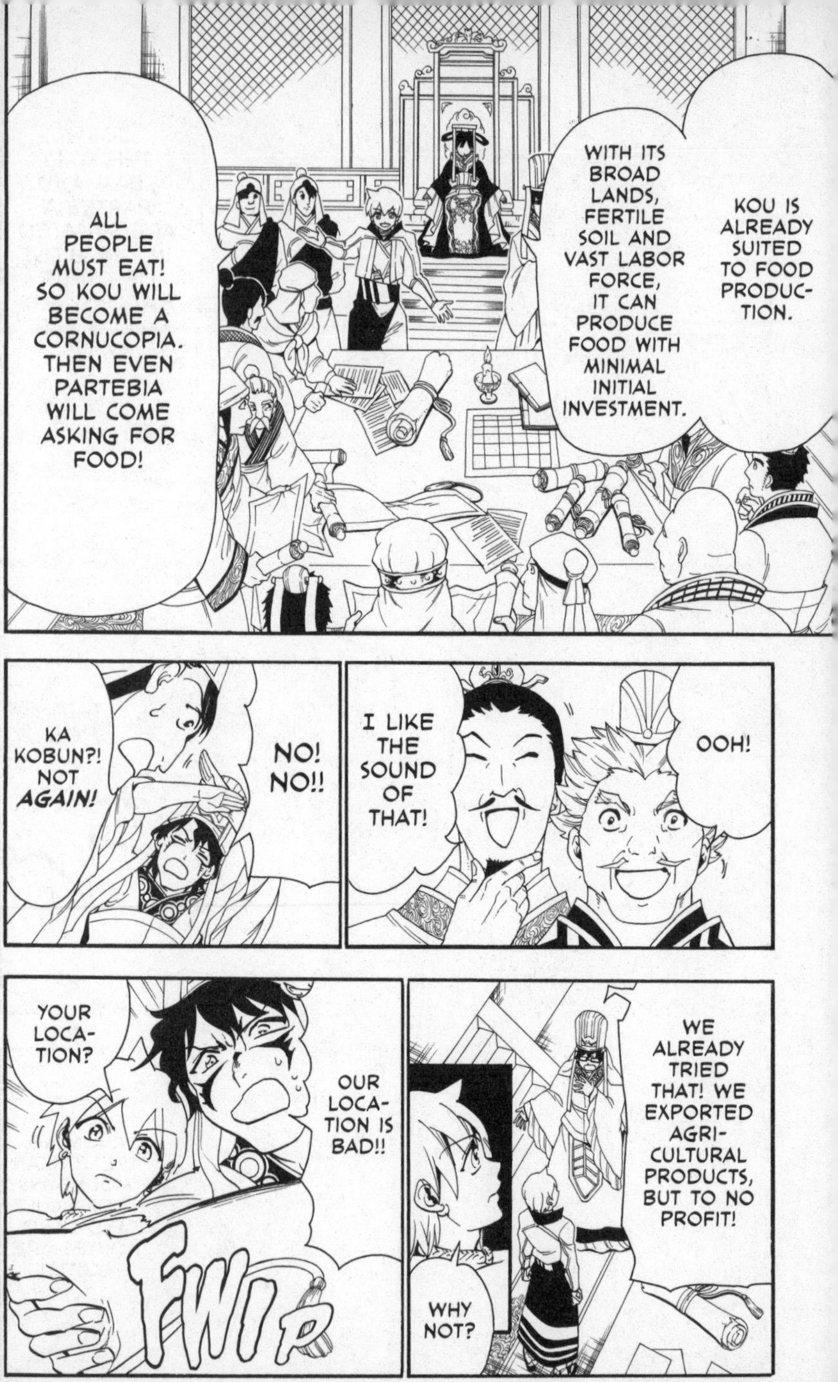
KOU IS ALREADY SUITED TO FOOD PRODUC-TION.
WITH ITS BROAD LANDS, FERTILE SOIL AND VAST LABOR FORCE, IT CAN PRODUCE FOOD WITH MINIMAL INITIAL INVESTMENT.
ALL PEOPLE MUST EAT! SO KOU WILL BECOME A CORNUCOPIA. THEN EVEN PARTEBIA WILL COME ASKING FOR FOOD!
OOH!
I LIKE THE SOUND OF THAT!
NO! NO!!
KA KOBUN?! NOT *AGAIN!*
WE ALREADY TRIED THAT! WE EXPORTED AGRI-CULTURAL PRODUCTS, BUT TO NO PROFIT!
WHY NOT?
OUR LOCA-TION IS BAD!!
YOUR LOCA-TION?
FWIP

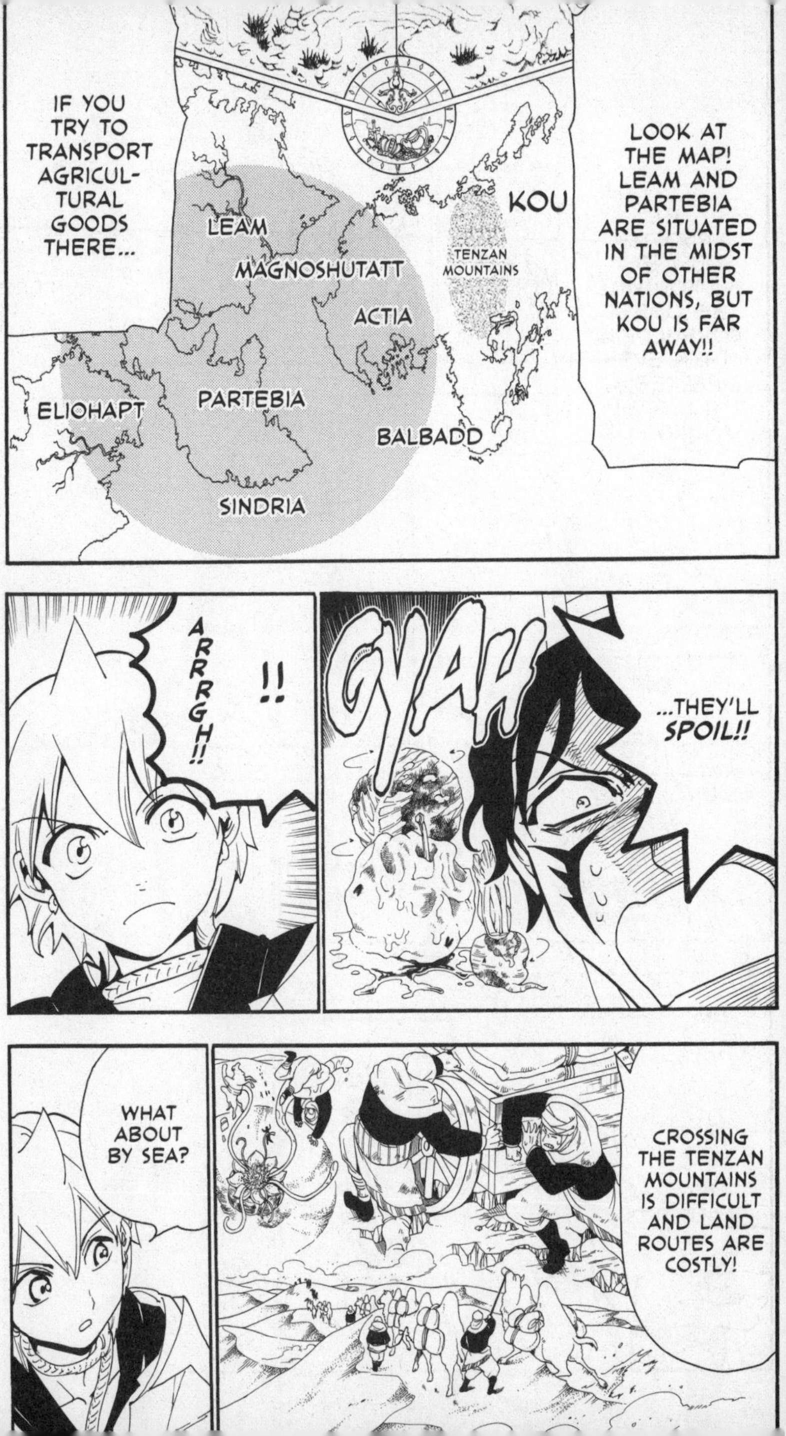
LOOK AT THE MAP! LEAM AND PARTEBIA ARE SITUATED IN THE MIDST OF OTHER NATIONS, BUT KOU IS FAR AWAY!!
KOU
TENZAN MOUNTAINS
LEAM
MAGNOSHUTATT
ACTIA
PARTEBIA
ELIOHAPT
BALBADD
SINDRIA
IF YOU TRY TO TRANSPORT AGRICUL-TURAL GOODS THERE...
GYAH
...THEY'LL *SPOIL!!*
ARRRGH!!
!!
CROSSING THE TENZAN MOUNTAINS IS DIFFICULT AND LAND ROUTES ARE COSTLY!
WHAT ABOUT BY SEA?

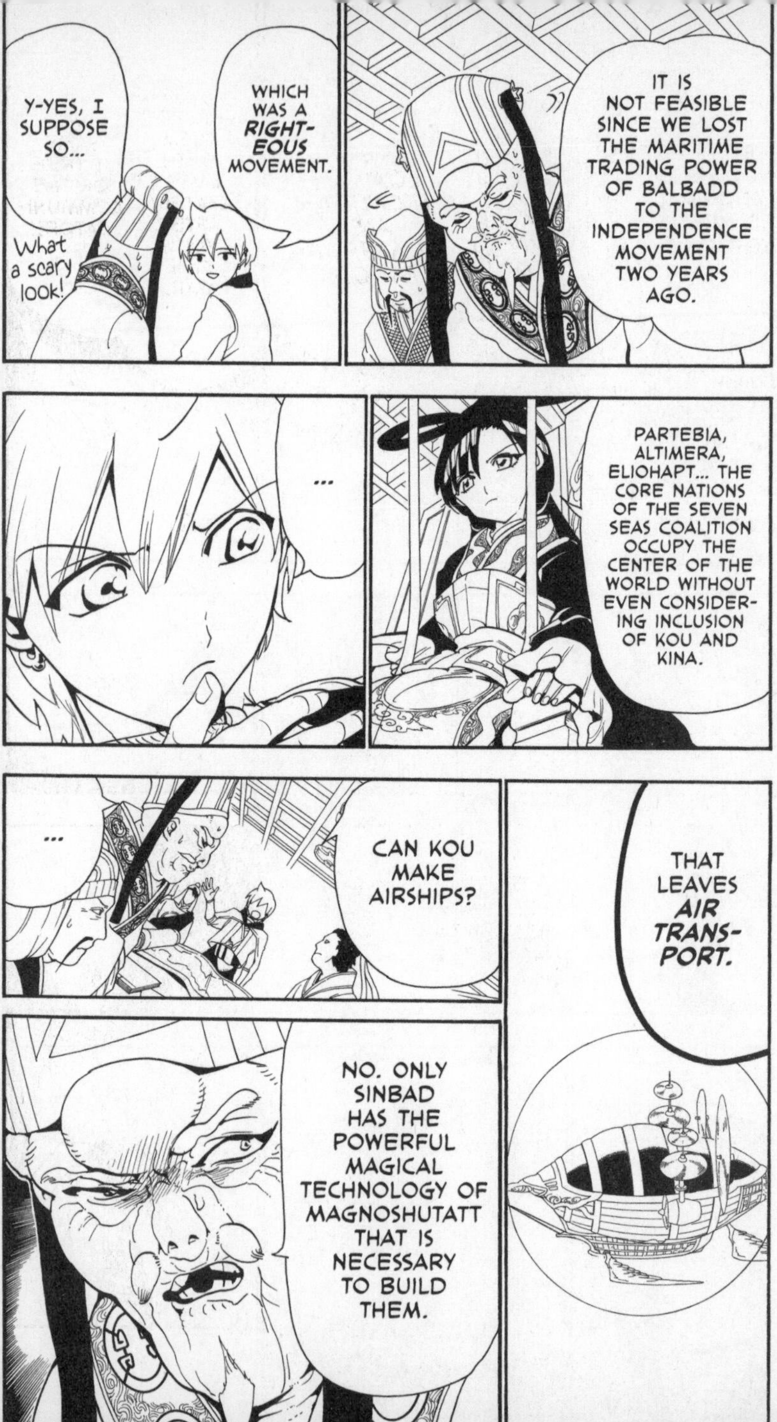
IT IS NOT FEASIBLE SINCE WE LOST THE MARITIME TRADING POWER OF BALBADD TO THE INDEPENDENCE MOVEMENT TWO YEARS AGO.
WHICH WAS A *RIGHTEOUS* MOVEMENT.
Y-YES, I SUPPOSE SO...
What a scary look!
PARTEBIA, ALTIMERA, ELIOHAPT... THE CORE NATIONS OF THE SEVEN SEAS COALITION OCCUPY THE CENTER OF THE WORLD WITHOUT EVEN CONSIDERING INCLUSION OF KOU AND KINA.
...
THAT LEAVES *AIR TRANSPORT.*
CAN KOU MAKE AIRSHIPS?
...
NO. ONLY SINBAD HAS THE POWERFUL MAGICAL TECHNOLOGY OF MAGNOSHUTATT THAT IS NECESSARY TO BUILD THEM.

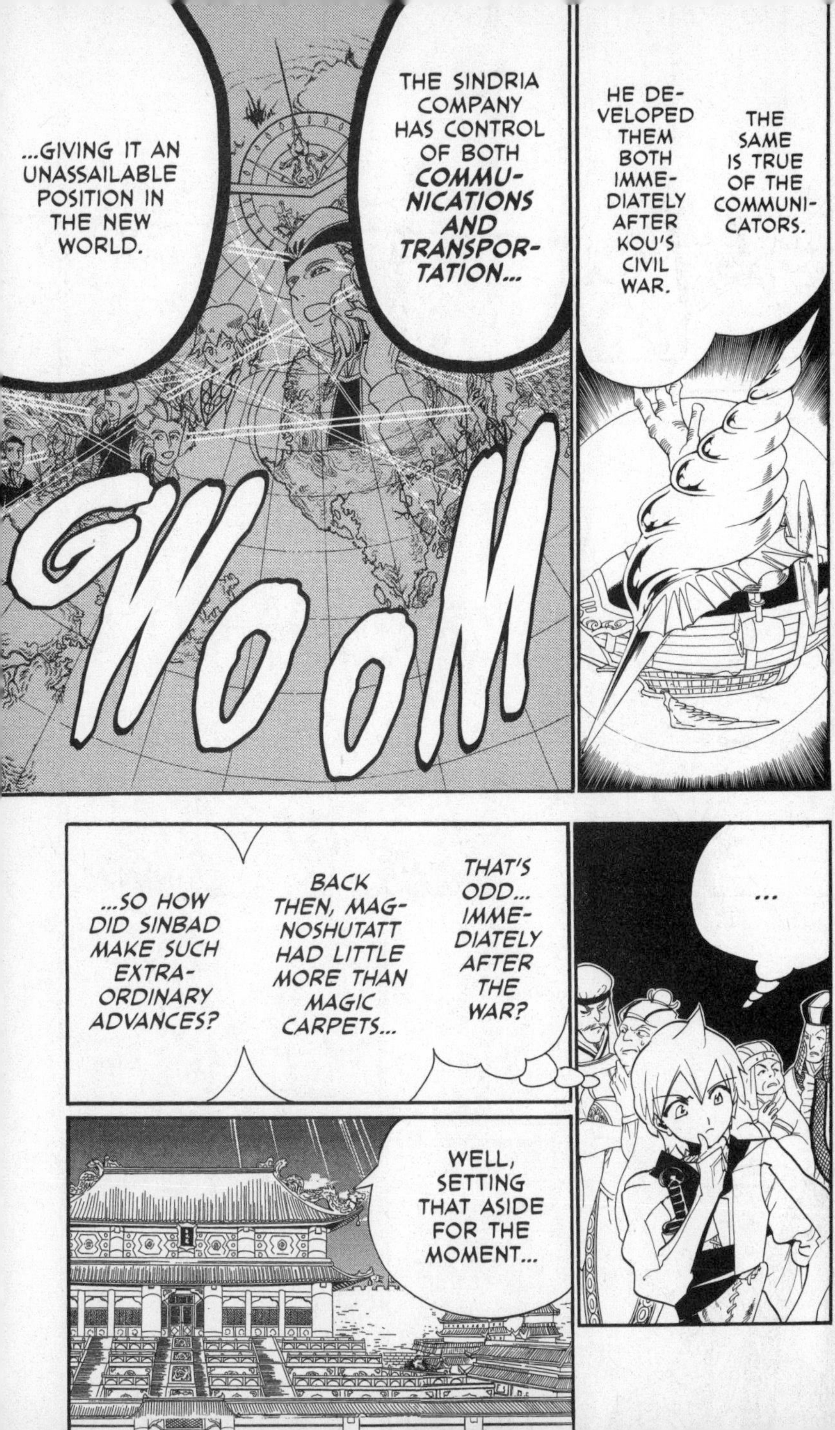
THE SAME IS TRUE OF THE COMMUNICATORS.
HE DEVELOPED THEM BOTH IMMEDIATELY AFTER KOU'S CIVIL WAR.
THE SINDRIA COMPANY HAS CONTROL OF BOTH ***COMMUNICATIONS AND TRANSPORTATION...***
...GIVING IT AN UNASSAILABLE POSITION IN THE NEW WORLD.
WOOM
...
THAT'S ODD... IMMEDIATELY AFTER THE WAR?
BACK THEN, MAGNOSHUTATT HAD LITTLE MORE THAN MAGIC CARPETS...
...SO HOW DID SINBAD MAKE SUCH EXTRAORDINARY ADVANCES?
WELL, SETTING THAT ASIDE FOR THE MOMENT...

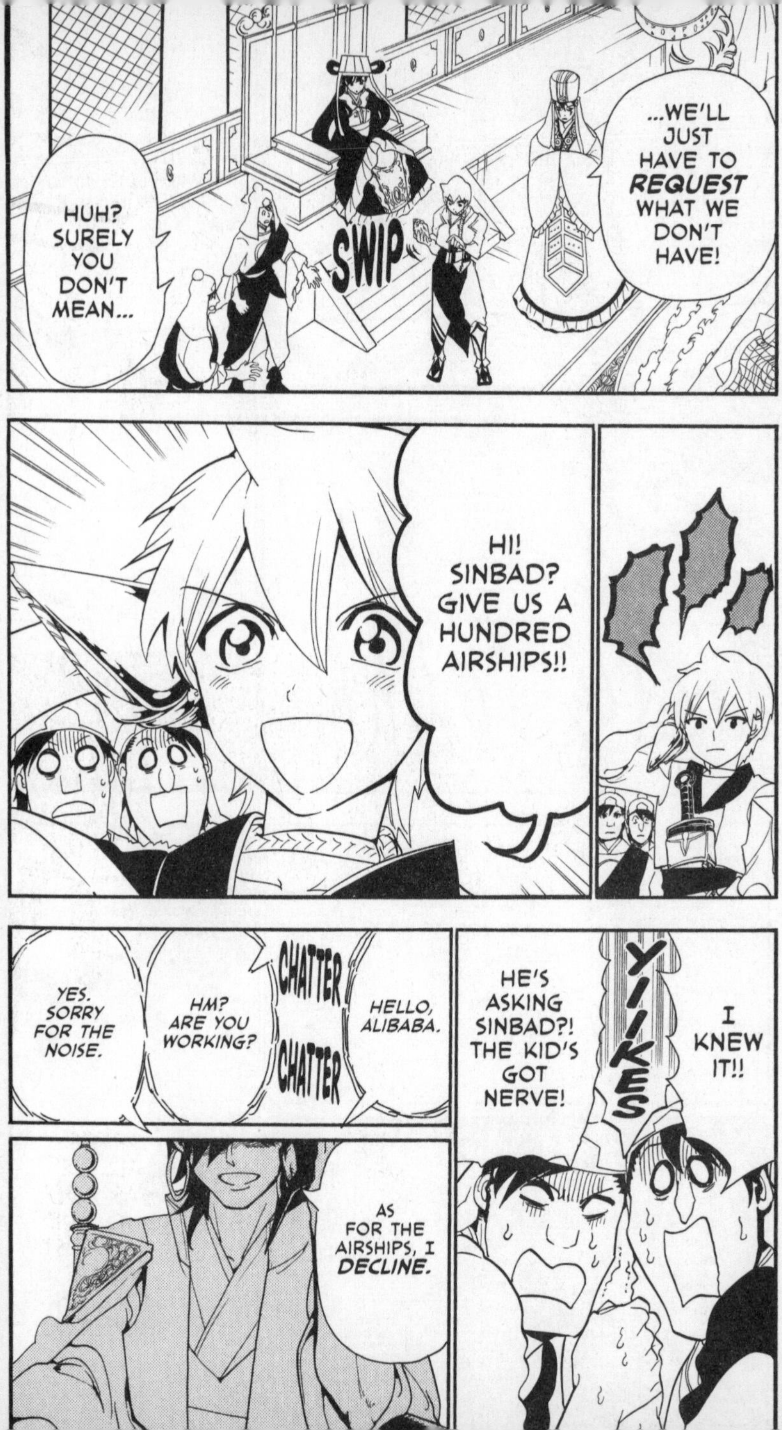

...WE'LL JUST HAVE TO REQUEST WHAT WE DON'T HAVE!
SWIP
HUH? SURELY YOU DON'T MEAN...
HI! SINBAD? GIVE US A HUNDRED AIRSHIPS!!
I KNEW IT!!
YIIKES
HE'S ASKING SINBAD?! THE KID'S GOT NERVE!
HELLO, ALIBABA.
CHATTER CHATTER
HM? ARE YOU WORKING?
YES. SORRY FOR THE NOISE.
AS FOR THE AIRSHIPS, I DECLINE.

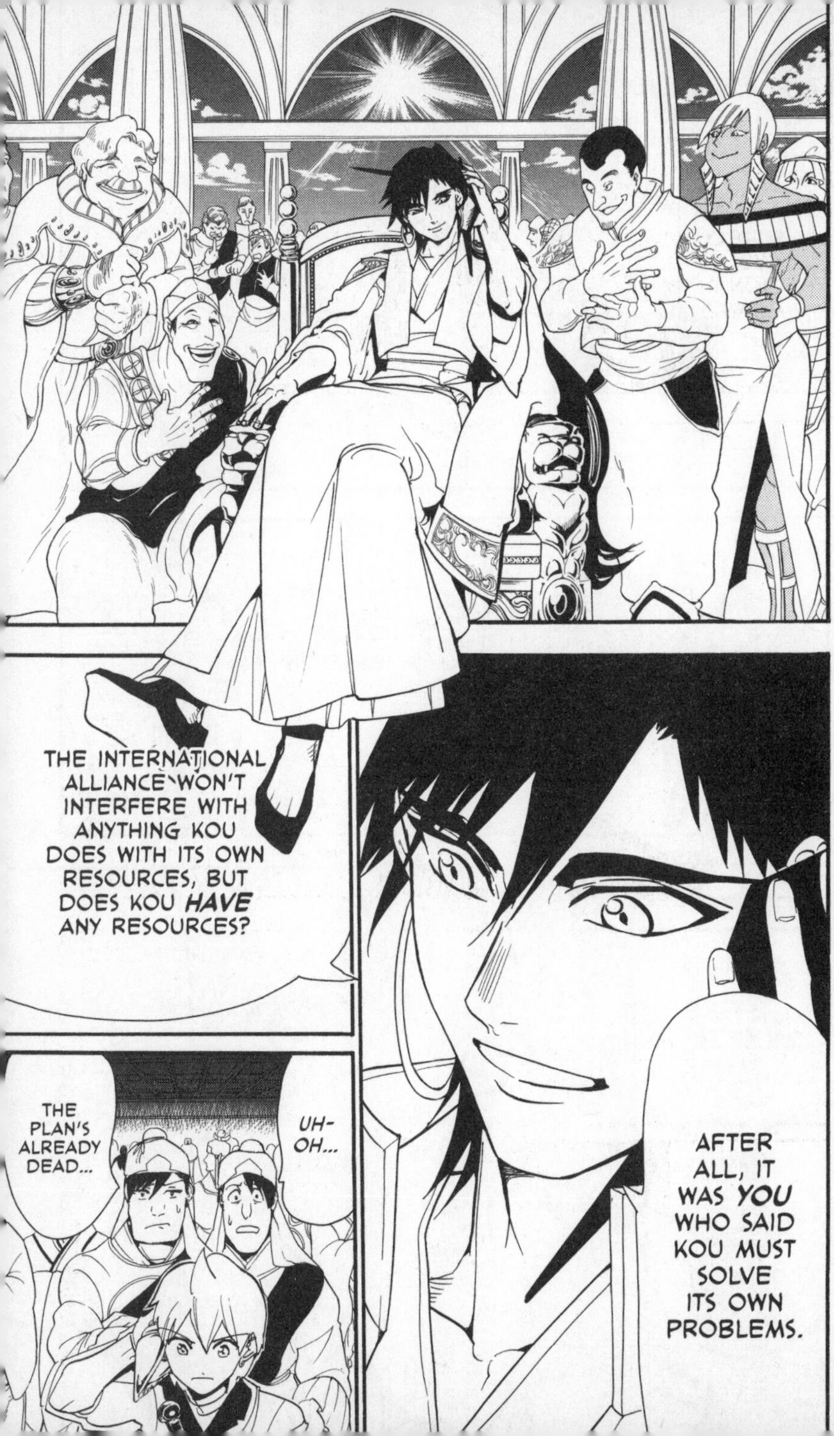
THE INTERNATIONAL ALLIANCE WON'T INTERFERE WITH ANYTHING KOU DOES WITH ITS OWN RESOURCES, BUT DOES KOU *HAVE* ANY RESOURCES?
AFTER ALL, IT WAS *YOU* WHO SAID KOU MUST SOLVE ITS OWN PROBLEMS.
UH-OH...
THE PLAN'S ALREADY DEAD...

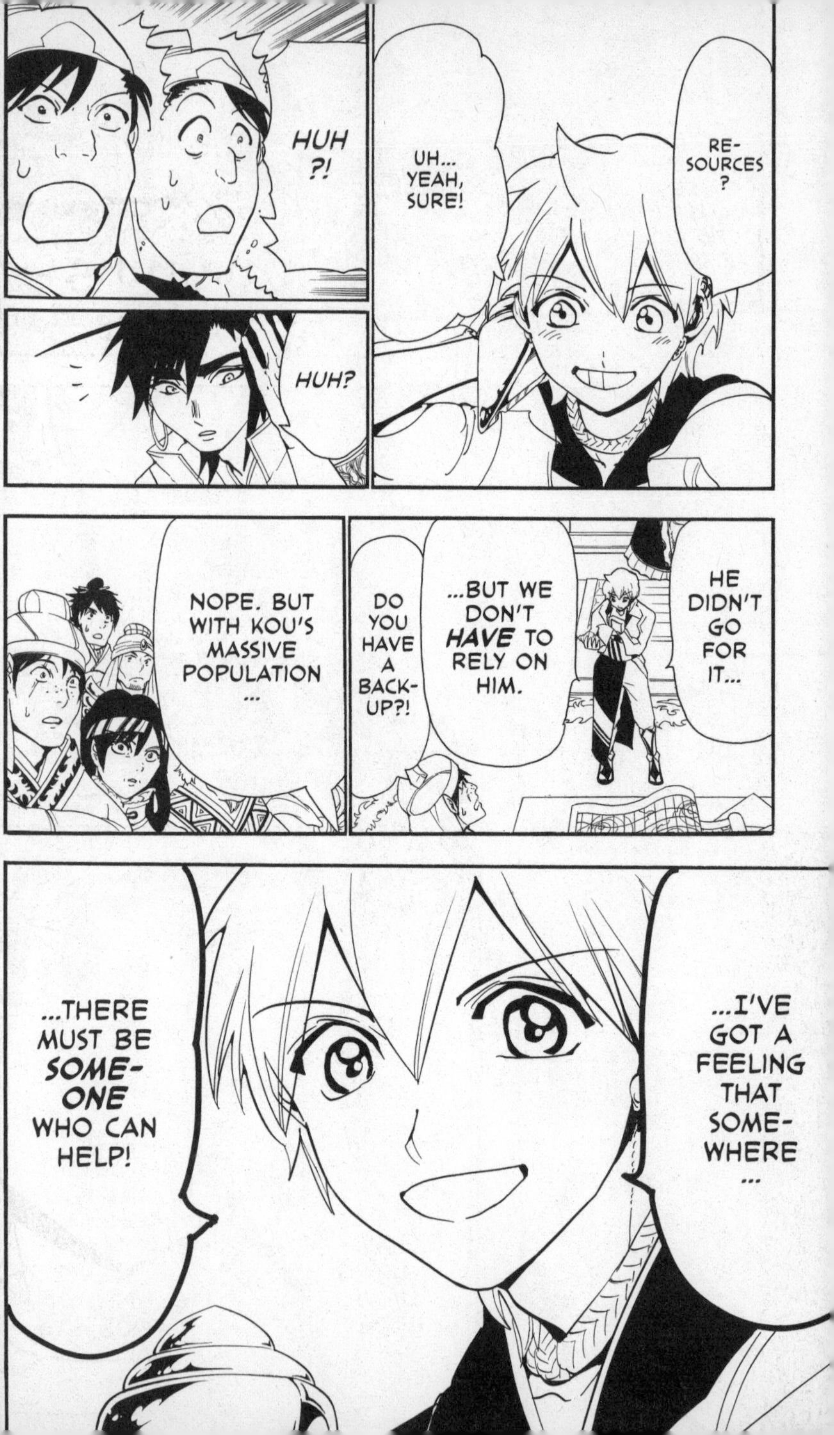
RE-SOURCES ?
UH... YEAH, SURE!
HUH ?!
HUH?
HE DIDN'T GO FOR IT...
...BUT WE DON'T *HAVE* TO RELY ON HIM.
DO YOU HAVE A BACK-UP?!
NOPE. BUT WITH KOU'S MASSIVE POPULATION ...
...I'VE GOT A FEELING THAT SOME-WHERE ...
...THERE MUST BE *SOME-ONE* WHO CAN HELP!

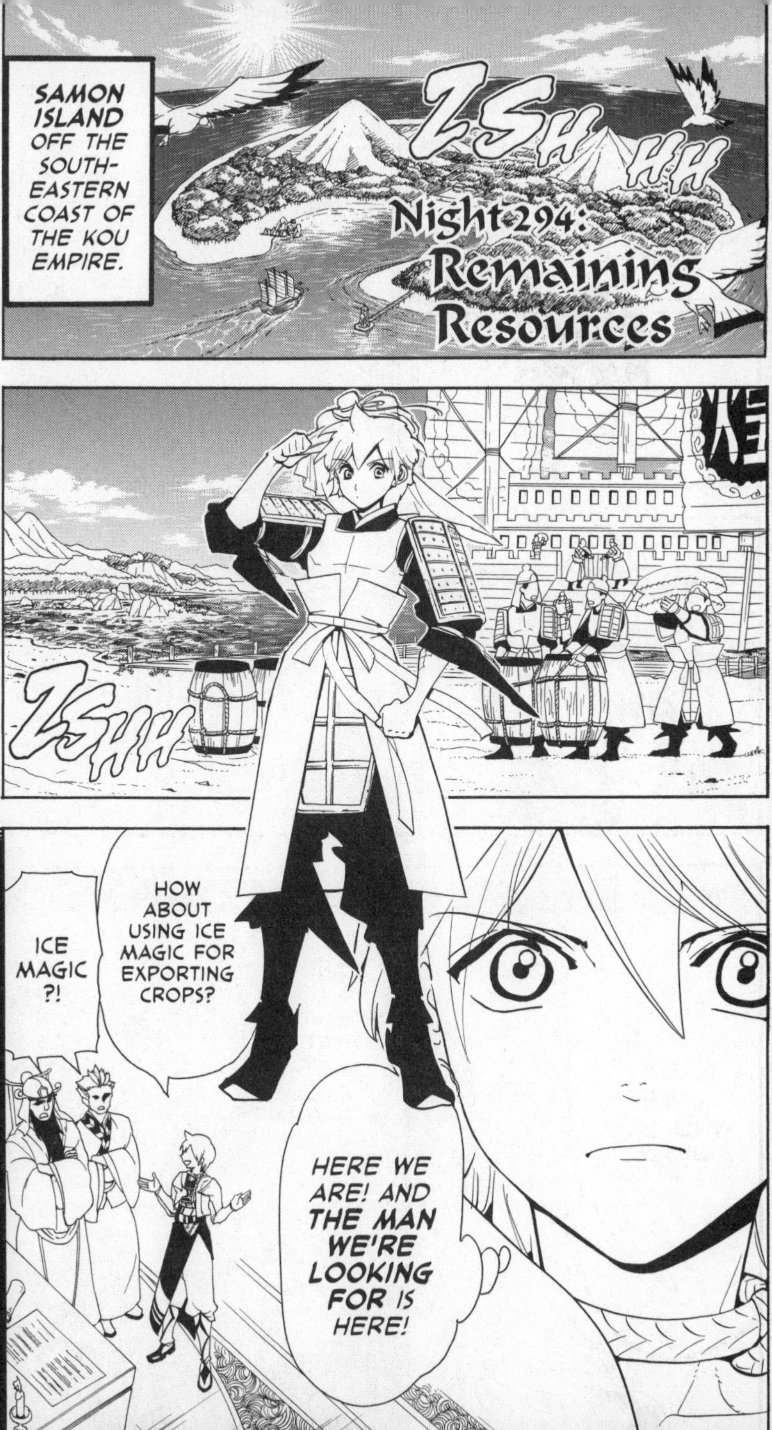
SAMON ISLAND OFF THE SOUTH-EASTERN COAST OF THE KOU EMPIRE.
ZSHHHH
Night 294: Remaining Resources
ZSHH
HOW ABOUT USING ICE MAGIC FOR EXPORTING CROPS?
ICE MAGIC ?!
HERE WE ARE! AND THE MAN WE'RE LOOKING FOR IS HERE!

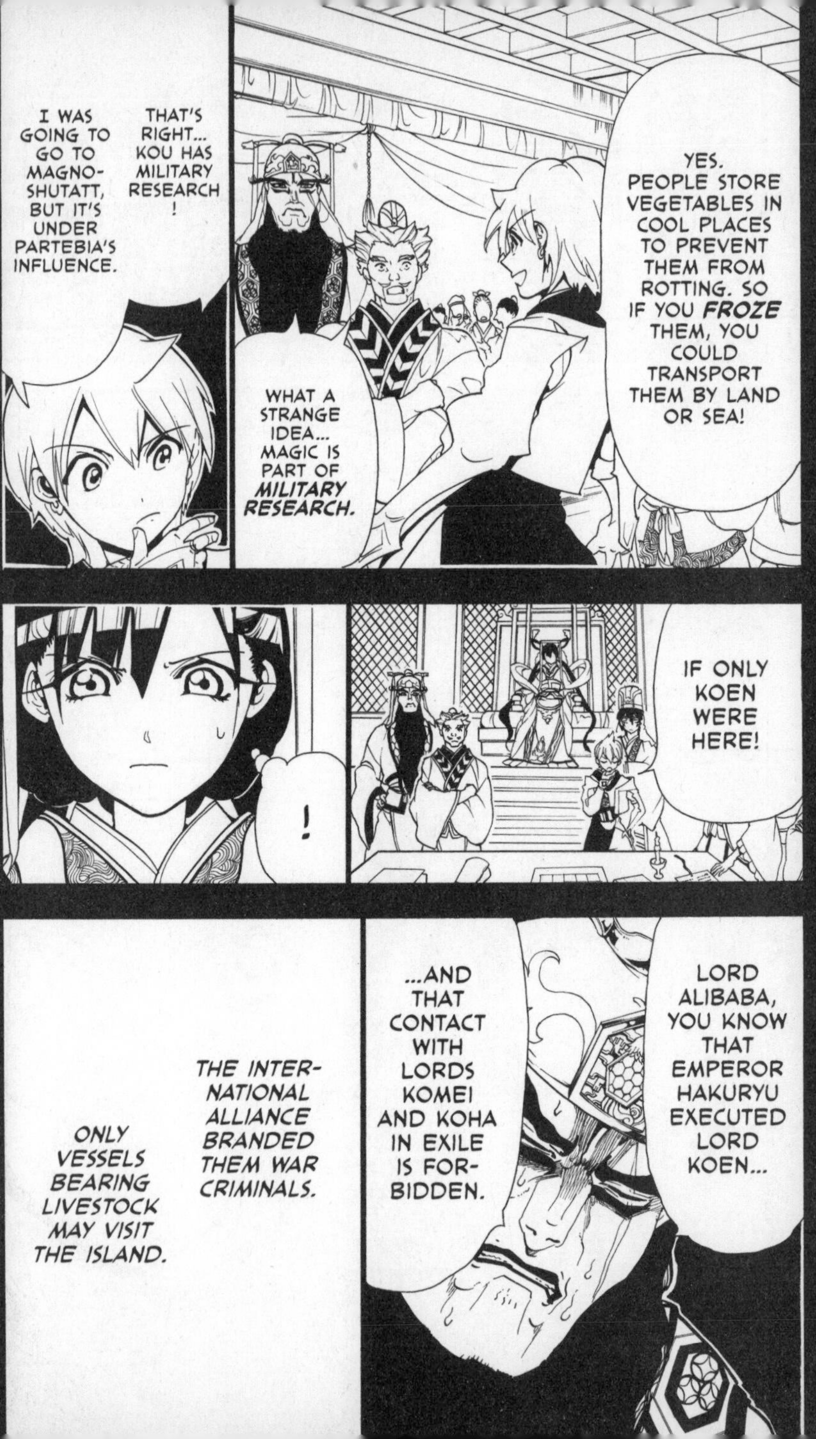
YES. PEOPLE STORE VEGETABLES IN COOL PLACES TO PREVENT THEM FROM ROTTING. SO IF YOU *FROZE* THEM, YOU COULD TRANSPORT THEM BY LAND OR SEA!
WHAT A STRANGE IDEA... MAGIC IS PART OF *MILITARY RESEARCH.*
THAT'S RIGHT... KOU HAS MILITARY RESEARCH!
I WAS GOING TO GO TO MAGNO-SHUTATT, BUT IT'S UNDER PARTEBIA'S INFLUENCE.
IF ONLY KOEN WERE HERE!
!
LORD ALIBABA, YOU KNOW THAT EMPEROR HAKURYU EXECUTED LORD KOEN...
...AND THAT CONTACT WITH LORDS KOMEI AND KOHA IN EXILE IS FOR-BIDDEN.
THE INTER-NATIONAL ALLIANCE BRANDED THEM WAR CRIMINALS.
ONLY VESSELS BEARING LIVESTOCK MAY VISIT THE ISLAND.

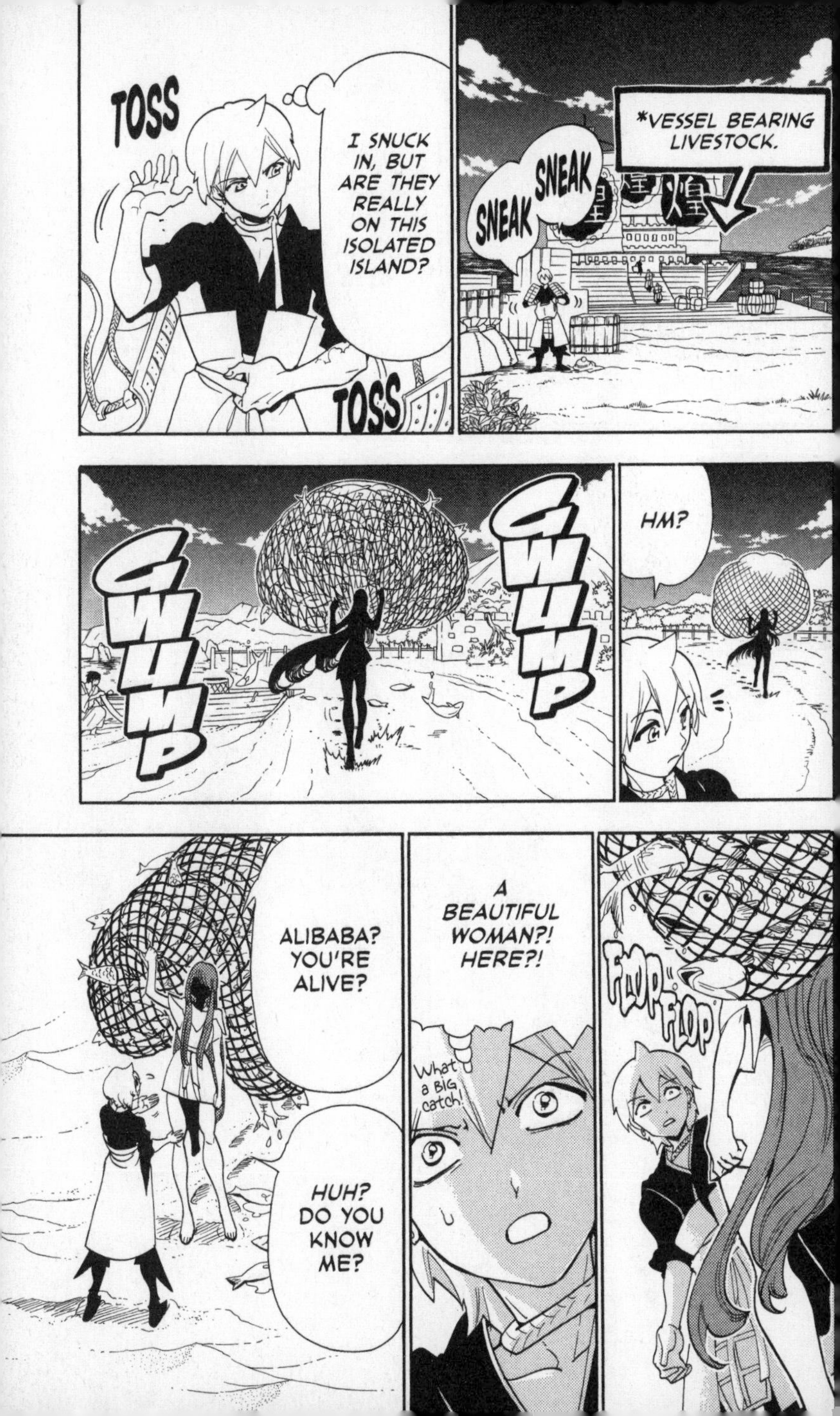
*VESSEL BEARING LIVESTOCK.
SNEAK
SNEAK
TOSS
I SNUCK IN, BUT ARE THEY REALLY ON THIS ISOLATED ISLAND?
TOSS
HM?
GWUMP
GWUMP
FLOP FLOP
A BEAUTIFUL WOMAN?! HERE?!
What a BIG catch!
ALIBABA? YOU'RE ALIVE?
HUH? DO YOU KNOW ME?

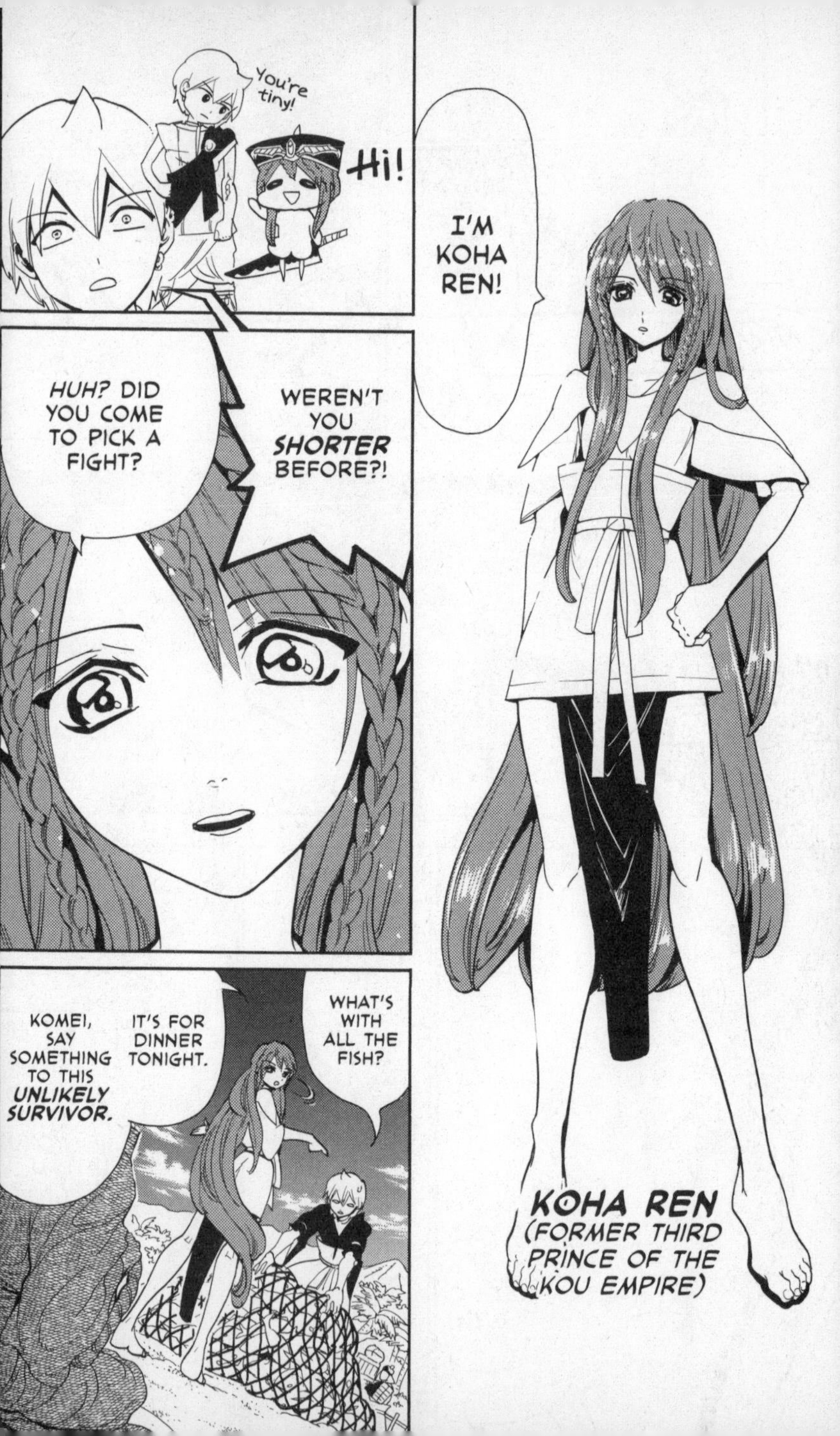
I'M KOHA REN!
KOHA REN (FORMER THIRD PRINCE OF THE KOU EMPIRE)
You're tiny!
Hi!
WEREN'T YOU SHORTER BEFORE?!
HUH? DID YOU COME TO PICK A FIGHT?
WHAT'S WITH ALL THE FISH?
IT'S FOR DINNER TONIGHT.
KOMEI, SAY SOMETHING TO THIS UNLIKELY SURVIVOR.

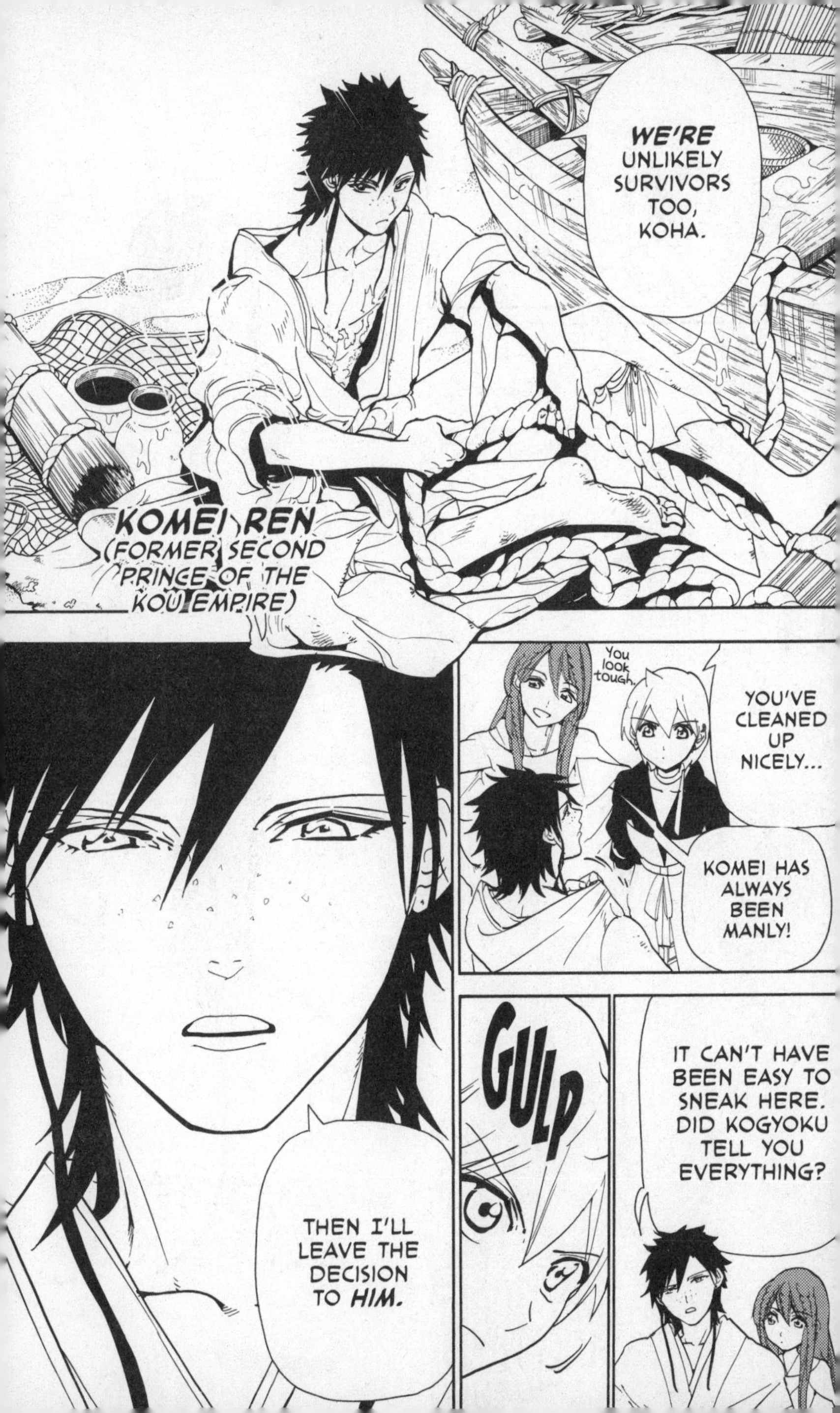
WE'RE UNLIKELY SURVIVORS TOO, KOHA.
KOMEI REN (FORMER SECOND PRINCE OF THE KOU EMPIRE)
YOU'VE CLEANED UP NICELY...
You look tough.
KOMEI HAS ALWAYS BEEN MANLY!
IT CAN'T HAVE BEEN EASY TO SNEAK HERE. DID KOGYOKU TELL YOU EVERYTHING?
GULP
THEN I'LL LEAVE THE DECISION TO HIM.

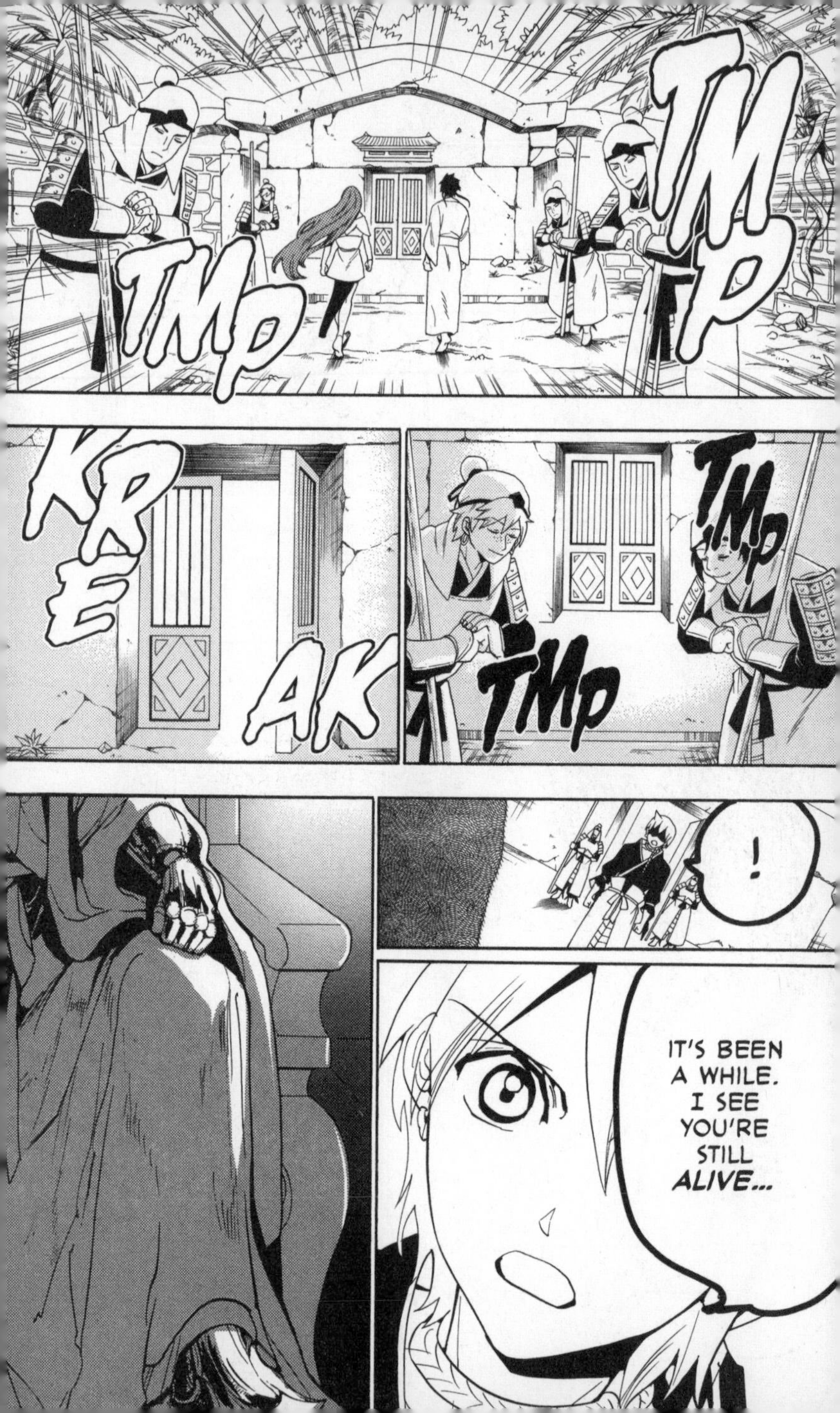
TMP
TMP
TMP
TMP
KREAK
!
IT'S BEEN A WHILE. I SEE YOU'RE STILL *ALIVE*...

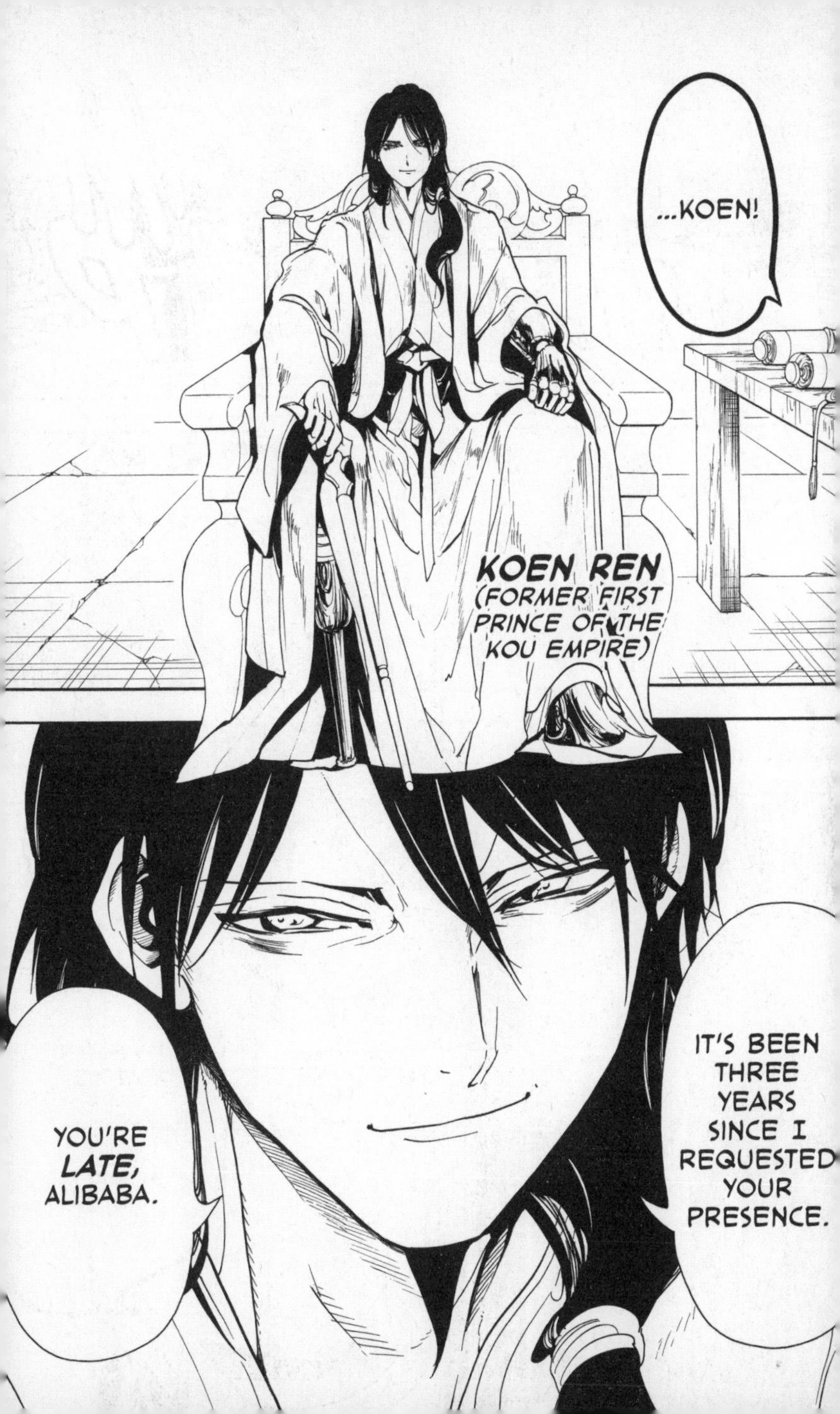
...KOEN!
KOEN REN
(FORMER FIRST PRINCE OF THE KOU EMPIRE)
IT'S BEEN THREE YEARS SINCE I REQUESTED YOUR PRESENCE.
YOU'RE *LATE,* ALIBABA.

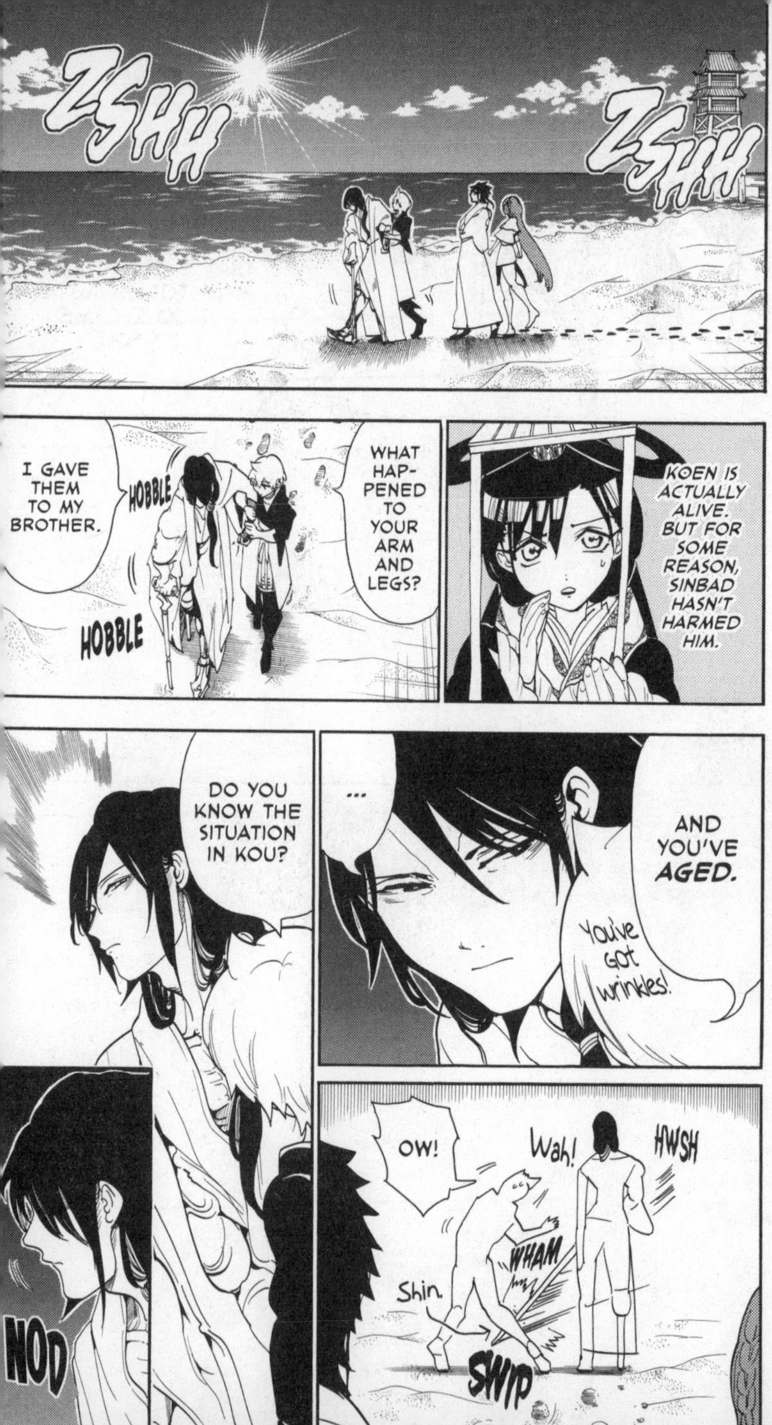

ZSHH
ZSHH
KOEN IS ACTUALLY ALIVE. BUT FOR SOME REASON, SINBAD HASN'T HARMED HIM.
WHAT HAP-PENED TO YOUR ARM AND LEGS?
HOBBLE
I GAVE THEM TO MY BROTHER.
HOBBLE
AND YOU'VE AGED.
You've got wrinkles!
...
HWSH
Wah!
OW!
WHAM
Shin.
SHIP
DO YOU KNOW THE SITUATION IN KOU?
NOD

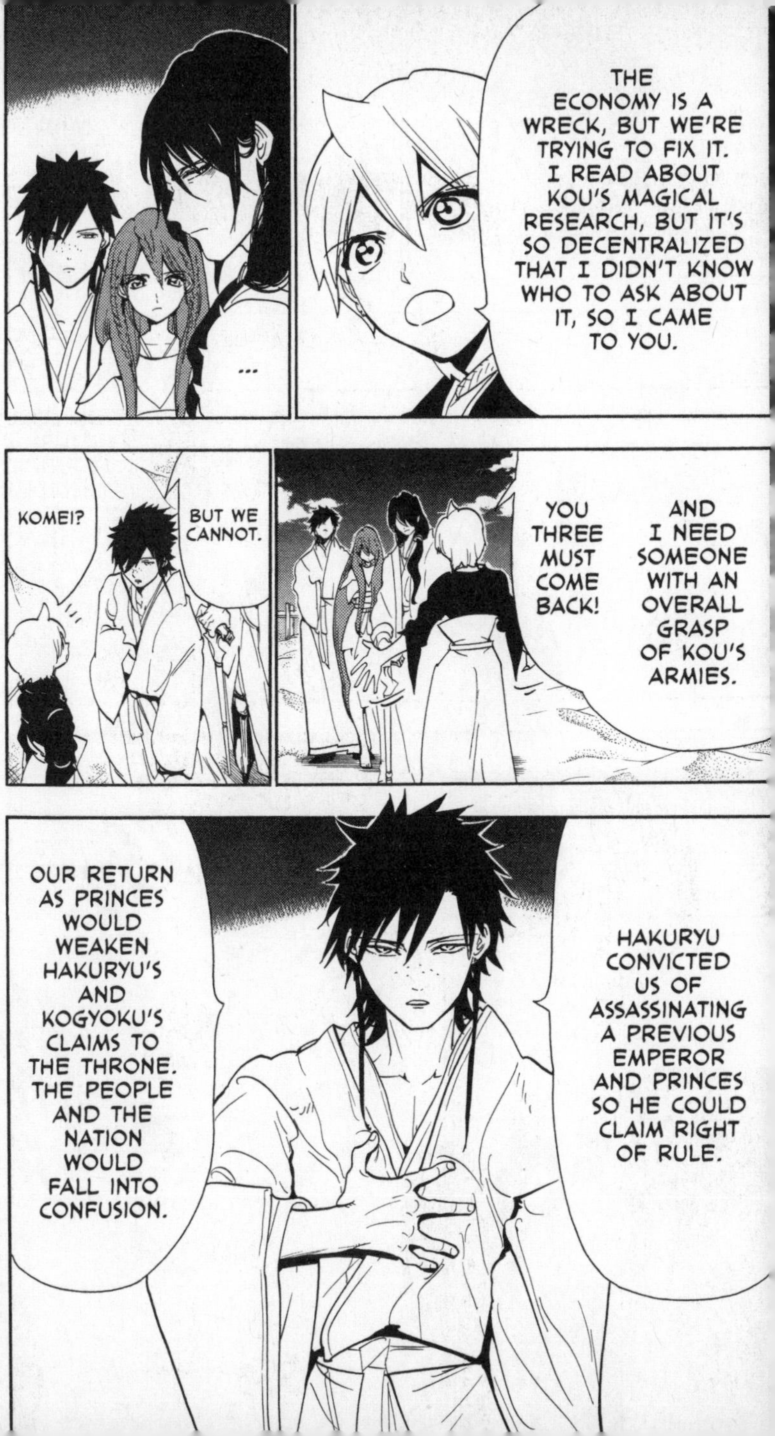
THE ECONOMY IS A WRECK, BUT WE'RE TRYING TO FIX IT. I READ ABOUT KOU'S MAGICAL RESEARCH, BUT IT'S SO DECENTRALIZED THAT I DIDN'T KNOW WHO TO ASK ABOUT IT, SO I CAME TO YOU.
...
AND I NEED SOMEONE WITH AN OVERALL GRASP OF KOU'S ARMIES.
YOU THREE MUST COME BACK!
BUT WE CANNOT.
KOMEI?
HAKURYU CONVICTED US OF ASSASSINATING A PREVIOUS EMPEROR AND PRINCES SO HE COULD CLAIM RIGHT OF RULE.
OUR RETURN AS PRINCES WOULD WEAKEN HAKURYU'S AND KOGYOKU'S CLAIMS TO THE THRONE. THE PEOPLE AND THE NATION WOULD FALL INTO CONFUSION.

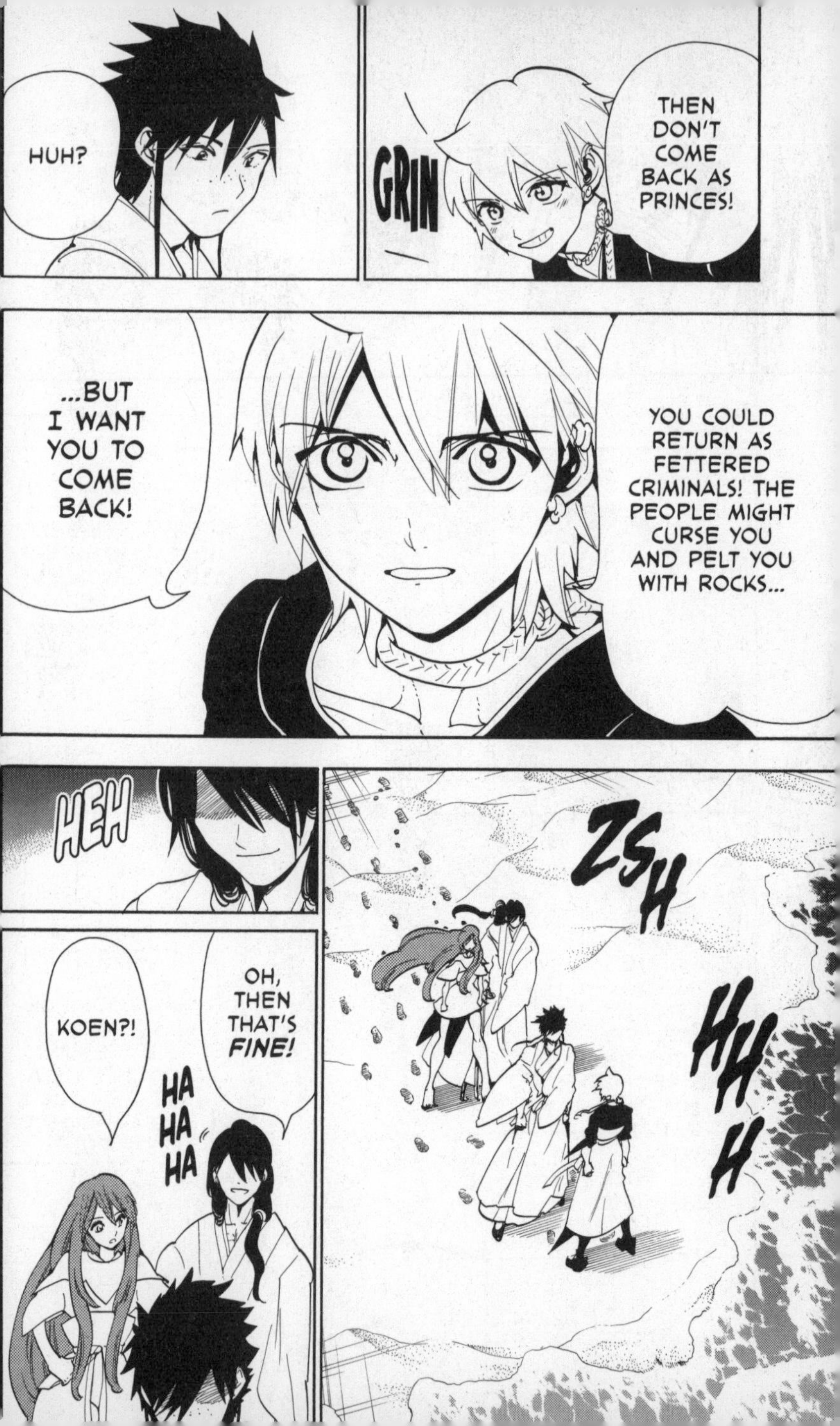
THEN DON'T COME BACK AS PRINCES!
GRIN
HUH?
YOU COULD RETURN AS FETTERED CRIMINALS! THE PEOPLE MIGHT CURSE YOU AND PELT YOU WITH ROCKS...
...BUT I WANT YOU TO COME BACK!
ZSH
HHHH
HEH
OH, THEN THAT'S *FINE!*
KOEN?!
HA HA HA

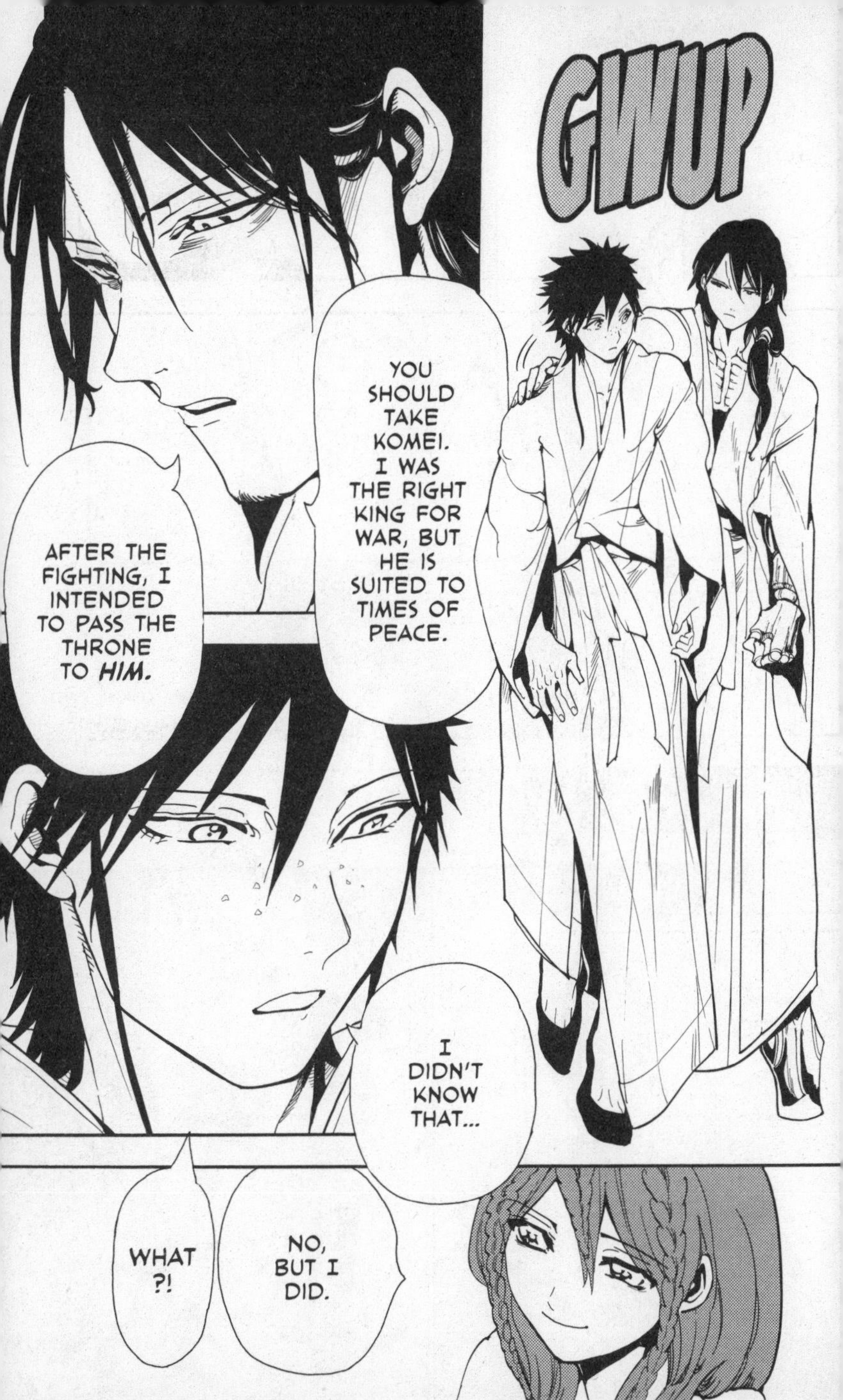

GWUP
YOU SHOULD TAKE KOMEI. I WAS THE RIGHT KING FOR WAR, BUT HE IS SUITED TO TIMES OF PEACE.
AFTER THE FIGHTING, I INTENDED TO PASS THE THRONE TO *HIM.*
I DIDN'T KNOW THAT...
NO, BUT I DID.
WHAT?!

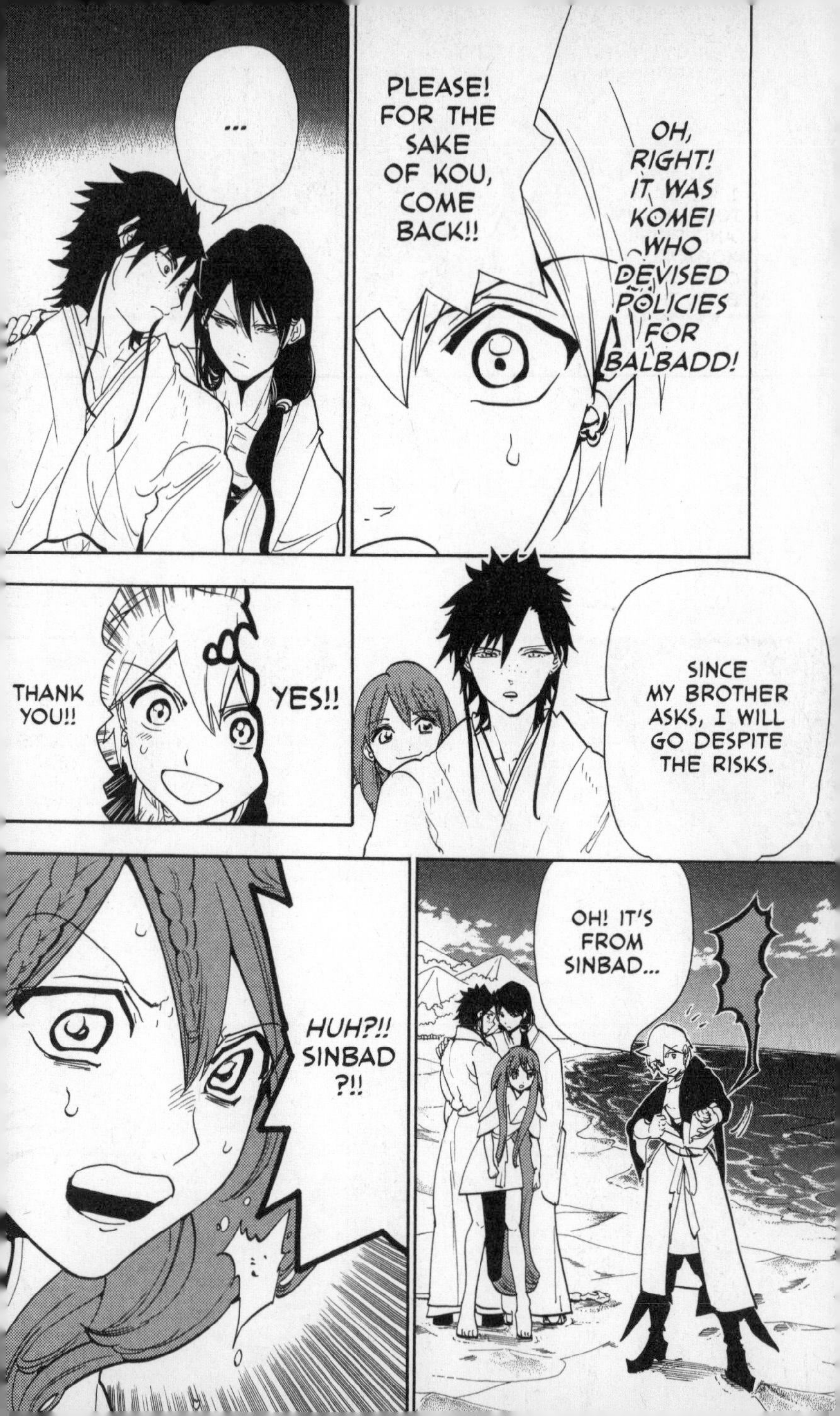

OH, RIGHT! IT WAS KOMEI WHO DEVISED POLICIES FOR BALBADD!
PLEASE! FOR THE SAKE OF KOU, COME BACK!!
...
SINCE MY BROTHER ASKS, I WILL GO DESPITE THE RISKS.
YES!!
THANK YOU!!
OH! IT'S FROM SINBAD...
HUH?!! SINBAD ?!!

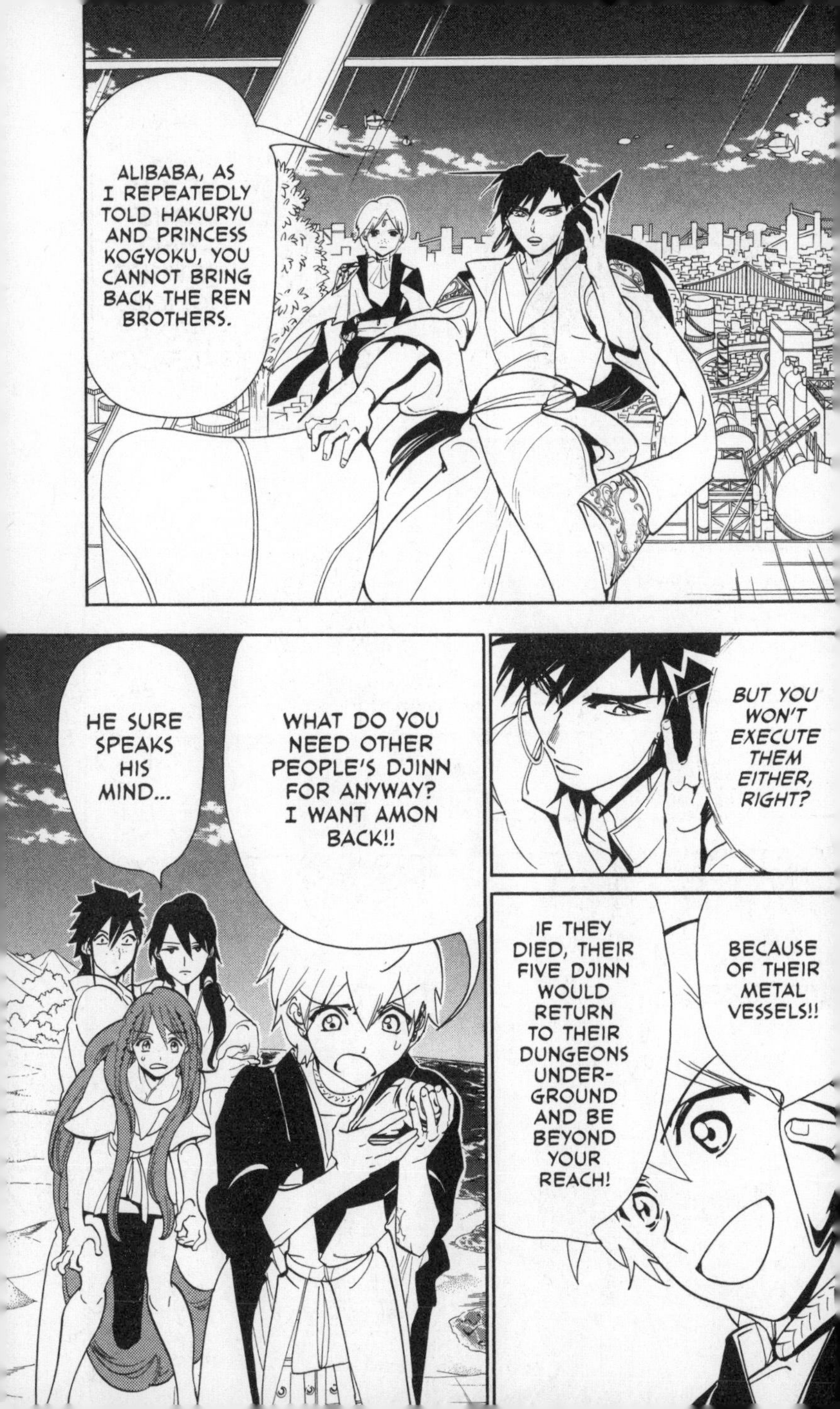
ALIBABA, AS I REPEATEDLY TOLD HAKURYU AND PRINCESS KOGYOKU, YOU CANNOT BRING BACK THE REN BROTHERS.
BUT YOU WON'T EXECUTE THEM EITHER, RIGHT?
BECAUSE OF THEIR METAL VESSELS!!
IF THEY DIED, THEIR FIVE DJINN WOULD RETURN TO THEIR DUNGEONS UNDER-GROUND AND BE BEYOND YOUR REACH!
WHAT DO YOU NEED OTHER PEOPLE'S DJINN FOR ANYWAY? I WANT AMON BACK!!
HE SURE SPEAKS HIS MIND...

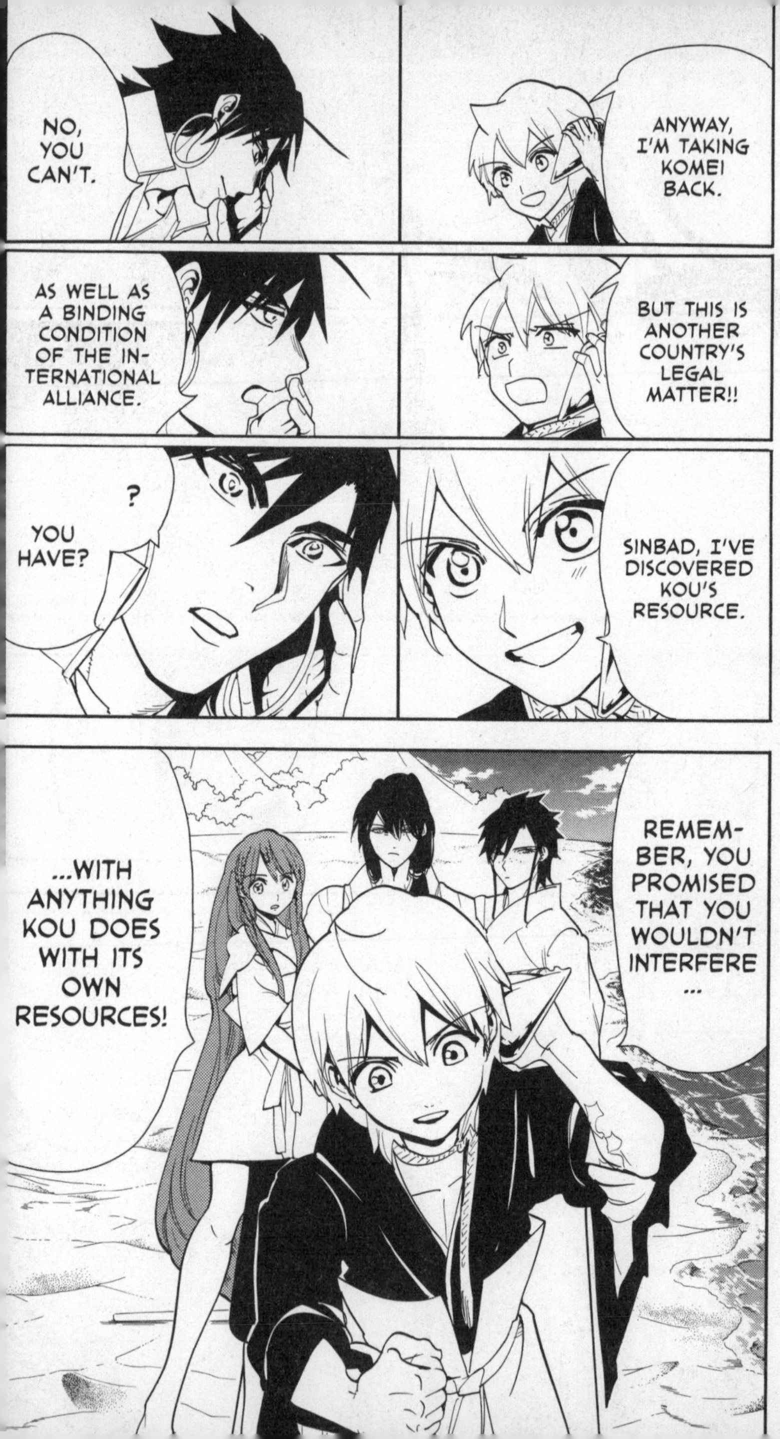
ANYWAY, I'M TAKING KOMEI BACK.
NO, YOU CAN'T.
BUT THIS IS ANOTHER COUNTRY'S LEGAL MATTER!!
AS WELL AS A BINDING CONDITION OF THE INTERNATIONAL ALLIANCE.
SINBAD, I'VE DISCOVERED KOU'S RESOURCE.
?
YOU HAVE?
REMEMBER, YOU PROMISED THAT YOU WOULDN'T INTERFERE ...
...WITH ANYTHING KOU DOES WITH ITS OWN RESOURCES!

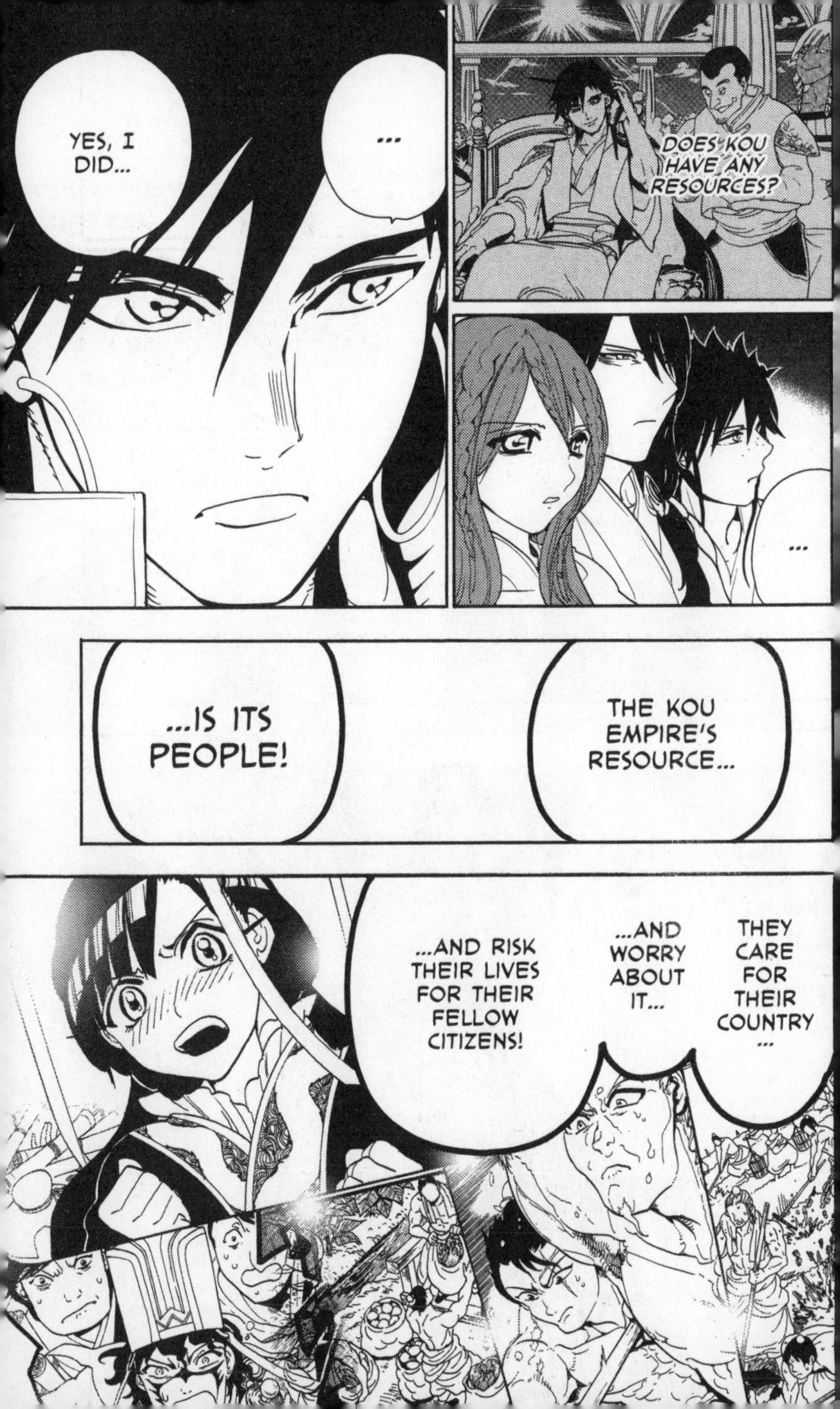
DOES KOU HAVE ANY RESOURCES?
...
...
YES, I DID...
THE KOU EMPIRE'S RESOURCE...
...IS ITS PEOPLE!
THEY CARE FOR THEIR COUNTRY...
...AND WORRY ABOUT IT...
...AND RISK THEIR LIVES FOR THEIR FELLOW CITIZENS!

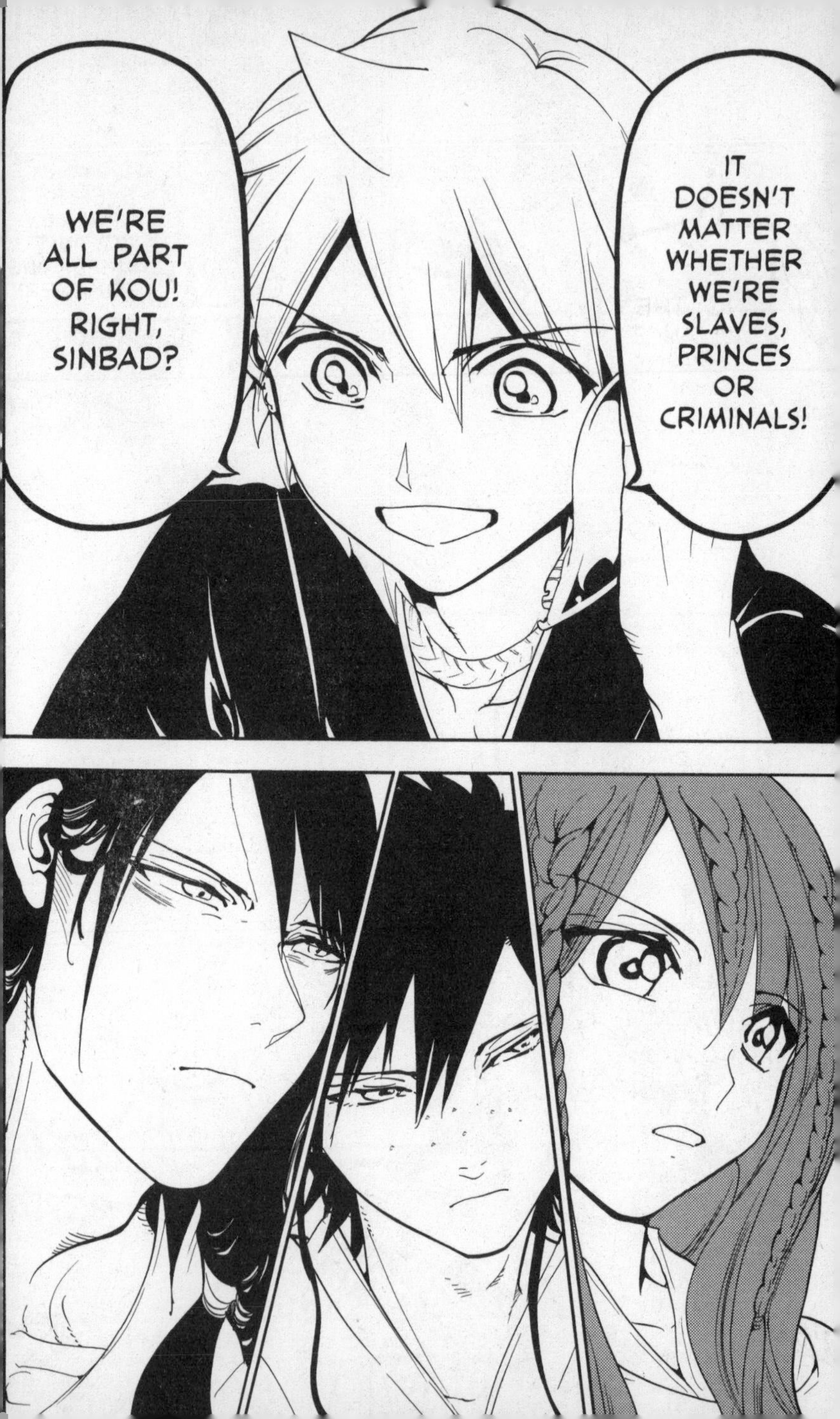
IT DOESN'T MATTER WHETHER WE'RE SLAVES, PRINCES OR CRIMINALS!
WE'RE ALL PART OF KOU! RIGHT, SINBAD?

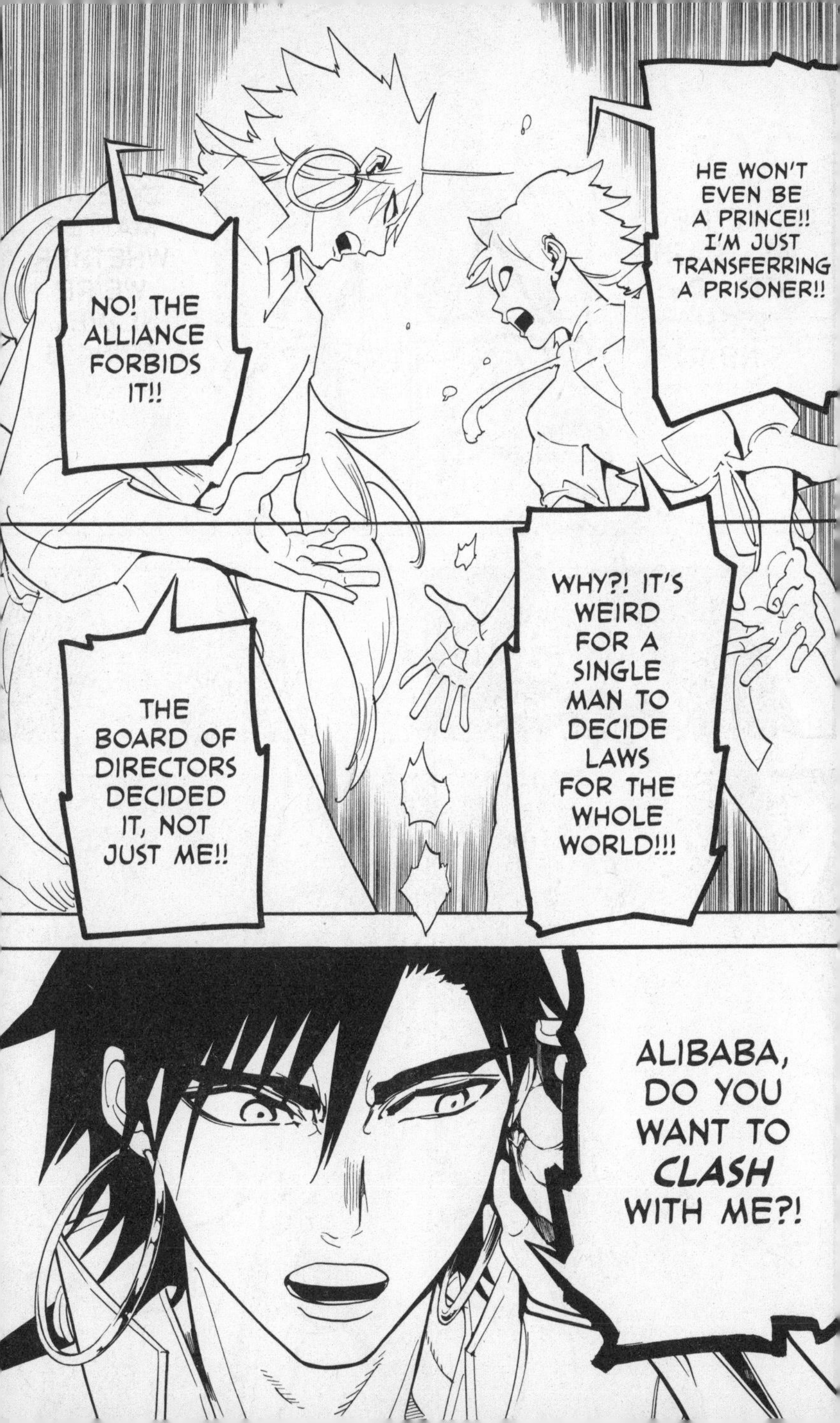
HE WON'T EVEN BE A PRINCE!! I'M JUST TRANSFERRING A PRISONER!!
NO! THE ALLIANCE FORBIDS IT!!
WHY?! IT'S WEIRD FOR A SINGLE MAN TO DECIDE LAWS FOR THE WHOLE WORLD!!!
THE BOARD OF DIRECTORS DECIDED IT, NOT JUST ME!!
ALIBABA, DO YOU WANT TO *CLASH* WITH ME?!

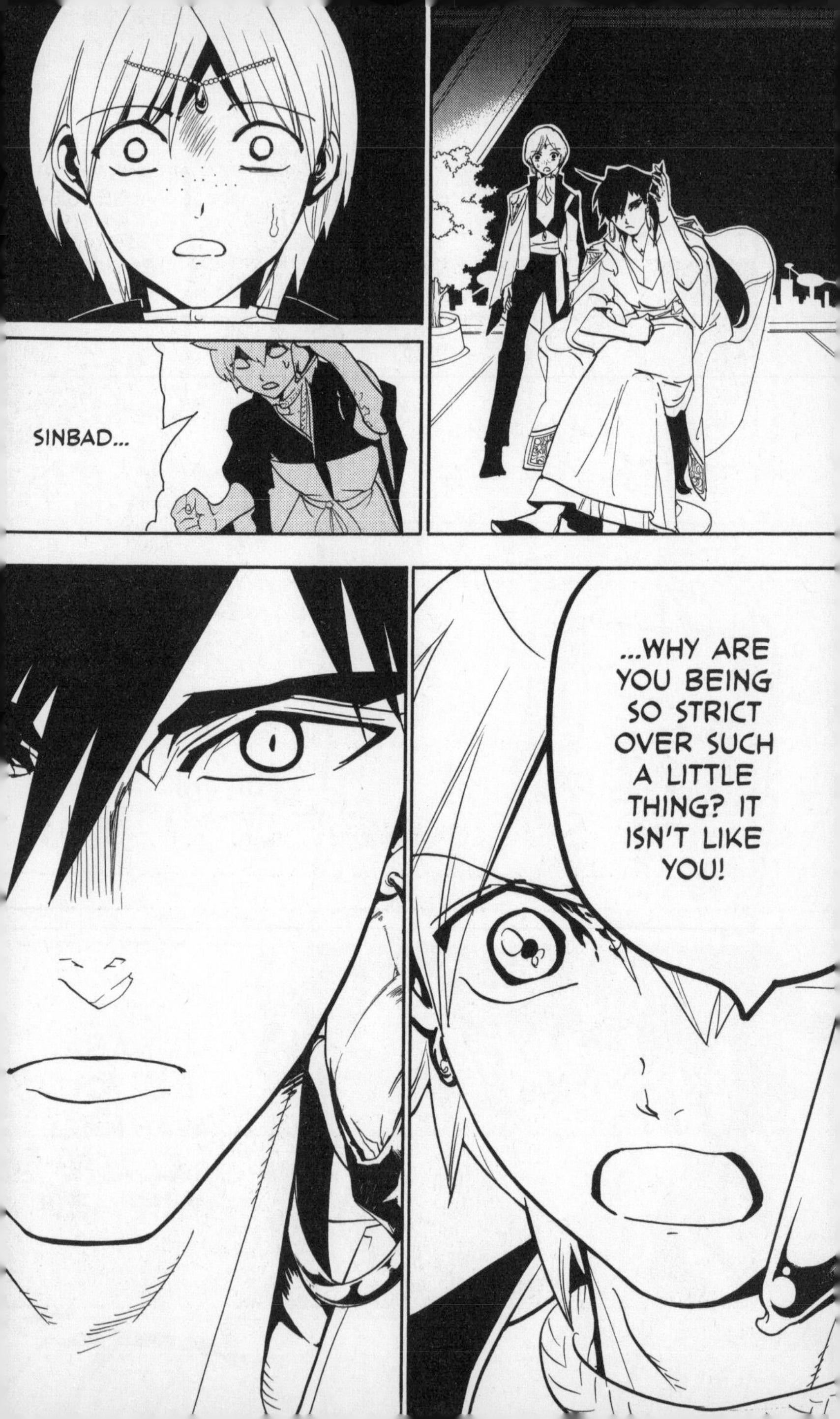
SINBAD...
...WHY ARE YOU BEING SO STRICT OVER SUCH A LITTLE THING? IT ISN'T LIKE YOU!

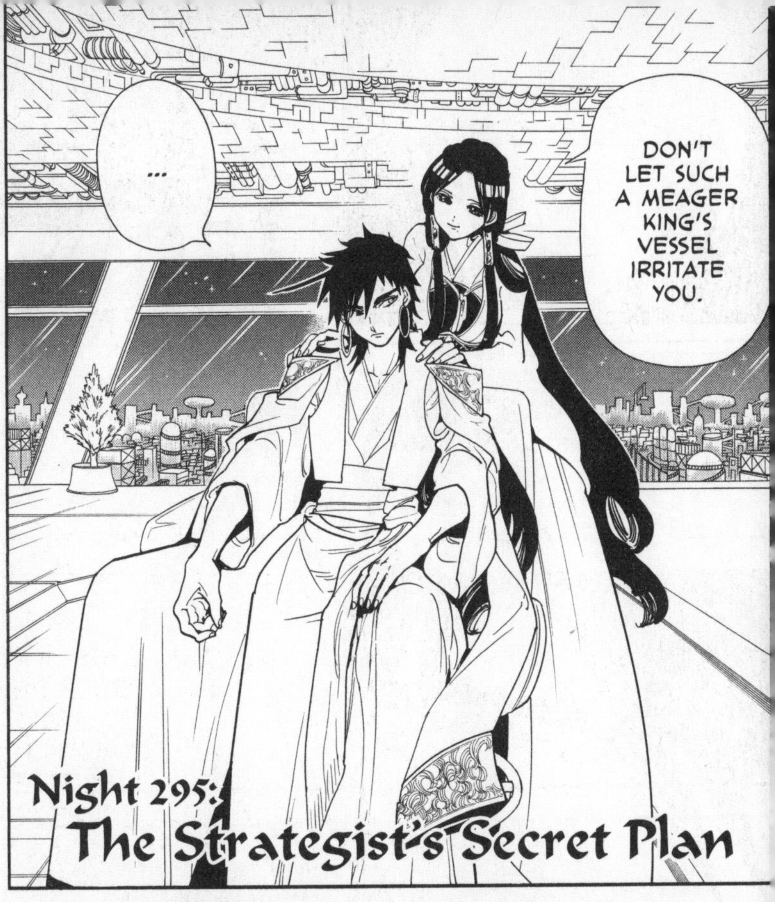
DON'T LET SUCH A MEAGER KING'S VESSEL IRRITATE YOU.
...

Night 295: The Strategist's Secret Plan

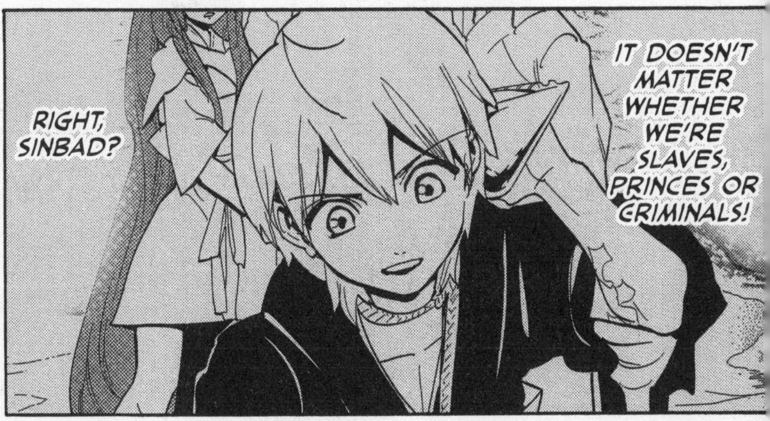
IT DOESN'T MATTER WHETHER WE'RE SLAVES, PRINCES OR CRIMINALS!
RIGHT, SINBAD?

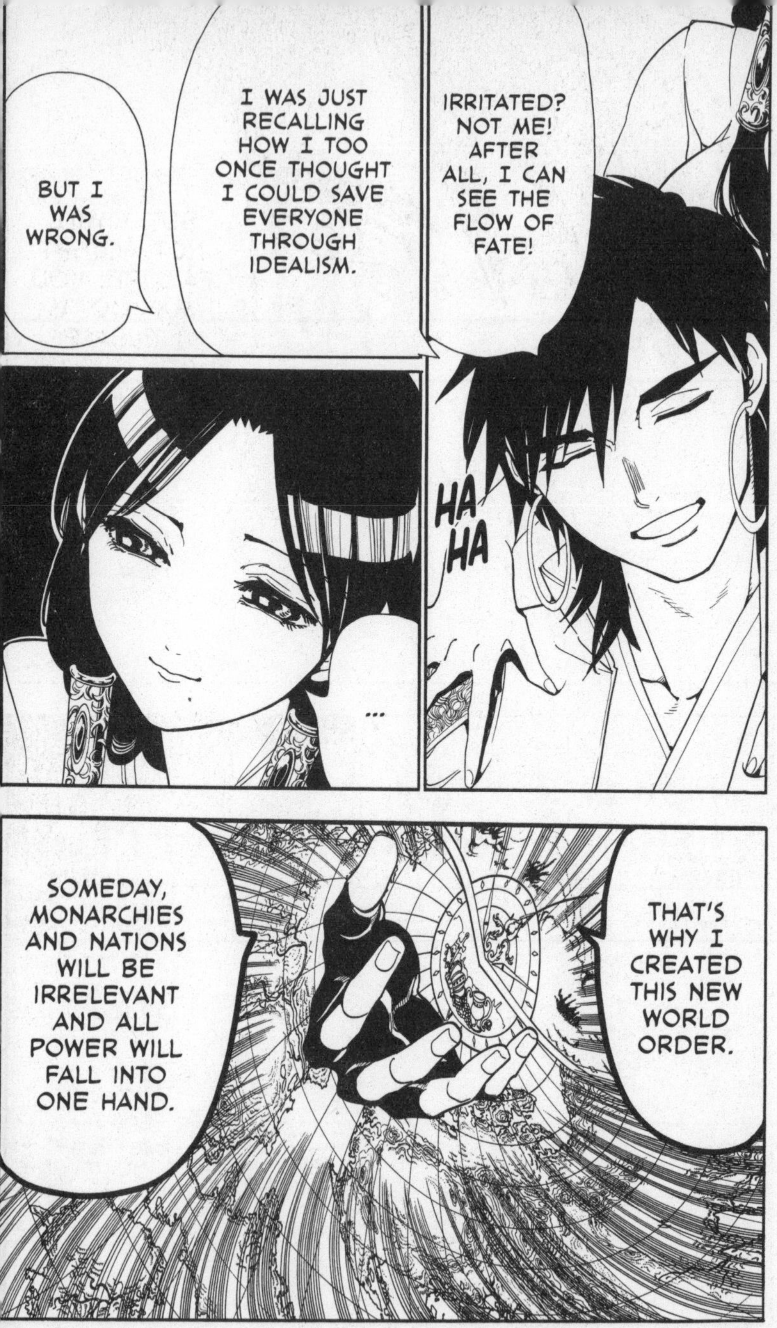
IRRITATED? NOT ME! AFTER ALL, I CAN SEE THE FLOW OF FATE!
I WAS JUST RECALLING HOW I TOO ONCE THOUGHT I COULD SAVE EVERYONE THROUGH IDEALISM.
BUT I WAS WRONG.
HA HA
...
THAT'S WHY I CREATED THIS NEW WORLD ORDER.
SOMEDAY, MONARCHIES AND NATIONS WILL BE IRRELEVANT AND ALL POWER WILL FALL INTO ONE HAND.

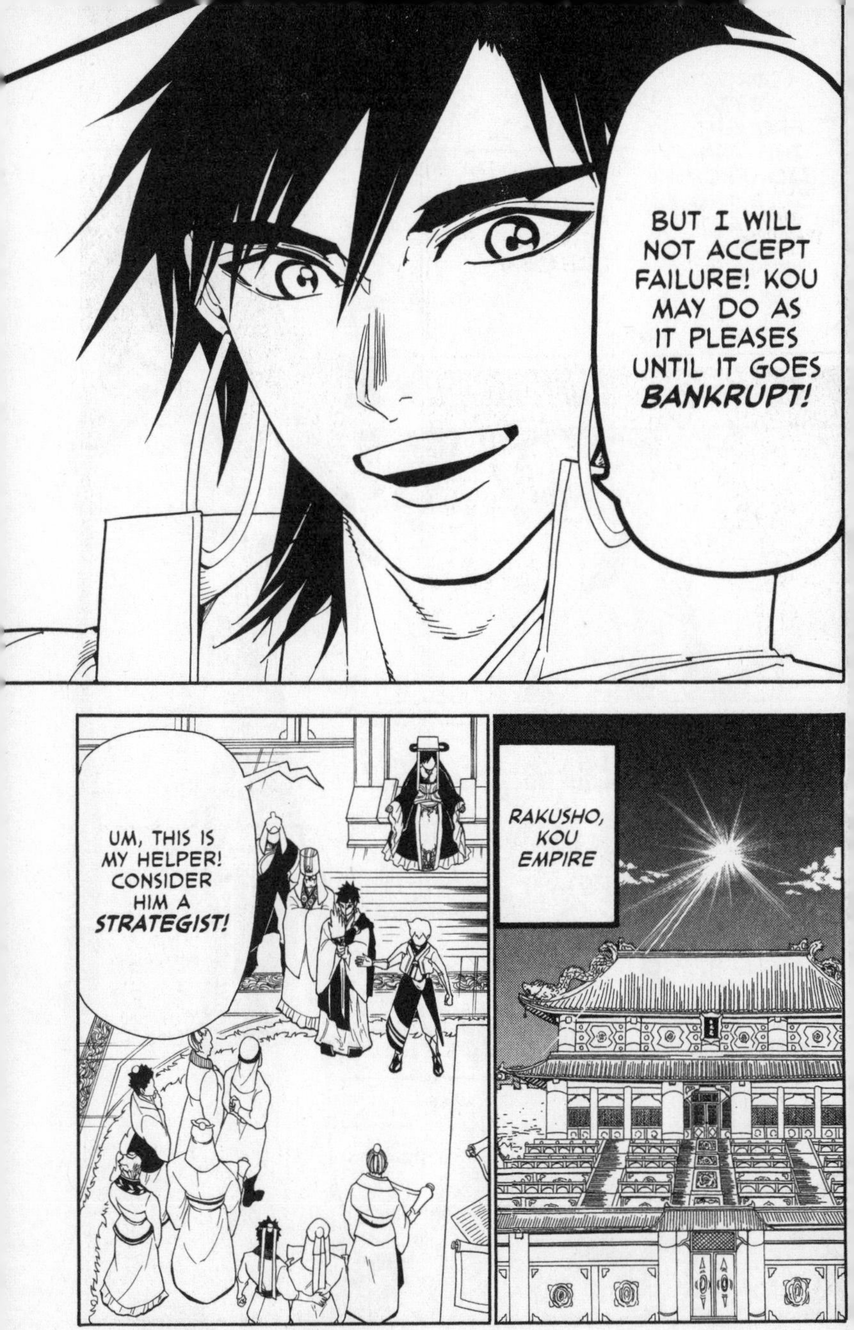
BUT I WILL NOT ACCEPT FAILURE! KOU MAY DO AS IT PLEASES UNTIL IT GOES **BANKRUPT!**
RAKUSHO, KOU EMPIRE
UM, THIS IS MY HELPER! CONSIDER HIM A **STRATEGIST!**

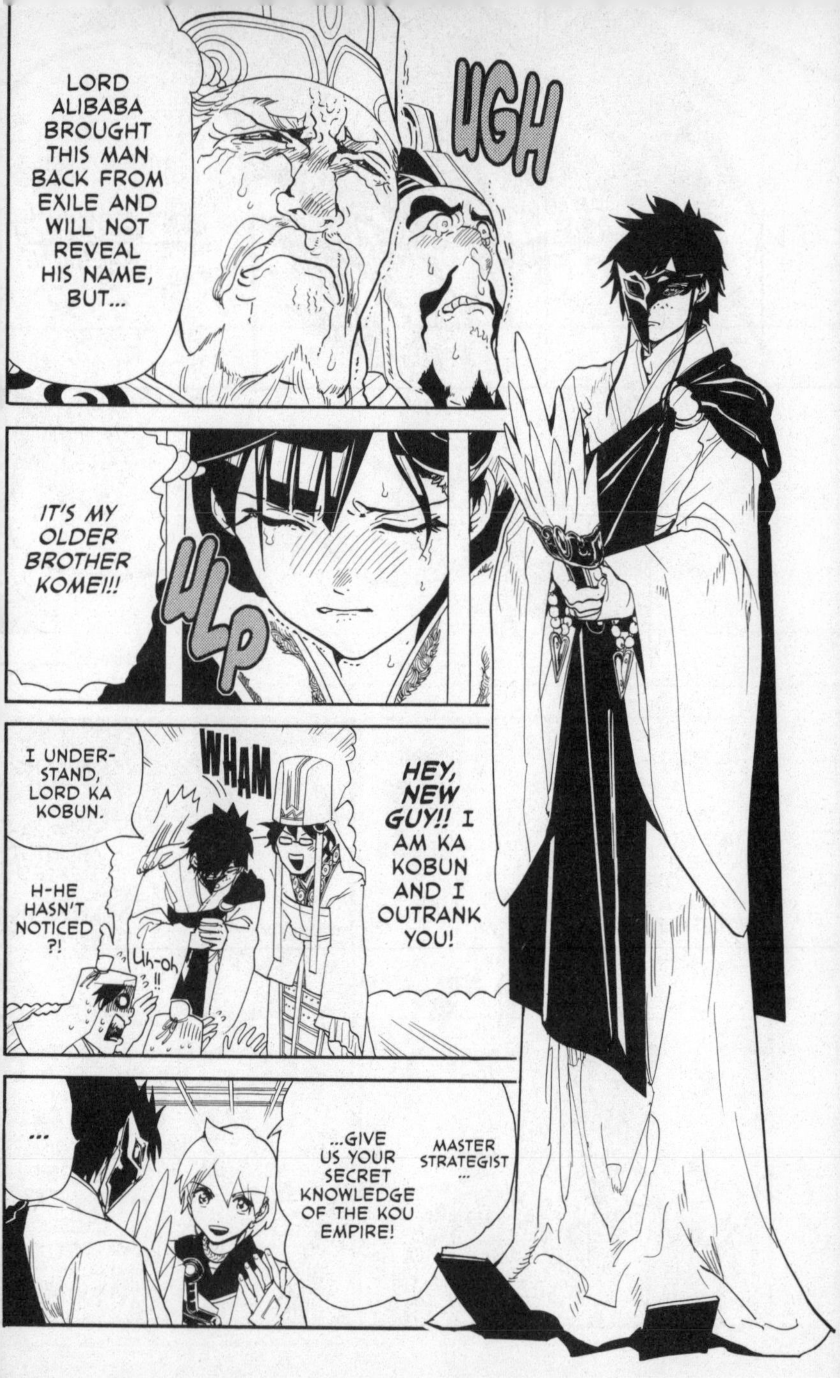
UGH
LORD ALIBABA BROUGHT THIS MAN BACK FROM EXILE AND WILL NOT REVEAL HIS NAME, BUT...
IT'S MY OLDER BROTHER KOMEI!!
ULP
WHAM
HEY, NEW GUY!! I AM KA KOBUN AND I OUTRANK YOU!
I UNDER-STAND, LORD KA KOBUN.
H-HE HASN'T NOTICED ?!
Uh-oh!!
MASTER STRATEGIST ...
...GIVE US YOUR SECRET KNOWLEDGE OF THE KOU EMPIRE!
...

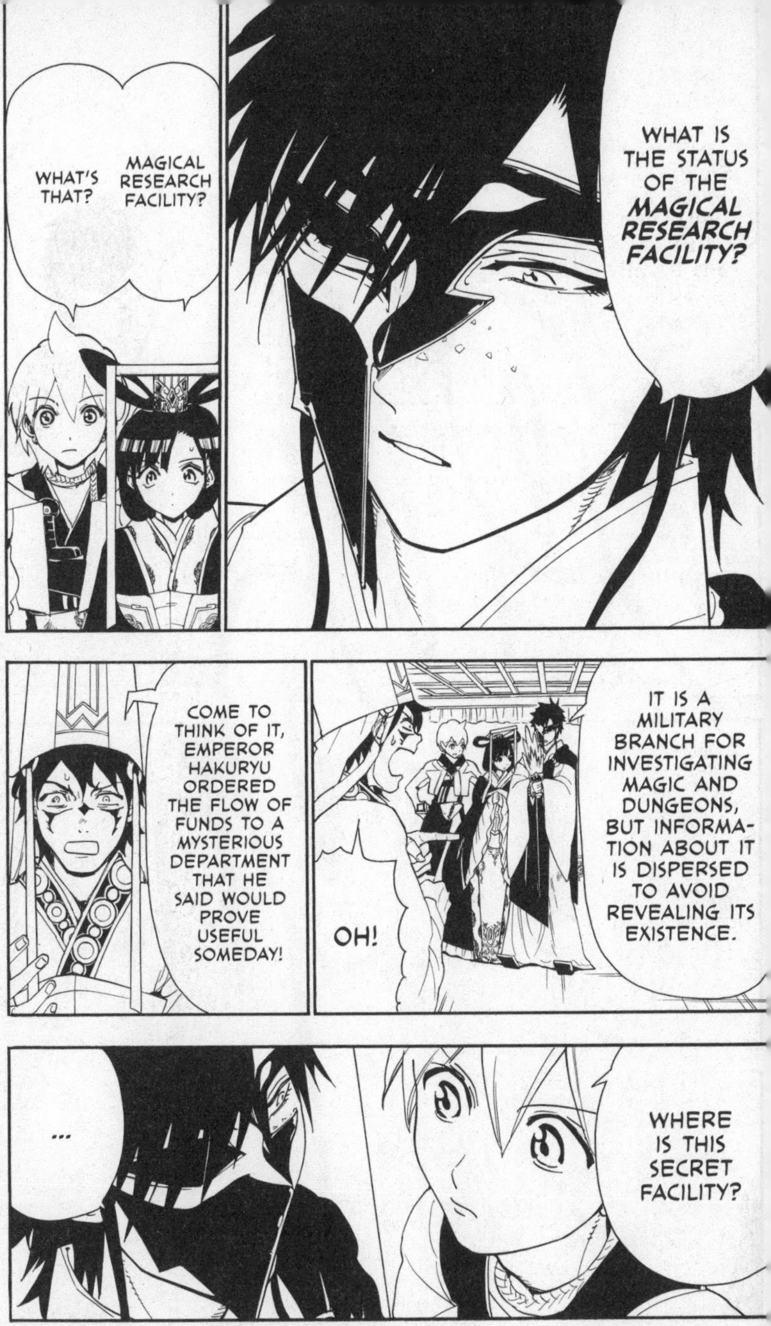
WHAT IS THE STATUS OF THE *MAGICAL RESEARCH FACILITY?*
MAGICAL RESEARCH FACILITY?
WHAT'S THAT?
IT IS A MILITARY BRANCH FOR INVESTIGATING MAGIC AND DUNGEONS, BUT INFORMATION ABOUT IT IS DISPERSED TO AVOID REVEALING ITS EXISTENCE.
OH!
COME TO THINK OF IT, EMPEROR HAKURYU ORDERED THE FLOW OF FUNDS TO A MYSTERIOUS DEPARTMENT THAT HE SAID WOULD PROVE USEFUL SOMEDAY!
WHERE IS THIS SECRET FACILITY?
...

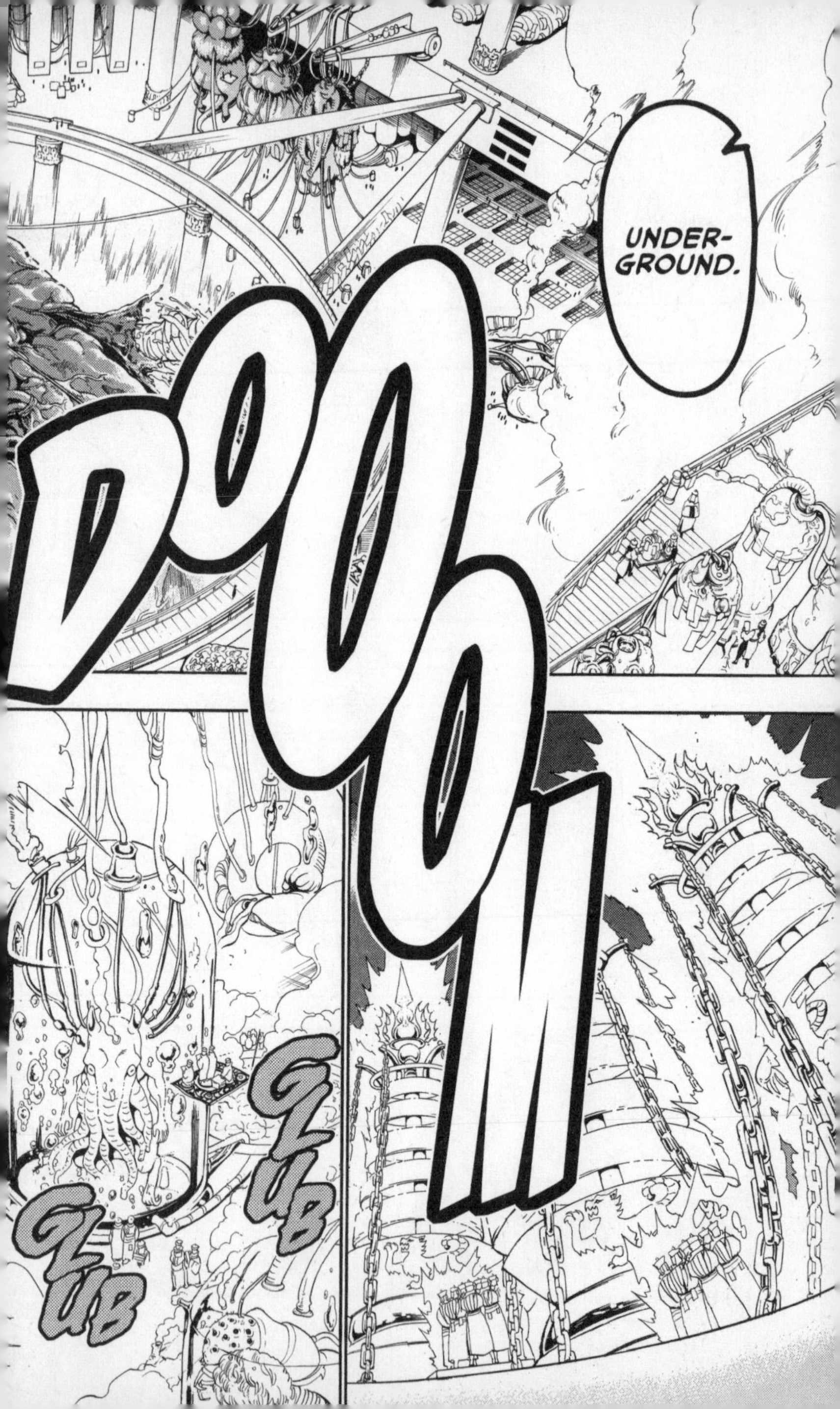
UNDER-GROUND.
DOOOM
GLUB GLUB

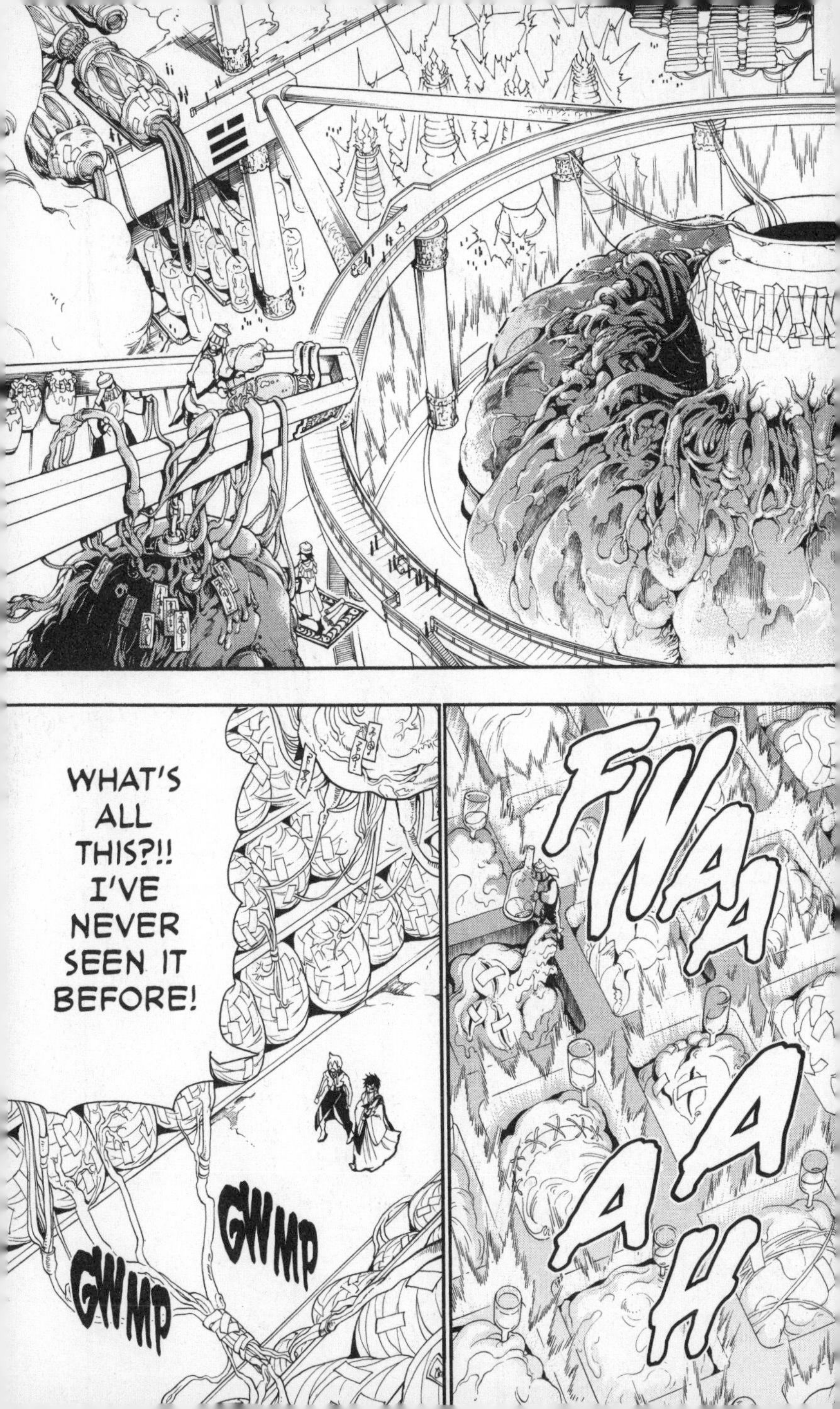
FWAAAAH
WHAT'S ALL THIS?!! I'VE NEVER SEEN IT BEFORE!
GWMP
GWMP

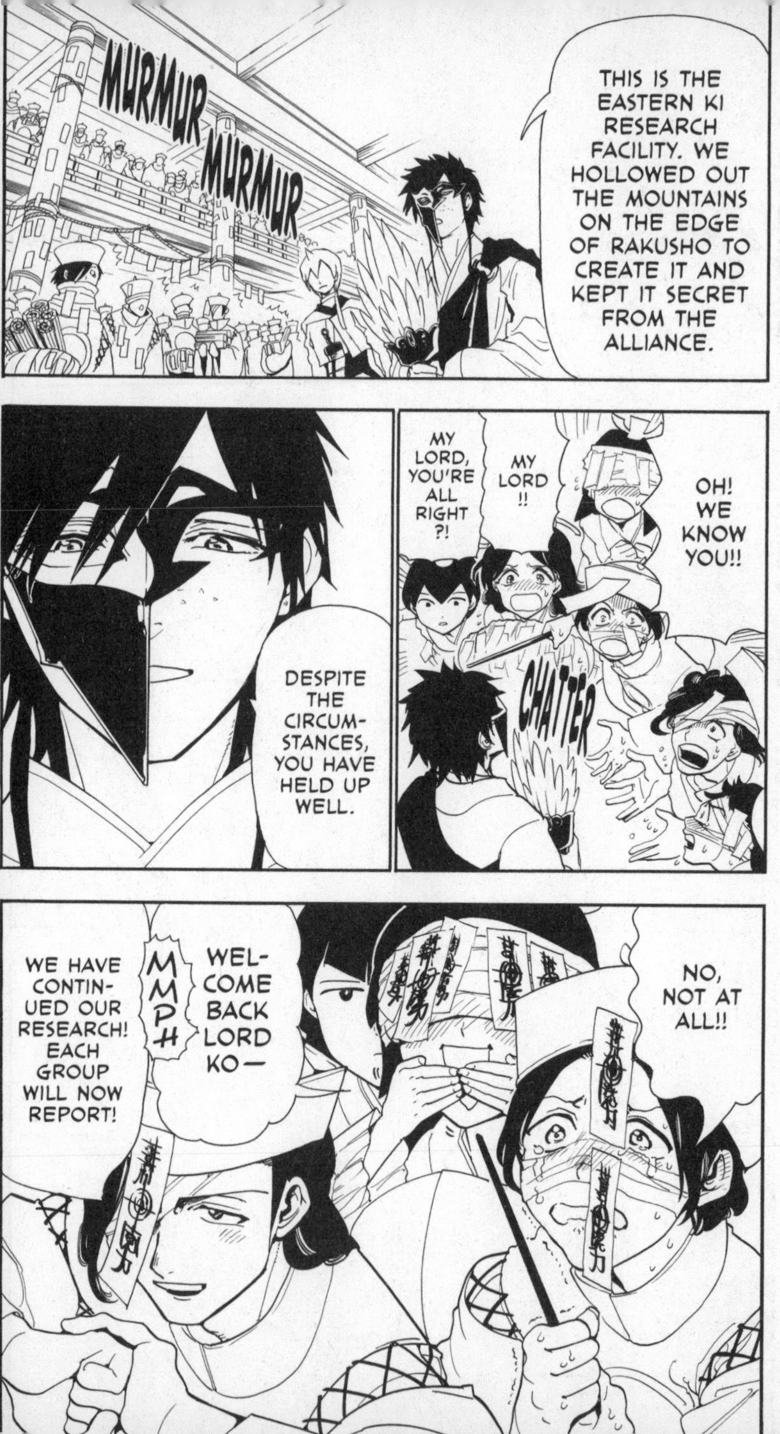
THIS IS THE EASTERN KI RESEARCH FACILITY. WE HOLLOWED OUT THE MOUNTAINS ON THE EDGE OF RAKUSHO TO CREATE IT AND KEPT IT SECRET FROM THE ALLIANCE.
MURMUR
MURMUR
OH! WE KNOW YOU!!
MY LORD!!
MY LORD, YOU'RE ALL RIGHT?!
CHATTER
DESPITE THE CIRCUM-STANCES, YOU HAVE HELD UP WELL.
NO, NOT AT ALL!!
WEL-COME BACK LORD KO—
MMPH
WE HAVE CONTIN-UED OUR RESEARCH! EACH GROUP WILL NOW REPORT!

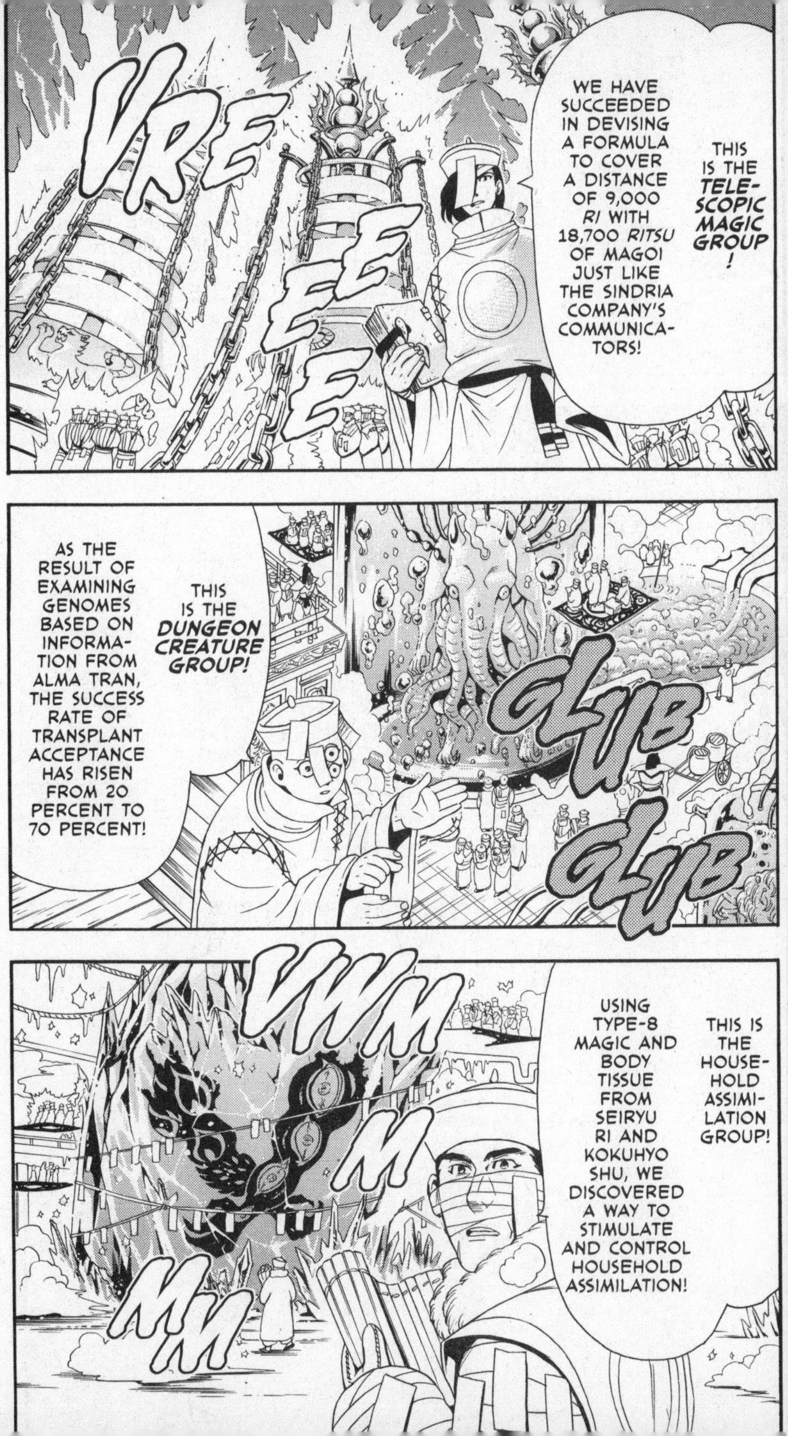
THIS IS THE TELESCOPIC MAGIC GROUP!
WE HAVE SUCCEEDED IN DEVISING A FORMULA TO COVER A DISTANCE OF 9,000 *RI* WITH 18,700 *RITSU* OF MAGOI JUST LIKE THE SINDRIA COMPANY'S COMMUNICATORS!
VREEEEE
THIS IS THE *DUNGEON CREATURE GROUP!*
AS THE RESULT OF EXAMINING GENOMES BASED ON INFORMATION FROM ALMA TRAN, THE SUCCESS RATE OF TRANSPLANT ACCEPTANCE HAS RISEN FROM 20 PERCENT TO 70 PERCENT!
GLUB GLUB
THIS IS THE HOUSEHOLD ASSIMILATION GROUP!
USING TYPE-8 MAGIC AND BODY TISSUE FROM SEIRYU RI AND KOKUHYO SHU, WE DISCOVERED A WAY TO STIMULATE AND CONTROL HOUSEHOLD ASSIMILATION!
VWMMMM

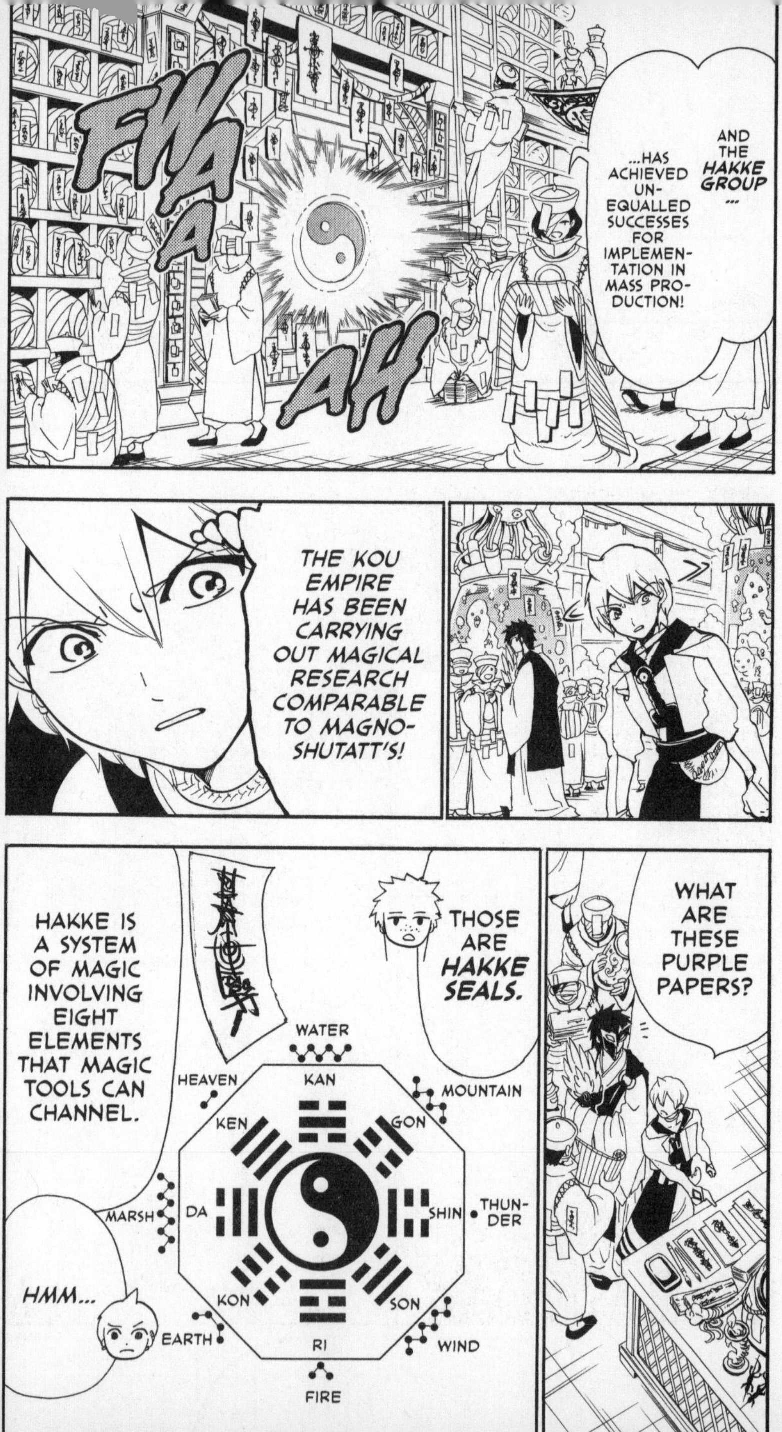
FWAAAH
AND THE HAKKE GROUP ...
...HAS ACHIEVED UN-EQUALLED SUCCESSES FOR IMPLEMENTATION IN MASS PRODUCTION!
THE KOU EMPIRE HAS BEEN CARRYING OUT MAGICAL RESEARCH COMPARABLE TO MAGNO-SHUTATT'S!
WHAT ARE THESE PURPLE PAPERS?
THOSE ARE HAKKE SEALS.
HAKKE IS A SYSTEM OF MAGIC INVOLVING EIGHT ELEMENTS THAT MAGIC TOOLS CAN CHANNEL.
WATER
KAN
HEAVEN
MOUNTAIN
KEN
GON
MARSH
DA
SHIN
THUNDER
KON
SON
EARTH
RI
WIND
FIRE
HMM...

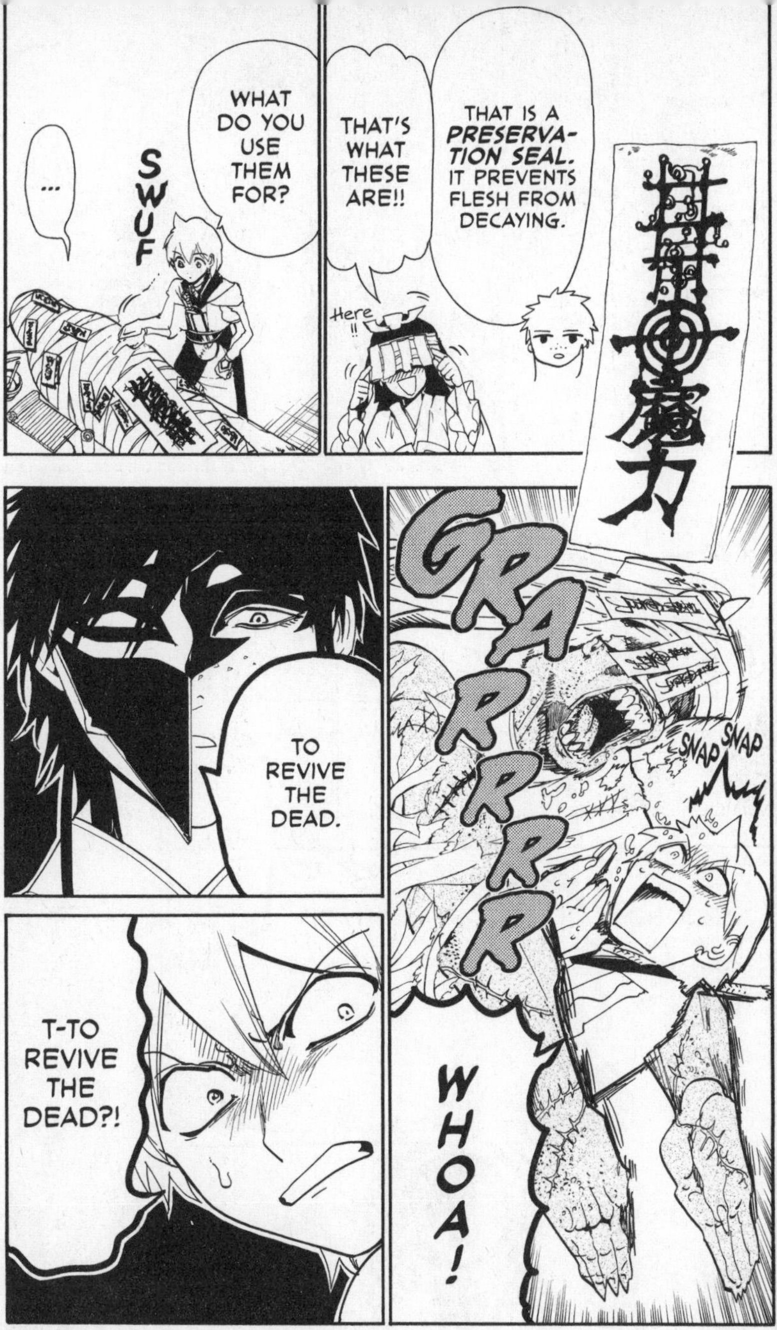
THAT IS A *PRESERVATION SEAL.* IT PREVENTS FLESH FROM DECAYING.
魔力
THAT'S WHAT THESE ARE!!
Here!!
WHAT DO YOU USE THEM FOR?
SWUF
...
GRARRRRR
SNAP SNAP
WHOA!
TO REVIVE THE DEAD.
T-TO REVIVE THE DEAD?!

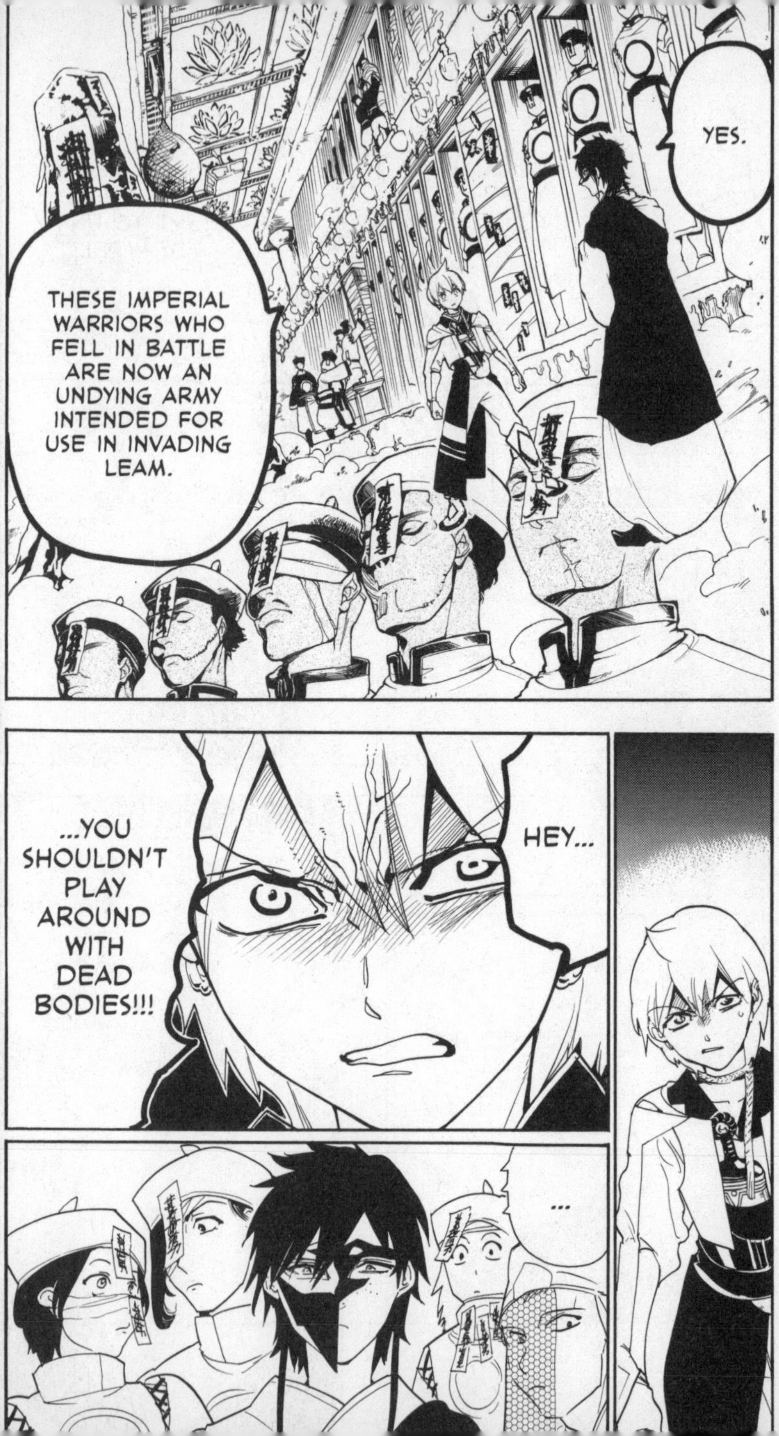
YES.
THESE IMPERIAL WARRIORS WHO FELL IN BATTLE ARE NOW AN UNDYING ARMY INTENDED FOR USE IN INVADING LEAM.
HEY...
...YOU SHOULDN'T PLAY AROUND WITH DEAD BODIES!!!
...

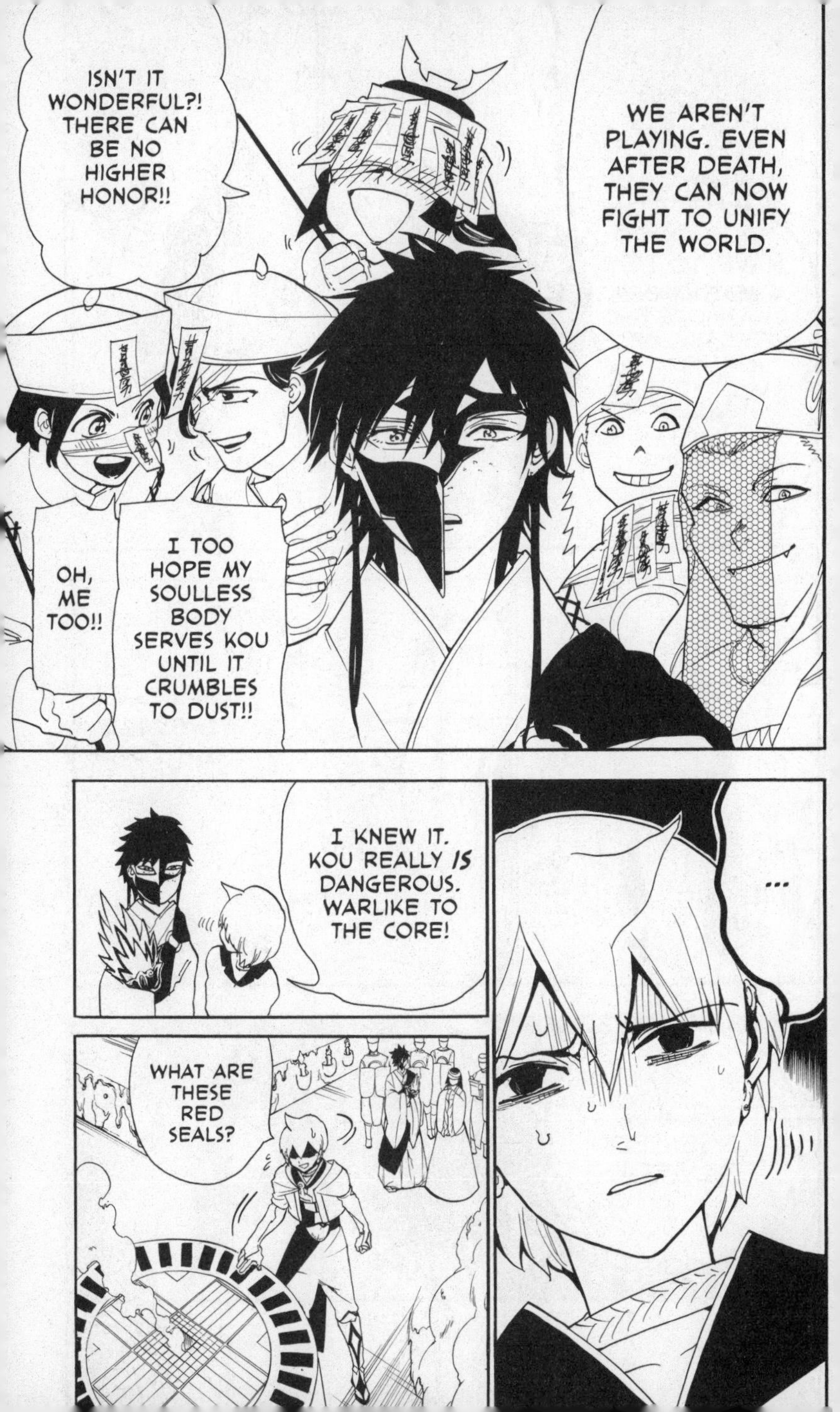

WE AREN'T PLAYING. EVEN AFTER DEATH, THEY CAN NOW FIGHT TO UNIFY THE WORLD.
ISN'T IT WONDERFUL?! THERE CAN BE NO HIGHER HONOR!!
I TOO HOPE MY SOULLESS BODY SERVES KOU UNTIL IT CRUMBLES TO DUST!!
OH, ME TOO!!
...
I KNEW IT. KOU REALLY *IS* DANGEROUS. WARLIKE TO THE CORE!
WHAT ARE THESE RED SEALS?

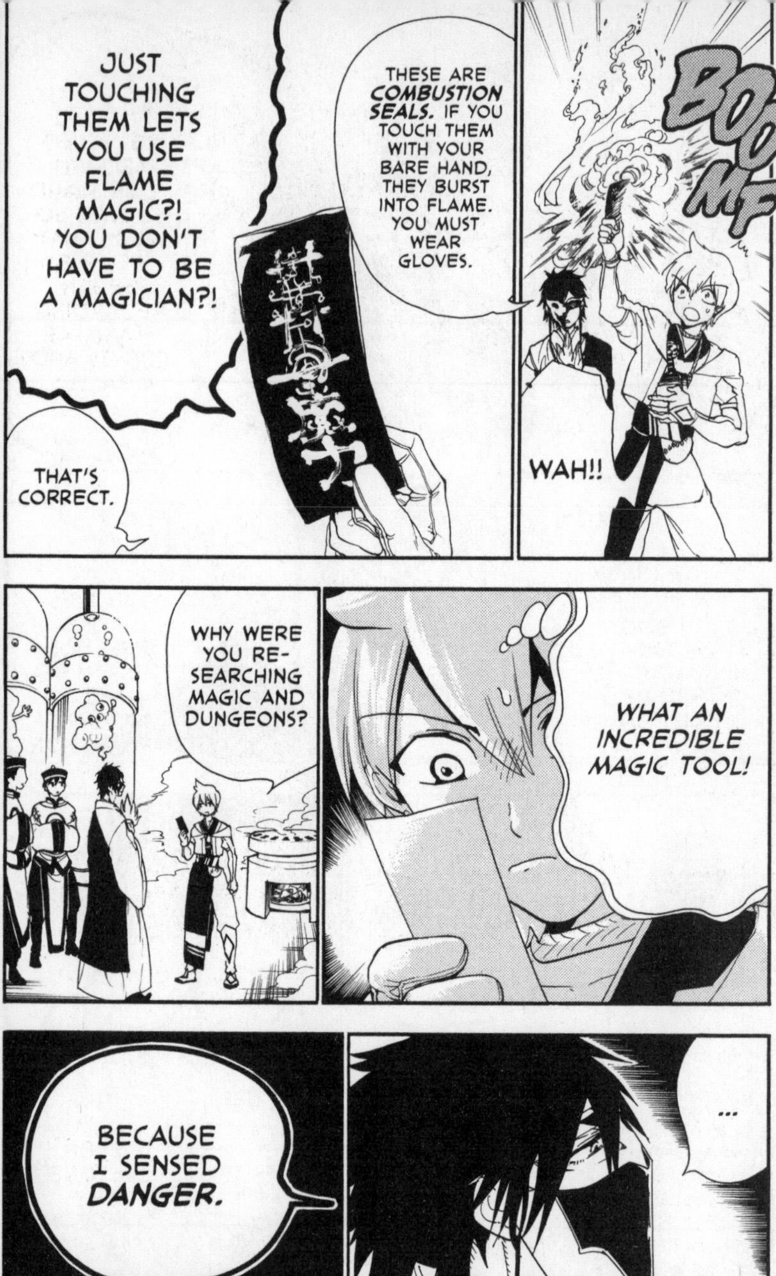
BOOMF
WAH!!
THESE ARE *COMBUSTION SEALS.* IF YOU TOUCH THEM WITH YOUR BARE HAND, THEY BURST INTO FLAME. YOU MUST WEAR GLOVES.
JUST TOUCHING THEM LETS YOU USE FLAME MAGIC?! YOU DON'T HAVE TO BE A MAGICIAN?!
THAT'S CORRECT.
WHAT AN INCREDIBLE MAGIC TOOL!
WHY WERE YOU RE-SEARCHING MAGIC AND DUNGEONS?
...
BECAUSE I SENSED *DANGER.*

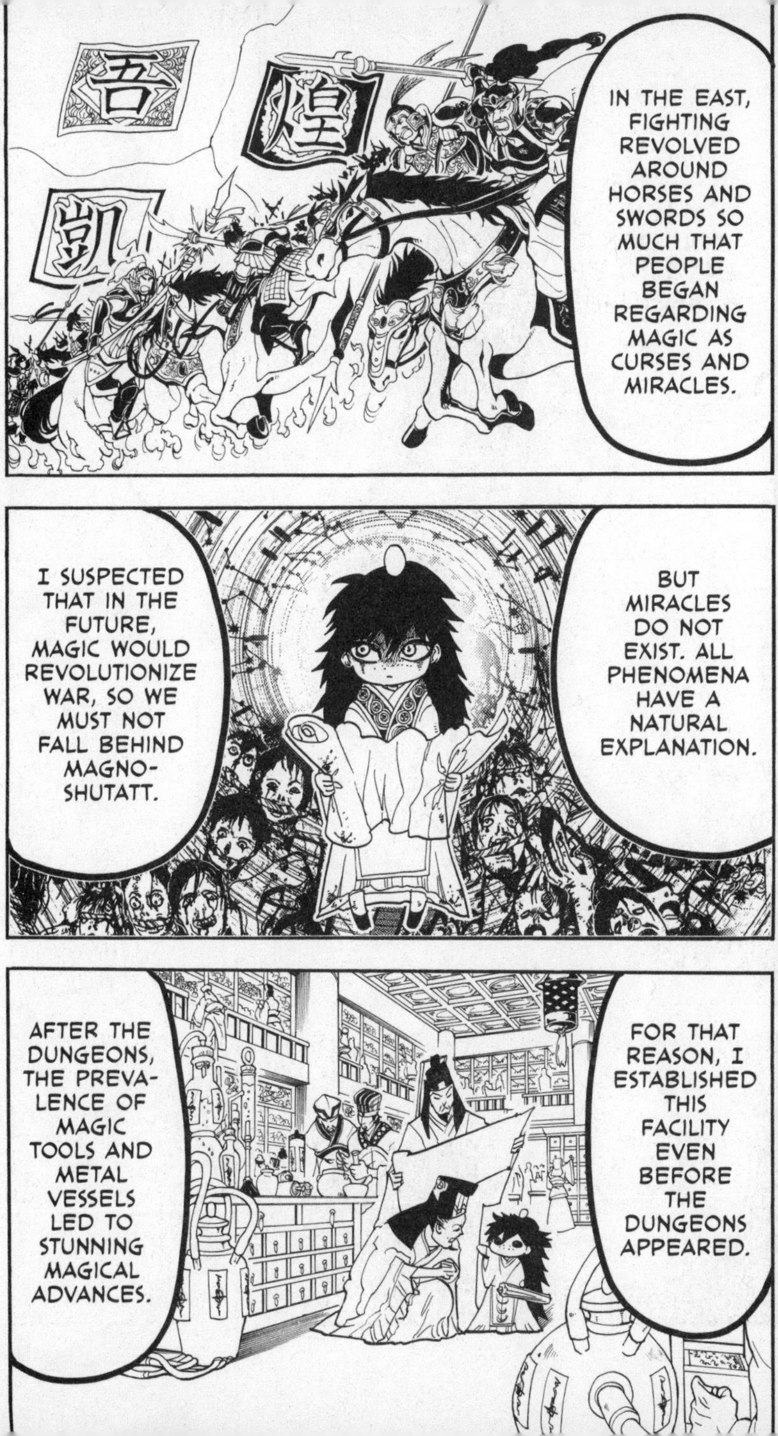
IN THE EAST, FIGHTING REVOLVED AROUND HORSES AND SWORDS SO MUCH THAT PEOPLE BEGAN REGARDING MAGIC AS CURSES AND MIRACLES.
煌
吾
凱
BUT MIRACLES DO NOT EXIST. ALL PHENOMENA HAVE A NATURAL EXPLANATION.
I SUSPECTED THAT IN THE FUTURE, MAGIC WOULD REVOLUTIONIZE WAR, SO WE MUST NOT FALL BEHIND MAGNO-SHUTATT.
FOR THAT REASON, I ESTABLISHED THIS FACILITY EVEN BEFORE THE DUNGEONS APPEARED.
AFTER THE DUNGEONS, THE PREVA-LENCE OF MAGIC TOOLS AND METAL VESSELS LED TO STUNNING MAGICAL ADVANCES.

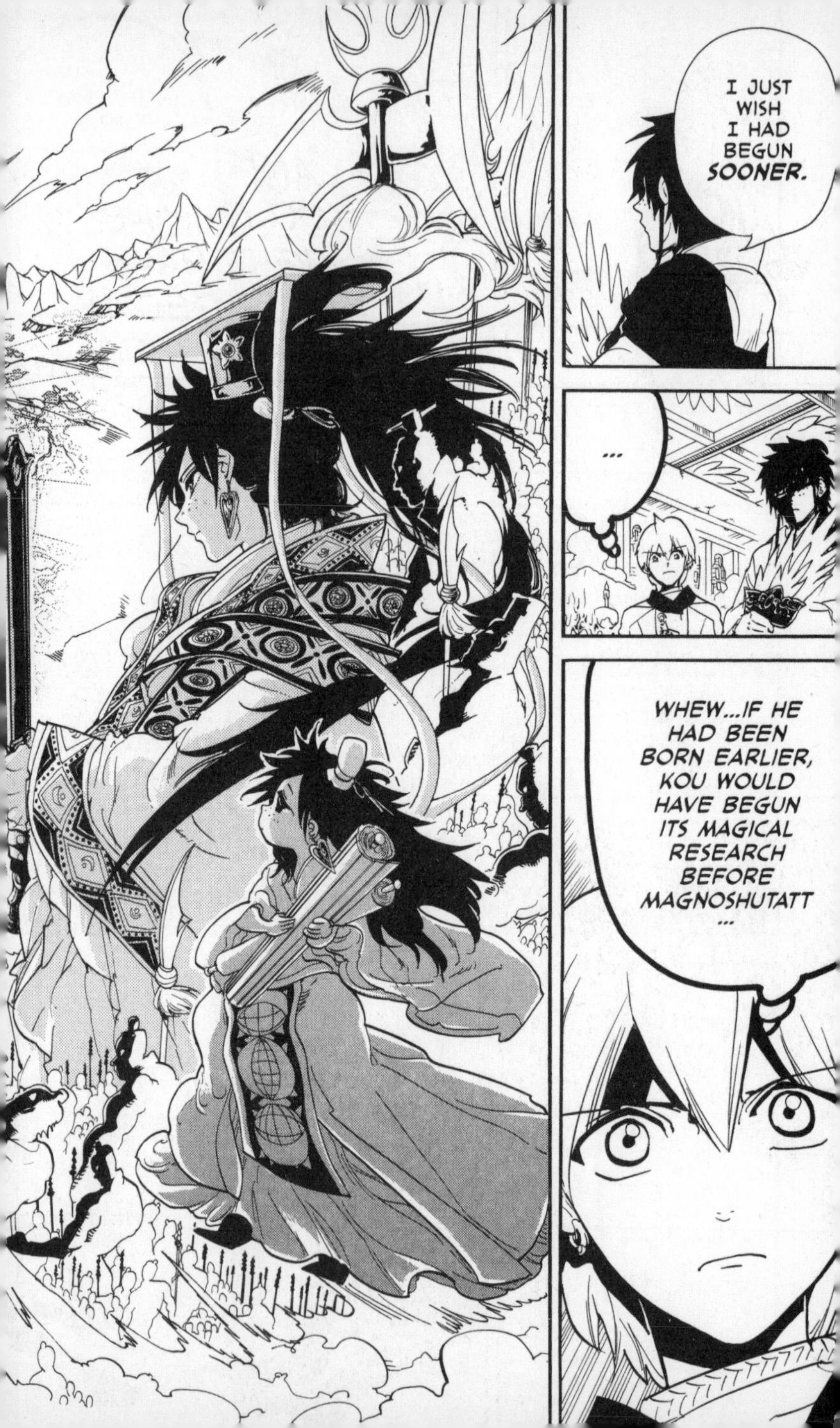
I JUST WISH I HAD BEGUN SOONER.
...
WHEW...IF HE HAD BEEN BORN EARLIER, KOU WOULD HAVE BEGUN ITS MAGICAL RESEARCH BEFORE MAGNOSHUTATT ...

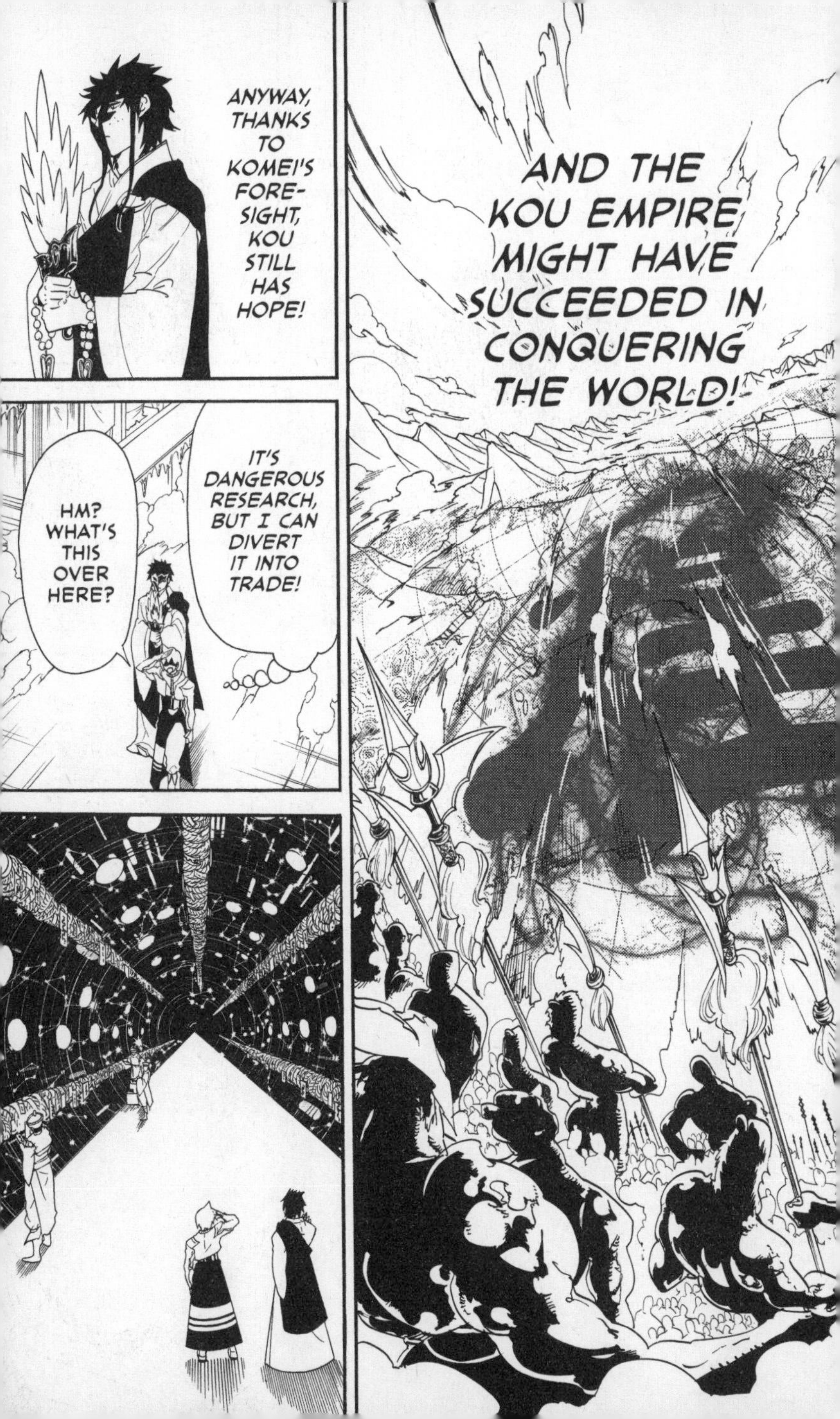
AND THE KOU EMPIRE MIGHT HAVE SUCCEEDED IN CONQUERING THE WORLD!
ANYWAY, THANKS TO KOMEI'S FORE-SIGHT, KOU STILL HAS HOPE!
IT'S DANGEROUS RESEARCH, BUT I CAN DIVERT IT INTO TRADE!
HM? WHAT'S THIS OVER HERE?

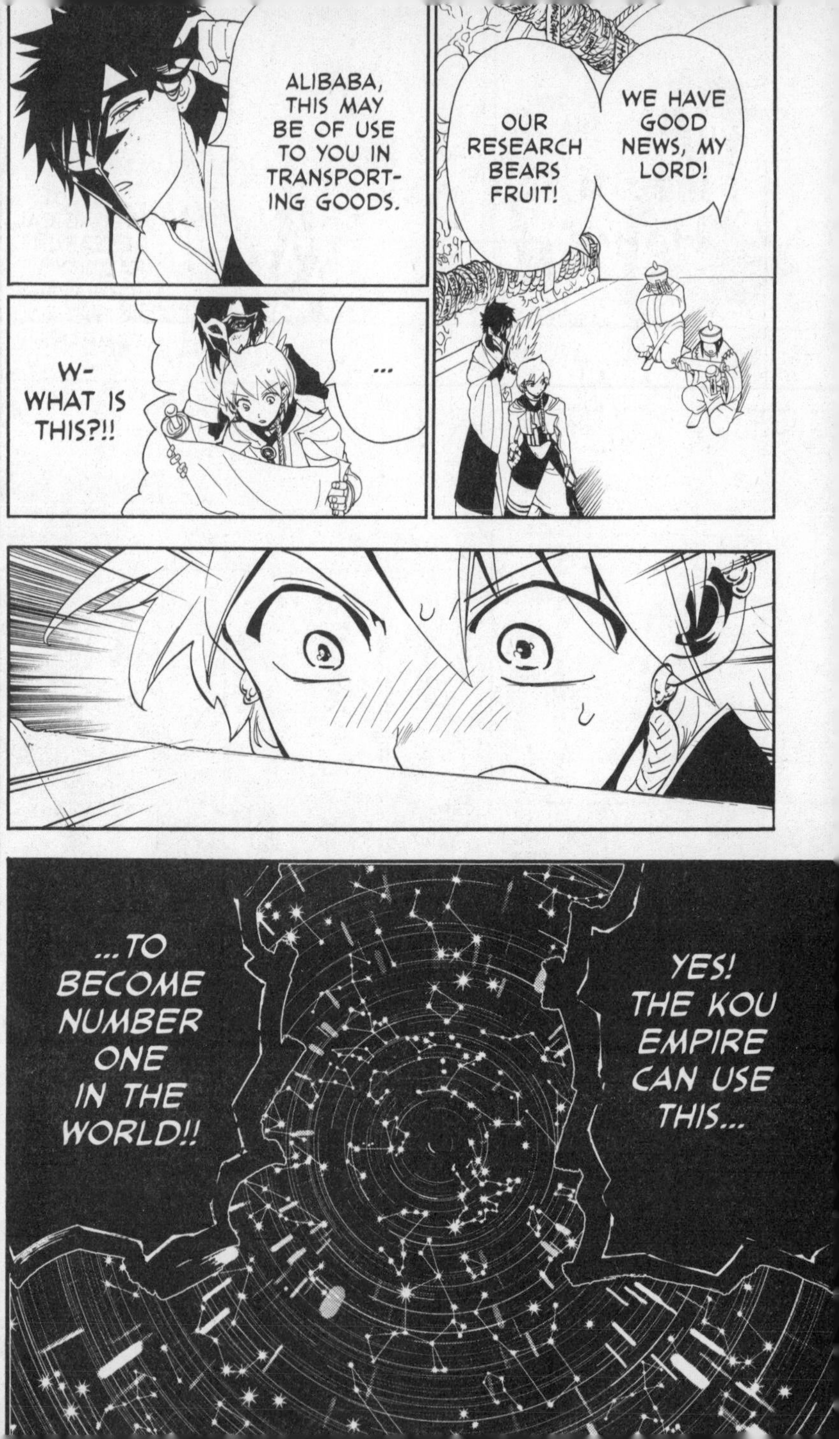
WE HAVE GOOD NEWS, MY LORD!
OUR RESEARCH BEARS FRUIT!
ALIBABA, THIS MAY BE OF USE TO YOU IN TRANSPORTING GOODS.
...
W-WHAT IS THIS?!!
YES! THE KOU EMPIRE CAN USE THIS...
...TO BECOME NUMBER ONE IN THE WORLD!!

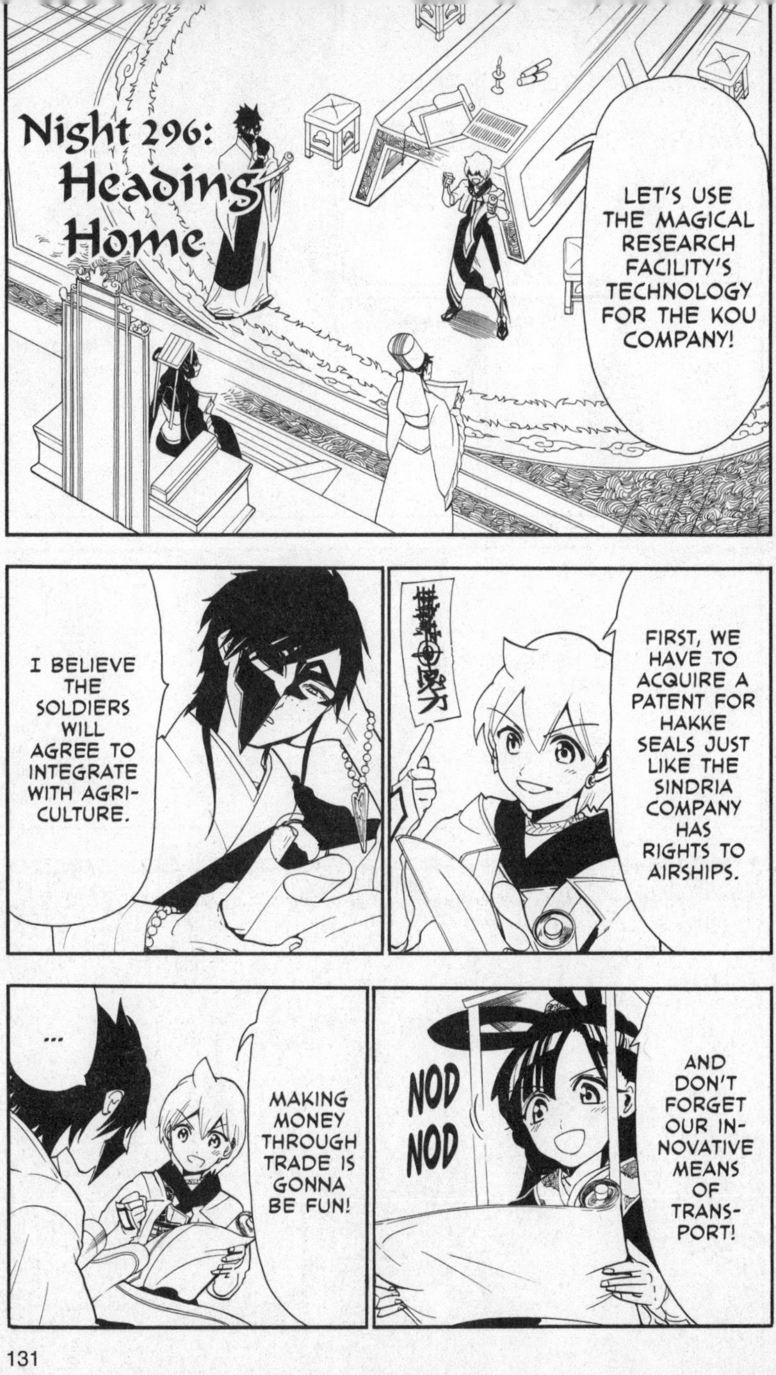
Night 296: Heading Home
LET'S USE THE MAGICAL RESEARCH FACILITY'S TECHNOLOGY FOR THE KOU COMPANY!
FIRST, WE HAVE TO ACQUIRE A PATENT FOR HAKKE SEALS JUST LIKE THE SINDRIA COMPANY HAS RIGHTS TO AIRSHIPS.
I BELIEVE THE SOLDIERS WILL AGREE TO INTEGRATE WITH AGRI-CULTURE.
AND DON'T FORGET OUR IN-NOVATIVE MEANS OF TRANS-PORT!
NOD NOD
MAKING MONEY THROUGH TRADE IS GONNA BE FUN!
...

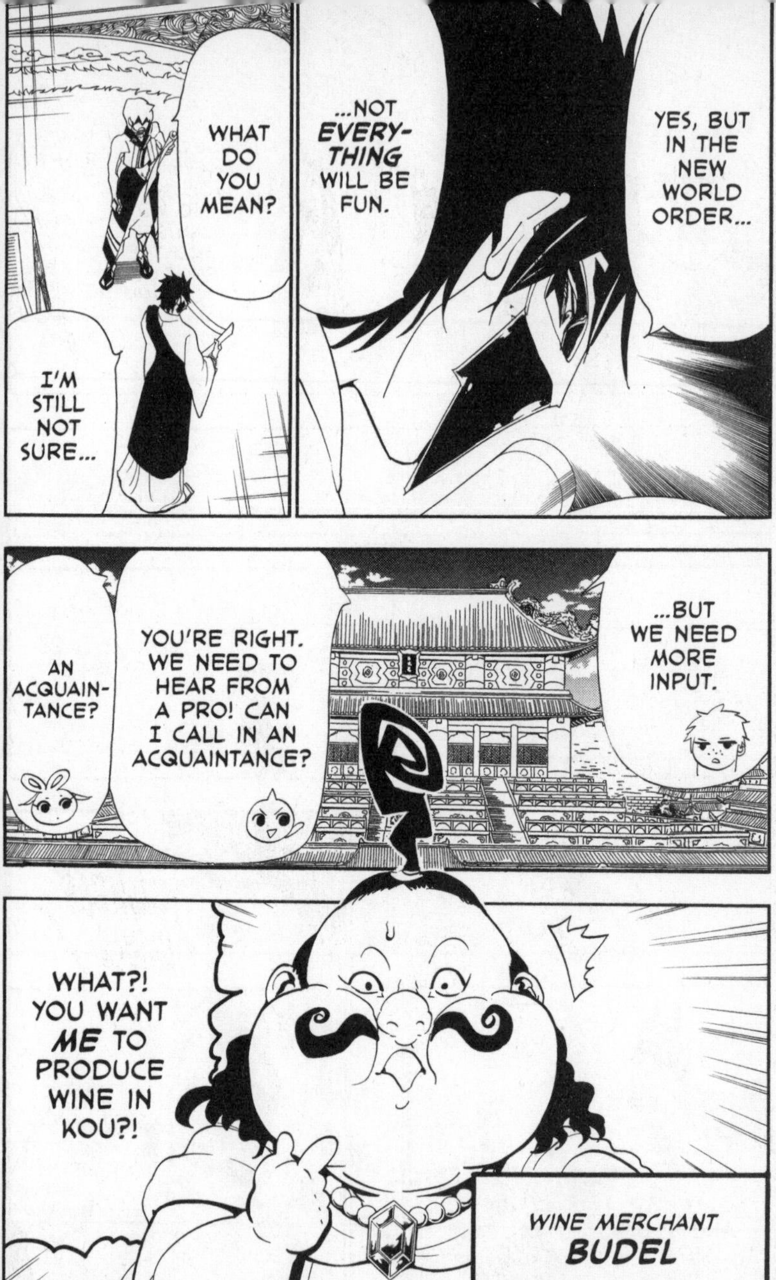

YES, BUT IN THE NEW WORLD ORDER...
...NOT *EVERYTHING* WILL BE FUN.
WHAT DO YOU MEAN?
I'M STILL NOT SURE...
...BUT WE NEED MORE INPUT.
YOU'RE RIGHT. WE NEED TO HEAR FROM A PRO! CAN I CALL IN AN ACQUAINTANCE?
AN ACQUAINTANCE?
WHAT?! YOU WANT *ME* TO PRODUCE WINE IN KOU?!
WINE MERCHANT ***BUDEL***

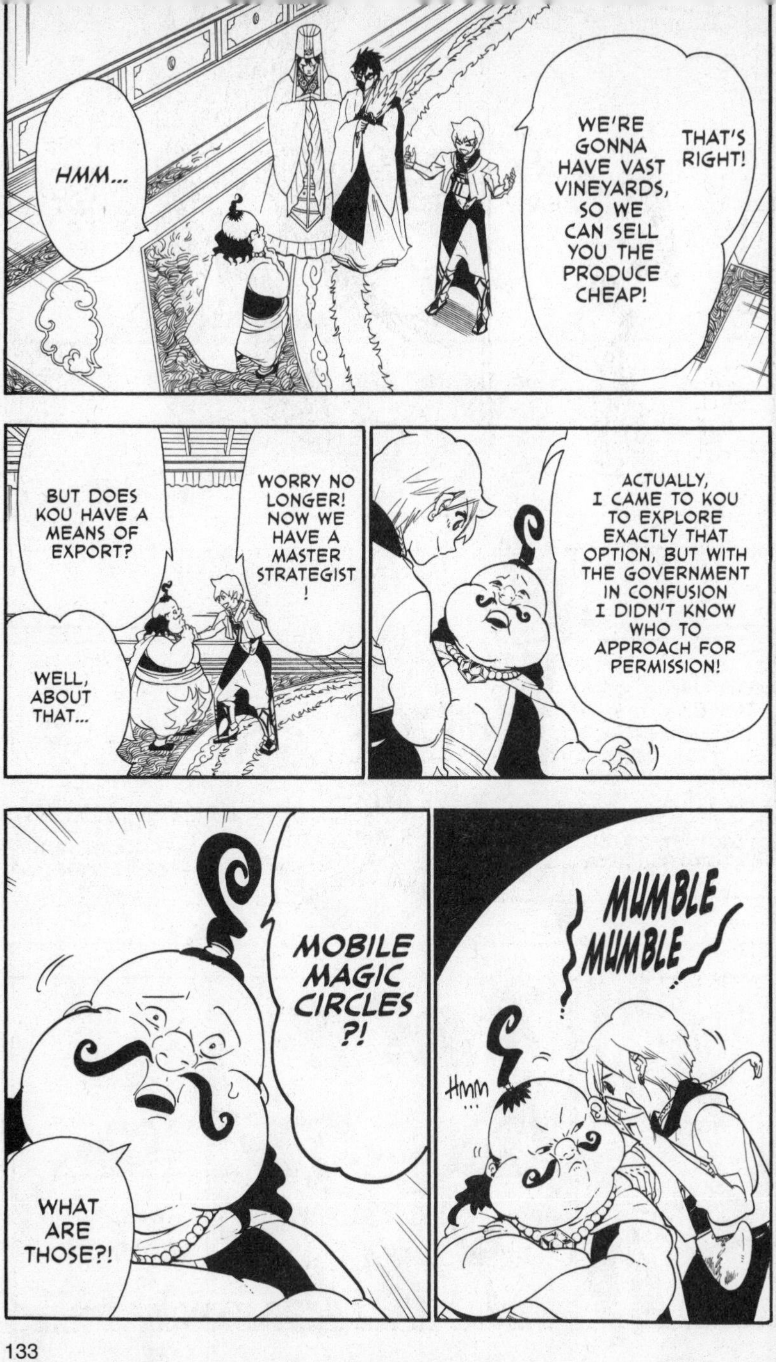
THAT'S RIGHT!
WE'RE GONNA HAVE VAST VINEYARDS, SO WE CAN SELL YOU THE PRODUCE CHEAP!
HMM...
ACTUALLY, I CAME TO KOU TO EXPLORE EXACTLY THAT OPTION, BUT WITH THE GOVERNMENT IN CONFUSION I DIDN'T KNOW WHO TO APPROACH FOR PERMISSION!
WORRY NO LONGER! NOW WE HAVE A MASTER STRATEGIST!
BUT DOES KOU HAVE A MEANS OF EXPORT?
WELL, ABOUT THAT...
MUMBLE MUMBLE
Hmm...
MOBILE MAGIC CIRCLES?!
WHAT ARE THOSE?!

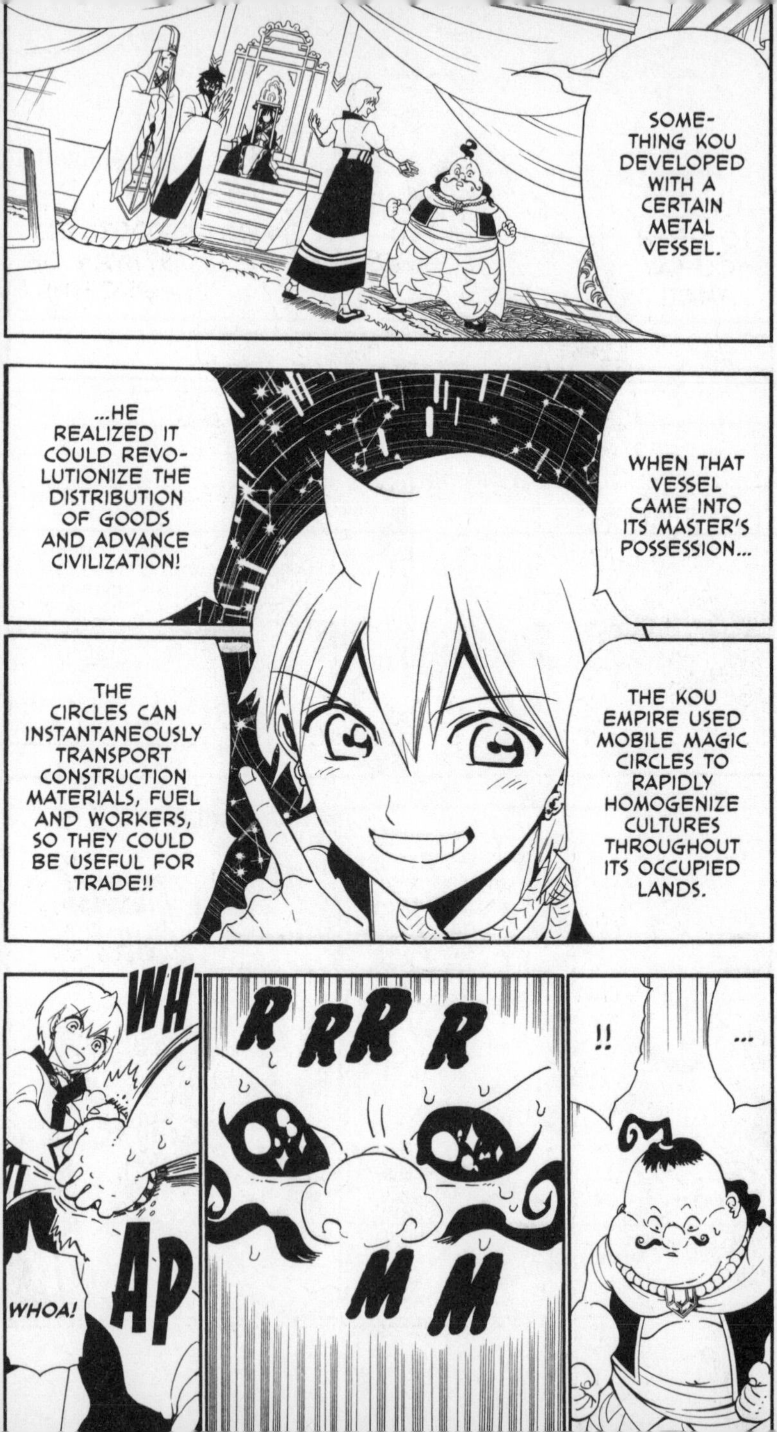
SOME-THING KOU DEVELOPED WITH A CERTAIN METAL VESSEL.
WHEN THAT VESSEL CAME INTO ITS MASTER'S POSSESSION...
...HE REALIZED IT COULD REVOLUTIONIZE THE DISTRIBUTION OF GOODS AND ADVANCE CIVILIZATION!
THE KOU EMPIRE USED MOBILE MAGIC CIRCLES TO RAPIDLY HOMOGENIZE CULTURES THROUGHOUT ITS OCCUPIED LANDS.
THE CIRCLES CAN INSTANTANEOUSLY TRANSPORT CONSTRUCTION MATERIALS, FUEL AND WORKERS, SO THEY COULD BE USEFUL FOR TRADE!!
...
!!
RRRR
MM
WH
AP
WHOA!

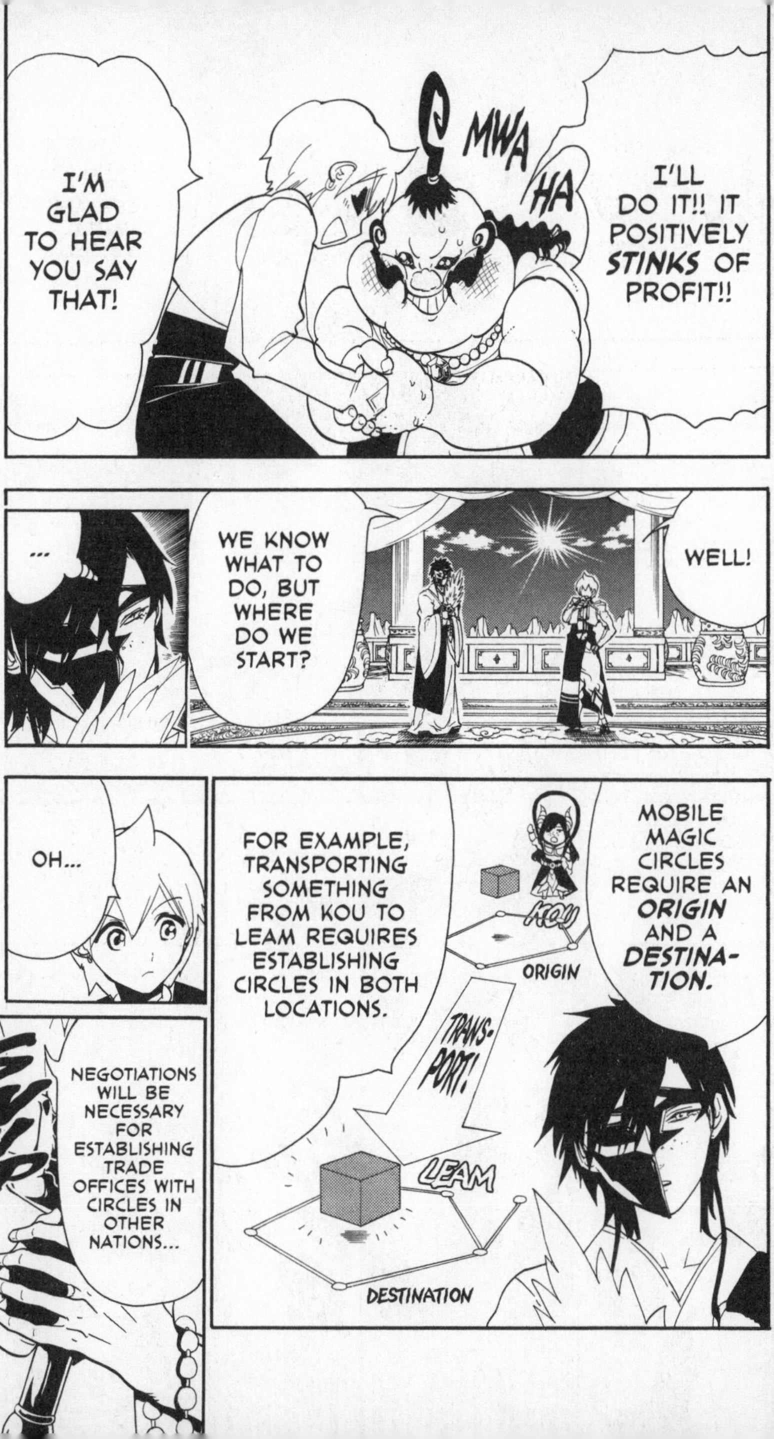
I'LL DO IT!! IT POSITIVELY STINKS OF PROFIT!!
MWA HA
I'M GLAD TO HEAR YOU SAY THAT!
WELL!
WE KNOW WHAT TO DO, BUT WHERE DO WE START?
...
MOBILE MAGIC CIRCLES REQUIRE AN ORIGIN AND A DESTINATION.
KOU
ORIGIN
FOR EXAMPLE, TRANSPORTING SOMETHING FROM KOU TO LEAM REQUIRES ESTABLISHING CIRCLES IN BOTH LOCATIONS.
TRANSPORT!
LEAM
DESTINATION
OH...
SWIP
NEGOTIATIONS WILL BE NECESSARY FOR ESTABLISHING TRADE OFFICES WITH CIRCLES IN OTHER NATIONS...

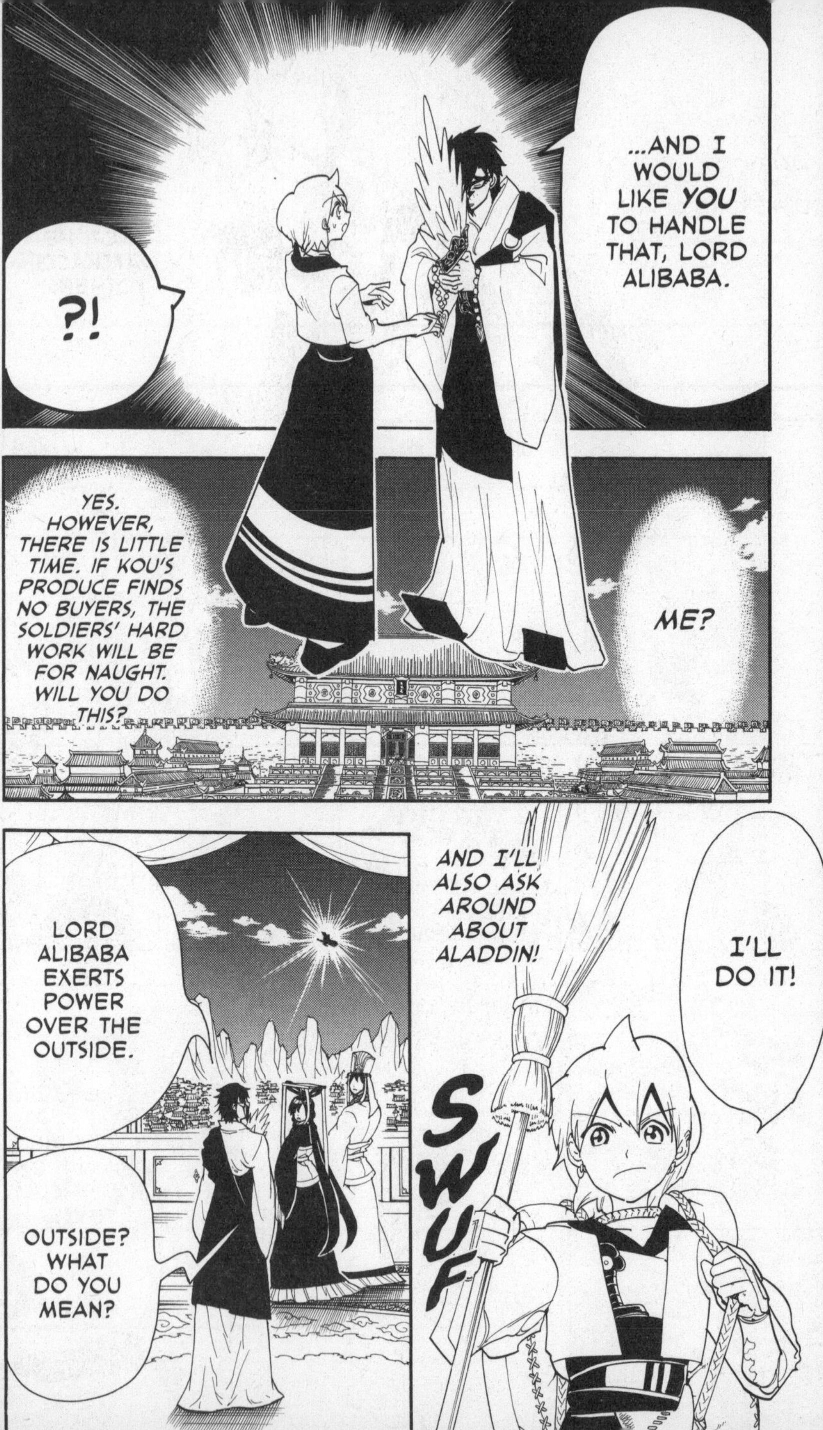
...AND I WOULD LIKE *YOU* TO HANDLE THAT, LORD ALIBABA.
?!
ME?
YES. HOWEVER, THERE IS LITTLE TIME. IF KOU'S PRODUCE FINDS NO BUYERS, THE SOLDIERS' HARD WORK WILL BE FOR NAUGHT. WILL YOU DO THIS?
I'LL DO IT!
AND I'LL ALSO ASK AROUND ABOUT ALADDIN!
SWUF
LORD ALIBABA EXERTS POWER OVER THE OUTSIDE.
OUTSIDE? WHAT DO YOU MEAN?

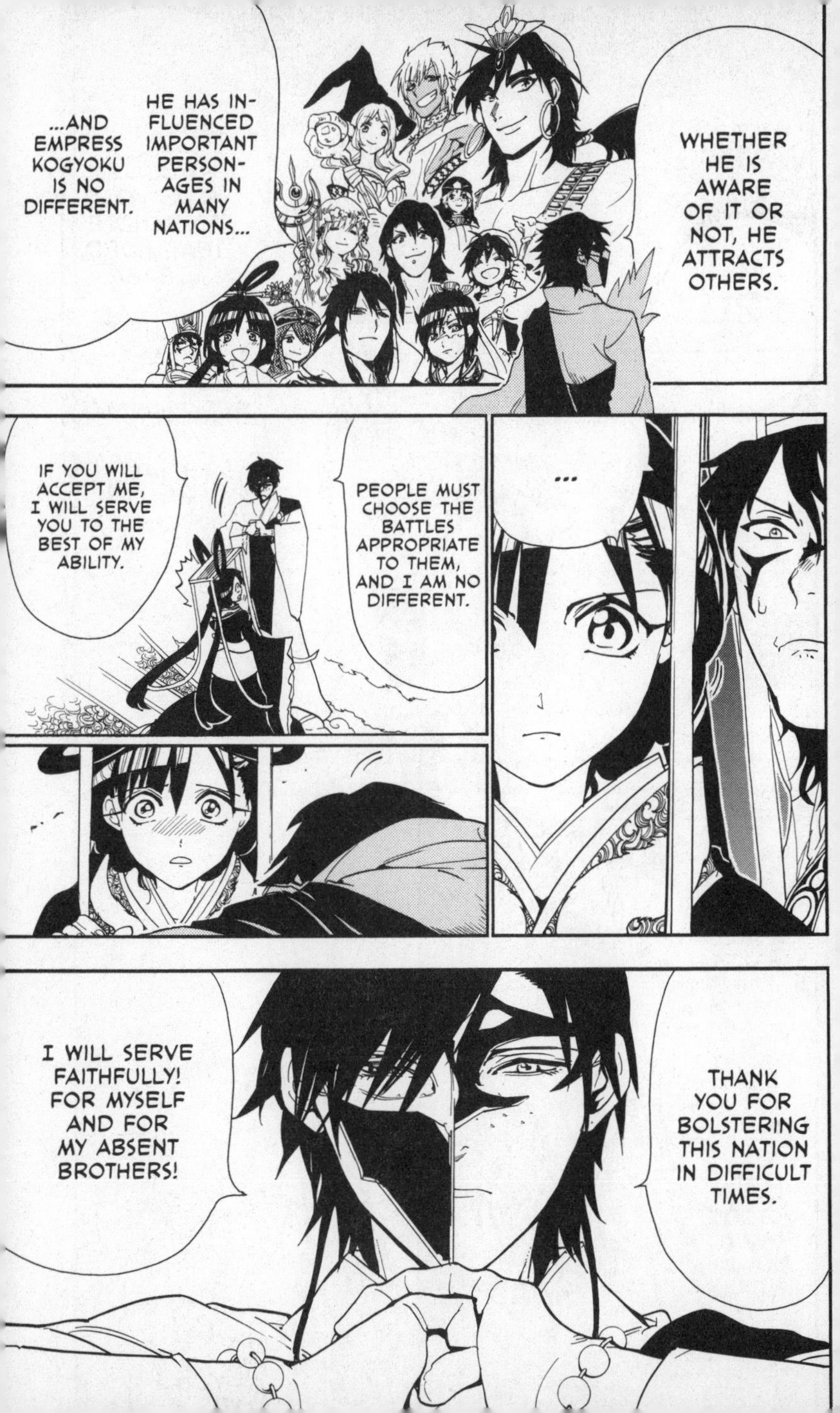
WHETHER HE IS AWARE OF IT OR NOT, HE ATTRACTS OTHERS.
HE HAS INFLUENCED IMPORTANT PERSONAGES IN MANY NATIONS...
...AND EMPRESS KOGYOKU IS NO DIFFERENT.
...
PEOPLE MUST CHOOSE THE BATTLES APPROPRIATE TO THEM, AND I AM NO DIFFERENT.
IF YOU WILL ACCEPT ME, I WILL SERVE YOU TO THE BEST OF MY ABILITY.
THANK YOU FOR BOLSTERING THIS NATION IN DIFFICULT TIMES.
I WILL SERVE FAITHFULLY! FOR MYSELF AND FOR MY ABSENT BROTHERS!

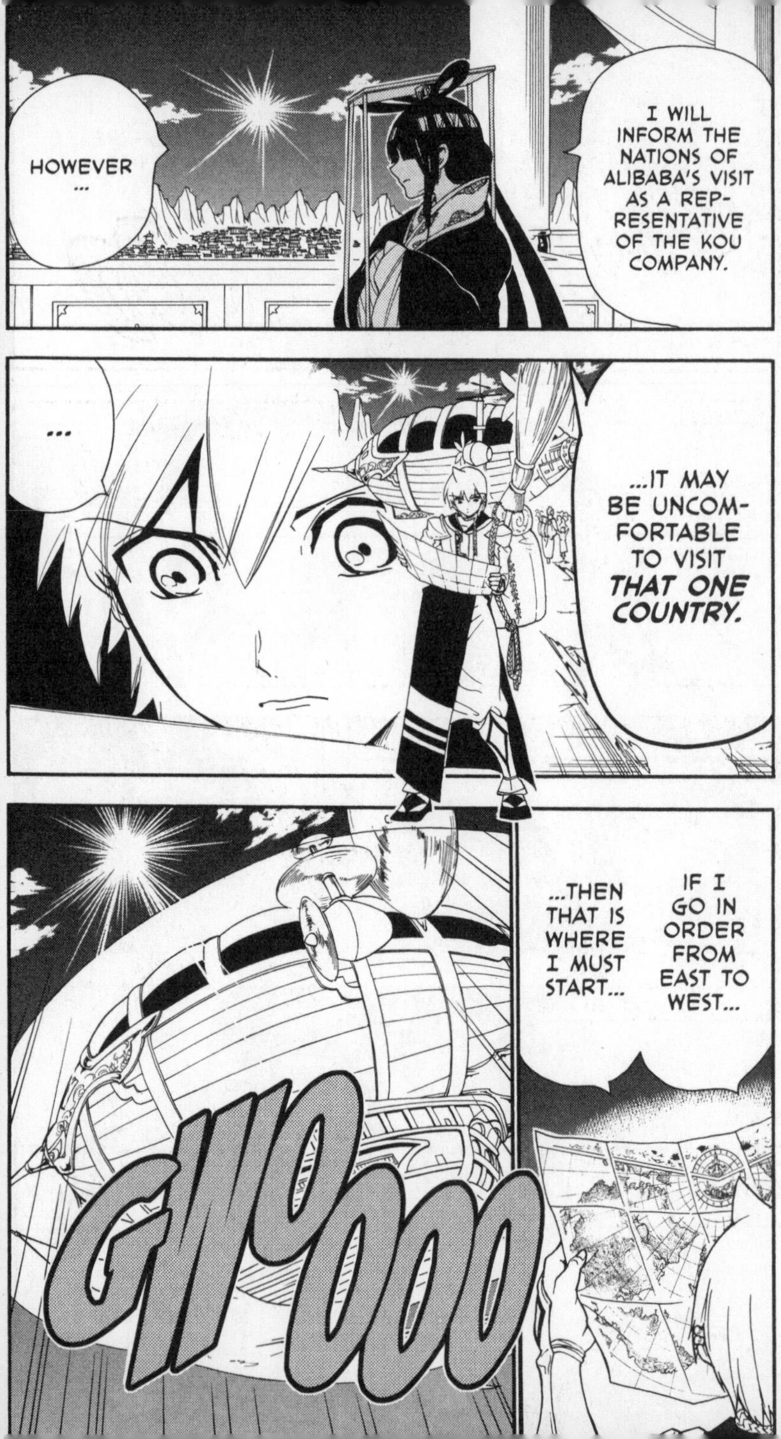
I WILL INFORM THE NATIONS OF ALIBABA'S VISIT AS A REPRESENTATIVE OF THE KOU COMPANY.
HOWEVER ...
...IT MAY BE UNCOMFORTABLE TO VISIT *THAT ONE COUNTRY.*
...
IF I GO IN ORDER FROM EAST TO WEST...
...THEN THAT IS WHERE I MUST START...
GWOOOO

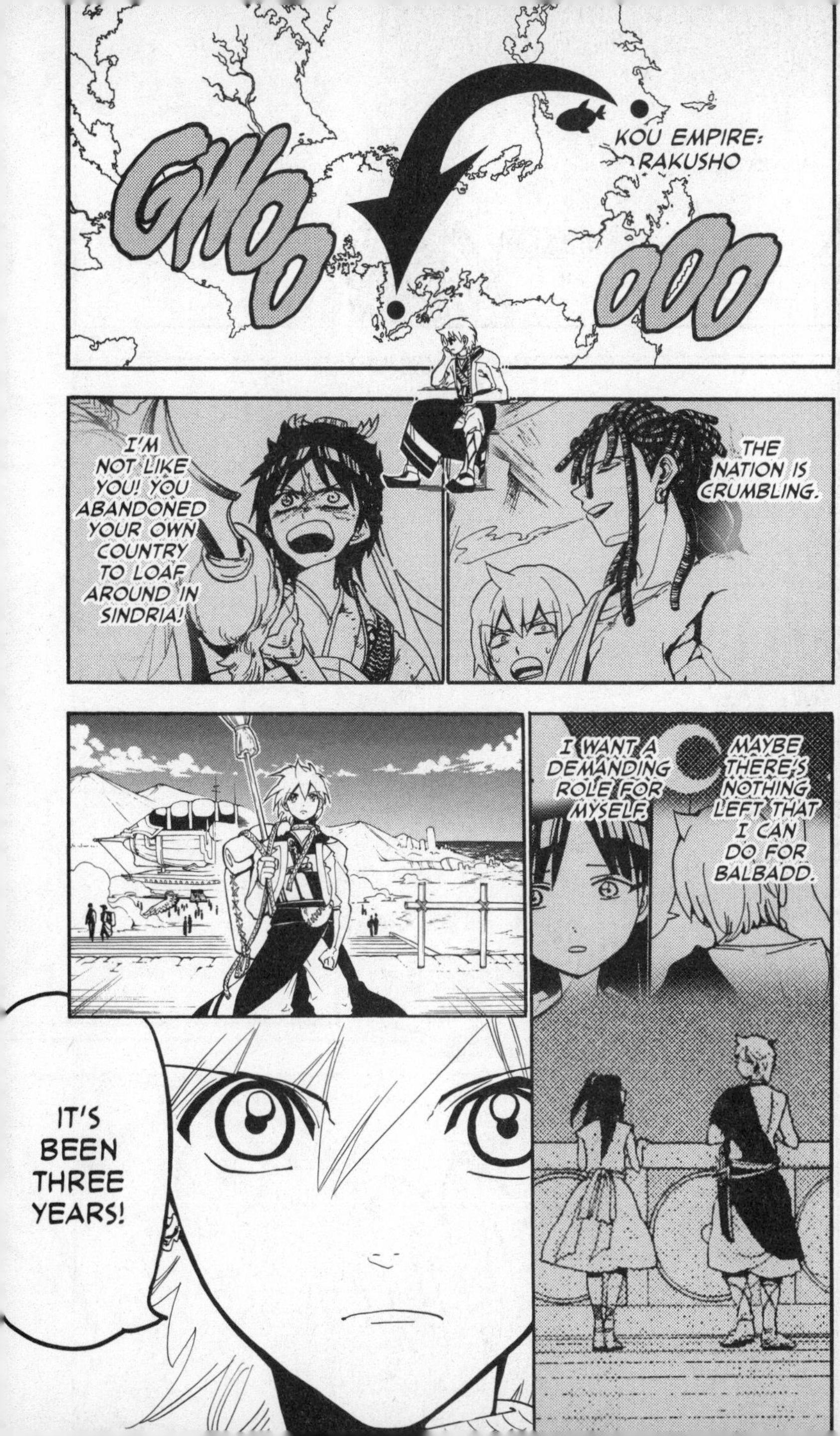
KOU EMPIRE: RAKUSHO
GWOOOOOOO
THE NATION IS CRUMBLING.
I'M NOT LIKE YOU! YOU ABANDONED YOUR OWN COUNTRY TO LOAF AROUND IN SINDRIA!
MAYBE THERE'S NOTHING LEFT THAT I CAN DO FOR BALBADD.
I WANT A DEMANDING ROLE FOR MYSELF.
IT'S BEEN THREE YEARS!

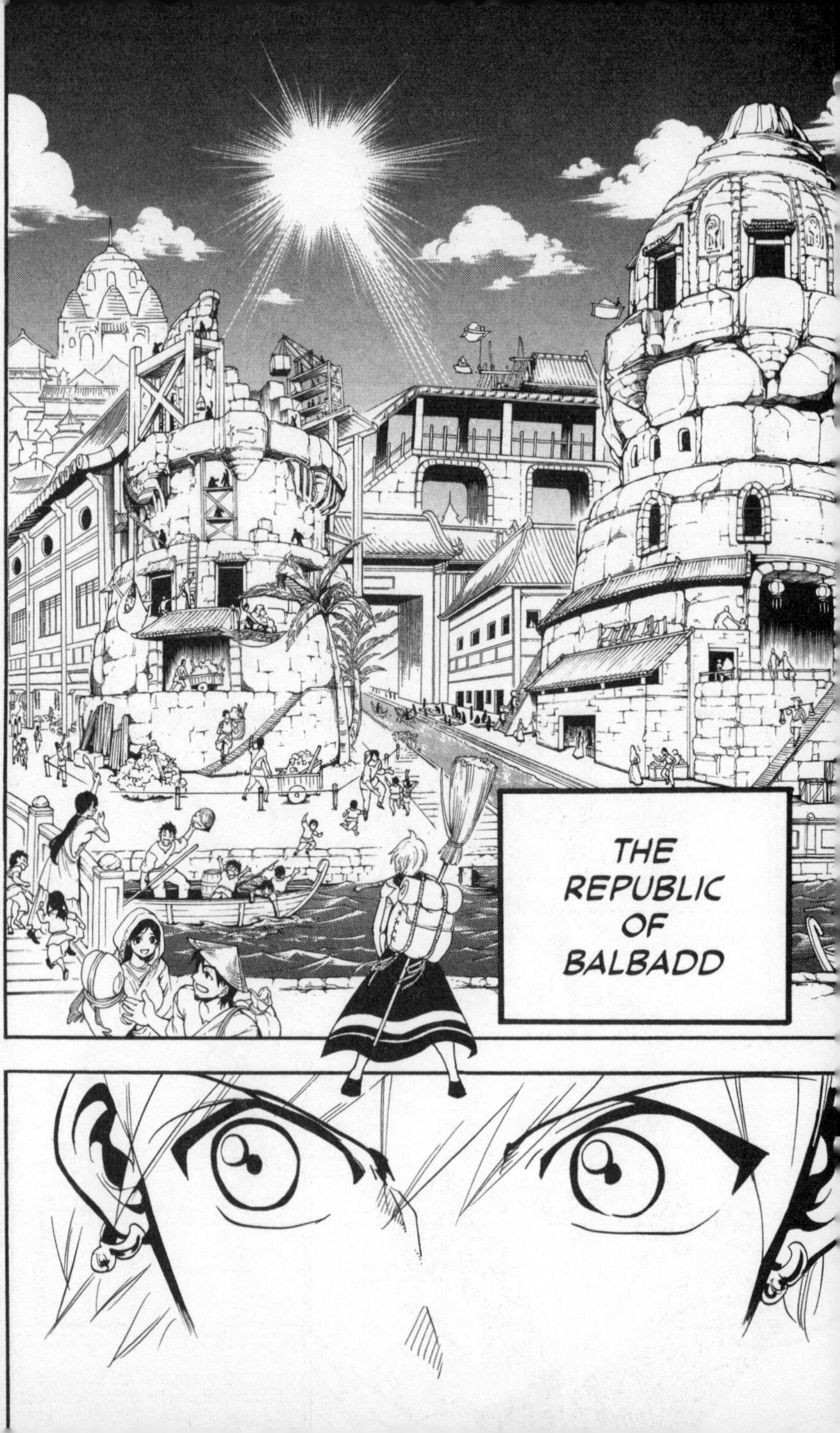
THE REPUBLIC OF BALBADD

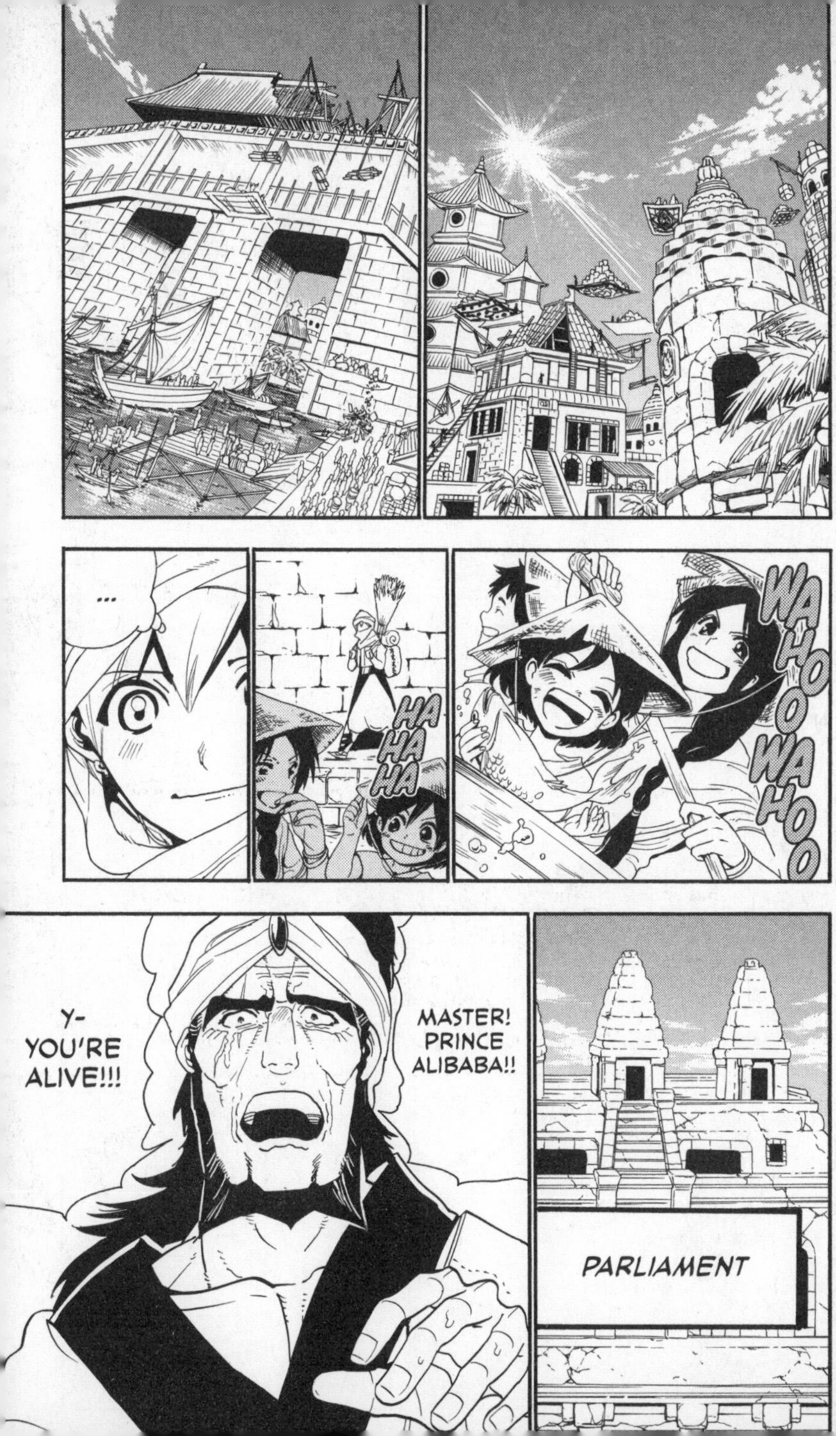
WAHOO WAHOO
HA HA HA HA
...
PARLIAMENT
MASTER! PRINCE ALIBABA!!
Y- YOU'RE ALIVE!!!

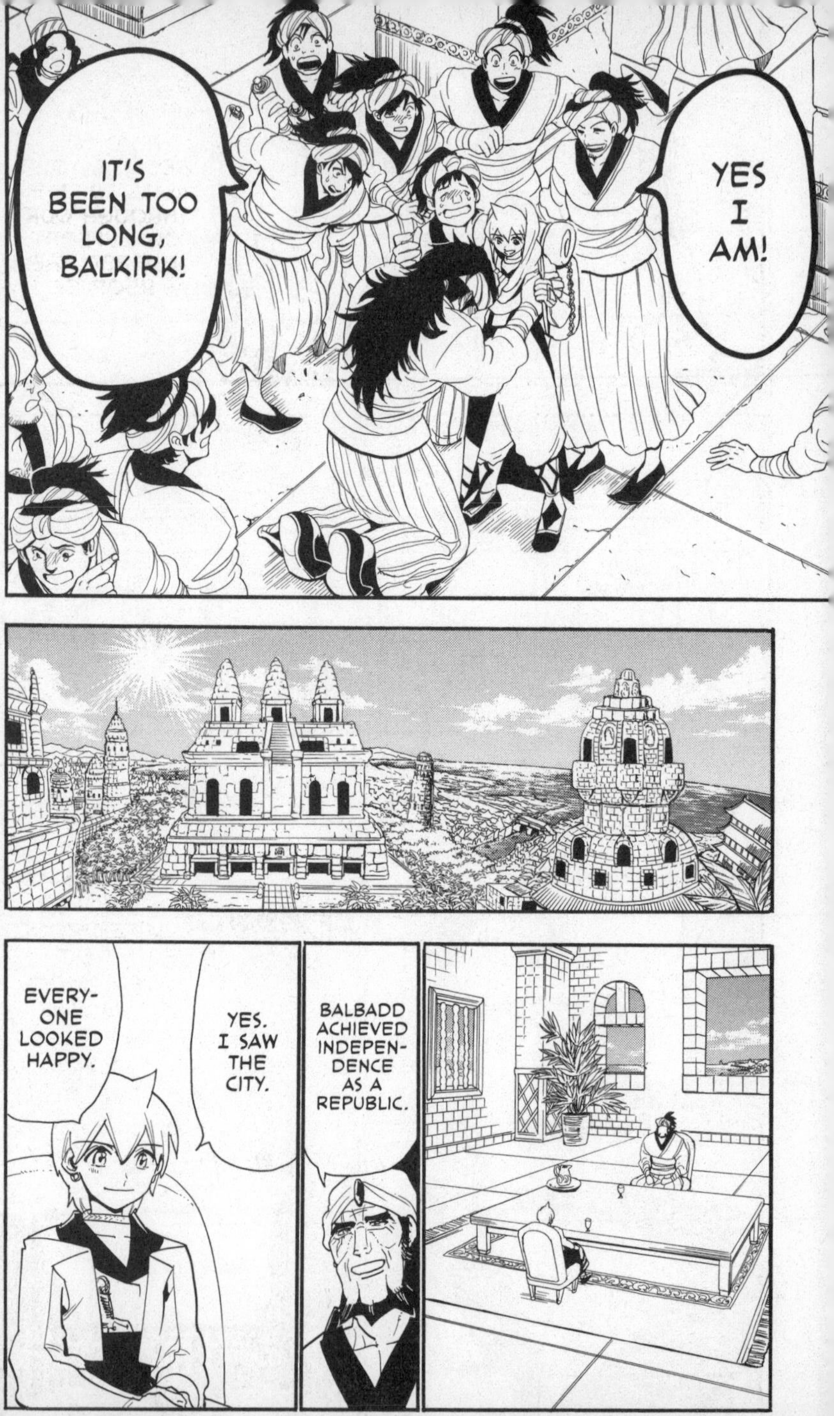
YES I AM!
IT'S BEEN TOO LONG, BALKIRK!
BALBADD ACHIEVED INDEPENDENCE AS A REPUBLIC.
YES. I SAW THE CITY.
EVERYONE LOOKED HAPPY.

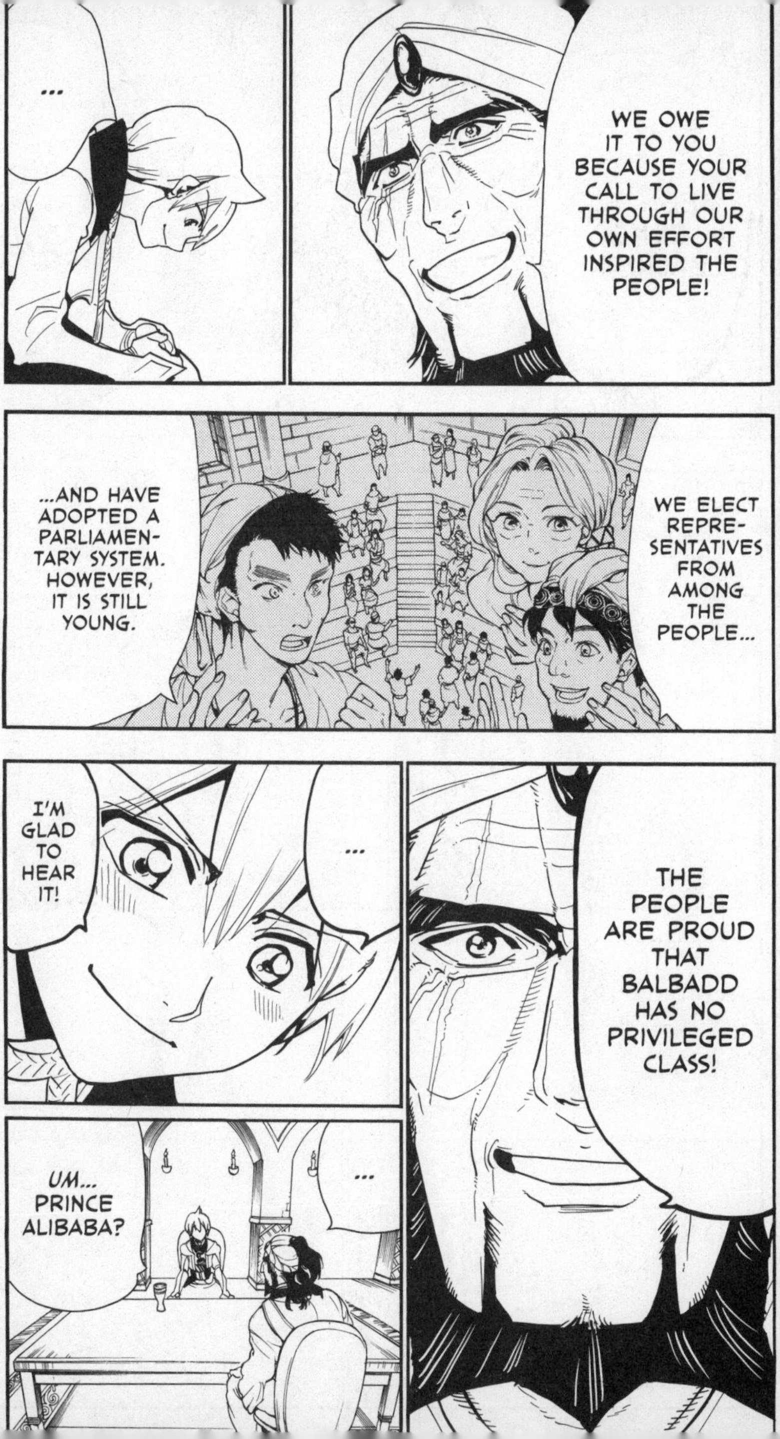
WE OWE IT TO YOU BECAUSE YOUR CALL TO LIVE THROUGH OUR OWN EFFORT INSPIRED THE PEOPLE!
...
WE ELECT REPRE-SENTATIVES FROM AMONG THE PEOPLE...
...AND HAVE ADOPTED A PARLIAMEN-TARY SYSTEM. HOWEVER, IT IS STILL YOUNG.
THE PEOPLE ARE PROUD THAT BALBADD HAS NO PRIVILEGED CLASS!
...
I'M GLAD TO HEAR IT!
...
UM... PRINCE ALIBABA?

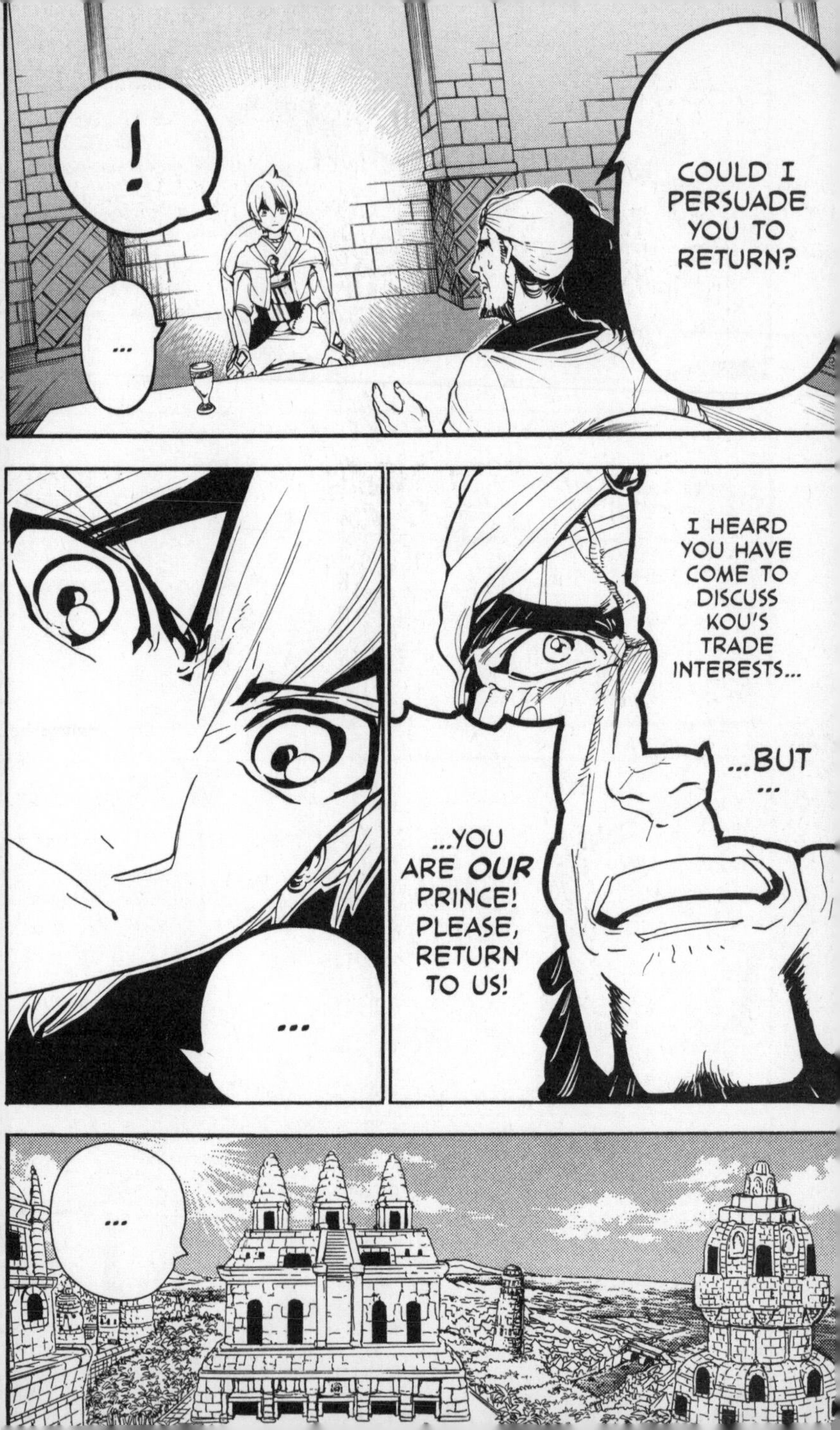
COULD I PERSUADE YOU TO RETURN?
!
...
I HEARD YOU HAVE COME TO DISCUSS KOU'S TRADE INTERESTS...
...BUT ...
...YOU ARE *OUR* PRINCE! PLEASE, RETURN TO US!
...
...

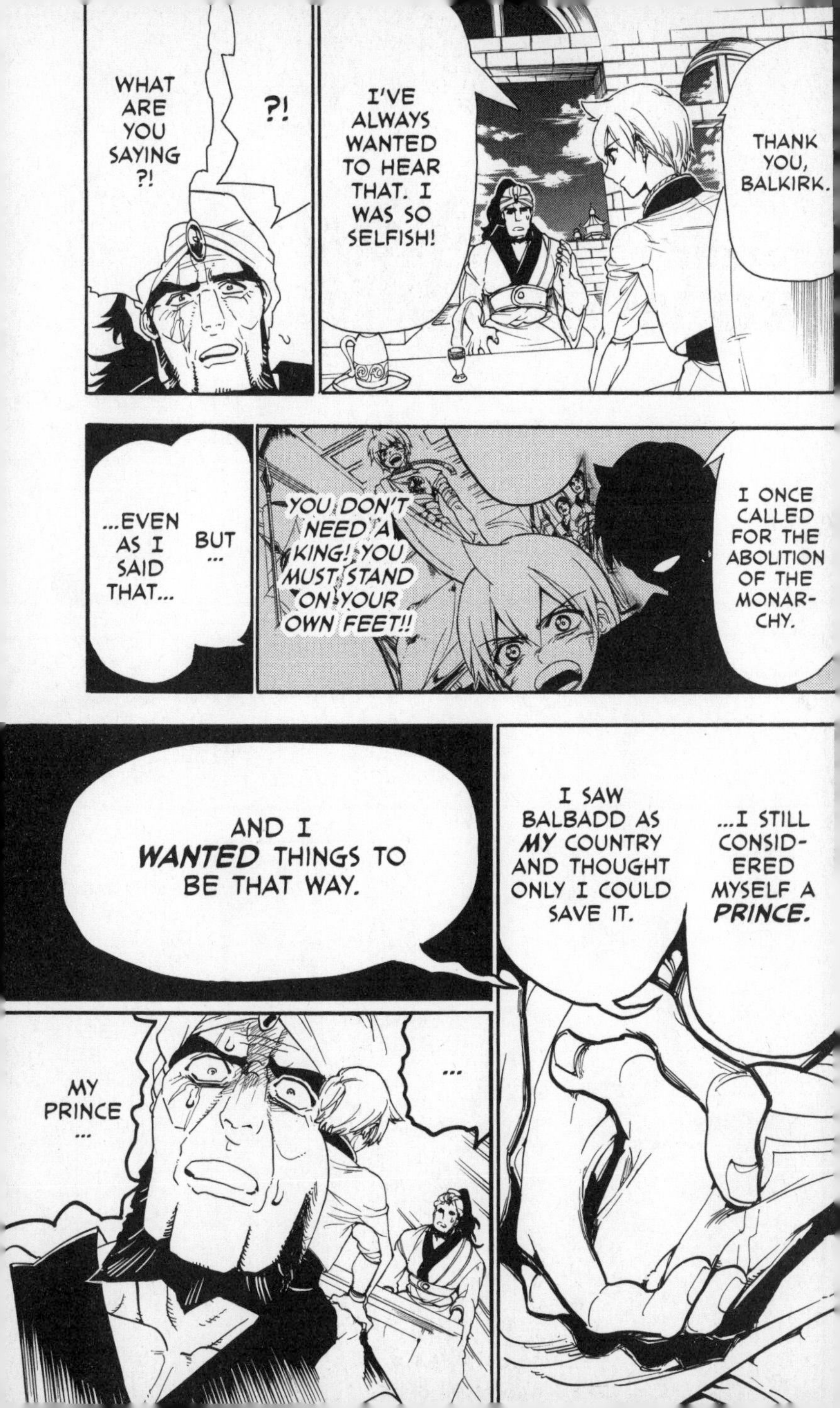
THANK YOU, BALKIRK.
I'VE ALWAYS WANTED TO HEAR THAT. I WAS SO SELFISH!
?!
WHAT ARE YOU SAYING ?!
I ONCE CALLED FOR THE ABOLITION OF THE MONAR-CHY.
YOU DON'T NEED A KING! YOU MUST STAND ON YOUR OWN FEET!!
BUT ...
...EVEN AS I SAID THAT...
...I STILL CONSID-ERED MYSELF A PRINCE.
I SAW BALBADD AS MY COUNTRY AND THOUGHT ONLY I COULD SAVE IT.
AND I WANTED THINGS TO BE THAT WAY.
...
MY PRINCE ...

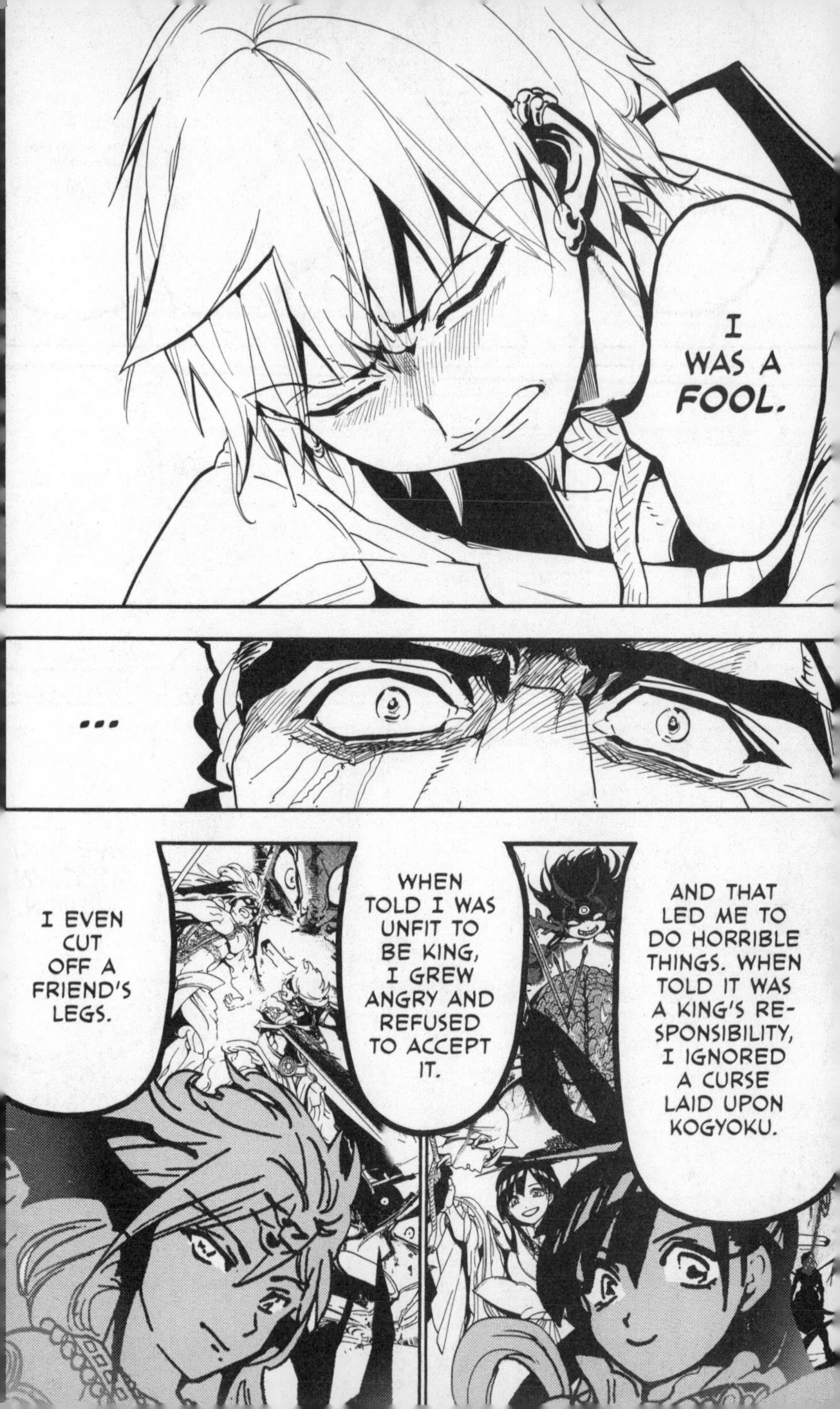
I WAS A *FOOL.*
...
AND THAT LED ME TO DO HORRIBLE THINGS. WHEN TOLD IT WAS A KING'S RE-SPONSIBILITY, I IGNORED A CURSE LAID UPON KOGYOKU.
WHEN TOLD I WAS UNFIT TO BE KING, I GREW ANGRY AND REFUSED TO ACCEPT IT.
I EVEN CUT OFF A FRIEND'S LEGS.

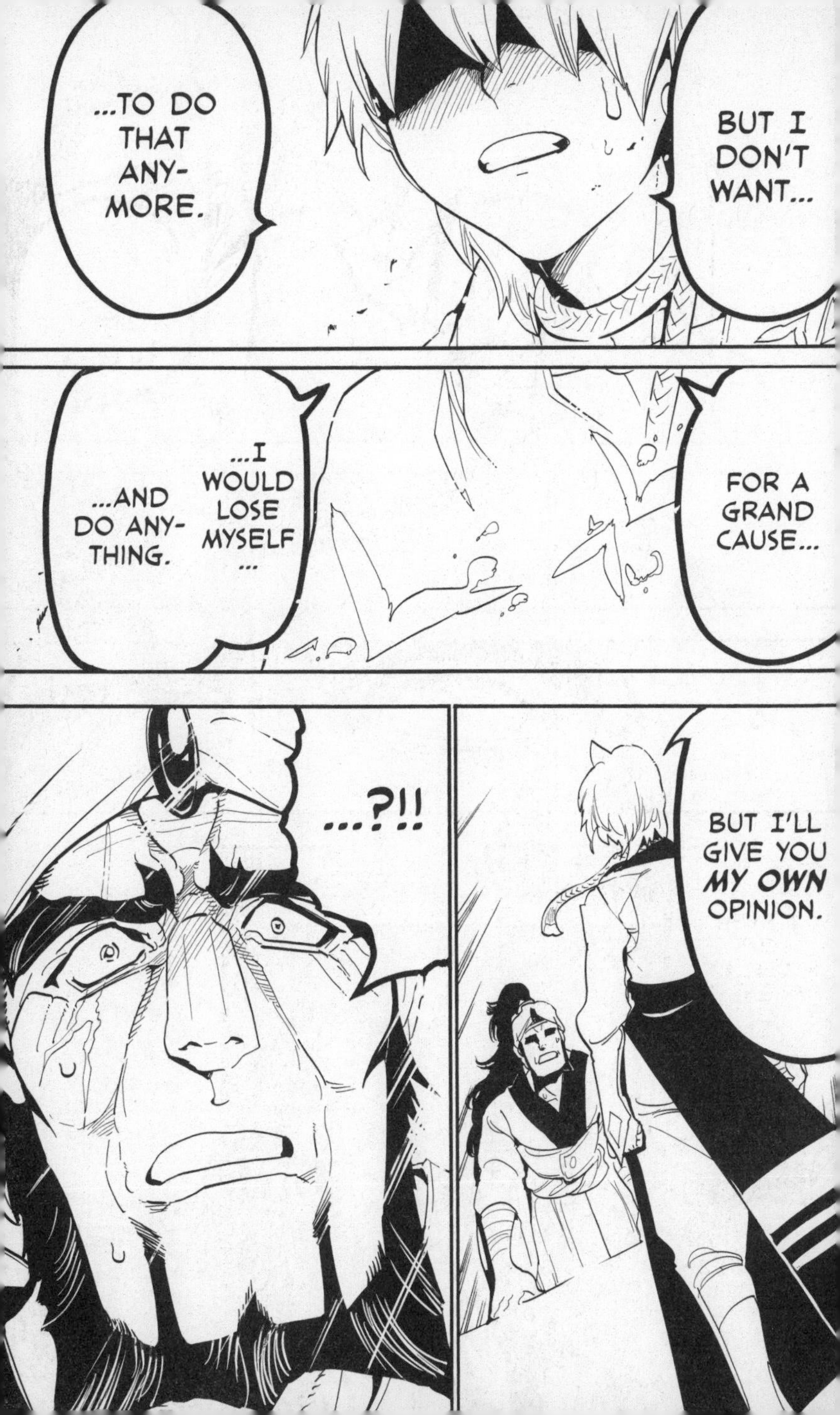
BUT I DON'T WANT...
...TO DO THAT ANYMORE.
FOR A GRAND CAUSE...
...I WOULD LOSE MYSELF...
...AND DO ANYTHING.
BUT I'LL GIVE YOU *MY OWN* OPINION.
...?!!

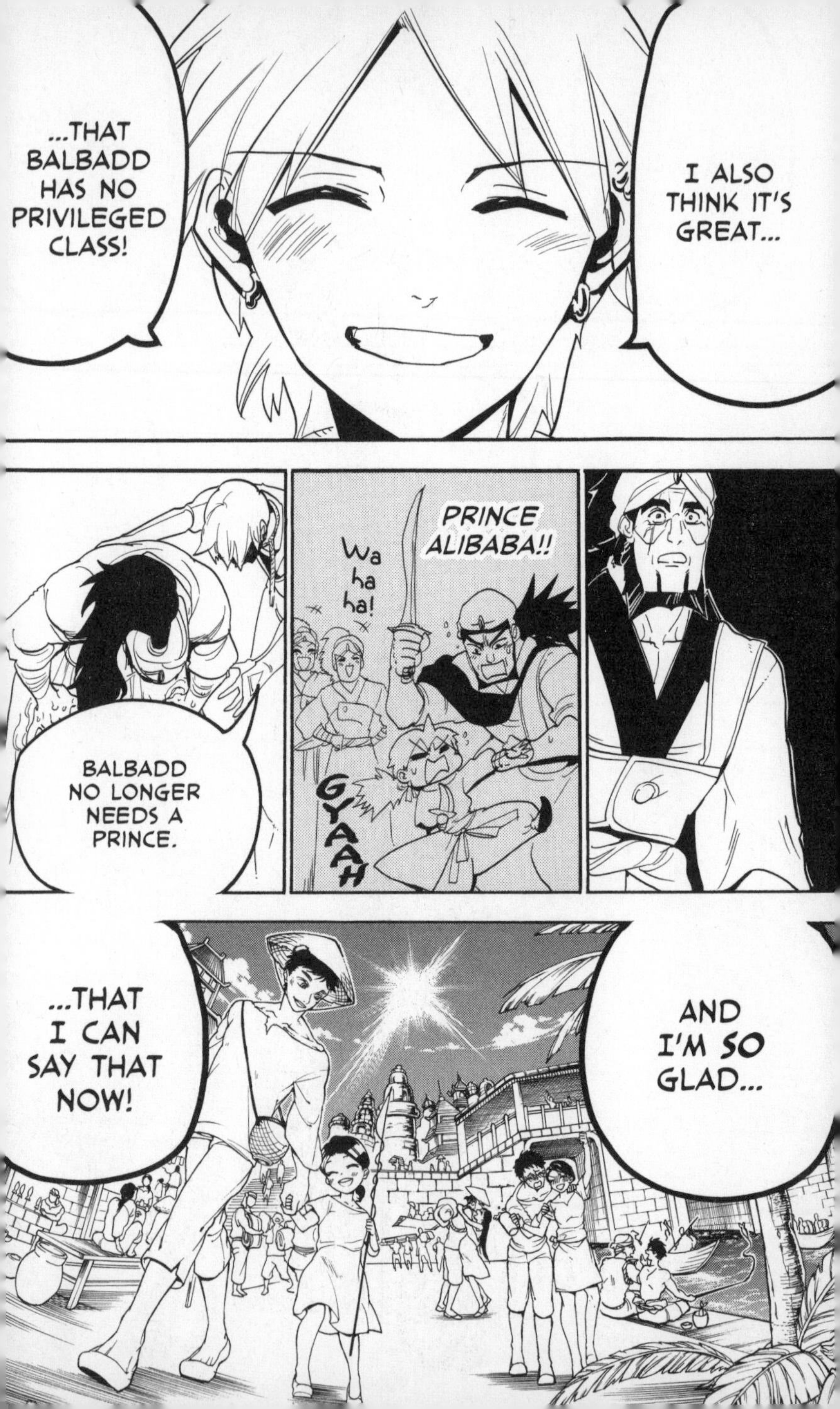
I ALSO THINK IT'S GREAT...
...THAT BALBADD HAS NO PRIVILEGED CLASS!
PRINCE ALIBABA!!
Wa ha ha!
GYAAH
BALBADD NO LONGER NEEDS A PRINCE.
AND I'M SO GLAD...
...THAT I CAN SAY THAT NOW!

Night 297: The Chance of Success

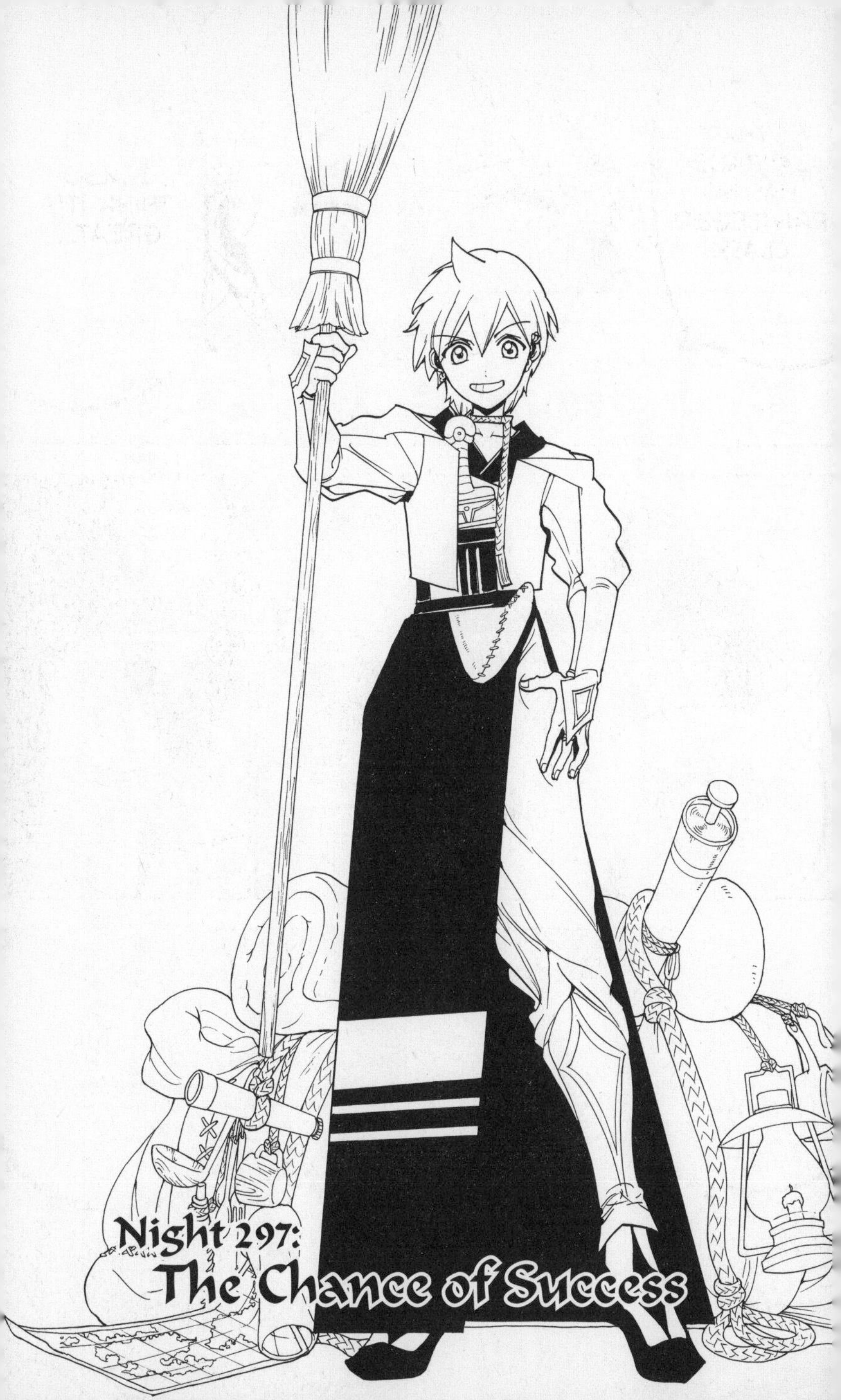

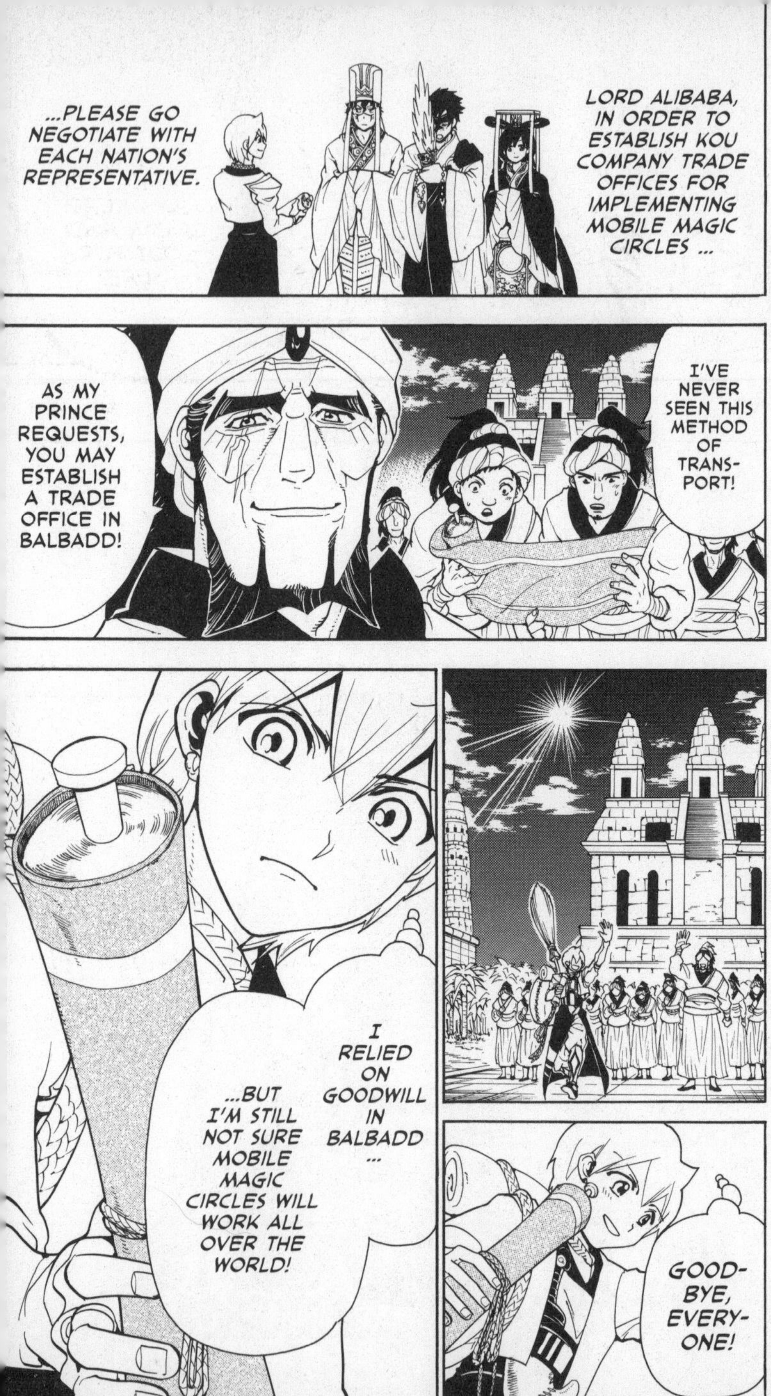
LORD ALIBABA, IN ORDER TO ESTABLISH KOU COMPANY TRADE OFFICES FOR IMPLEMENTING MOBILE MAGIC CIRCLES ...
...PLEASE GO NEGOTIATE WITH EACH NATION'S REPRESENTATIVE.
I'VE NEVER SEEN THIS METHOD OF TRANS-PORT!
AS MY PRINCE REQUESTS, YOU MAY ESTABLISH A TRADE OFFICE IN BALBADD!
GOOD-BYE, EVERY-ONE!
I RELIED ON GOODWILL IN BALBADD ...
...BUT I'M STILL NOT SURE MOBILE MAGIC CIRCLES WILL WORK ALL OVER THE WORLD!

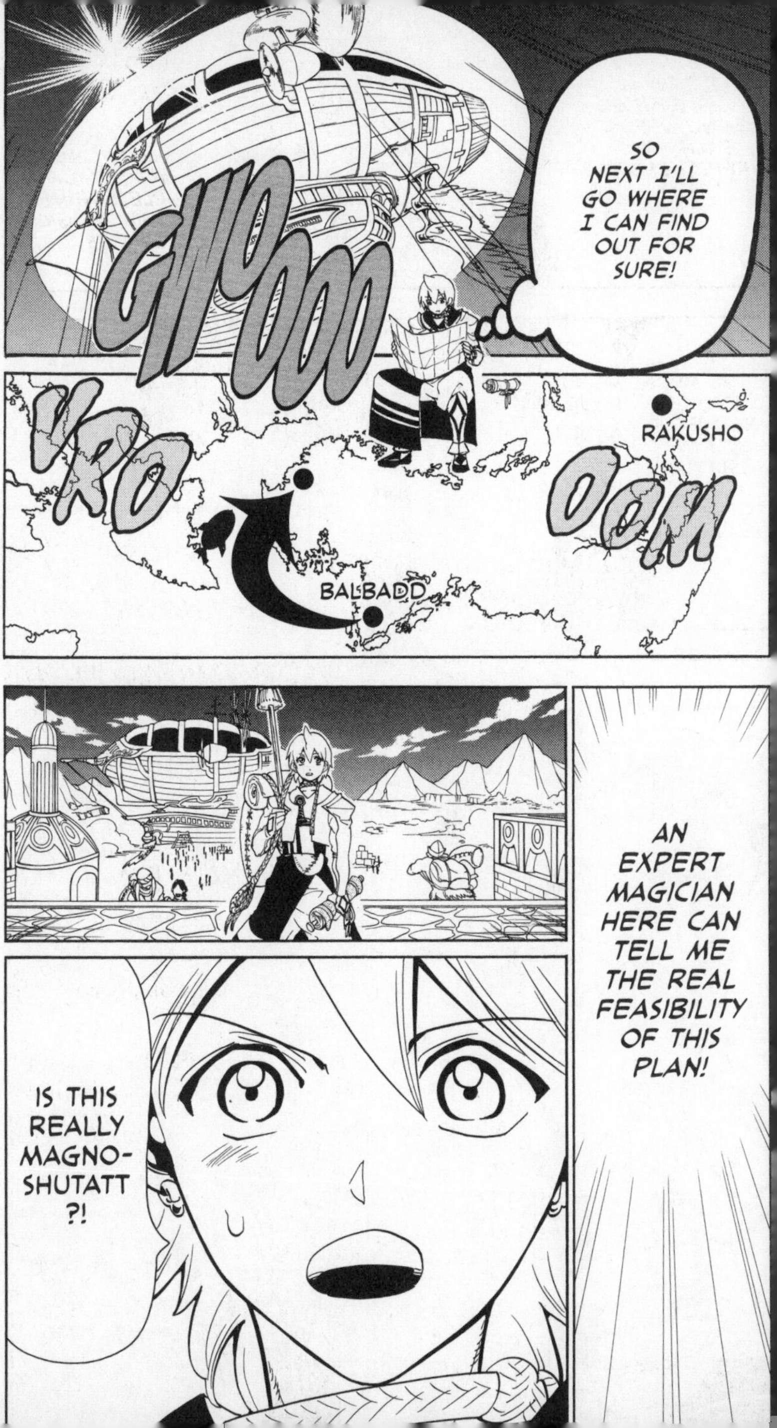
GWOOOO
SO NEXT I'LL GO WHERE I CAN FIND OUT FOR SURE!
RAKUSHO
VRO
OOM
BALBADD
AN EXPERT MAGICIAN HERE CAN TELL ME THE REAL FEASIBILITY OF THIS PLAN!
IS THIS REALLY MAGNO-SHUTATT?!

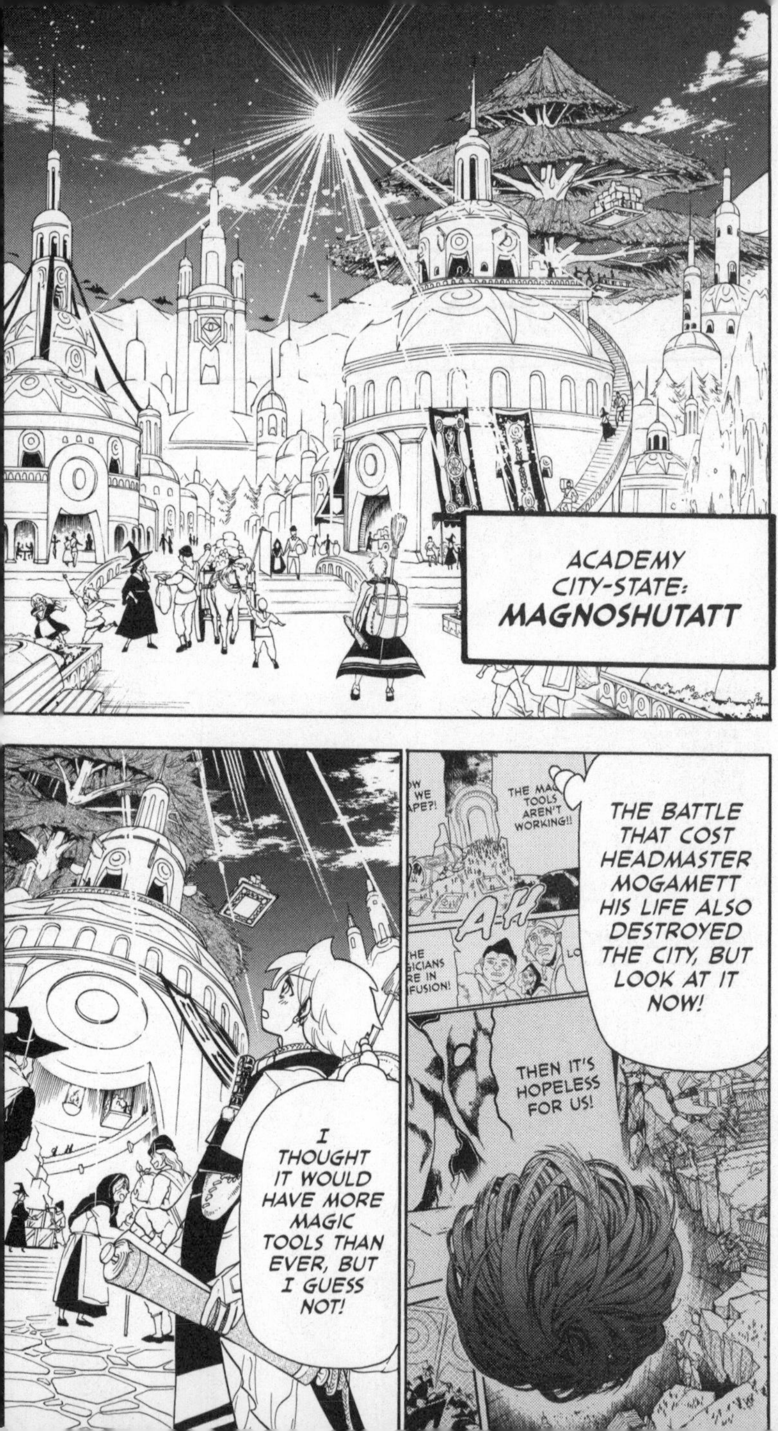
ACADEMY CITY-STATE: MAGNOSHUTATT
THE BATTLE THAT COST HEADMASTER MOGAMETT HIS LIFE ALSO DESTROYED THE CITY, BUT LOOK AT IT NOW!
TOOLS AREN'T WORKING!!
A-H
THEN IT'S HOPELESS FOR US!
I THOUGHT IT WOULD HAVE MORE MAGIC TOOLS THAN EVER, BUT I GUESS NOT!

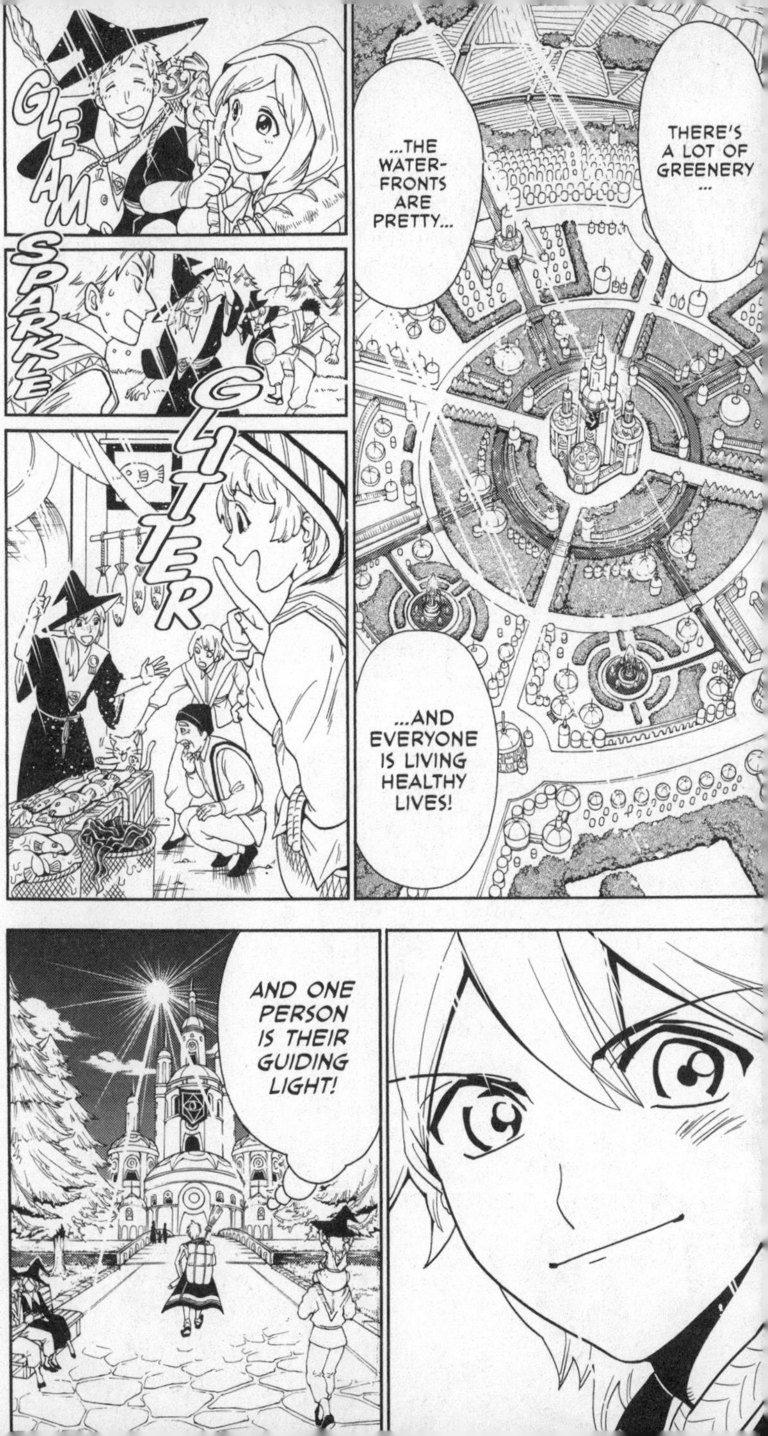
THERE'S A LOT OF GREENERY ...
...THE WATER-FRONTS ARE PRETTY...
...AND EVERYONE IS LIVING HEALTHY LIVES!
GLEAM
SPARKLE
GLITTER
AND ONE PERSON IS THEIR GUIDING LIGHT!

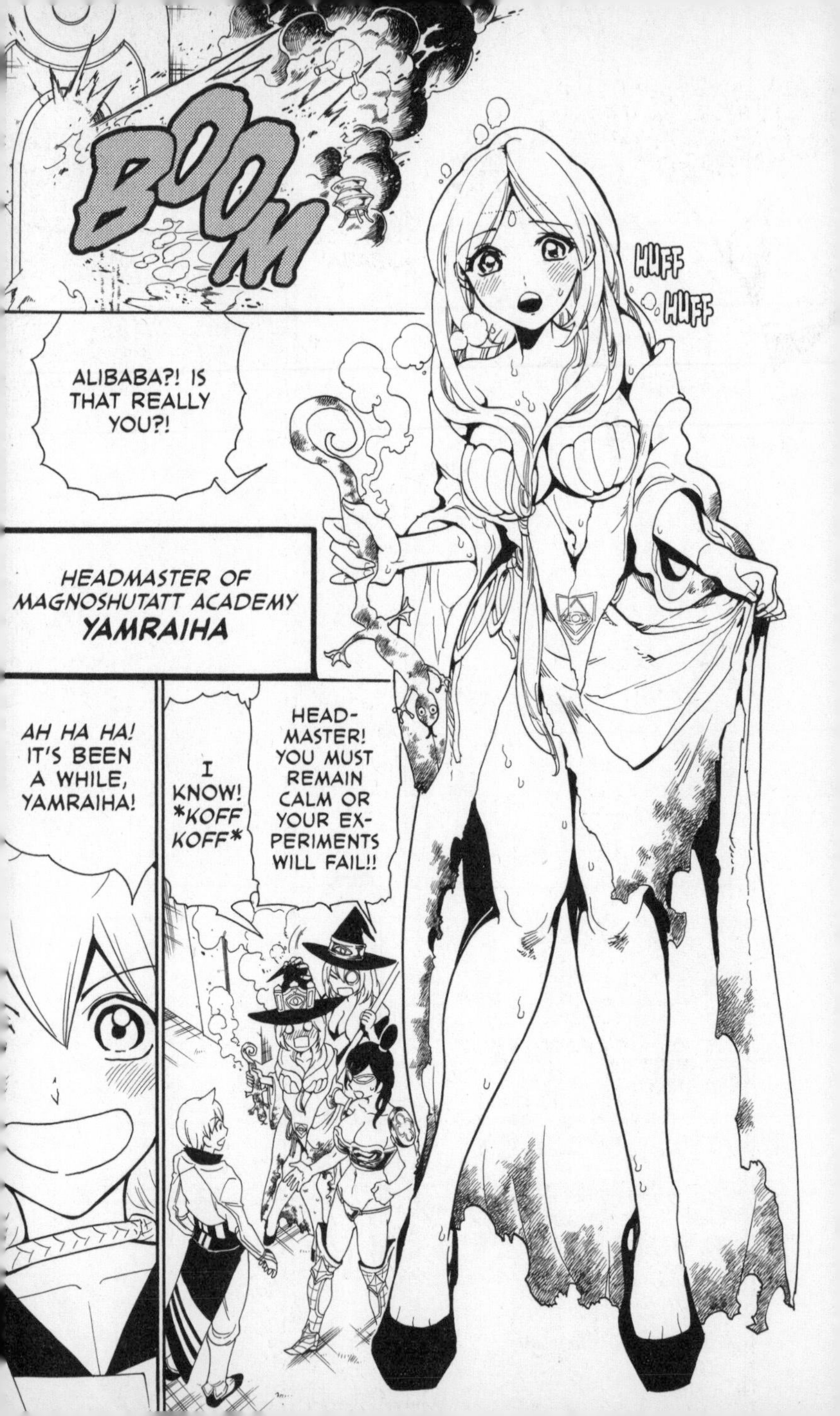
BOOM
HUFF HUFF
ALIBABA?! IS THAT REALLY YOU?!
HEADMASTER OF MAGNOSHUTATT ACADEMY
YAMRAIHA
HEAD-MASTER! YOU MUST REMAIN CALM OR YOUR EX-PERIMENTS WILL FAIL!!
I KNOW! *KOFF KOFF*
AH HA HA! IT'S BEEN A WHILE, YAMRAIHA!

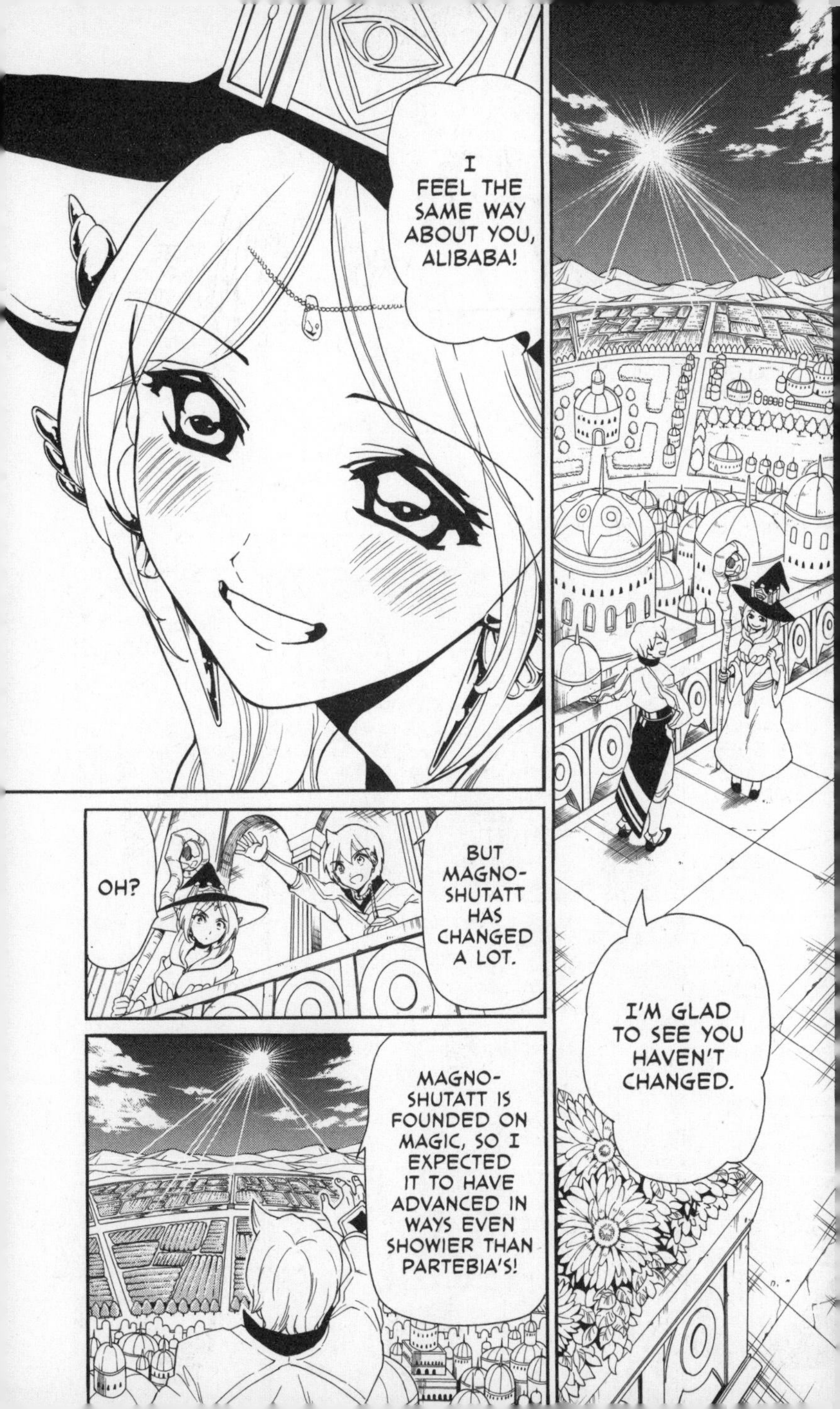
I'M GLAD TO SEE YOU HAVEN'T CHANGED.
I FEEL THE SAME WAY ABOUT YOU, ALIBABA!
BUT MAGNOSHUTATT HAS CHANGED A LOT.
OH?
MAGNOSHUTATT IS FOUNDED ON MAGIC, SO I EXPECTED IT TO HAVE ADVANCED IN WAYS EVEN SHOWIER THAN PARTEBIA'S!

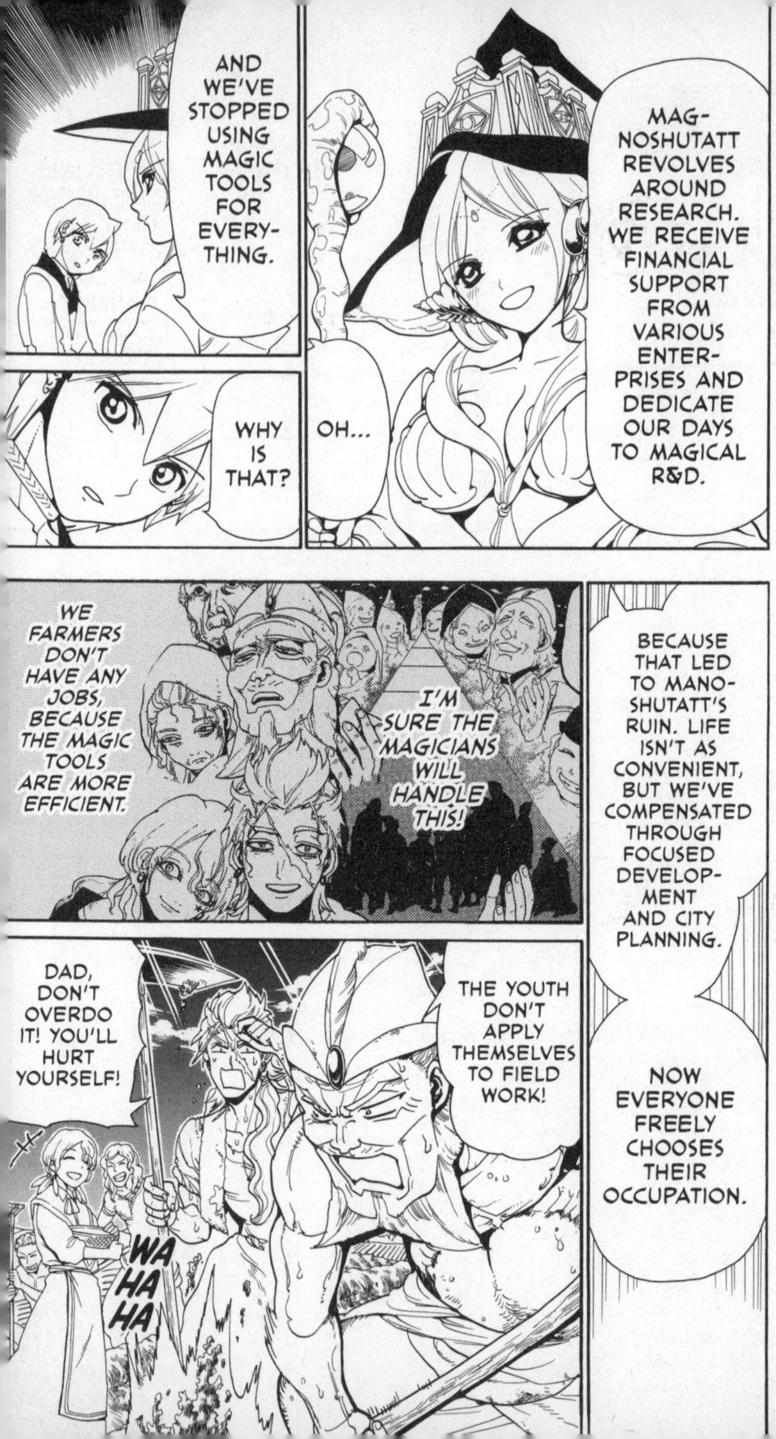
MAG-NOSHUTATT REVOLVES AROUND RESEARCH. WE RECEIVE FINANCIAL SUPPORT FROM VARIOUS ENTER-PRISES AND DEDICATE OUR DAYS TO MAGICAL R&D.
OH...
AND WE'VE STOPPED USING MAGIC TOOLS FOR EVERY-THING.
WHY IS THAT?
BECAUSE THAT LED TO MANO-SHUTATT'S RUIN. LIFE ISN'T AS CONVENIENT, BUT WE'VE COMPENSATED THROUGH FOCUSED DEVELOP-MENT AND CITY PLANNING.
NOW EVERYONE FREELY CHOOSES THEIR OCCUPATION.
WE FARMERS DON'T HAVE ANY JOBS, BECAUSE THE MAGIC TOOLS ARE MORE EFFICIENT.
I'M SURE THE MAGICIANS WILL HANDLE THIS!
THE YOUTH DON'T APPLY THEMSELVES TO FIELD WORK!
DAD, DON'T OVERDO IT! YOU'LL HURT YOURSELF!
WA HA HA

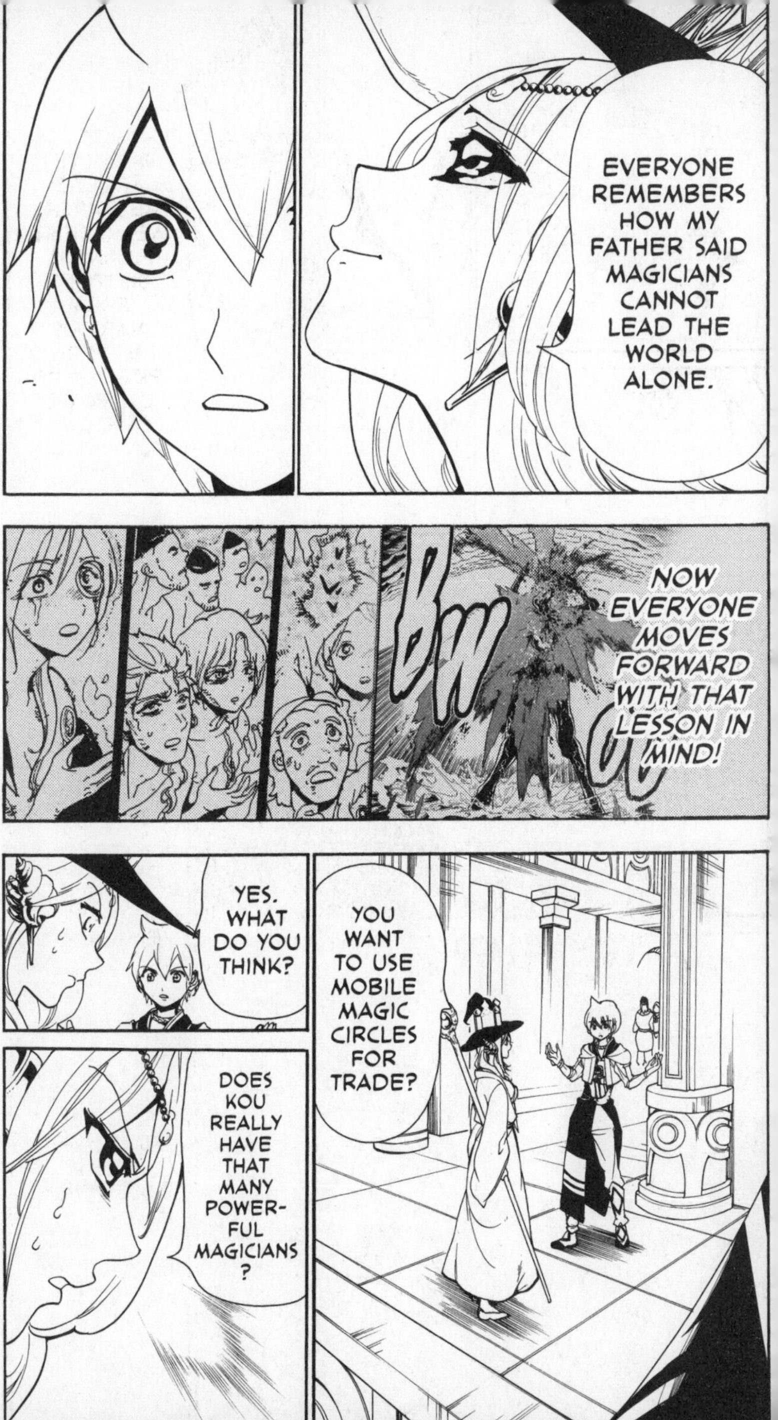
EVERYONE REMEMBERS HOW MY FATHER SAID MAGICIANS CANNOT LEAD THE WORLD ALONE.
NOW EVERYONE MOVES FORWARD WITH THAT LESSON IN MIND!
YOU WANT TO USE MOBILE MAGIC CIRCLES FOR TRADE?
YES. WHAT DO YOU THINK?
DOES KOU REALLY HAVE THAT MANY POWERFUL MAGICIANS?

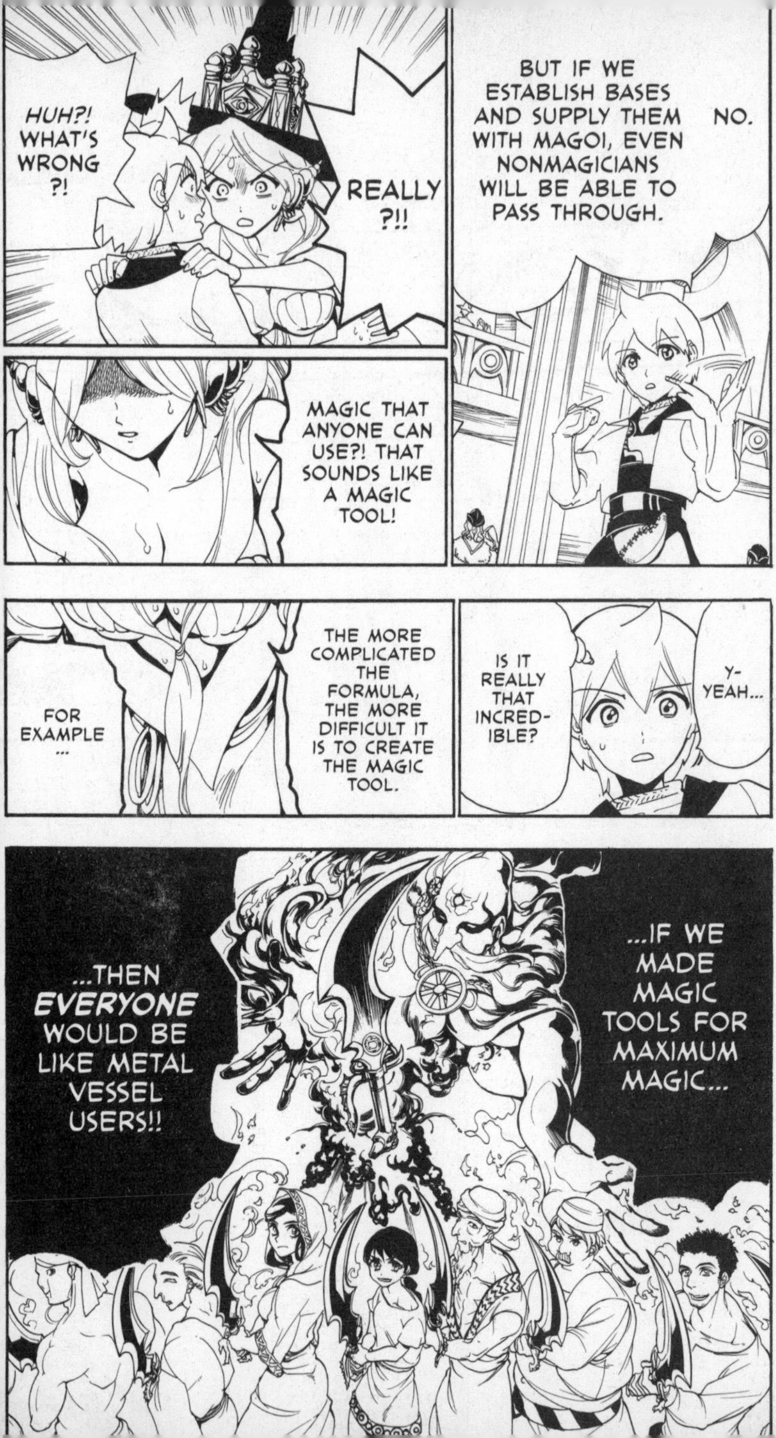
NO.
BUT IF WE ESTABLISH BASES AND SUPPLY THEM WITH MAGOI, EVEN NONMAGICIANS WILL BE ABLE TO PASS THROUGH.
REALLY ?!!
HUH?! WHAT'S WRONG ?!
MAGIC THAT ANYONE CAN USE?! THAT SOUNDS LIKE A MAGIC TOOL!
Y- YEAH...
IS IT REALLY THAT INCRED- IBLE?
THE MORE COMPLICATED THE FORMULA, THE MORE DIFFICULT IT IS TO CREATE THE MAGIC TOOL.
FOR EXAMPLE ...
...IF WE MADE MAGIC TOOLS FOR MAXIMUM MAGIC...
...THEN *EVERYONE* WOULD BE LIKE METAL VESSEL USERS!!

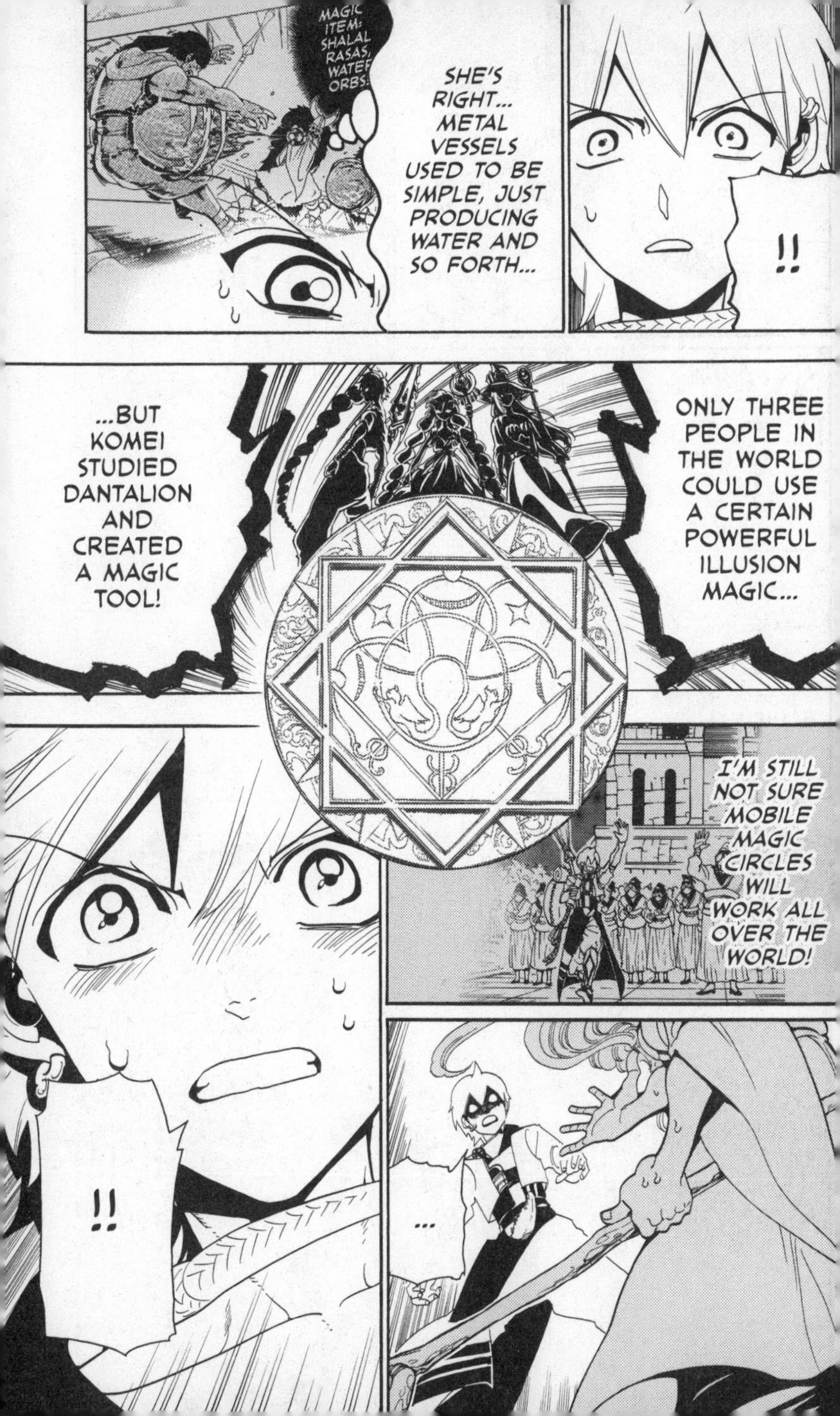
!!
SHE'S RIGHT... METAL VESSELS USED TO BE SIMPLE, JUST PRODUCING WATER AND SO FORTH...
MAGIC ITEM: SHALAL RASAS, WATER ORBS!
ONLY THREE PEOPLE IN THE WORLD COULD USE A CERTAIN POWERFUL ILLUSION MAGIC...
...BUT KOMEI STUDIED DANTALION AND CREATED A MAGIC TOOL!
I'M STILL NOT SURE MOBILE MAGIC CIRCLES WILL WORK ALL OVER THE WORLD!
...
!!

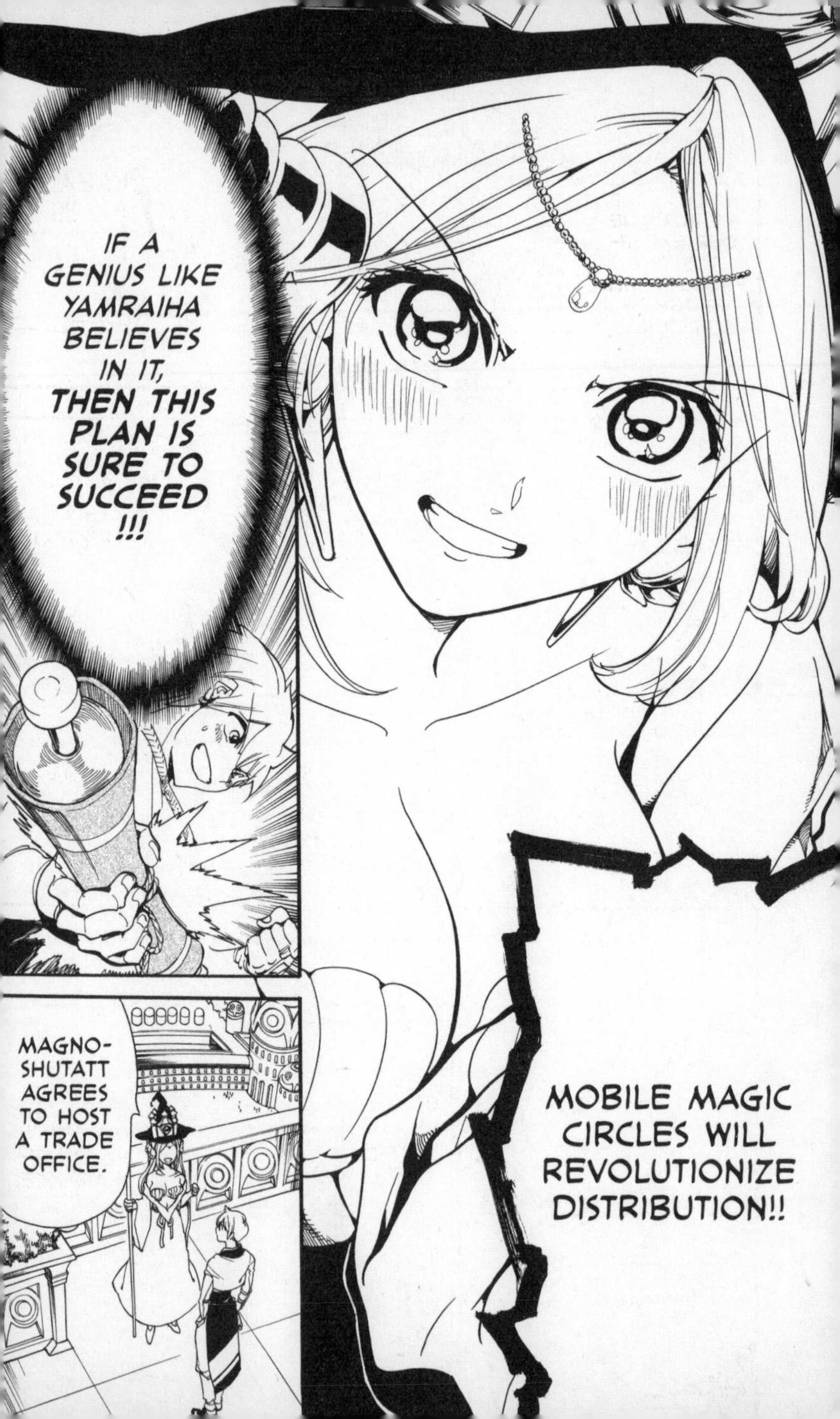
MOBILE MAGIC CIRCLES WILL REVOLUTIONIZE DISTRIBUTION!!
IF A GENIUS LIKE YAMRAIHA BELIEVES IN IT, THEN THIS PLAN IS SURE TO SUCCEED!!!
MAGNO-SHUTATT AGREES TO HOST A TRADE OFFICE.

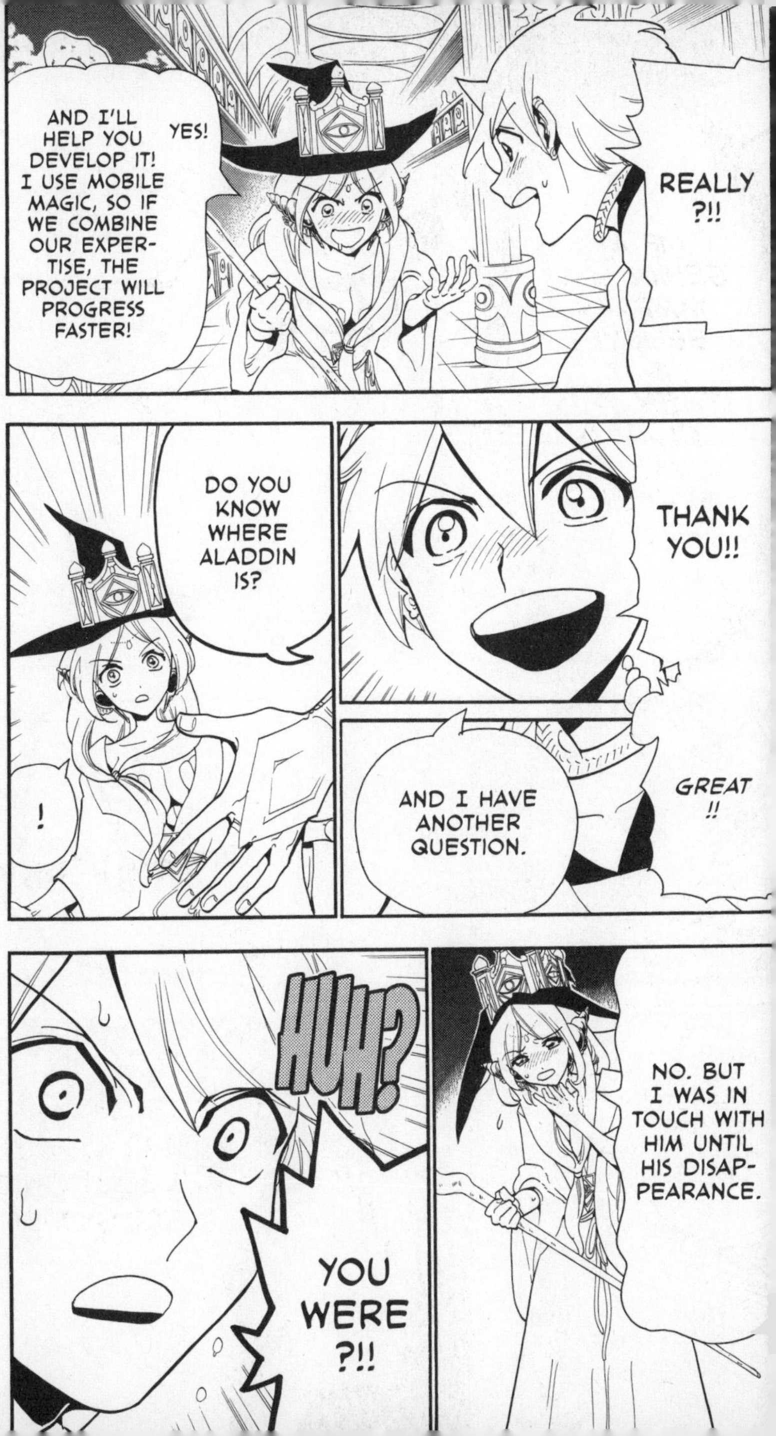
REALLY ?!!
YES!
AND I'LL HELP YOU DEVELOP IT! I USE MOBILE MAGIC, SO IF WE COMBINE OUR EXPERTISE, THE PROJECT WILL PROGRESS FASTER!
THANK YOU!!
GREAT !!
AND I HAVE ANOTHER QUESTION.
DO YOU KNOW WHERE ALADDIN IS?
!
NO. BUT I WAS IN TOUCH WITH HIM UNTIL HIS DISAPPEARANCE.
HUH?
YOU WERE ?!!

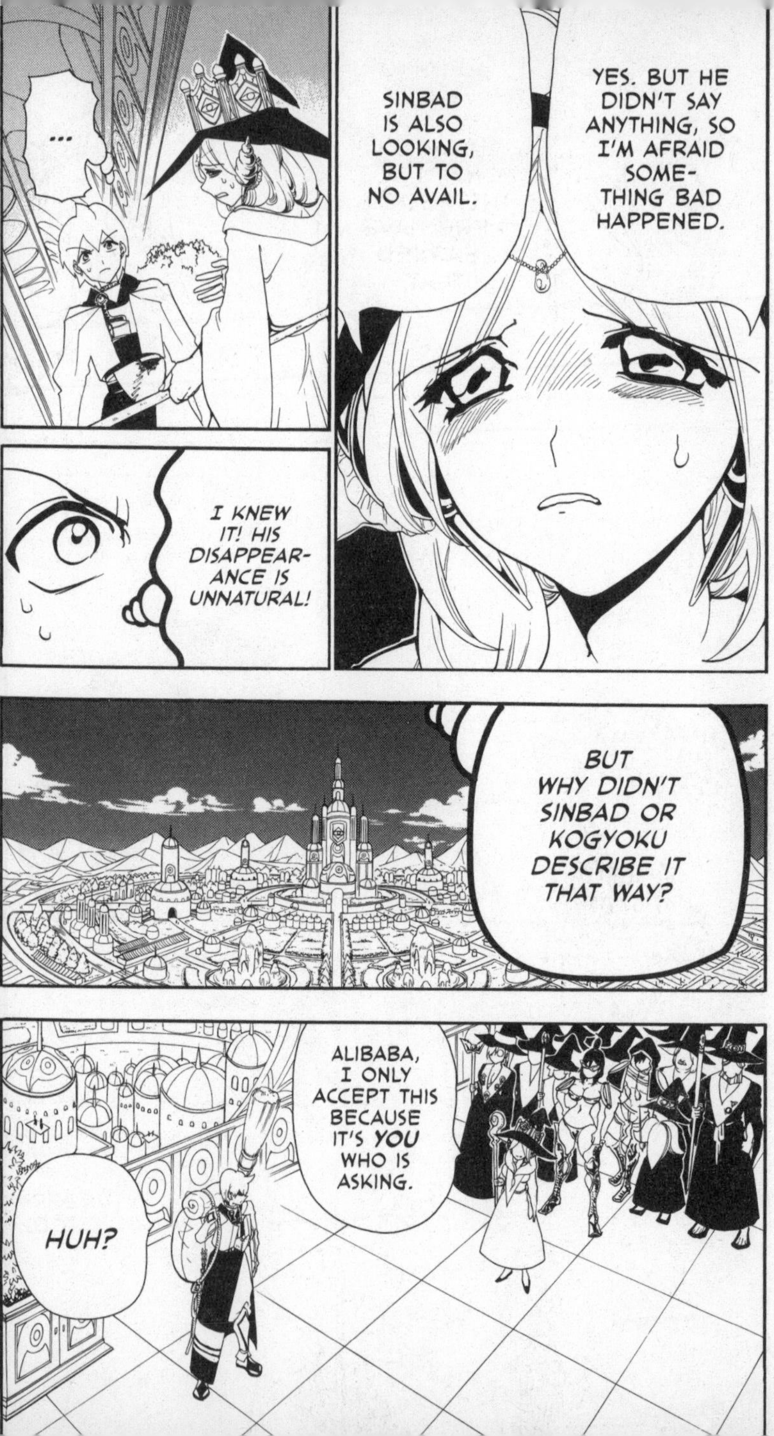
YES. BUT HE DIDN'T SAY ANYTHING, SO I'M AFRAID SOME-THING BAD HAPPENED.
SINBAD IS ALSO LOOKING, BUT TO NO AVAIL.
...
I KNEW IT! HIS DISAPPEAR-ANCE IS UNNATURAL!
BUT WHY DIDN'T SINBAD OR KOGYOKU DESCRIBE IT THAT WAY?
ALIBABA, I ONLY ACCEPT THIS BECAUSE IT'S YOU WHO IS ASKING.
HUH?

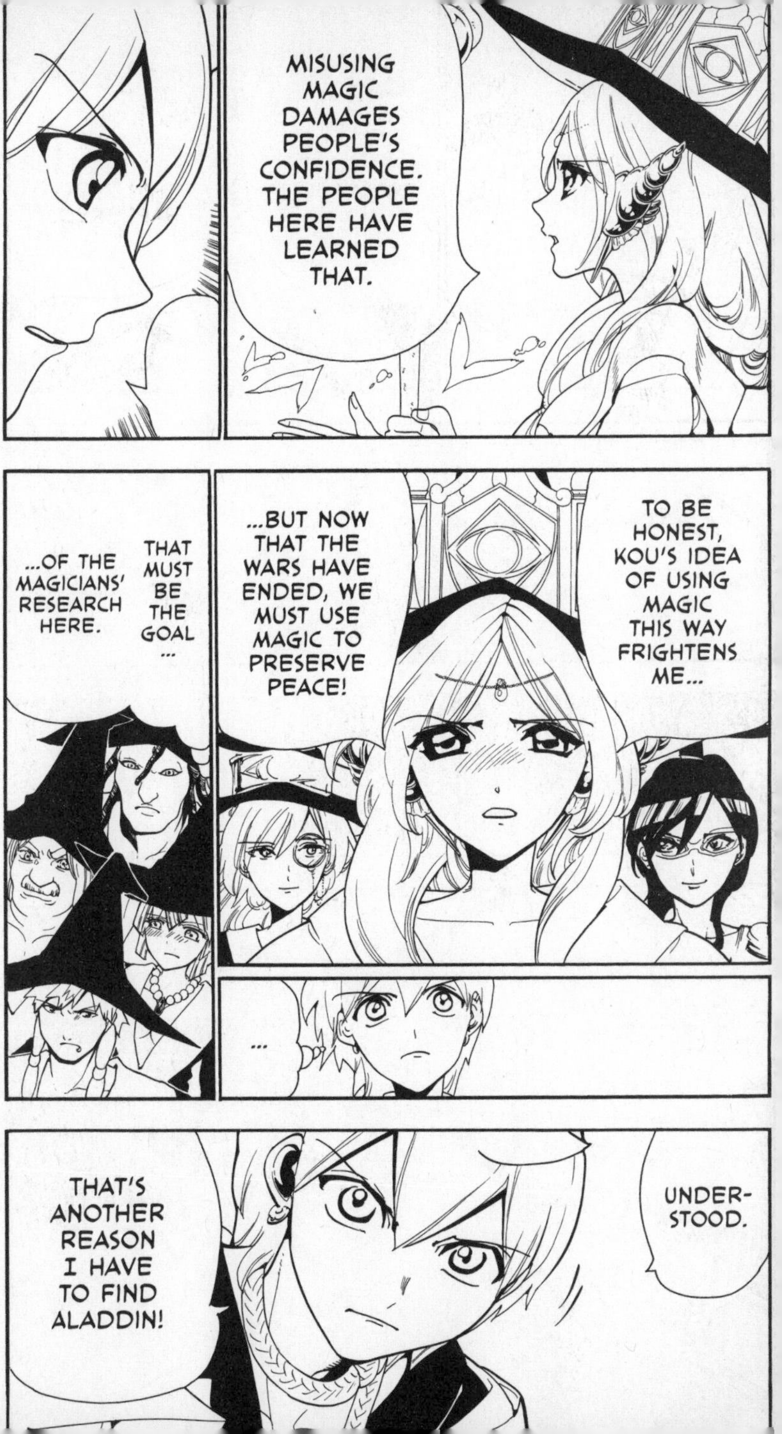
MISUSING MAGIC DAMAGES PEOPLE'S CONFIDENCE. THE PEOPLE HERE HAVE LEARNED THAT.
TO BE HONEST, KOU'S IDEA OF USING MAGIC THIS WAY FRIGHTENS ME...
...BUT NOW THAT THE WARS HAVE ENDED, WE MUST USE MAGIC TO PRESERVE PEACE!
...
THAT MUST BE THE GOAL...
...OF THE MAGICIANS' RESEARCH HERE.
UNDER-STOOD.
THAT'S ANOTHER REASON I HAVE TO FIND ALADDIN!

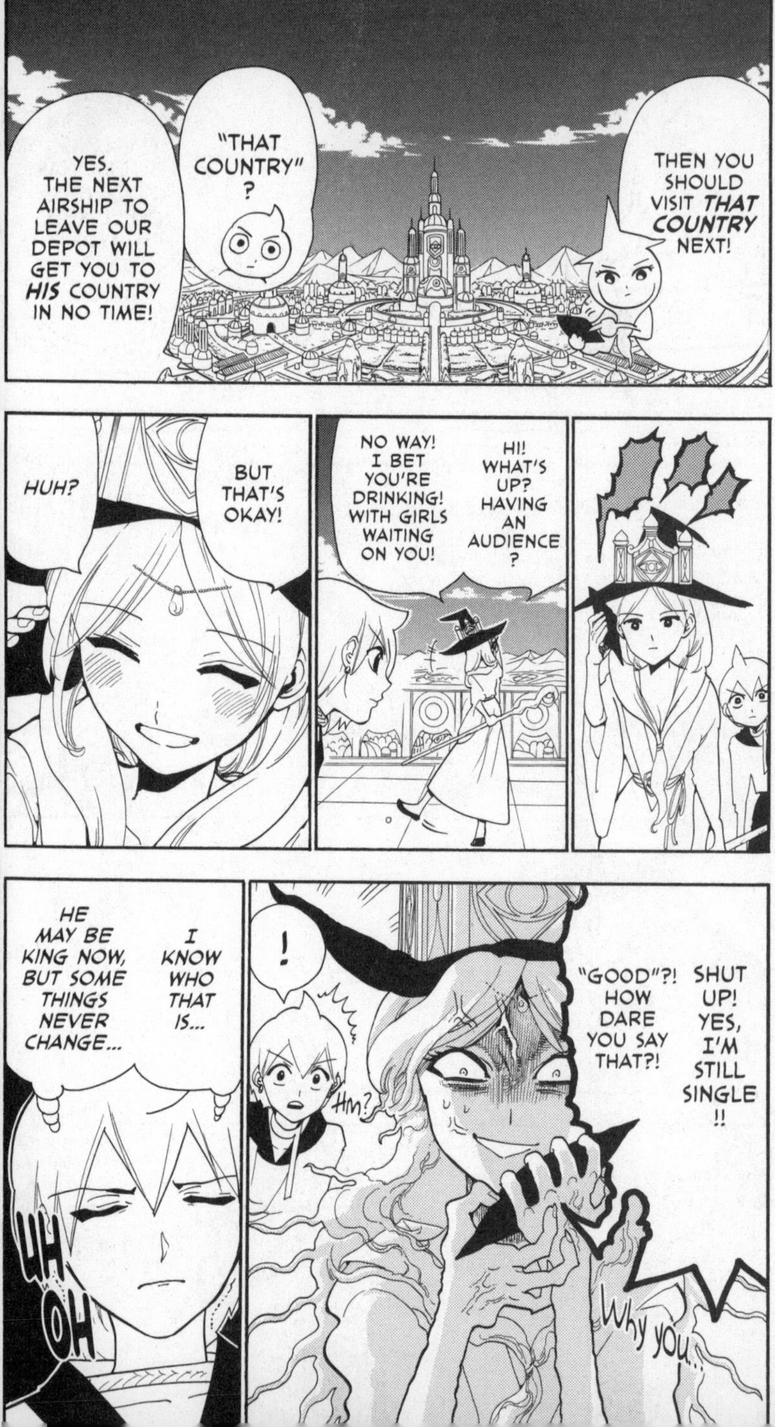
THEN YOU SHOULD VISIT *THAT COUNTRY* NEXT!
"THAT COUNTRY"?
YES. THE NEXT AIRSHIP TO LEAVE OUR DEPOT WILL GET YOU TO *HIS* COUNTRY IN NO TIME!
HI! WHAT'S UP? HAVING AN AUDIENCE?
NO WAY! I BET YOU'RE DRINKING! WITH GIRLS WAITING ON YOU!
BUT THAT'S OKAY!
HUH?
SHUT UP! YES, I'M STILL SINGLE!!
"GOOD"?! HOW DARE YOU SAY THAT?!
!
Hm?
Why you...
I KNOW WHO THAT IS...
HE MAY BE KING NOW, BUT SOME THINGS NEVER CHANGE...
UH OH

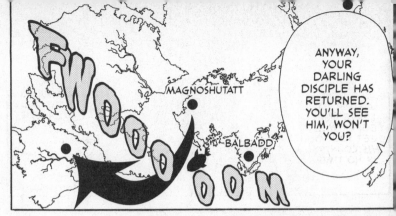

ANYWAY, YOUR DARLING DISCIPLE HAS RETURNED. YOU'LL SEE HIM, WON'T YOU?

MAGNOSHUTATT

BALBADD

FWOOOOOOM

THE KINGDOM OF ELIOHAPT

CHATTER

CHATTER

DADUM

DOOOM

HELLO, ALIBABA!

M-MASTER ...

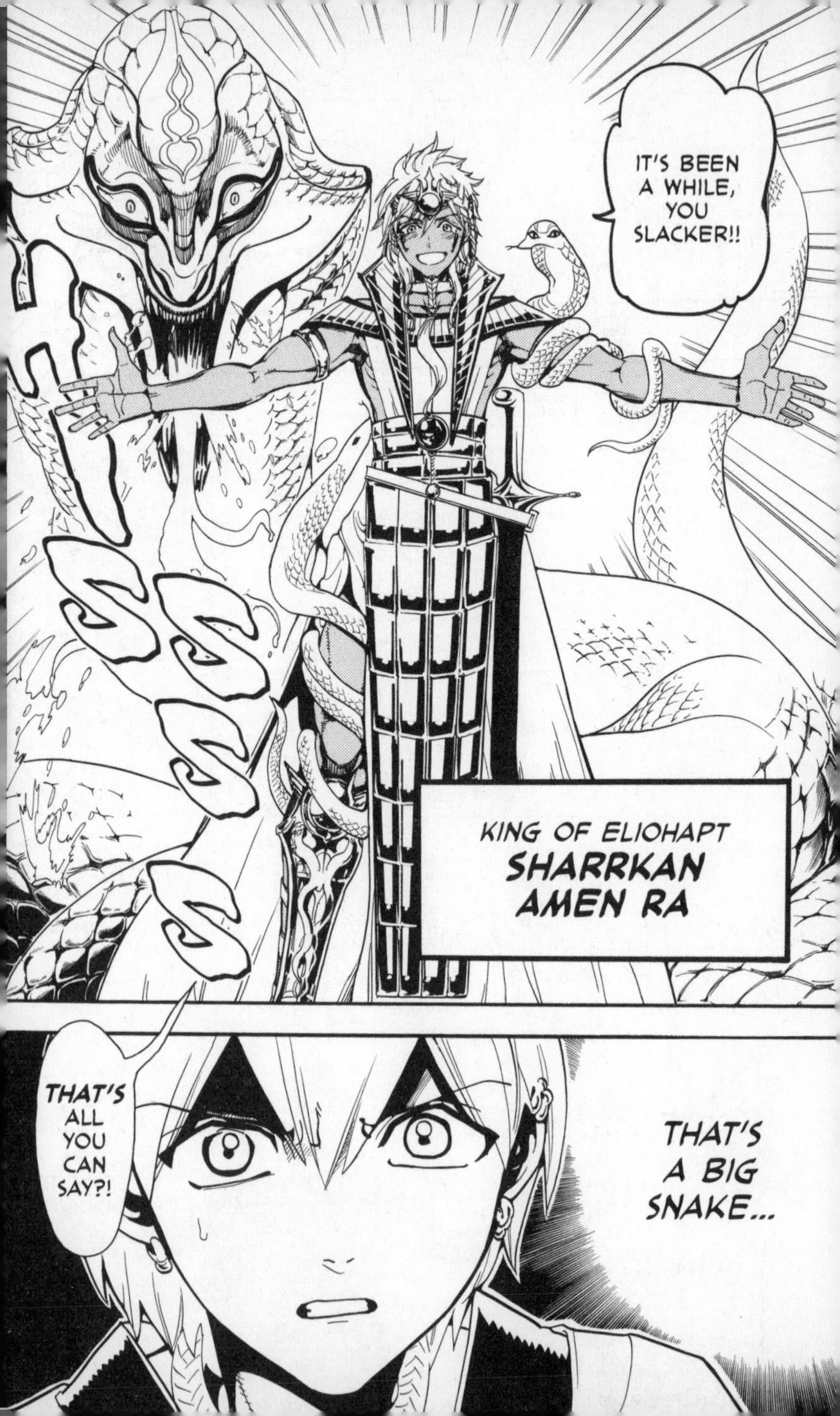
IT'S BEEN A WHILE, YOU SLACKER!!
KING OF ELIOHAPT
SHARRKAN AMEN RA
THAT'S A BIG SNAKE...
THAT'S ALL YOU CAN SAY?!

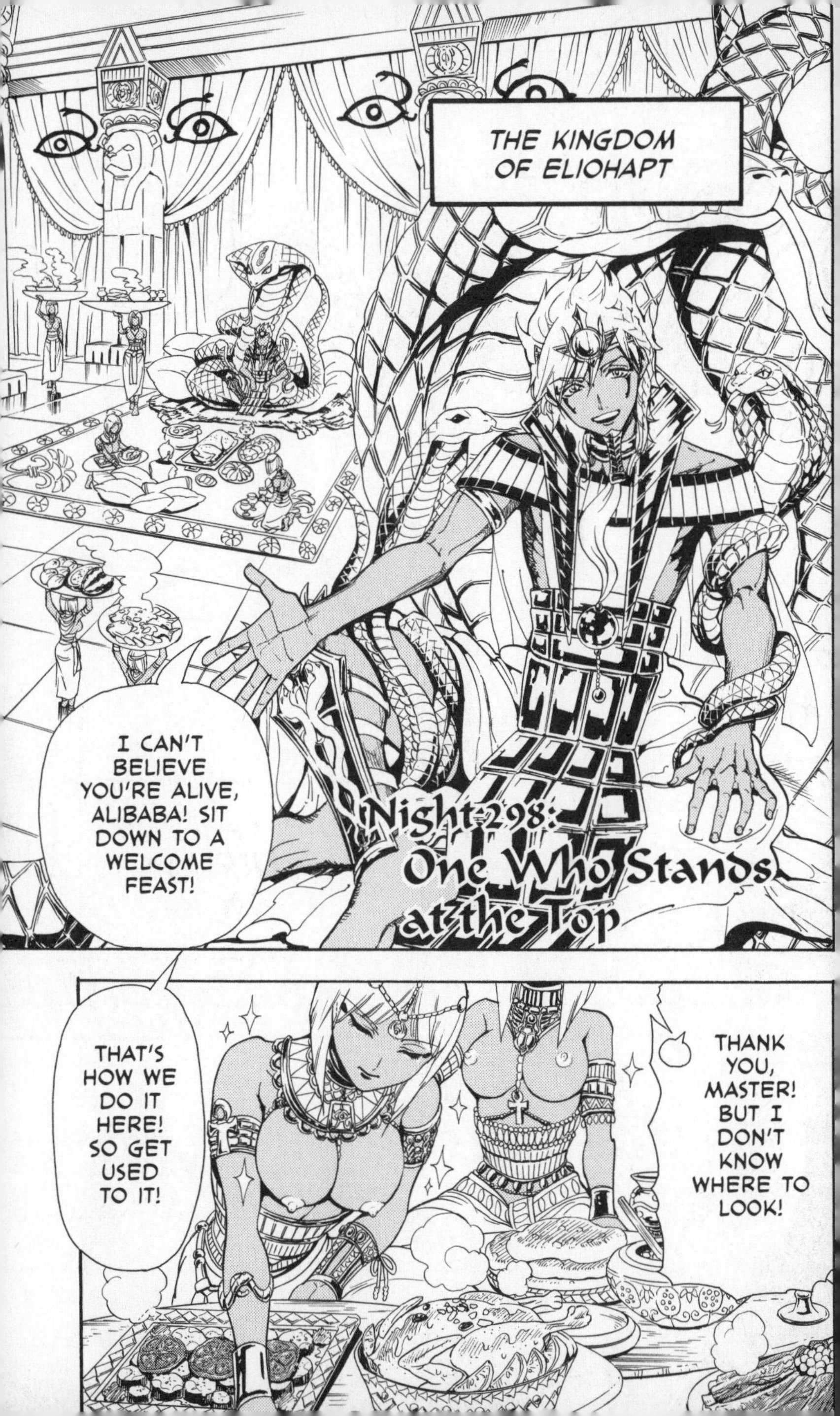
THE KINGDOM OF ELIOHAPT
I CAN'T BELIEVE YOU'RE ALIVE, ALIBABA! SIT DOWN TO A WELCOME FEAST!
Night 298: One Who Stands at the Top
THANK YOU, MASTER! BUT I DON'T KNOW WHERE TO LOOK!
THAT'S HOW WE DO IT HERE! SO GET USED TO IT!

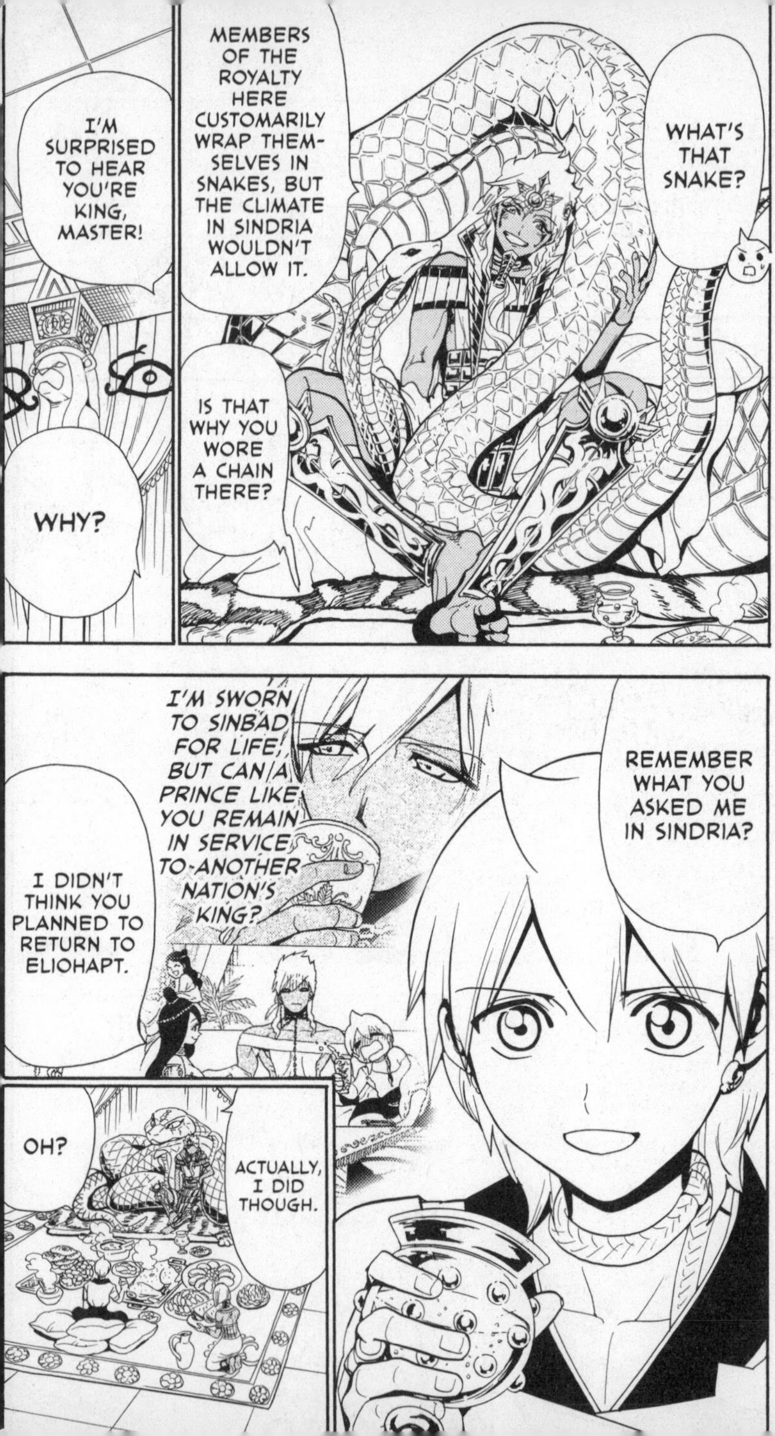
WHAT'S THAT SNAKE?
MEMBERS OF THE ROYALTY HERE CUSTOMARILY WRAP THEM-SELVES IN SNAKES, BUT THE CLIMATE IN SINDRIA WOULDN'T ALLOW IT.
IS THAT WHY YOU WORE A CHAIN THERE?
I'M SURPRISED TO HEAR YOU'RE KING, MASTER!
WHY?
REMEMBER WHAT YOU ASKED ME IN SINDRIA?
I'M SWORN TO SINBAD FOR LIFE, BUT CAN A PRINCE LIKE YOU REMAIN IN SERVICE TO ANOTHER NATION'S KING?
I DIDN'T THINK YOU PLANNED TO RETURN TO ELIOHAPT.
ACTUALLY, I DID THOUGH.
OH?

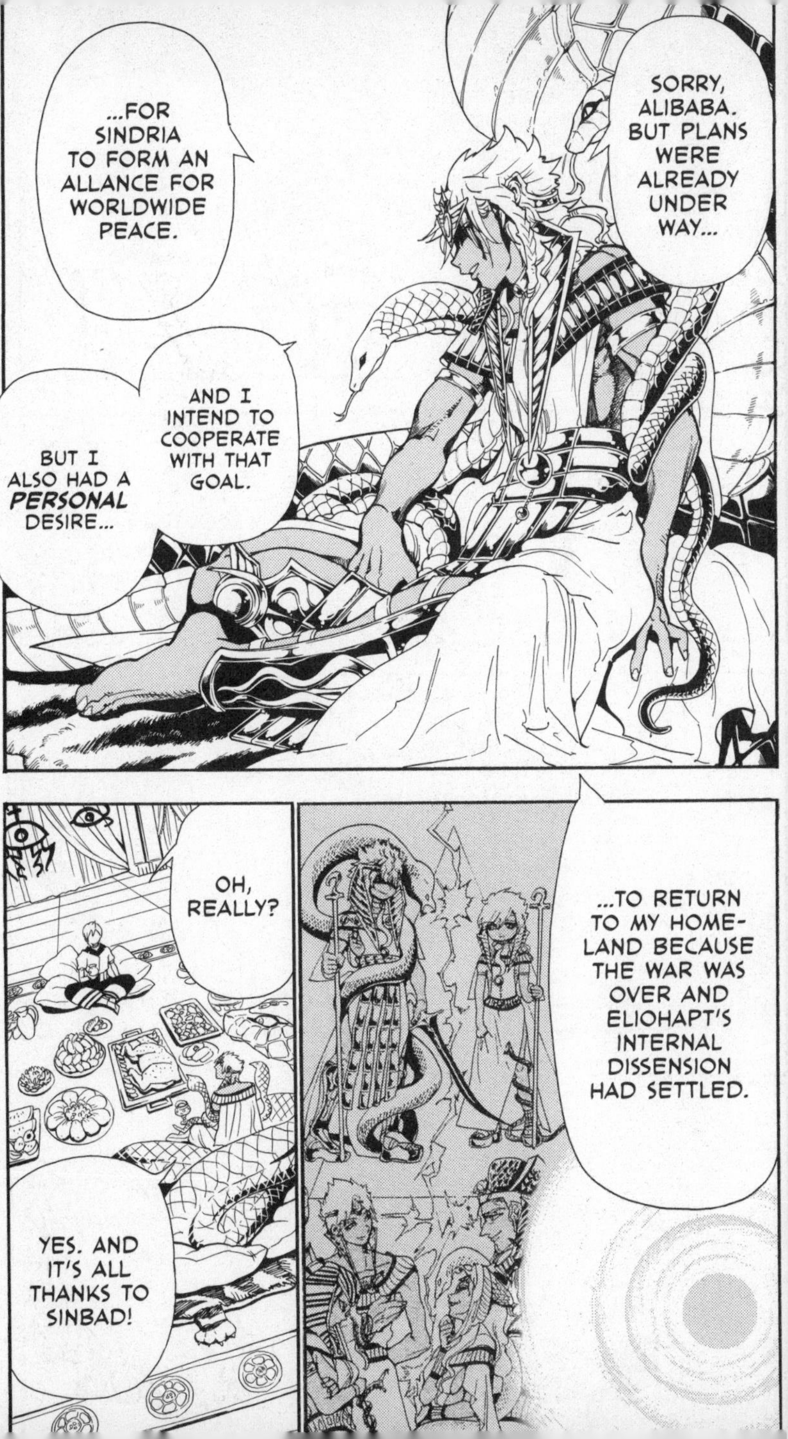
SORRY, ALIBABA. BUT PLANS WERE ALREADY UNDER WAY...
...FOR SINDRIA TO FORM AN ALLANCE FOR WORLDWIDE PEACE.
AND I INTEND TO COOPERATE WITH THAT GOAL.
BUT I ALSO HAD A *PERSONAL* DESIRE...
...TO RETURN TO MY HOME-LAND BECAUSE THE WAR WAS OVER AND ELIOHAPT'S INTERNAL DISSENSION HAD SETTLED.
OH, REALLY?
YES. AND IT'S ALL THANKS TO SINBAD!

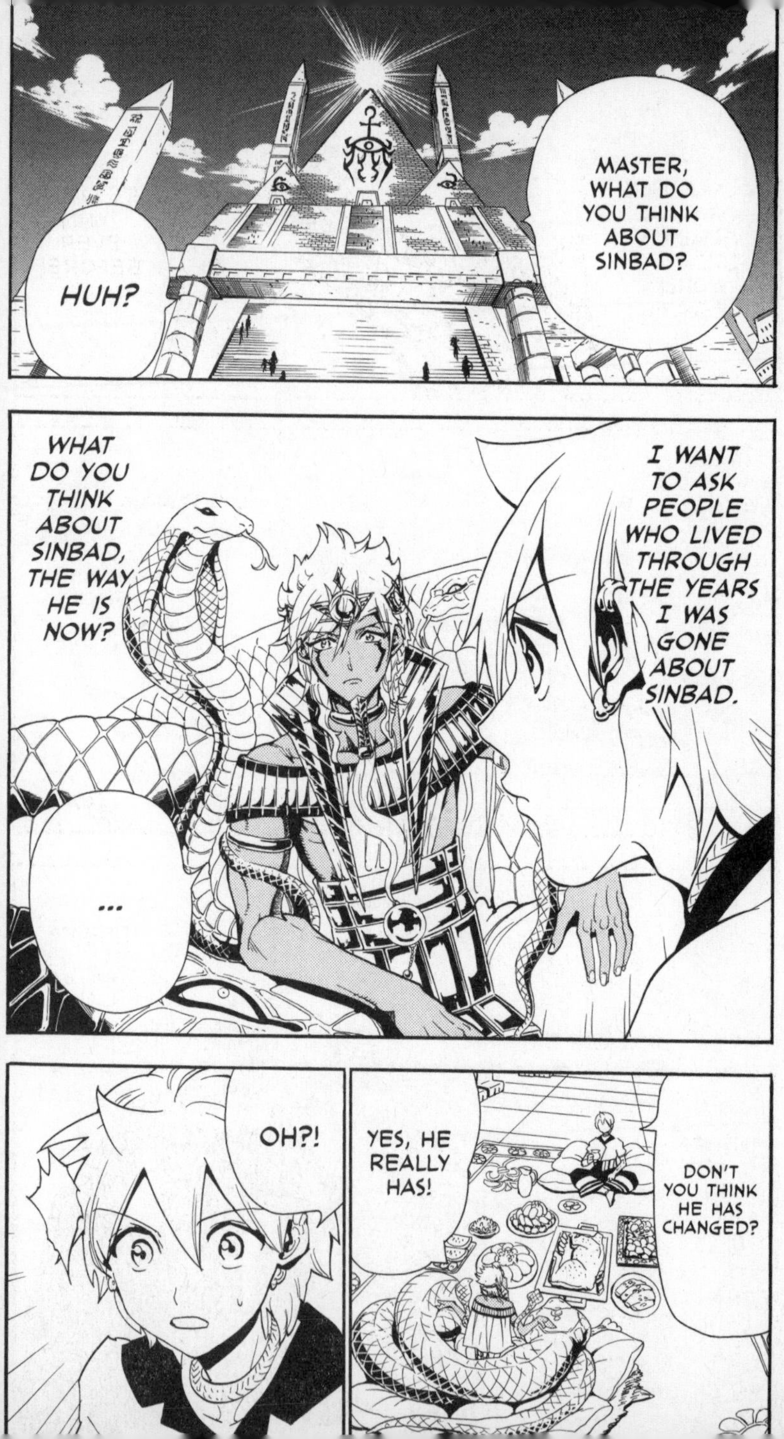
MASTER, WHAT DO YOU THINK ABOUT SINBAD?
HUH?
I WANT TO ASK PEOPLE WHO LIVED THROUGH THE YEARS I WAS GONE ABOUT SINBAD.
WHAT DO YOU THINK ABOUT SINBAD, THE WAY HE IS NOW?
...
DON'T YOU THINK HE HAS CHANGED?
YES, HE REALLY HAS!
OH?!

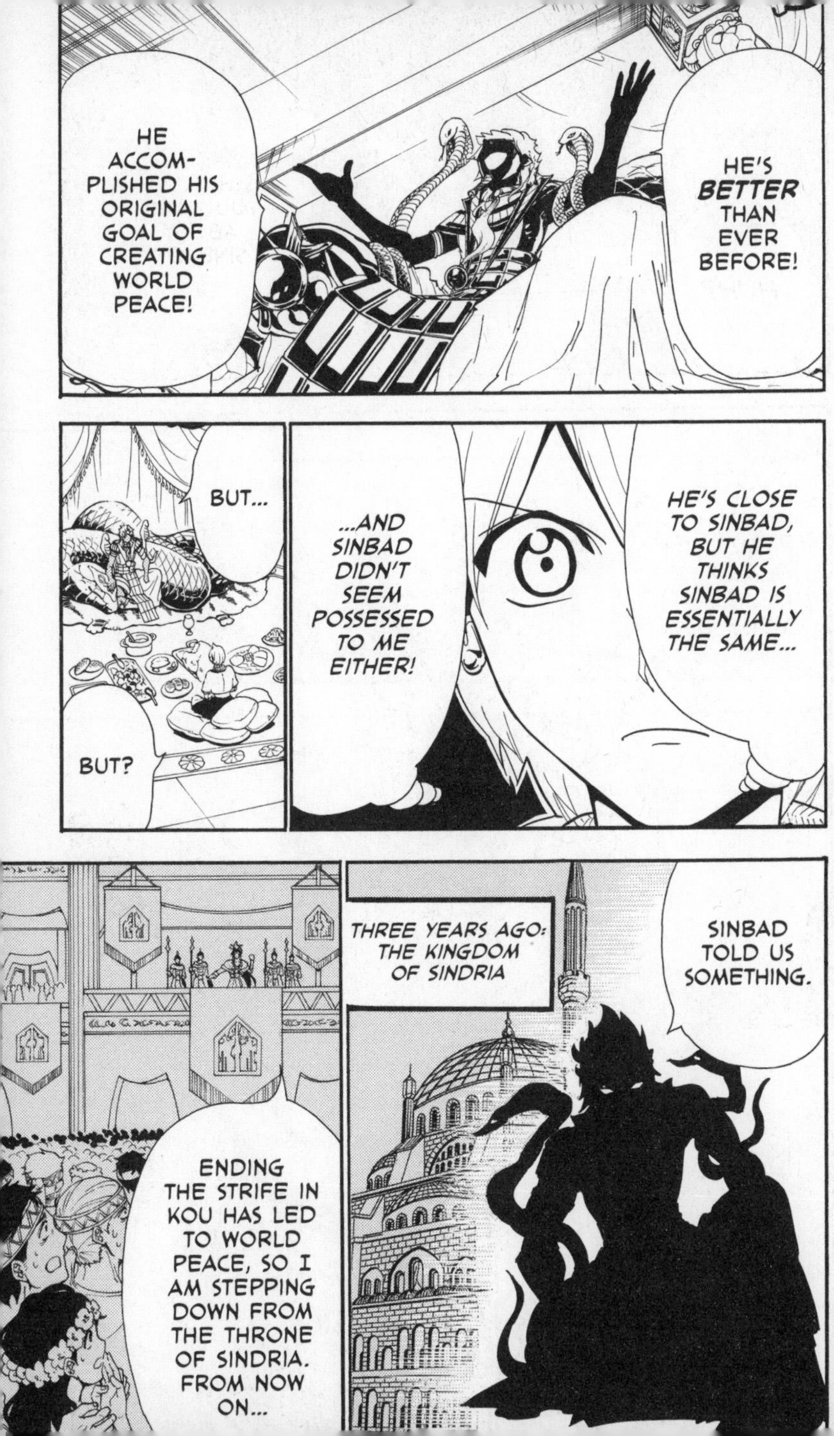
HE'S *BETTER* THAN EVER BEFORE!
HE ACCOM-PLISHED HIS ORIGINAL GOAL OF CREATING WORLD PEACE!
HE'S CLOSE TO SINBAD, BUT HE THINKS SINBAD IS ESSENTIALLY THE SAME...
...AND SINBAD DIDN'T SEEM POSSESSED TO ME EITHER!
BUT...
BUT?
SINBAD TOLD US SOMETHING.
THREE YEARS AGO: THE KINGDOM OF SINDRIA
ENDING THE STRIFE IN KOU HAS LED TO WORLD PEACE, SO I AM STEPPING DOWN FROM THE THRONE OF SINDRIA. FROM NOW ON...

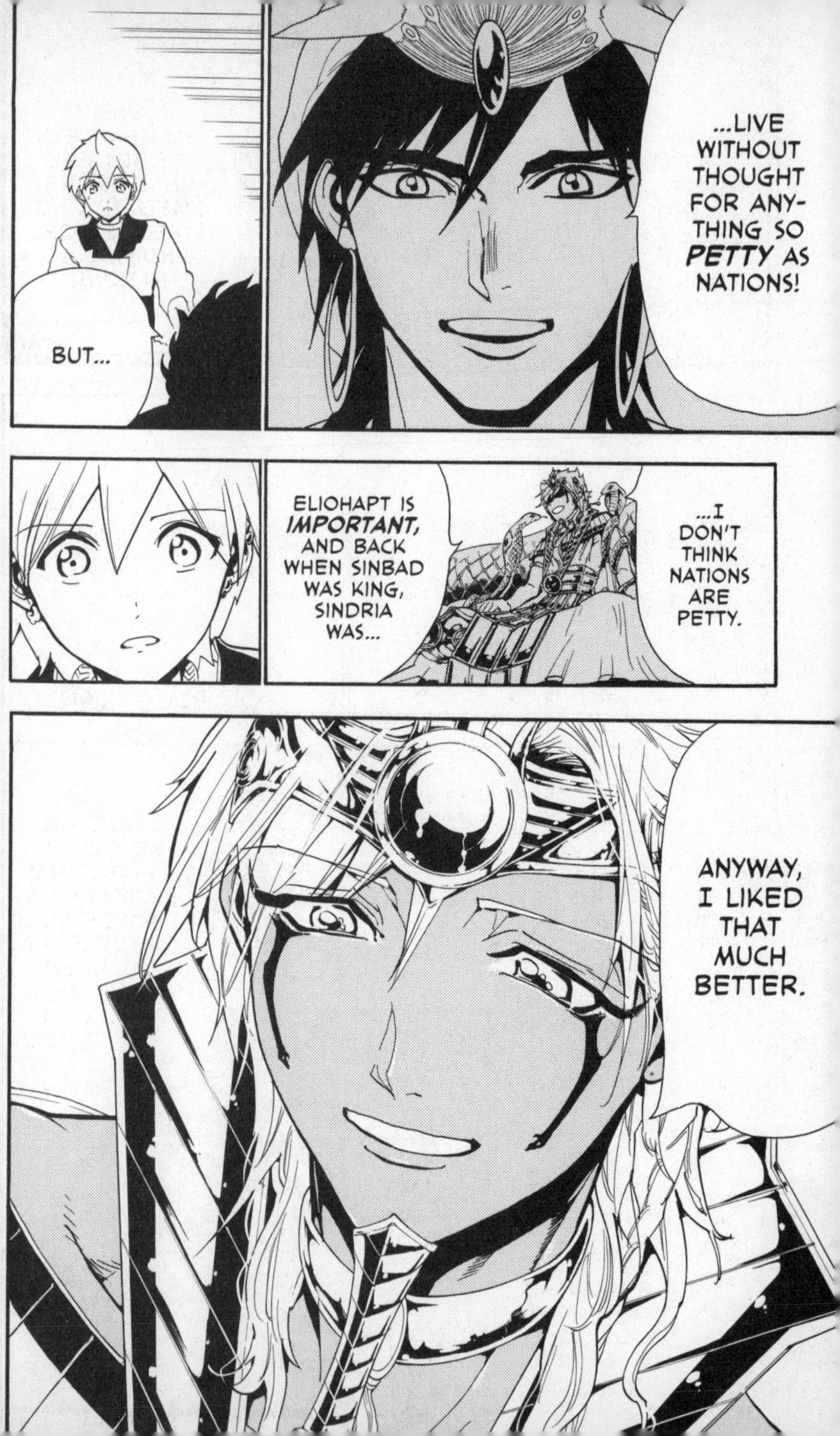
...LIVE WITHOUT THOUGHT FOR ANY-THING SO *PETTY* AS NATIONS!
BUT...
...I DON'T THINK NATIONS ARE PETTY.
ELIOHAPT IS *IMPORTANT,* AND BACK WHEN SINBAD WAS KING, SINDRIA WAS...
ANYWAY, I LIKED THAT MUCH BETTER.

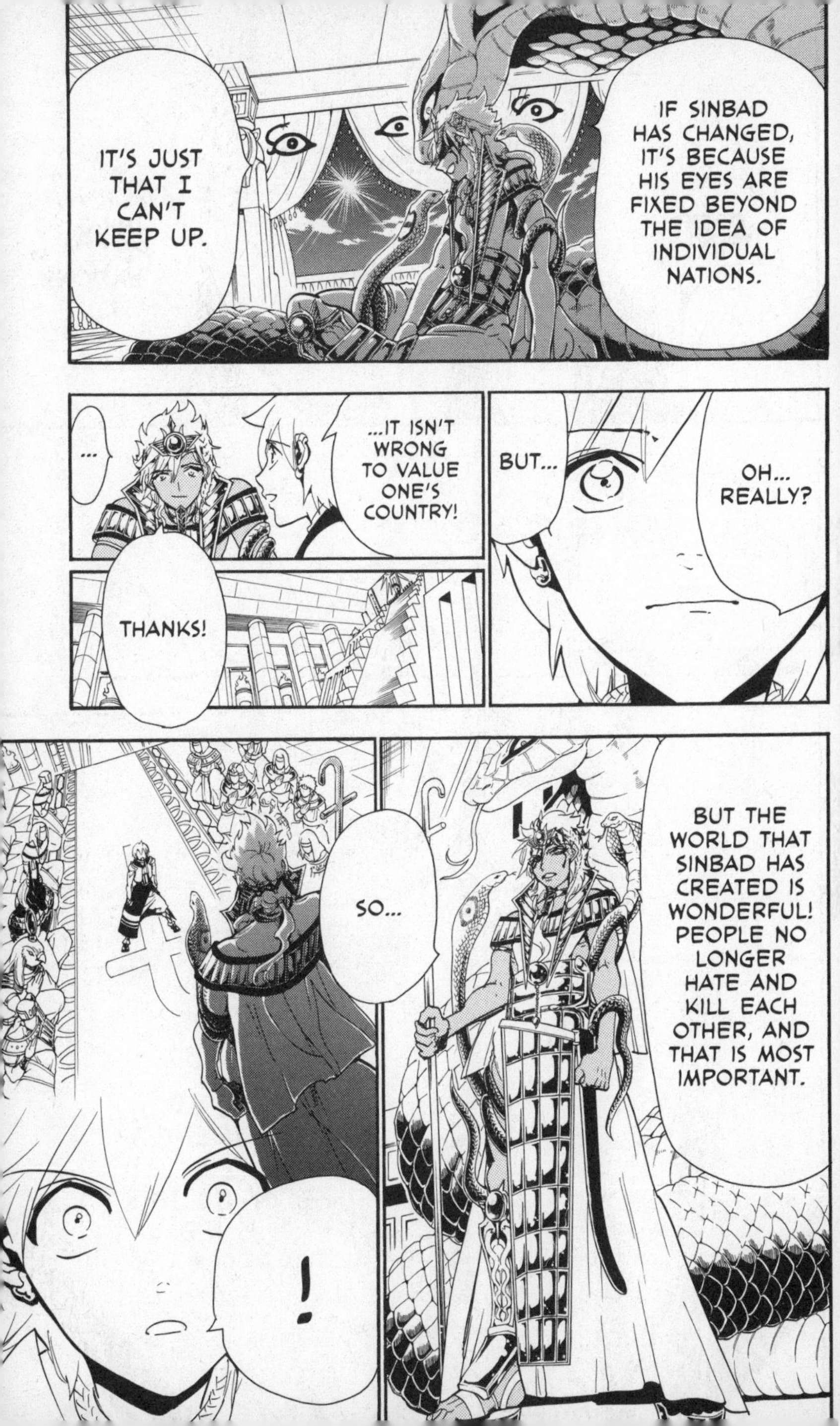
IF SINBAD HAS CHANGED, IT'S BECAUSE HIS EYES ARE FIXED BEYOND THE IDEA OF INDIVIDUAL NATIONS.
IT'S JUST THAT I CAN'T KEEP UP.
OH... REALLY?
BUT...
...IT ISN'T WRONG TO VALUE ONE'S COUNTRY!
...
THANKS!
BUT THE WORLD THAT SINBAD HAS CREATED IS WONDERFUL! PEOPLE NO LONGER HATE AND KILL EACH OTHER, AND THAT IS MOST IMPORTANT.
SO...
!

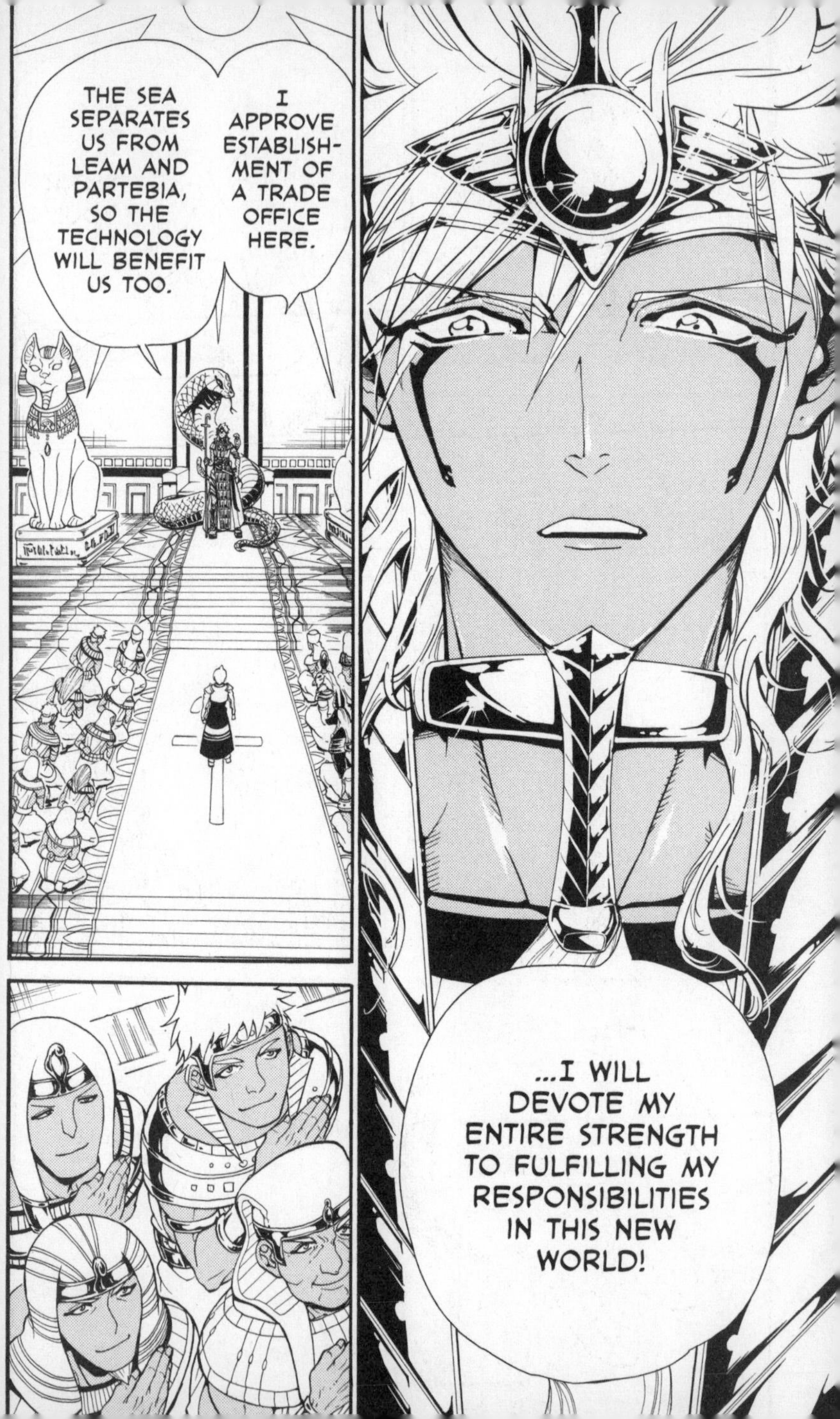
...I WILL DEVOTE MY ENTIRE STRENGTH TO FULFILLING MY RESPONSIBILITIES IN THIS NEW WORLD!
I APPROVE ESTABLISHMENT OF A TRADE OFFICE HERE.
THE SEA SEPARATES US FROM LEAM AND PARTEBIA, SO THE TECHNOLOGY WILL BENEFIT US TOO.

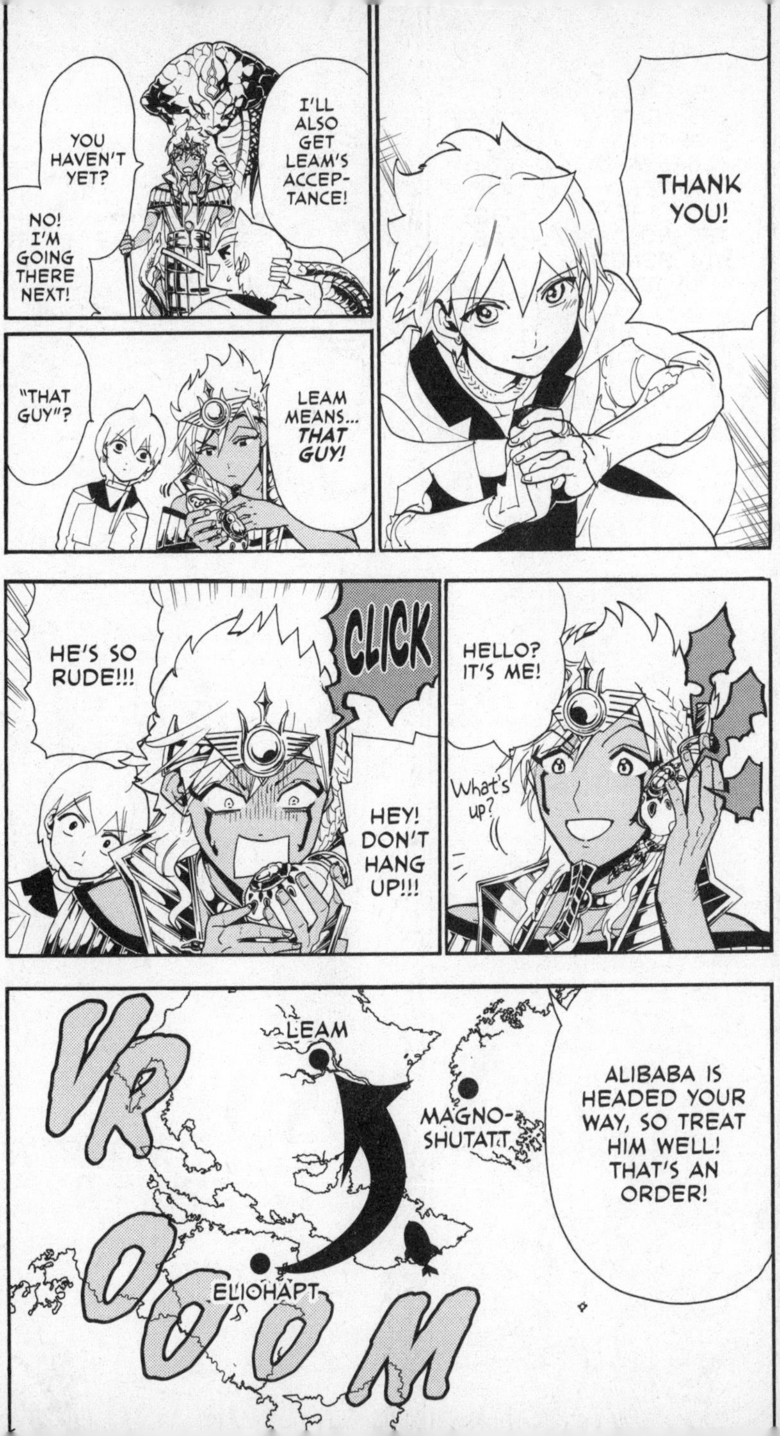
THANK YOU!
I'LL ALSO GET LEAM'S ACCEP-TANCE!
YOU HAVEN'T YET?
NO! I'M GOING THERE NEXT!
LEAM MEANS... *THAT GUY!*
"THAT GUY"?
HELLO? IT'S ME!
What's up?
CLICK
HEY! DON'T HANG UP!!!
HE'S SO RUDE!!!
ALIBABA IS HEADED YOUR WAY, SO TREAT HIM WELL! THAT'S AN ORDER!
LEAM
MAGNO-SHUTATT
ELIOHAPT
VROOOOM

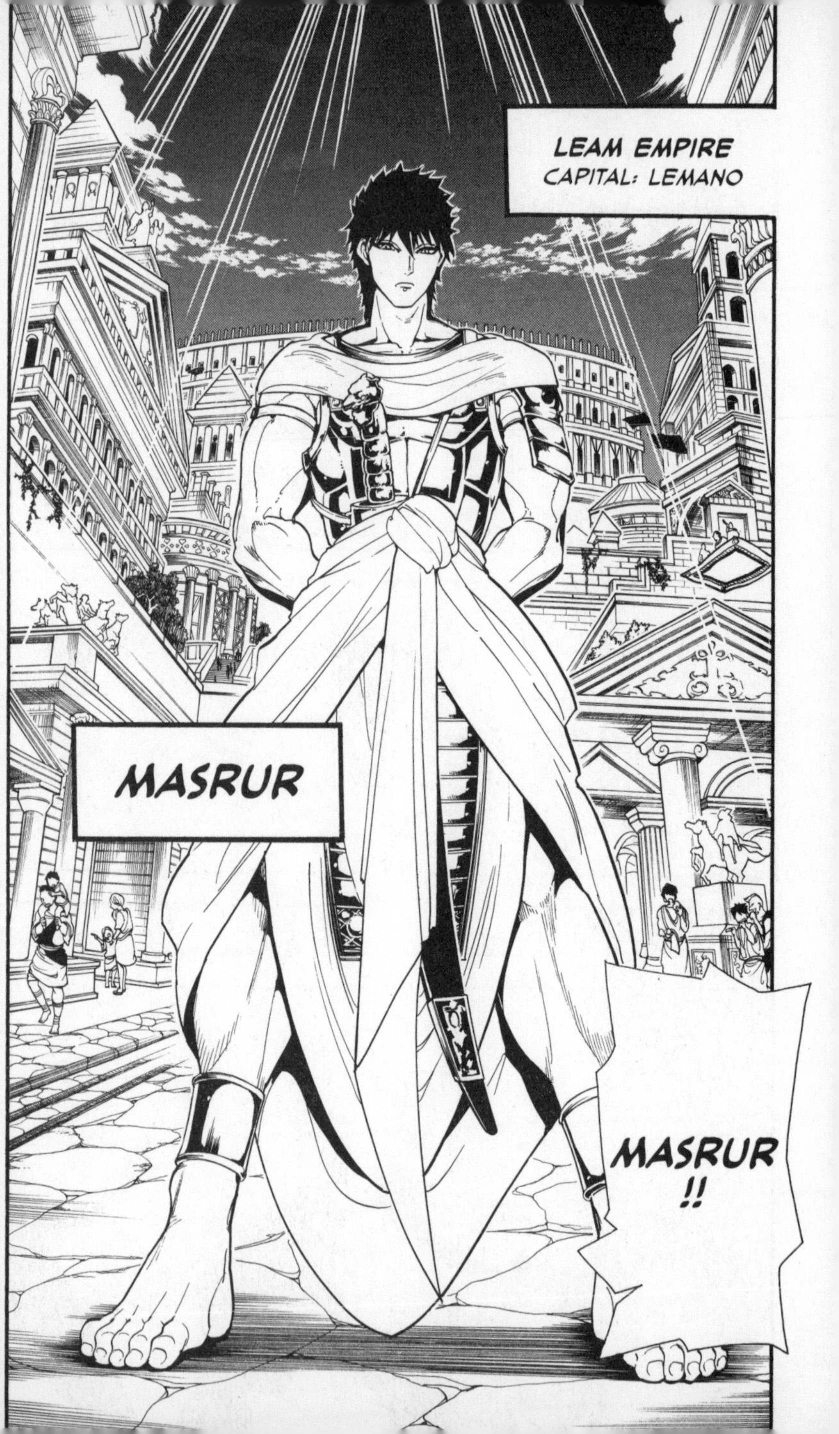
LEAM EMPIRE
CAPITAL: LEMANO
MASRUR
MASRUR !!

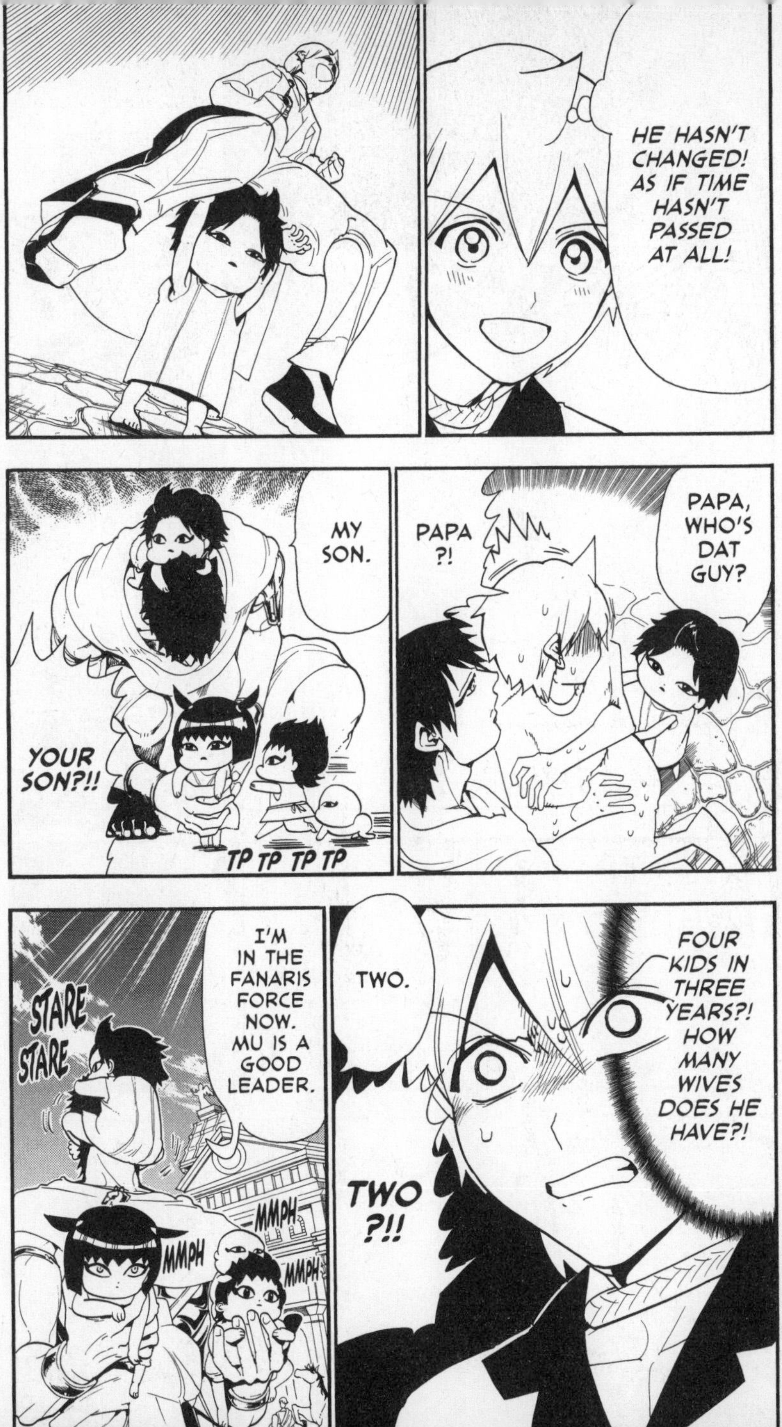
HE HASN'T CHANGED! AS IF TIME HASN'T PASSED AT ALL!
PAPA, WHO'S DAT GUY?
PAPA ?!
MY SON.
YOUR SON?!!
TP TP TP TP
FOUR KIDS IN THREE YEARS?! HOW MANY WIVES DOES HE HAVE?!
TWO.
TWO ?!!
I'M IN THE FANARIS FORCE NOW. MU IS A GOOD LEADER.
STARE
STARE
MMPH
MMPH
MMPH

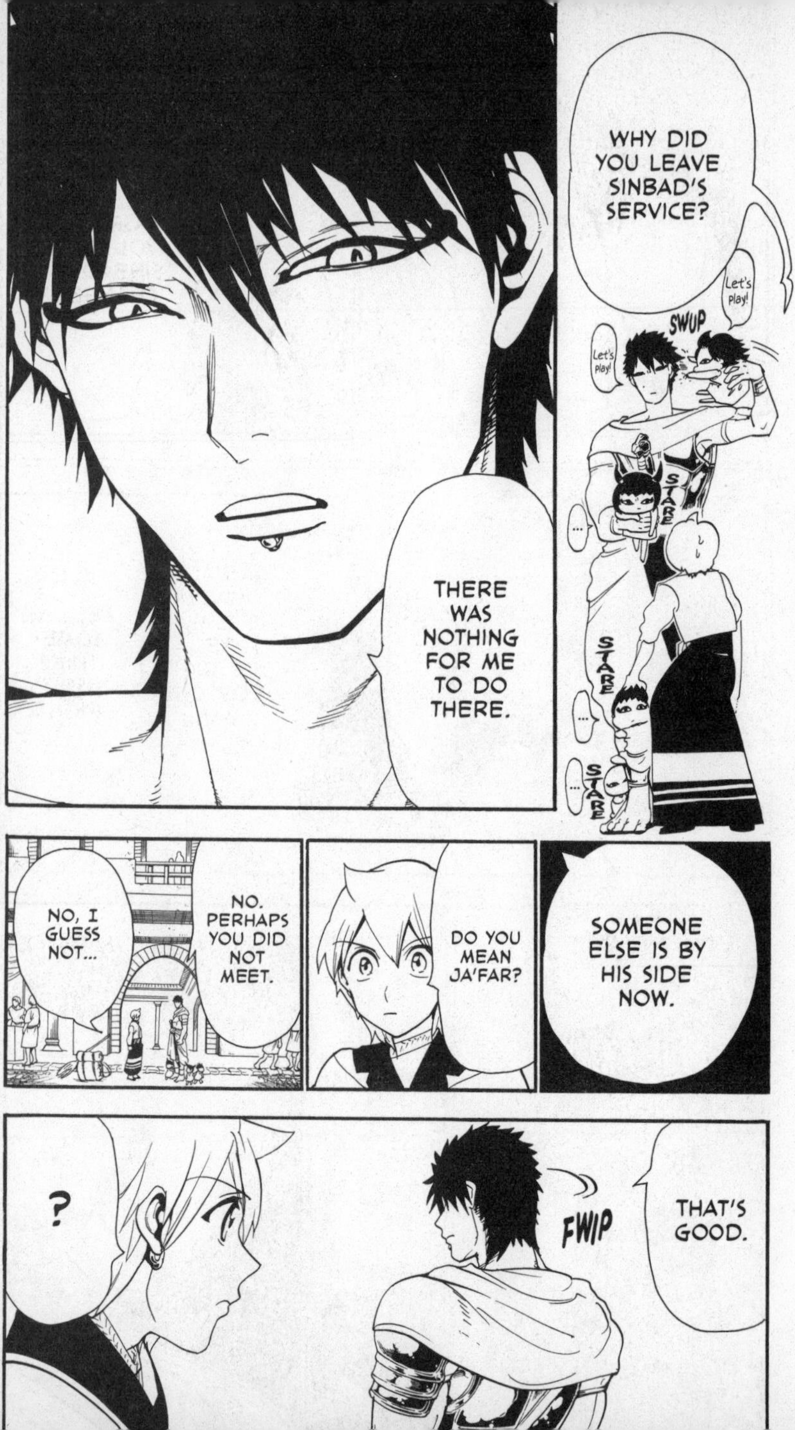

WHY DID YOU LEAVE SINBAD'S SERVICE?
Let's play!
SWUP
Let's play!
STARE
...
STARE
...
STARE
...
THERE WAS NOTHING FOR ME TO DO THERE.
SOMEONE ELSE IS BY HIS SIDE NOW.
DO YOU MEAN JA'FAR?
NO. PERHAPS YOU DID NOT MEET.
NO, I GUESS NOT...
THAT'S GOOD.
FWIP
?

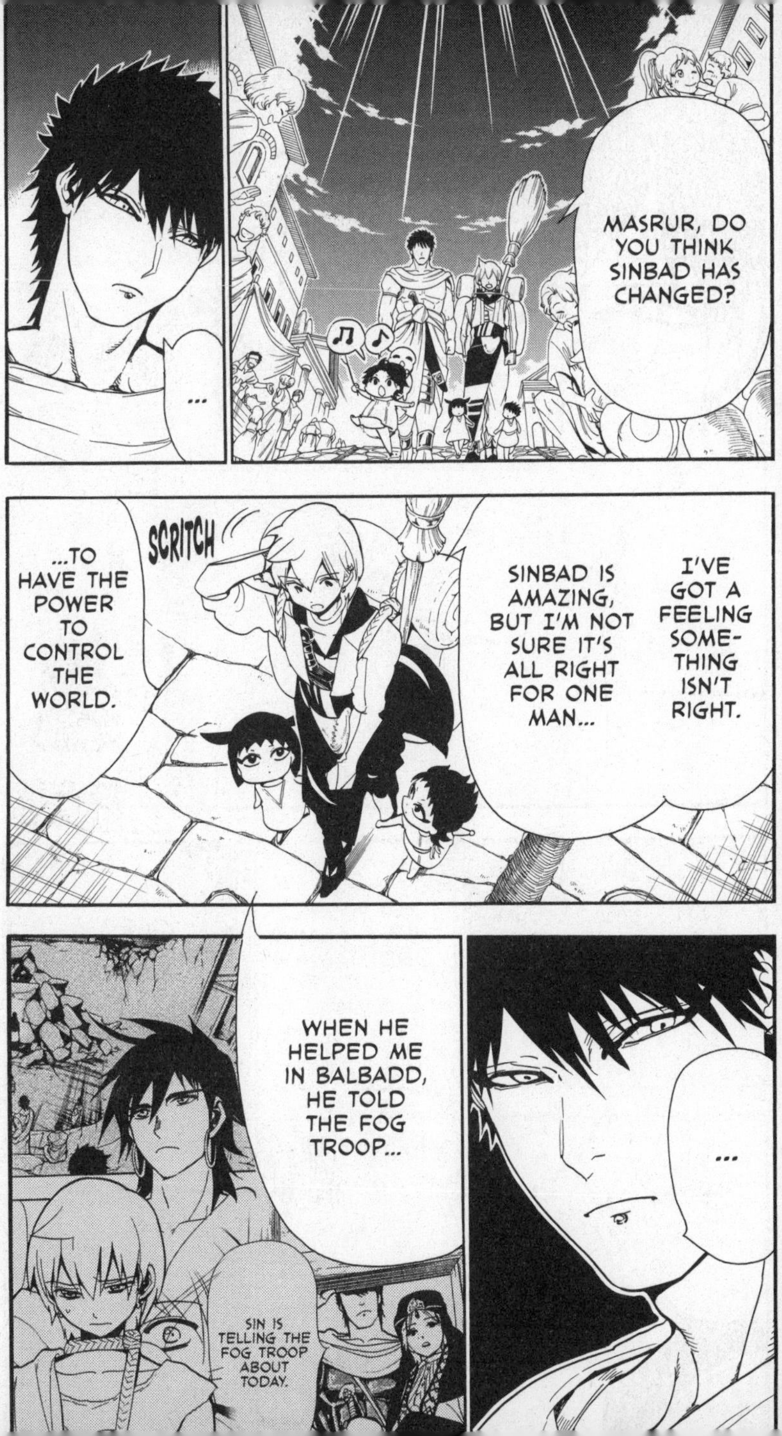
MASRUR, DO YOU THINK SINBAD HAS CHANGED?
...
I'VE GOT A FEELING SOMETHING ISN'T RIGHT.
SINBAD IS AMAZING, BUT I'M NOT SURE IT'S ALL RIGHT FOR ONE MAN...
SCRITCH
...TO HAVE THE POWER TO CONTROL THE WORLD.
...
WHEN HE HELPED ME IN BALBADD, HE TOLD THE FOG TROOP...
SIN IS TELLING THE FOG TROOP ABOUT TODAY.

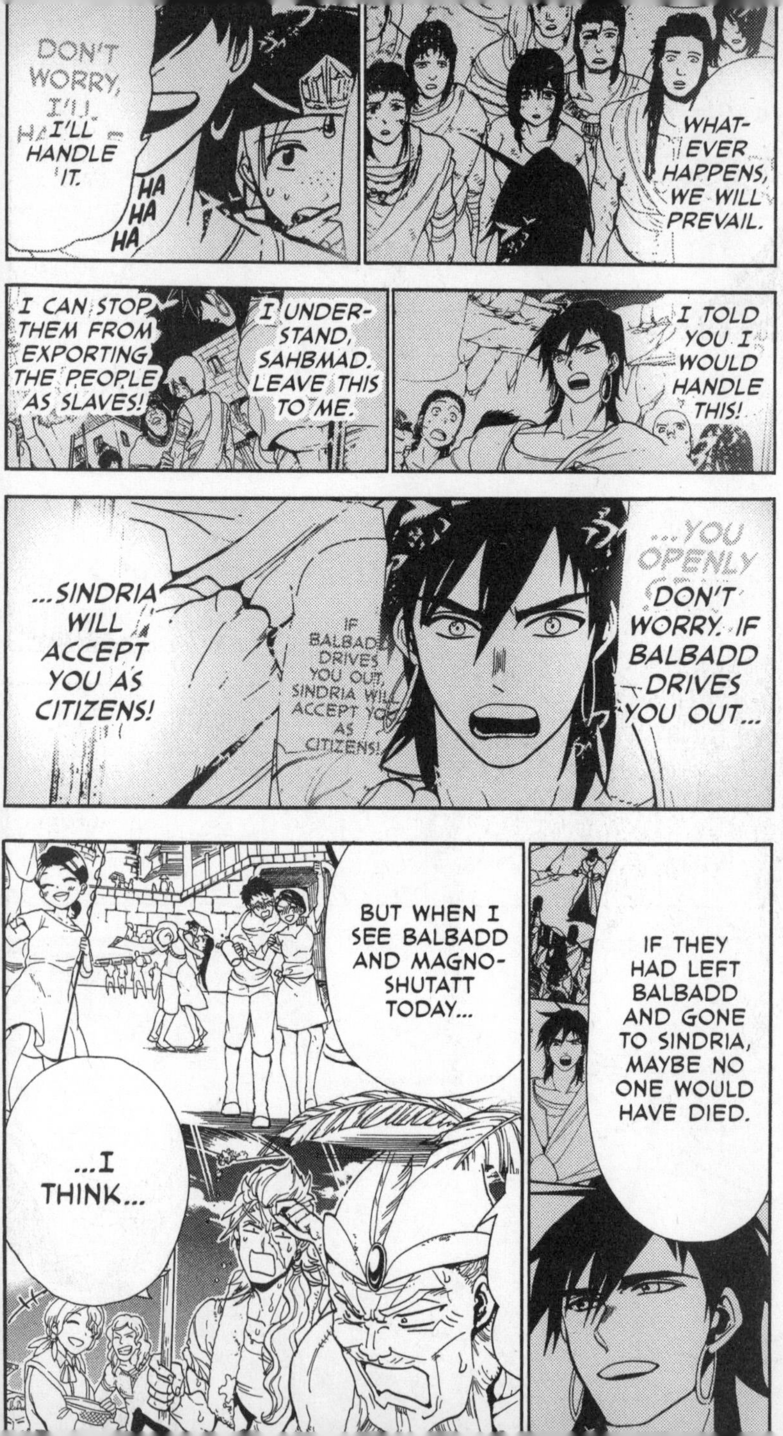
WHAT-EVER HAPPENS, WE WILL PREVAIL.
DON'T WORRY, I'LL...
I'LL HANDLE IT.
HA HA HA
I TOLD YOU I WOULD HANDLE THIS!
I UNDER-STAND, SAHBMAD. LEAVE THIS TO ME.
I CAN STOP THEM FROM EXPORTING THE PEOPLE AS SLAVES!
...YOU OPENLY
DON'T WORRY. IF BALBADD DRIVES YOU OUT...
IF BALBADD DRIVES YOU OUT, SINDRIA WILL ACCEPT YO AS CITIZENS!
...SINDRIA WILL ACCEPT YOU AS CITIZENS!
IF THEY HAD LEFT BALBADD AND GONE TO SINDRIA, MAYBE NO ONE WOULD HAVE DIED.
BUT WHEN I SEE BALBADD AND MAGNO-SHUTATT TODAY...
...I THINK...

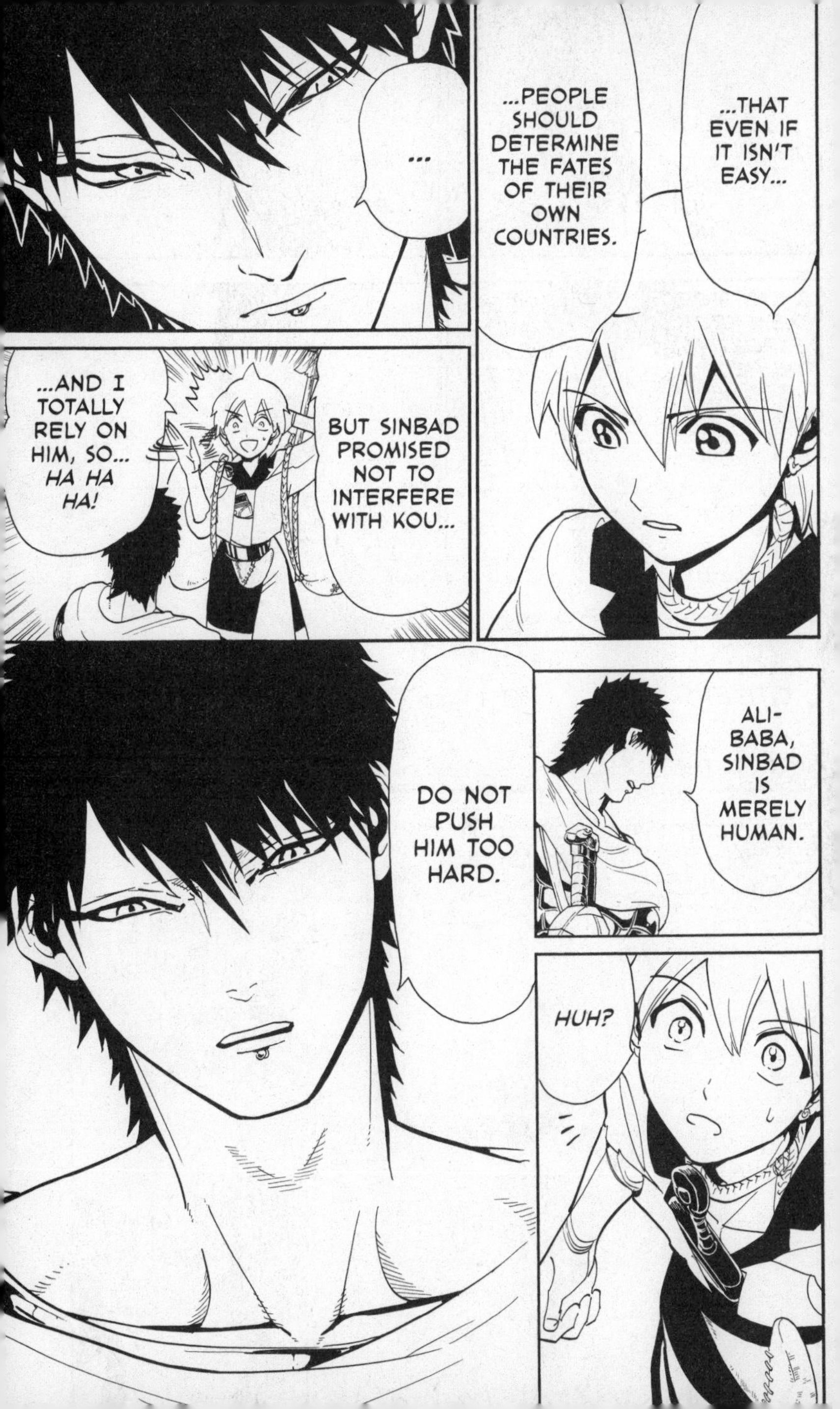

...THAT EVEN IF IT ISN'T EASY...
...PEOPLE SHOULD DETERMINE THE FATES OF THEIR OWN COUNTRIES.
...
BUT SINBAD PROMISED NOT TO INTERFERE WITH KOU...
...AND I TOTALLY RELY ON HIM, SO... *HA HA HA!*
ALI-BABA, SINBAD IS MERELY HUMAN.
HUH?
DO NOT PUSH HIM TOO HARD.

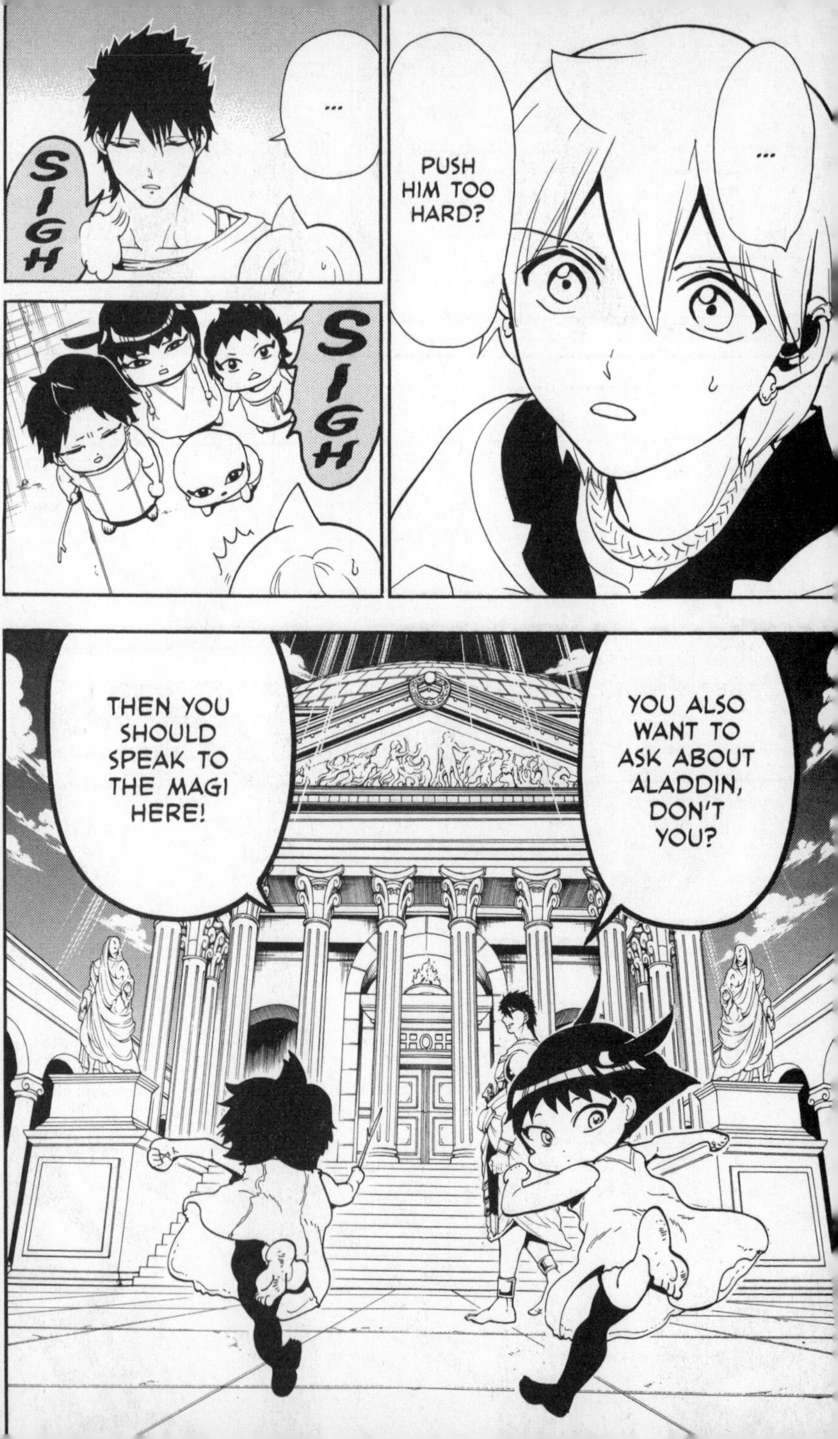
...
PUSH HIM TOO HARD?
...
SIGH
SIGH
YOU ALSO WANT TO ASK ABOUT ALADDIN, DON'T YOU?
THEN YOU SHOULD SPEAK TO THE MAGI HERE!

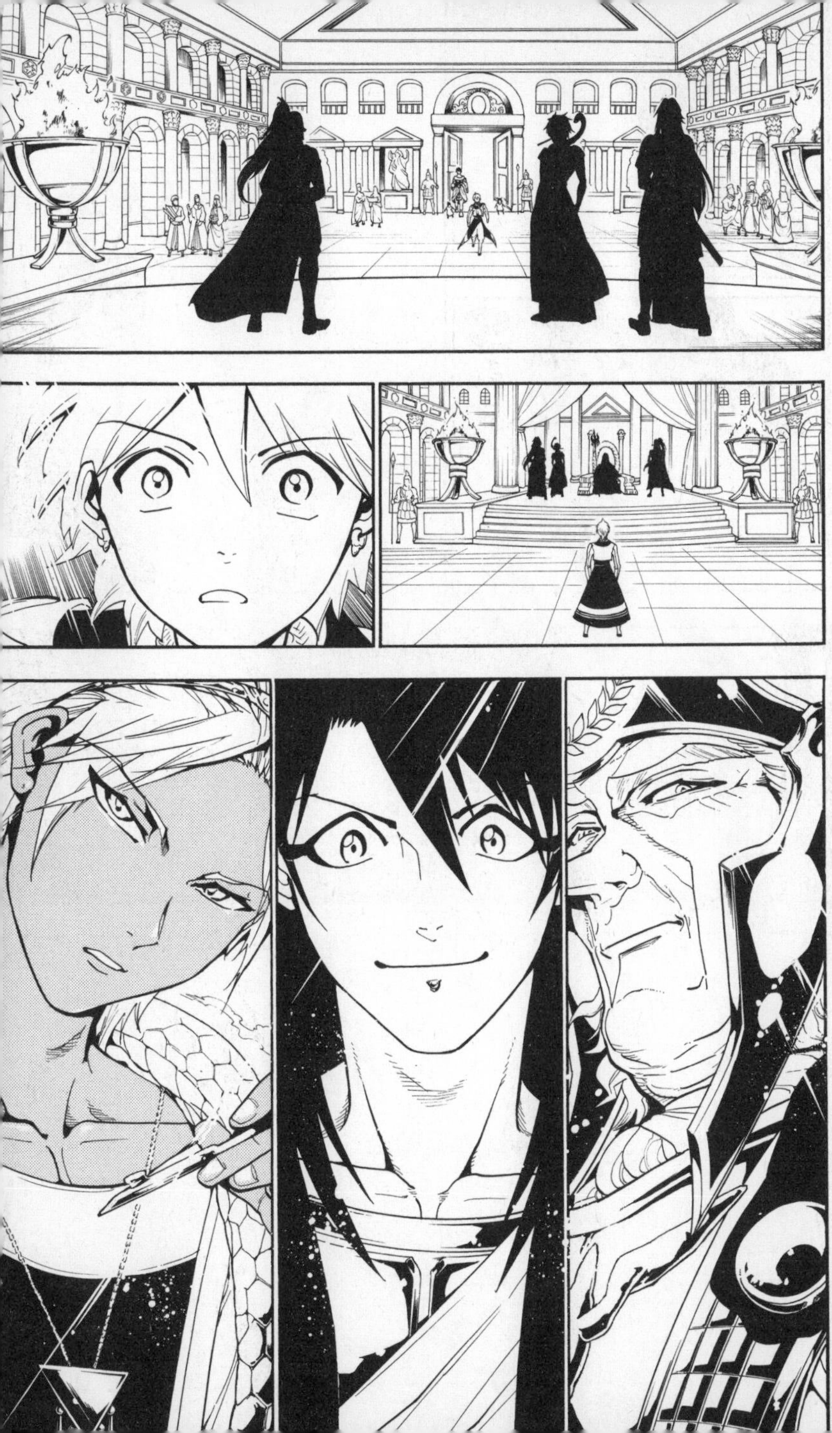

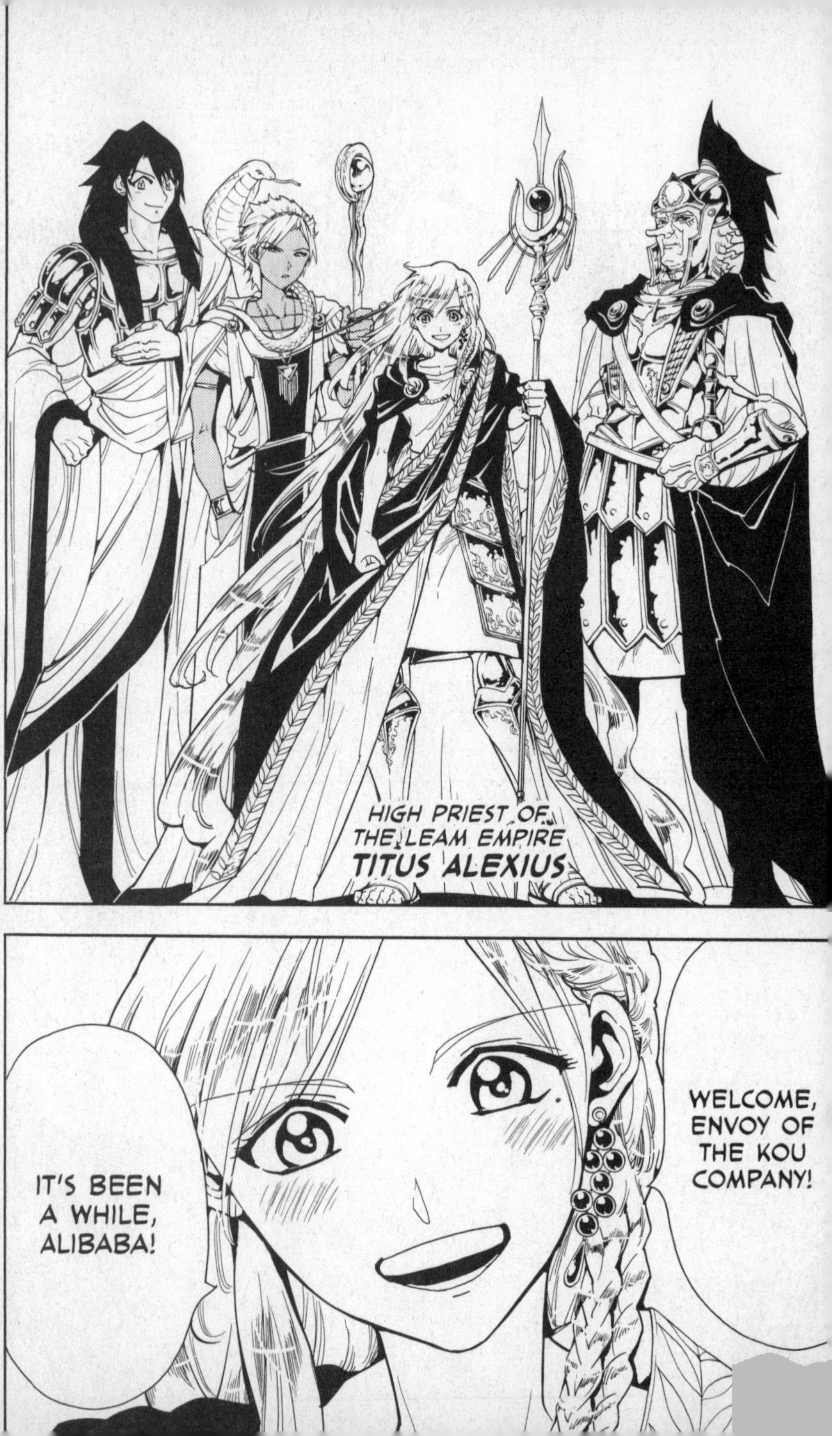
HIGH PRIEST OF THE LEAM EMPIRE
TITUS ALEXIUS
WELCOME, ENVOY OF THE KOU COMPANY!
IT'S BEEN A WHILE, ALIBABA!

MAGI
The labyrinth of magic
30

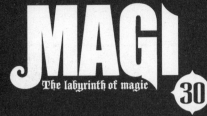

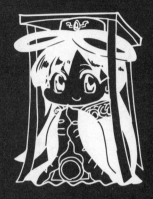

Staff

Story & Art
Shinobu Ohtaka

Regular Assistants
Hiro Maizima
Yuiko Akiyama
Megi
Aya Umoto
Mami Yoshida
Yuka Otsuji

Editors
Kazuaki Ishibashi
Makoto Ishiwata

Sales & Promotion
Tsunato Imamoto
Yuta Uchiyama

Designer
Hajime Tokushige + Bay Bridge Studio

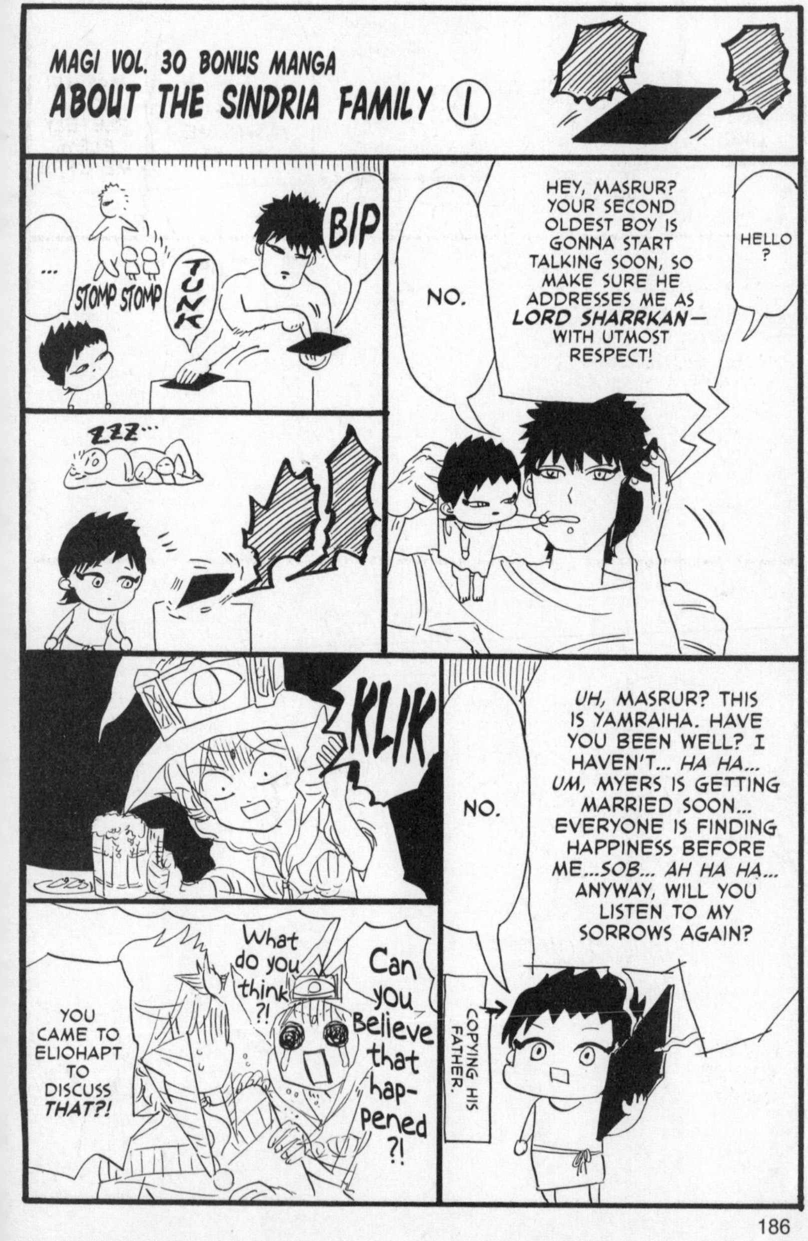
MAGI VOL. 30 BONUS MANGA
ABOUT THE SINDRIA FAMILY ①
HELLO?
HEY, MASRUR? YOUR SECOND OLDEST BOY IS GONNA START TALKING SOON, SO MAKE SURE HE ADDRESSES ME AS *LORD SHARRKAN*—WITH UTMOST RESPECT!
NO.
BIP
TUNK
STOMP STOMP
...
ZZZ...
UH, MASRUR? THIS IS YAMRAIHA. HAVE YOU BEEN WELL? I HAVEN'T... *HA HA...* *UM,* MYERS IS GETTING MARRIED SOON... EVERYONE IS FINDING HAPPINESS BEFORE ME...*SOB*... *AH HA HA...* ANYWAY, WILL YOU LISTEN TO MY SORROWS AGAIN?
NO.
COPYING HIS FATHER.
KLIK
Can you Believe that hap-pened?!
What do you think?!
YOU CAME TO ELIOHAPT TO DISCUSS *THAT?!*

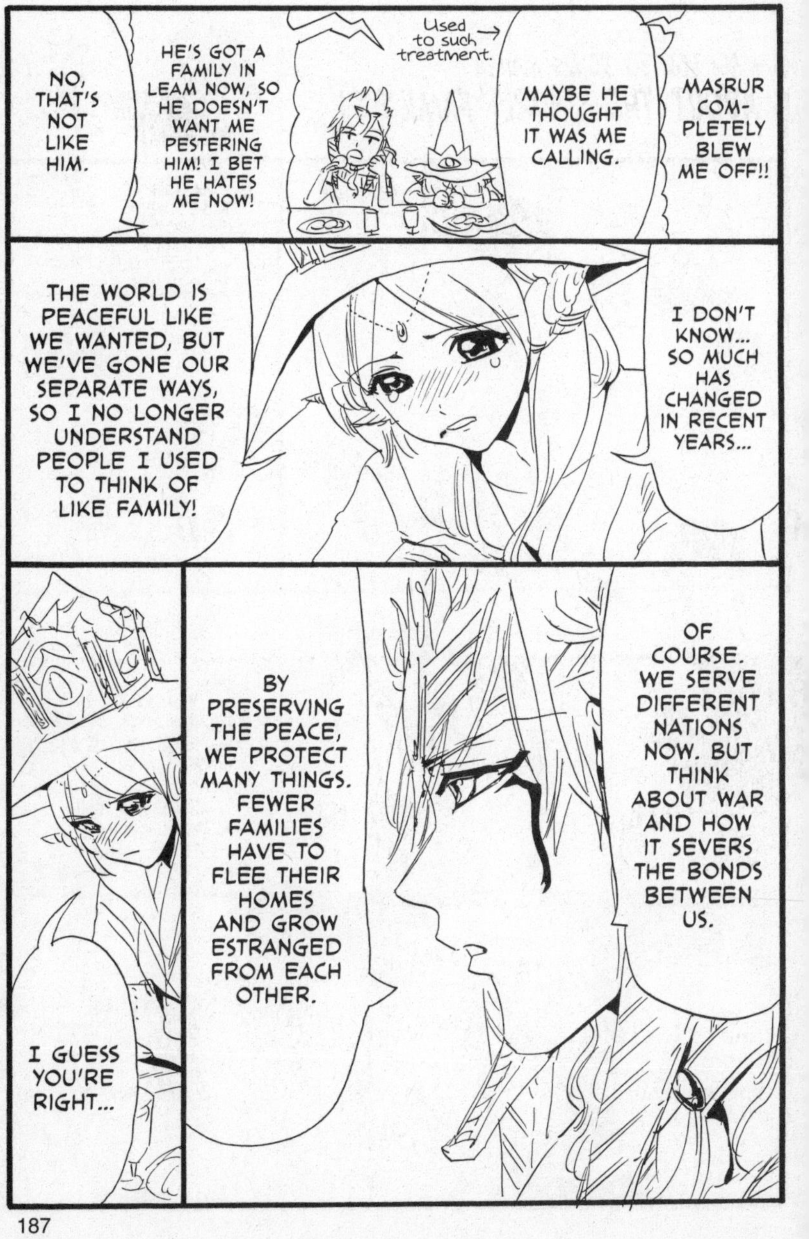
MASRUR COMPLETELY BLEW ME OFF!!
MAYBE HE THOUGHT IT WAS ME CALLING.
Used to such treatment.
HE'S GOT A FAMILY IN LEAM NOW, SO HE DOESN'T WANT ME PESTERING HIM! I BET HE HATES ME NOW!
NO, THAT'S NOT LIKE HIM.
I DON'T KNOW... SO MUCH HAS CHANGED IN RECENT YEARS...
THE WORLD IS PEACEFUL LIKE WE WANTED, BUT WE'VE GONE OUR SEPARATE WAYS, SO I NO LONGER UNDERSTAND PEOPLE I USED TO THINK OF LIKE FAMILY!
OF COURSE. WE SERVE DIFFERENT NATIONS NOW. BUT THINK ABOUT WAR AND HOW IT SEVERS THE BONDS BETWEEN US.
BY PRESERVING THE PEACE, WE PROTECT MANY THINGS. FEWER FAMILIES HAVE TO FLEE THEIR HOMES AND GROW ESTRANGED FROM EACH OTHER.
I GUESS YOU'RE RIGHT...

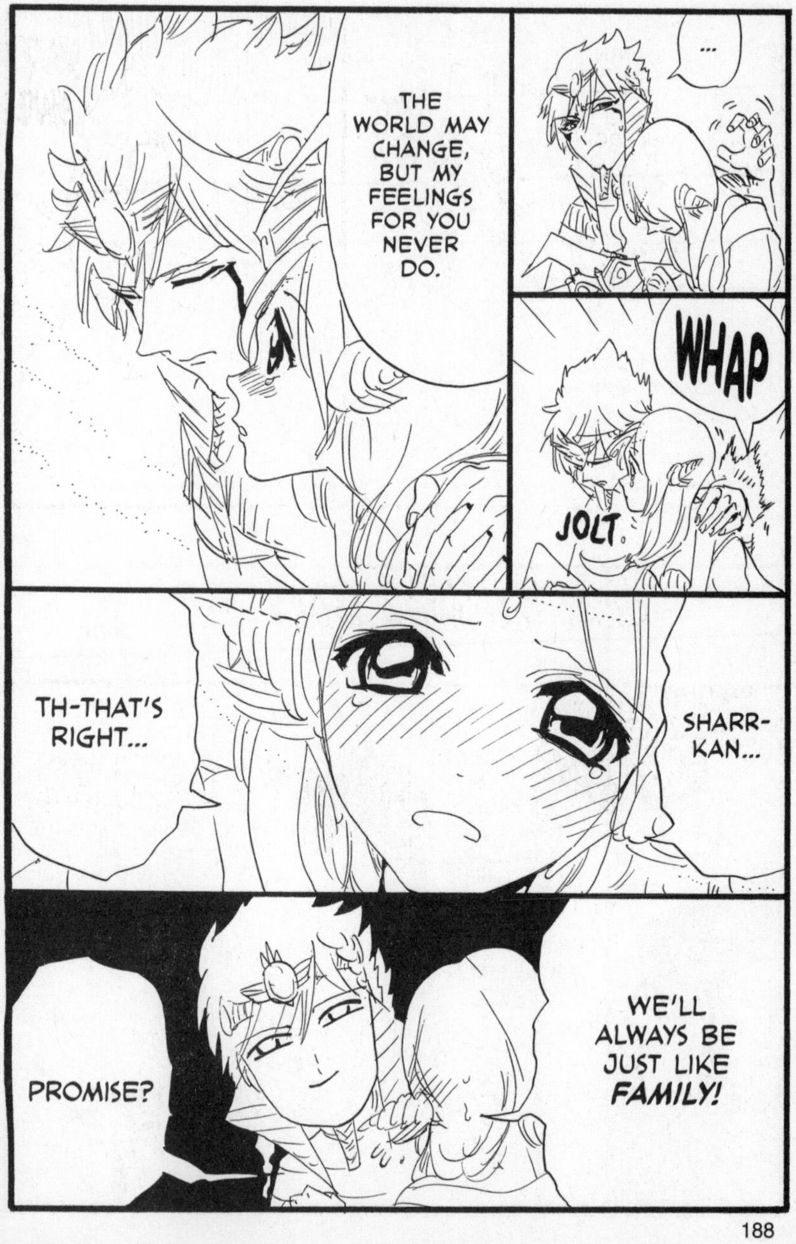
...
WHAP
JOLT.
THE WORLD MAY CHANGE, BUT MY FEELINGS FOR YOU NEVER DO.
SHARR-KAN...
TH-THAT'S RIGHT...
WE'LL ALWAYS BE JUST LIKE *FAMILY!*
PROMISE?

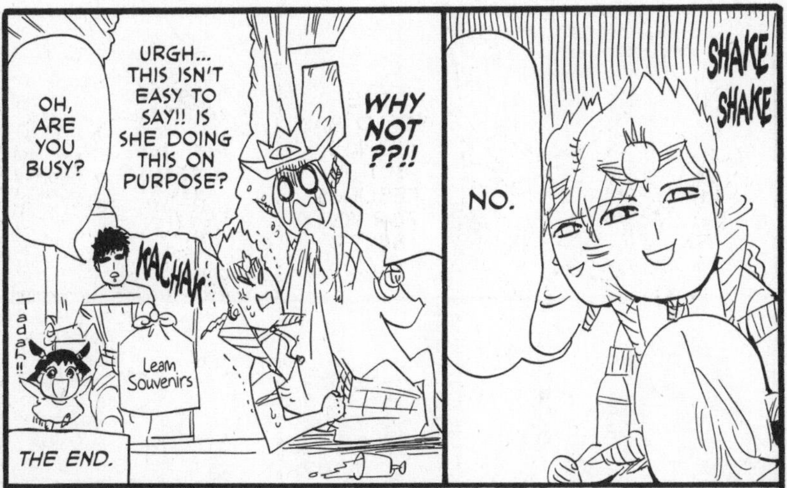
SHAKE SHAKE
NO.
WHY NOT ??!!
URGH... THIS ISN'T EASY TO SAY!! IS SHE DOING THIS ON PURPOSE?
OH, ARE YOU BUSY?
KACHAK
Tadah!!
Leam Souvenirs
THE END.

MAGI VOL. 30 BONUS MANGA

ABOUT THE SINDRIA FAMILY ②

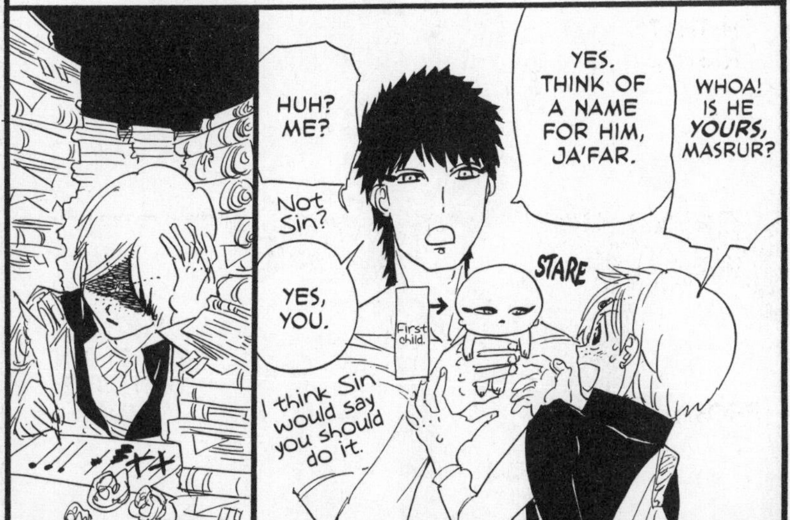
WHOA! IS HE *YOURS,* MASRUR?
YES. THINK OF A NAME FOR HIM, JA'FAR.
HUH? ME?
Not Sin?
STARE
YES, YOU.
First child.
I think Sin would say you should do it.

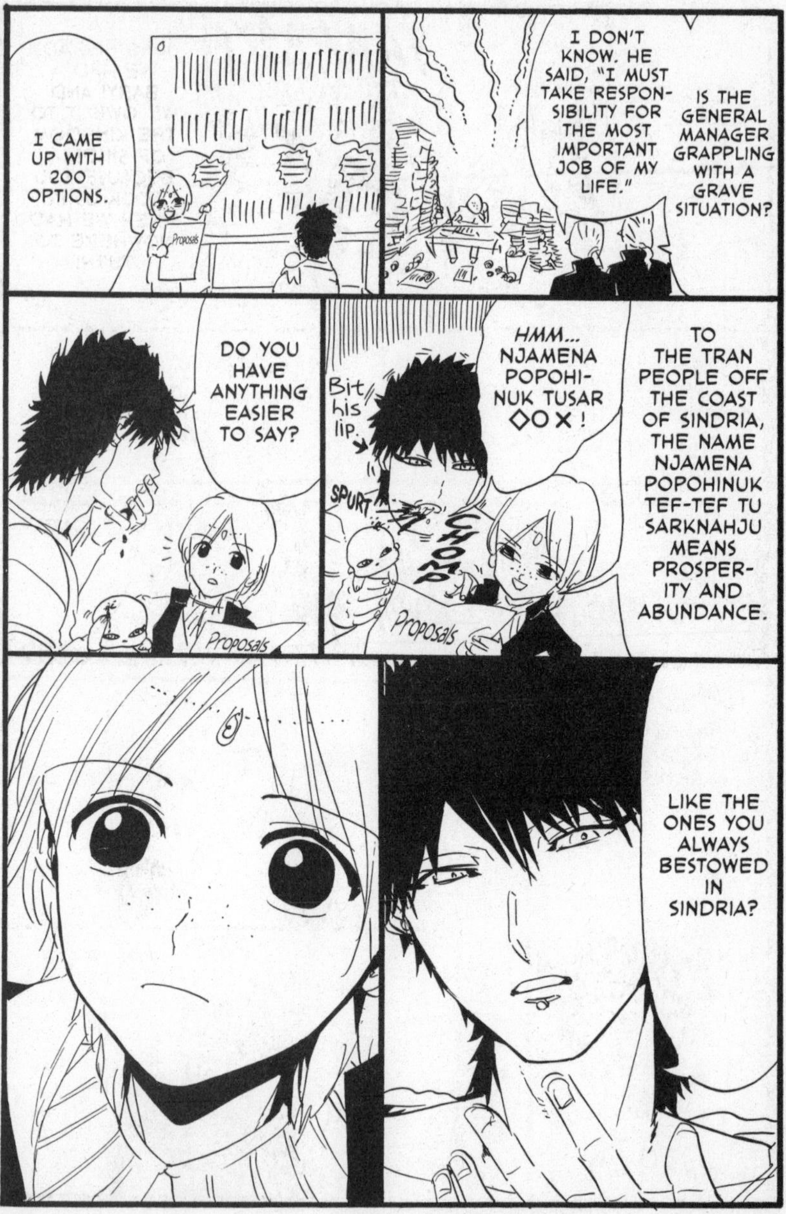
IS THE GENERAL MANAGER GRAPPLING WITH A GRAVE SITUATION?
I DON'T KNOW. HE SAID, "I MUST TAKE RESPONSIBILITY FOR THE MOST IMPORTANT JOB OF MY LIFE."
I CAME UP WITH 200 OPTIONS.
Proposals
TO THE TRAN PEOPLE OFF THE COAST OF SINDRIA, THE NAME NJAMENA POPOHINUK TEF-TEF TU SARKNAHJU MEANS PROSPERITY AND ABUNDANCE.
HMM... NJAMENA POPOHI-NUK TUSAR ◇O×!
Bit his lip.
SPURT
CHOMP
Proposals
DO YOU HAVE ANYTHING EASIER TO SAY?
Proposals
LIKE THE ONES YOU ALWAYS BESTOWED IN SINDRIA?

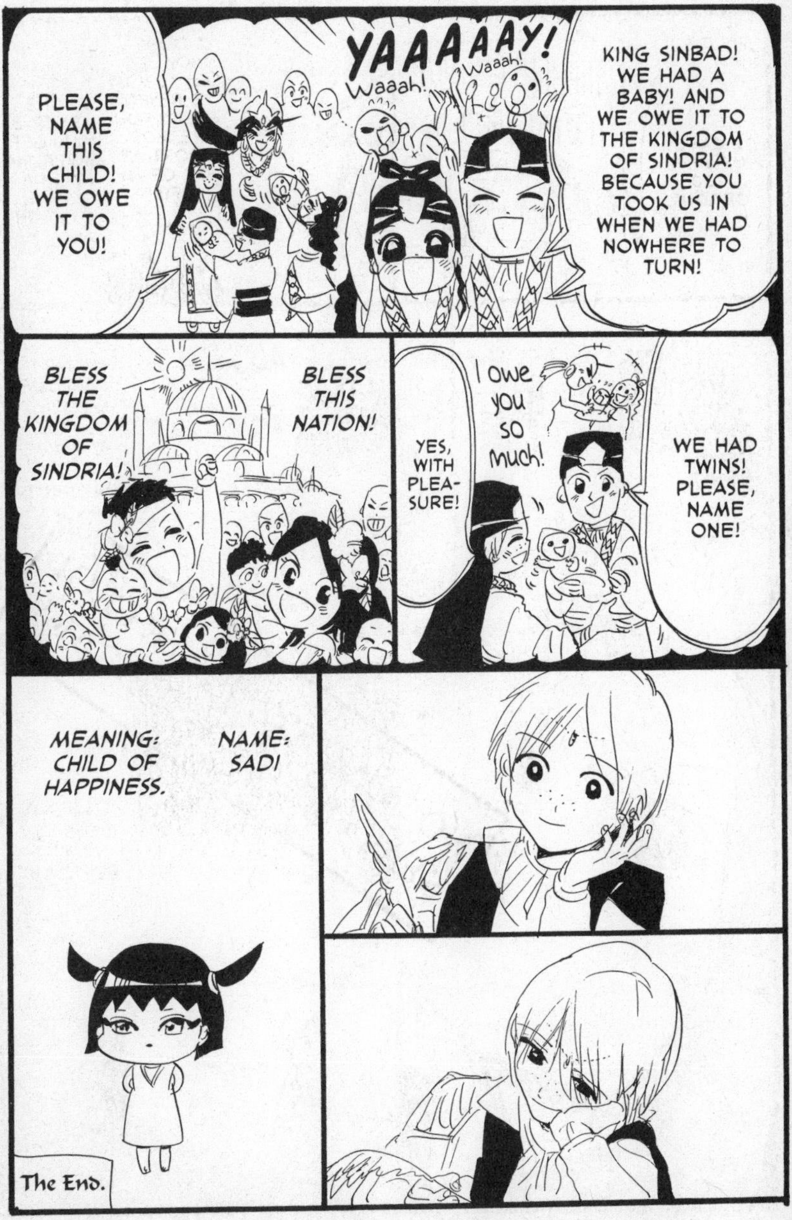
KING SINBAD! WE HAD A BABY! AND WE OWE IT TO THE KINGDOM OF SINDRIA! BECAUSE YOU TOOK US IN WHEN WE HAD NOWHERE TO TURN!
YAAAAAY!
Waaah!
Waaah!
PLEASE, NAME THIS CHILD! WE OWE IT TO YOU!
WE HAD TWINS! PLEASE, NAME ONE!
I owe you so much!
YES, WITH PLEA-SURE!
BLESS THIS NATION!
BLESS THE KINGDOM OF SINDRIA!
NAME: SADI
MEANING: CHILD OF HAPPINESS.
The End.

You're reading the
WRONG WAY

MAGI reads from right to left, starting in the upper-right corner. Japanese is read from **right** to **left**, meaning that action, sound effects, and word-balloon order are completely reversed from English order.

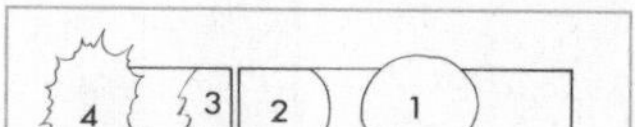
1
1
2
2
3
4
3
5
6
4
7
8
5
9
142

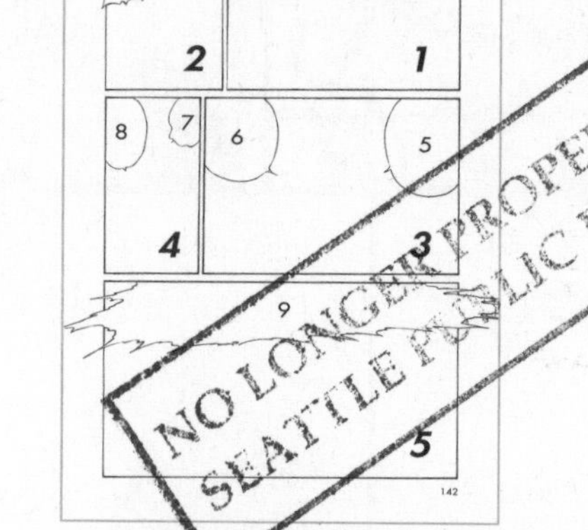

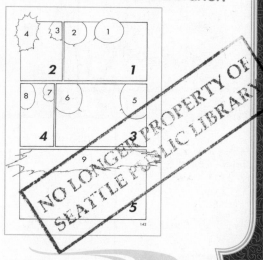